DATE DUE

DEMCO 38-296

Federalists Reconsidered

FEDERALISTS
RECONSIDERED

Edited by DORON BEN-ATAR AND BARBARA B. OBERG

UNIVERSITY PRESS OF VIRGINIA • *Charlottesville and London*

For notice of previous publication, see chapter 2, notes, and chapter 11, notes.

THE UNIVERSITY PRESS OF VIRGINIA
© 1998 by the Rector and Visitors of the University of Virginia
All rights reserved
Printed in the United States of America

First published 1998

⊚ The paper used in this publication meets the minimum requirements
of the American National Standard for Information Sciences—Permanence of
Paper for Printed Library Materials, ANSI Z39.48-1984.

Library of Congress Cataloging-in-Publication Data

Federalists reconsidered / edited by Doron Ben-Atar and Barbara B.
  Oberg.
      p.   cm.
    Includes bibliographical references and index.
    ISBN 0-8139-1819-7 (cloth : alk. paper). — ISBN 0-8139-1863-4
(paper : alk. paper)
      1. United States—Politics and government—1798–1809. 2. Federal
Party (U.S.) 3. Political culture—United States—History—18th
century. 4. Political parties—United States—History—18th
century. I. Ben-Atar, Doron S. II. Oberg, Barbara B.
E310.F43   1999
306.2'0973'09033—dc21   98-34195
                                                                CIP

Contents

PART I: *Age of Federalism*

PART II: *Federalism and the Origins of American Political Culture*

PART III: *Varieties of Federalism*

Illustrations

ACKNOWLEDGMENTS

OUR FIRST acknowledgment and gratitude naturally go to the authors of the chapters included in this volume. Their intellectual vigor, enthusiasm, and patience create the collection. We are grateful for the generosity of Fordham University's Research Expense Grant Program. The contributions of several other people have strengthened the book, and we offer them our thanks. Fredrika J. Teute, Jan Lewis, and Peter Onuf made perceptive comments on an earlier version of the manuscript, and we took their suggestions to heart. Herbert Sloan, John P. Kaminski, and Eric Papenfuse gave us the benefit of their careful reading. And finally, our spouses, Jo Ben-Atar and Perry Leavell, offered respectively their sophisticated computer skills and sweeping understanding of American history.

Introduction

The Paradoxical Legacy of the Federalists

Doron Ben-Atar and Barbara B. Oberg

THE FEDERALISTS took an untried confederacy and successfully established its domestic and international legitimacy. They breathed life and meaning into the new central government. They brought order to the chaotic national finances and guided the country through a decade of great commercial prosperity. Under the leadership of George Washington and Alexander Hamilton, they boldly contained the Whiskey Rebellion, enthusiastically supported western development, and skillfully averted threatening entanglements with Great Britain, Spain, and France. In short, during their first decade in politics, the Federalists laid the foundations for economic growth, continental expansion, and the union of the states.

Still, most historians of the early American republic have cast the Federalists as either fallen heroes innocently gone astray or traitors guilty of ruthless apostasy. As historians see it, by 1798 the Federalists turned to subverting the very government and institutions they had established. Horrified by the excesses of the French Revolution, men like Robert Goodloe Harper and Harrison Gray Otis moved to check the opposition, passing the Alien and Sedition Acts and raising an army of potentially Herculean proportions. In 1800 the party failed to present a cohesive unified alternative to the Jeffersonians. As a humiliated John Adams put it, the Federalists "killed themselves and the national President . . . at one shot, and then . . . indicted me for murder."[1]

Rebuffed by the election of 1800—the story continues—the Federalists desperately tried to supplant the people's choice and arrange Aaron Burr's election as president. Their failure to accomplish this signaled the end of the party's life as a constructive political force on the national level and its lapse "into waspish parochialism."[2] Moving into the opposition,

the Federalists objected to the greatest bargain in the annals of real estate
—the Louisiana Purchase. Then, in a delusional "frenzy" reminiscent of
the "witchcraft and Quaker mania," they callously promoted secessionist
schemes and subverted the national government's "foreign policy."[3]
Finally, in their darkest hour, some party members renounced the War of
1812 and committed treason.

Federalists can be seen as the victims of their own successes. Their
policies, enacted in the face of strong Jeffersonian opposition, "helped to
create a competitive, fiercely individualist social environment."[4] After the
disintegration of old social and economic ties, any expectation that men
and women would remain dependent on their betters was unreasonable
and anachronistic. By 1800 the party existed, as Gordon S. Wood put it,
"essentially on borrowed time."[5] The Federalists' close association with
the founding of the nation led them to imagine that they owned it. When
their political fortunes suddenly improved following the public outrage
over the XYZ affair in 1797–98, they championed a domestic program
that undermined "the very principle—the sovereignty of the people—
that had enabled them a dozen years before to ride down the opposition
to their new Constitution."[6] They stubbornly refused to adjust to the
emerging democratic political culture. Twice in a period of two years
their maneuvers brought the nation to the brink of disunion and civil
war. Their attempt during the Quasi-War with France to muzzle the opposition with the Alien and Sedition Acts in 1798 moved Jefferson, in the
Kentucky Resolutions, to advocate nullification. Two years later, in response
to the Federalists' Burr maneuver, Republican leaders in Virginia and
Pennsylvania considered raising an army and marching on the nation's
capital to place Jefferson at the helm.[7] By the time President Adams
slipped out of Washington on the morning of March 4, 1801, the men
who had founded the first modern republic seemed to have turned on
their own creation. Federalism became synonymous with contempt for
republican values and political vindictiveness.

But have historians drawn only a partial picture? The great debate of the
last three decades over how liberal capitalism replaced republicanism as
the dominant American ideology largely ignored the voices of the Federalists. Nearly three decades ago pathbreaking studies by David Hackett
Fischer, Linda K. Kerber, and James M. Banner showed that Federalist
leaders at both the national and local level were committed to republican
ideals and that Federalism continued to exist as a dynamic political and
cultural influence long after it ceased to be a major player in national
politics.[8] Since their work, however, studies of the transformation of

American political culture from the Revolution to the Jacksonian era have focused primarily on the victorious Jeffersonians, who evolved together with the United States into the party of capitalism, individualism, free labor, and slavery. The Federalists, it seems, simply were not part of the "'dominant' mode of cultural hegemony from 1790 to 1820."[9] Rather, by rejecting popular politics and vociferously lamenting the erosion of public deference, they were branded the American incarnation of the British court party—a group associated with English monarchism, aristocratic manipulation, political corruption, and careless disregard for the popular will.[10]

The chapters in this volume provide evidence that there is much more to the Federalists than the political and diplomatic intrigues of the 1790s. Federalism indeed originated on the federal level. Yet its narrative permeated politics at all levels and lingered long after the party lost hope of regaining power at the national level. American political culture was fashioned in a dialogue. Deeply conservative, self-destructive, and anachronistic though they were, the Federalists nevertheless advanced an alternative course that survived long after the "death" of the party.

Federalism grew out of national and international politics, and we begin by examining the "Age of Federalism." The men who supported the Constitution drafted in Philadelphia in the summer of 1787 called themselves Federalists and their opponents Anti-Federalists. When political parties emerged in the 1790s, supporters of the administration, hoping to capitalize on the legitimacy conferred by the Constitution, conceptualized the political map in terms of the battle over ratification. They too called themselves Federalists and their opponents Anti-Federalists. But the coalitions of the late 1780s did not last into the constitutional era. James Madison, the intellectual force behind the constitutional movement, was also the founder and leader of the Republican opposition, while Anti-Federalist leaders like Patrick Henry, Luther Martin, and John Marshall became staunch Federalists.

The Federalists' loyalty to the spirit of the Constitution partially explains their hostility to the appearance of an opposition. They interpreted the political battles of the early republic through the prism of the contest over ratification. The Constitution, after all, was constructed in part to prevent the development of political parties. Madison himself praised "its tendency to break and control the violence of faction."[11] The Jeffersonian campaign against Alexander Hamilton's finances fostered the spirit of "a faction . . . subversive of the principles of good government and dangerous to the union, peace and happiness of the country."[12]

The first order of business for the Washington administration was to solidify a distinct American identity in the former British colonies. "Do the people of the United States form a nation?" asked Associate Justice of the Supreme Court James Wilson in 1793. Indeed, the only bond that seemed to unify the United States in the 1790s was a vague allegiance to the Constitution. That document, however, merely constructed a "roof without walls."[13] The Federalists had to persuade the residents of the various states and the unorganized trans-Appalachian region that the men and women under the loose jurisdiction of the government indeed constituted a people.

The success of the experiment in nation making depended upon the Federalists' ability to bind the loyalty of the former British subjects to the idea of the nation and to its governing elite. The struggle over who would be included in the body politic was crucial in determining the nature of the new political community. As Rogers Smith explains, American identity came to be defined by ascriptive conceptions of inborn and unalterable characteristics. The nativist exclusiveness of the Alien and Sedition Acts reflected the Federalists' growing fear over their shrinking authority in an increasingly ethnically and culturally diverse society. They tried to exclude the "other" from the body politic and offered a restrictive definition of national identity. Citizenship became a matter of birth, heritage, and natural allegiance in which certain ethnic backgrounds were defined as more truly American than others. These measures, ironically, fostered the strange political alliance between southern slaveholding planters and northern and mid-Atlantic immigrant farmers and workers that propelled the Jeffersonians to power in 1800. In the end, the Federalists defined themselves right out of American nationalism.

It was Alexander Hamilton whose vision and diplomacy polarized early national politics. Hostility to his financial program and pro-British diplomacy, particularly his blueprint for the Bank of the United States and his antipathy to the French Revolution, galvanized the Jeffersonian opposition. Proponents of Washington's administration united under the Federalist standard, arguing the necessity of centralizing power and stabilizing national finances in order to prevent a return to the localism, disorder, and international humiliation of the 1780s. Partisan lines were drawn somewhat more clearly after France declared war on Great Britain in February 1793. Jefferson applauded the French for carrying on the republican enterprise and justified the violent turn of the French Revolution by arguing that the "liberty of the whole earth" was at stake and that rather than have the Revolution fail, he would prefer to see "half the earth desolated."[14] The Federalists, on the other hand, were horrified by the violent turn of events in Paris. They also believed that American interests and the credibility of the new government depended on the maintenance of good relations with Great Britain, which was by far the republic's most important trading partner: 90 percent of American imports came from the British Empire, and over 90 percent of federal revenue came from customs duties on those imports.

It is no coincidence that the first party system emerged at the beginning of the wars of the French Revolution and expired a few years after the Congress of Vienna. France and Britain, in their attempt to starve each other into submission, seized American ships, confiscated American goods, and scornfully violated American sovereignty. Neither the Federalists nor the Republicans favored direct military intervention. Both believed, however, that the future of the republic depended on the outcome of the conflict. Unlike the Republicans, Federalists were willing to tolerate British violations of American neutrality and occasional seizures of American ships and goods because Britain protected the republic from "an open hell, still ringing with agonies and blasphemies, still smoking with sufferings and crimes."[15] And indeed popular participation in the partisan struggles centered around issues of diplomacy. In 1795 the Jeffersonians took to the streets to protest the Jay Treaty, which they maintained placed the United States in the British camp. Three years later, when Franco-American relations had descended into open hostilities, Federalists rode the crest of patriotism to gain control of Congress and try to eliminate the opposition.

Doron Ben-Atar and Herbert Sloan rethink Hamilton's putative submissive loyalty to Great Britain and the success of his financial plan. Ben-Atar challenges the standard view of Hamilton as an apologist for, if not an active agent of, British economic and diplomatic domination. Hamilton indeed appreciated the source of Britain's power. During the Philadelphia Convention he described the British constitution as "the best in the world" and urged the delegates to adopt much of it.[16] But he had no intention of turning the United States into a British satellite. On the contrary, he wanted the young republic to become strong enough to challenge British economic dominance in North America. Britain was to be the model, not the master. Like many of his contemporaries, Hamilton believed that Britain owed its power to its industrial economy. Developing American manufacturing seemed the best way to rid the young nation of its dependence on British imports. The infant manufacturers of the United States, however, were technologically inferior to British industries and could compete in neither quality nor price. To remedy American inferiority Hamilton proposed that the government orchestrate the transfer of technology across the Atlantic by smuggling advanced machinery and encouraging the migration of experienced workers. British officials were alarmed by the plan and its endorsement of technology piracy and industrial espionage. Hamilton nevertheless asked Congress to enact an industrialization program that threatened the supposed foundation of Britain's power—its industrial superiority.

Heading the list of Federalist achievements was the creation of the economic foundations for the transition to industrial capitalism that occurred early in the nineteenth century. Hamilton's plan to pay the Revolutionary War debt won public confidence in government securities and provided capital needed to fuel economic growth. The Bank of the United States stabilized the nation's finances by establishing an agency to regulate the currency and institute a common circulating medium. Yet, as Sloan reminds us, Hamilton's funding system was too bold for late eighteenth-century America. Before he left office in January 1795, Hamilton submitted to Congress a report on the state of American credit in which he all but admitted that his fiscal policy had failed to establish public credit on a "secure and lasting basis."

Why was Hamilton so disillusioned with a system that even his rivals kept intact after they came to power in 1800? He was alarmed, Sloan argues, by Congress's failure to establish a domestic tax structure capable of supporting an assertive government and its decision to rely on customs duties to support the entire operation of government. Borrowing from Dutch bankers during times of crisis, as the Continental Congress had done, was no longer possible: France had established a puppet regime in the Netherlands that was unlikely to finance the United States at a time when Franco-American relations were rapidly deteriorating. Attempts to raise money through excise precipitated the two semirevolts of the 1790s, the Whiskey and Fries rebellions. The Federalist effort to put the nation's finances on a sound footing failed because Hamilton did not appreciate the reluctance of Americans to tax themselves. As Jefferson admitted, taxes were among the primary reasons for the Federalists' defeat in 1800. The Republicans, in contrast, seductively offered to eliminate all internal taxes.

Andrew Cayton concludes the opening section of this volume by examining the way in which the Federalists successfully integrated the unorganized Northwest into the American body politic. Keeping the western lands within the Union depended on the Federalists' ability to accomplish several objectives: to instill in western inhabitants a sense of American nationhood; to persuade the residents of towns in the Ohio Valley to consider themselves members of one American national family; and to impress upon them that they would be better off as part of the United States than as subjects of England, Spain, or France or as independent enemies. The performance of the federal government in the late 1780s and early 1790s could hardly have been reassuring on those points. It had failed to solve the two major problems faced by white westerners— attacks by Indians and Spain's closure of the Mississippi River to American navigation and shipment of goods in 1784. Westerners might rightly have asked, as Cayton writes, why they should remain loyal to a government that could not solve the fundamental problems of its people. Indeed, Federalist leaders worried that the trans-Appalachian region would become a separate political entity. Rufus King was so certain in 1786 that the West would not be part of the United States that he saw every emigrant to the West as "forever lost to the Confederacy."[17]

The Federalists constructed an American nationalism that met the needs and desires of western settlers. Their elaborate plan for colonizing the West and their willingness to use national power (both coercion and diplomacy) to implement it made them "the most thorough-going radicals in the 'western world' in the late eighteenth century." By the mid-1790s the Federalists had defeated the Indians, established their authority by suppressing the Whiskey Rebellion, and signed treaties with Spain and England to secure the commercial routes of the region. As Cayton writes, "Flags, forts, uniforms, and cannon were visible and welcome manifestations of federal authority in the Northwest Territory." The lasting imperial legacy of the Federalists is the establishment of a transcendent and expansive American identity, eager and ready to march across the continent. As Eric J. Hobsbawm put it, "There is nothing like being an imperial people to make a population conscious of its collective existence as such."[18]

The second section explores "The Origins of American Political Culture." The Federalists are often depicted as the conservative alternative of the era—patricians who tried to stem the tide of participatory politics. What, we ask, was the meaning of their political conservatism? It had very little to do with the modern political understanding of the term, as the successful appropriation of the Jeffersonian legacy by modern conservatives suggests.[19] Like present-day critics of liberalism, the Jeffersonians charged that the Federalists were elitist and called for a more open and responsive political order. To the Jeffersonians, the government under Federalist control seemed a corrupt, money-hungry monster, an interest group in itself. And the Federalists' positions on race and gender, their distrust of the free market, and their cultural elitism are reminiscent of contemporary liberalism. Reversing the labels, however, and equating the Jeffersonians with modern conservatives and the Federalists with modern liberals is equally misleading and anachronistic. The Federalists interpreted the Revolutionary mandate to mean the creation of a representative government responsive to, yet independent of, the popular will. They were nationalists who respected local autonomy. They were aristocrats competing in a new political world for the votes of ordinary individuals. Their political plan, however, continued to conform to "the paradox of Rousseau—all government was the people's and yet the people never directly governed." Committed to the idea that members of the elite were the natural rulers, the Federalists propagated a political culture that in celebration and ritual cultivated "conservative respect for the better sort."[20]

Unlike European conservatives, the Federalists did not question the right of the people to express their political preference through the ballot and were content with the popular will as long as it confirmed their view of social hierarchy. The same people who favored a strong central government as a check against the danger posed to liberty and property by the dictates of popular government went on to campaign for the support of the people and proved that they could, at least momentarily, out-democrat the Jeffersonians. The first congressional party caucus was held by members of the opposition in order to block ratification of the Jay Treaty. Republicans took their battle to the streets, denouncing the agreement in newspapers, issuing pamphlets, organizing petitions, and rallying the public against what they saw as humiliating American concessions to Great Britain. "The cry against the treaty," Washington wrote in 1795, "is like a mad dog; and everyone . . . seems engaged in running it down."[21] Initially, the Federalists insisted on keeping secret the terms of the treaty and conducting the debate exclusively among the political elite. As the process moved forward, however, they recognized the need for a counter public campaign. The business community organized support for the treaty. Federalists orchestrated public meetings to protest the threat of the Republican-controlled House of Representatives not to vote the money to implement the treaty and organized a counter petition campaign that found support for the treaty even among such supposedly loyal Republican constituents as western farmers and urban artisans. By the late 1790s the Federalists seemed to master popular politics. In March 1798 President John Adams submitted the XYZ dispatches to Congress. They revealed that not only had France seized American ships and refused to negotiate with the designated American delegations, but the French foreign minister had demanded a personal bribe from the United States as a precondition to negotiations. The Federalists' overwhelming electoral victory in 1798 proved that they had indeed mastered participatory politics.[22]

Federalist immersion in popular politics was not confined to national issues. After Jefferson's ascendance, Federalist party organizers remained active even in the South, where the party routinely garnered 20 to 40 percent of the votes. Many southern Federalists "ran for office using every possible method of winning votes." Young Federalists "tried to create popularly oriented vote-seeking political organization which might defeat Jefferson with his own weapons."[23] But their embrace of a participatory style of politics, as David Waldstreicher demonstrates, was hardly democratic. Federalist political culture played upon gendered rhetoric, nationalist symbols, Christian practices, and homophobic sentiments. The medium was indeed the message in the sense that political style conveyed a set of political commitments and partisan loyalties. Their ultimate goal was the maintenance of a hierarchical and deferential social order that would make the nation federal in style and substance.

Success depended upon the Federalists' ability to win and retain the allegiance of the public. When the French Revolution shook the foundations of American politics, they quickly realized that they must not leave the streets to their rivals. Their problem, however, was trying to persuade their supporters to get behind the slogan of staying out of politics. The Federalists developed what Waldstreicher calls "the style of antistyle." They were quick to label the results of the election of 1800 as the victory of style over substance, and they blamed the Republicans for degrading civic discourse and for replacing natural leaders with political managers who manipulated the public.

While the Federalists refused to let go of their elitist vision, their political opponents successfully fought for the rights of white men. The Republican victory over Federalism, however, meant the elevation of one group at the expense of the others: women, slaves, and Indians. The same Republican ethos that "countenanced a purportedly egalitarian community of enfranchised men . . . had another more conservative face . . . [which] countenanced inequality and relations of power between masters and their dependents."[24] Ironically, the party that sought to stem the tide of popular politics proved far more open to the rights of Indians, women, and African Americans than their Jeffersonian opponents, who championed individual freedom and participatory politics.

Rosemarie Zagarri challenges the view that hostility to the participation of women in the political arena was especially strong among conservatives of the early republic. Federalists were significantly more receptive than the Jeffersonians to the inclusion of women in the political process. Federalist politicians took the lead in soliciting women's votes in New Jersey, the only state that permitted women to vote. Federalists invited women to political gatherings, where speakers addressed women's social and cultural responsibilities in the polity. Zagarri's conclusions are reinforced by Waldstreicher's evidence that women actively participated in the court politics of Federalism. The triumph of the Jeffersonians, the relocation of the nation's capital to Washington, D.C., where there was no resident elite to match those in New York and Philadelphia, and the elimination of the "corrupt court" eroded an important public arena for female activism. While the Jeffersonians marched women toward separate spheres, Zagarri concludes, the Federalists allowed them a certain degree of political participation.[25]

Similarly, as Paul Finkelman shows, Federalists were more sensitive than Jeffersonians to the plight of African Americans. Manasseh Cutler and Nathan Dane, proponents of the prohibition on slavery in the Northwest Ordinance, became Federalists. The Washington and Adams administrations aided the rebelling slaves of St. Domingue, to the horror of England, France, and the Jeffersonians. Both the leaders and the members of northern antislavery societies were overwhelmingly Federalist.[26] The remnants of the northern Federalists led the battle to restrict the expansion of slavery during the Missouri controversy of 1819–21. And the pro-slavery forces recognized this reality and charged "that the entire movement was a Federalist plot."[27] Indeed, the Republicans successfully defeated the restrictionist forces primarily through a rhetorical identification of pro-restriction with the Federalist party of the War of 1812. Only traitors who were willing to betray their country during its darkest moments would oppose the admission of Missouri, they insisted.

Seizing upon the Federalist support for the rights of slaves and free Africans, Jeffersonian candidates introduced race into their electoral campaigns. Free blacks clearly comprehended who stood for freedom and who for slavery: soon after Massachusetts allowed African Americans to vote in 1811, for example, their support for Federalist candidates in 1812 brought about a Republican defeat in Salem. New York's free blacks faithfully voted for the Federalist ticket. The few North Carolina blacks who voted until they were disenfranchised in 1835 also sided with the Federalists. As Finkelman explains, blacks recognized that the Federalists' foreign and domestic policies were favorable to them and that they had no political alternative: "Jefferson's was the party of slavery."

Zagarri's and Finkelman's analyses of the Federalists' positions on gender and race show the kinder face of their conservative elitism. Andrew Siegel's analysis of the ideology of Connecticut Federalists and Cayton's arguments on the colonization of the West reinforce this view. Connecticut Federalists opposed the Louisiana Purchase because it gave new life to the institution of slavery. Federalists encouraged the migration of women to the West, believing that the presence of families there would counter the wildness of the frontiersmen. They called for fair treatment of Indians and tried to prohibit the spread of slavery into the region. The defeat of the Federalist vision by the new democratic order spelled a diminished status for women, Indians, and Africans.

These same Federalists who advocated greater respect for Indian rights, spoke against slavery, and addressed women as participants in the polity saw nothing inconsistent in upholding a social order that denied equality to Indians, blacks, and women and imposed on white men property qualifications for voting. They sharply distinguished between an abstract moral community composed of all human beings and a concrete political community whose membership was limited. They assumed that the better should govern. Power, however, involved an obligation to assist those less capable of protecting themselves: women, nonelite white males, African slaves, and Indians. The Republicans promised to remove government from peoples' lives. The Federalists, on the other hand, were committed to the idea that government was necessary to protect the weak.

Was there a class dimension to the division between Federalists and Jeffersonians? Federalists supposedly represented mercantile and financial circles while Republicans spoke for farmers and workers. The leaders of both parties, however, came from the upper socioeconomic echelon. Ironically, Republican leaders often came from even more privileged backgrounds. On the national level, for example, Jefferson and Madison were planter aristocrats by birth while Hamilton and Adams were parvenu self-made men. Similar patterns appear in the composition of New York's congressional delegations from 1789 to 1803, where Republicans tended to come from more privileged and wealthier families. Republicans in New York and Pennsylvania championed the new commercial banking of the age. In fact, the Federalist insistence on a limited and controlled banking policy alienated artisans and small merchants, who transferred their support to the Republicans. On the other hand, New York City election results from 1800 show the Federalists running strong in wards "where assessments were high, houses were large, lots were scarce and addresses were fashionable."[28] In sum, the partisan divisions of the early republic do not conform to any clear-cut socioeconomic alignment.

Federalist policies nevertheless benefited the upper class and facilitated the growth of market capitalism. Hamiltonian financing of the Continental war debt benefited the 2 percent of white men who held government securities in 1790. Most of these men were Philadelphia, Boston, and New York merchants, and Hamilton's policy successfully tied them to the federal government. Many others who stood to gain from the establishment of an effective central government also joined the Federalist ranks. As Joyce Appleby put it, the "underlying issue was . . . class"; Jeffersonians "unified ordinary voters through a vision of classlessness," whereas the Federalists stood for the "permanence of social classes."[29]

After acquiring wealth and status, Federalists turned to worrying about the political, social, and cultural excesses brought about by market capitalism. Their response, as Steven Watts explains, included "collusion and uneasiness, participation and rejection." To illustrate this tension Watts offers three short intellectual biographies of prominent New Englanders as archetypes of distinct groups of Federalists: poet Timothy Dwight represents traditional clerical Federalism, John Adams the politically moderate wing of the party, and Massachusetts politician Josiah Quincy the young dissenters whose treasonable actions during the War of 1812 sealed the party's political fate. All three figures fashioned an uncertain view of their surroundings and adopted "a deeply troubled creed of ambivalence, despair, and guilt that encouraged the ascendancy of liberal capitalism while lamenting its consequences." The Federalists, then, had hoped to regulate the market economy in a way that would allow Americans to enjoy the prosperity it ushered in while preserving the stability and hierarchy of the precapitalist world. They were no match for the emerging capitalist order that dramatically altered the U.S. economy, society, and politics. Unable to control the forces that were shaping their world, in the end the Federalists retreated from public life.

The concluding section offers a taste of the diversity of Federalism that transcended national politics and lasted into the third decade of the nineteenth century. Three case studies in the "Varieties of Federalism" focus on Federalists in Philadelphia, Connecticut, and the frontier. Keith Arbour examines one fanatical high Federalist's vicious anti-Republican campaign in the turbulent 1790s. Andrew Siegel analyzes the complex ideology that took Connecticut Federalists to the brink of secession in the winter of 1814–15. Alan Taylor looks at the personal political imperatives of a northern rural context.

The nasty turn of the French Revolution and the growing popularity of the Jeffersonian opposition shook the faith of some Federalists that participatory politics could be controlled and contained. The most extreme exponent of this mood, pamphleteer William Cobbett of Philadelphia, launched a virulent campaign against imagined agents of French Jacobinism in America. Born in England, Cobbett flirted briefly with republican ideas and even spent some time in revolutionary France before migrating to America in 1794. Here he aligned himself with the most extreme anti-Jeffersonian positions, issuing attacks so fierce that Federalists from Fisher Ames to John and Abigail Adams found them offensive. Yet his pamphlets, which sold well, offer us a glimpse into the anxious minds of the party's most virulent supporters.

Writing as "Peter Porcupine," Cobbett sought to discredit the Jeffersonians by attacking the reputation of Benjamin Franklin, dead since 1790. Franklin's legacy was indisputably claimed by the Republicans. The first extended attack on the Jay Treaty, published in March 1795 under the title *Letters of Franklin*, intimated that had Franklin been alive he would have been outraged by the Federalist submission to Britain. Cobbett in turn seized on the connection between Franklin's Francophilia and the French Revolution as a way to attack the Jeffersonians, the American incarnation of Jacobinism. In the cultural expression of the political battles of the 1790s, the historical Franklin came to symbolize the ideology and culture that threatened aristocratic hegemony. If Franklin was a "whoremaster, a hypocrite and an infidel," then the opposition that was closely associated with his legacy was tainted by the very same evils.

Neither Cobbett's fanaticism nor the election of 1800 mortally wounded Federalism. As late as 1816 the party controlled the state governments of Maryland, Connecticut, Delaware, and Massachusetts and garnered between 40 and 50 percent of the votes cast that year in New Jersey, New York, Rhode Island, New Hampshire, and Vermont. Andrew

Siegel's study of the social and political thought of Connecticut Federalists in the first two decades of the nineteenth century portrays a vibrant political force subscribing to a complex and forward-looking set of political ideas. Federalists dominated the state's politics, and it was no coincidence that the Federalists chose Hartford as the meeting place for their bold and controversial convention in 1814. In every presidential contest from 1796 to 1816, Connecticut cast all of its electoral votes for the Federalist nominee. Until 1818 both the state's Governor's Council and its delegation to the House of Representatives were composed only of Federalists. In short, Connecticut Federalists hardly acted like timid, retreating have-beens.

Committed to republican ideology, they worried about French-modeled revolutionary republicanism overtaking the fragile American government. They interpreted the legacy of the Revolution in a restorational manner—i.e., returning to the liberty protected by time-tested institutions and practices. The Jeffersonians, they charged, embraced the concept of a new beginning and licensed anarchy. Connecticut Federalists "drew a stark line between liberty and license and portrayed the latter as the violent enemy of the republic." Their opposition to the War of 1812 originated in their conviction that the Jefferson and Madison administrations undertook policies which bordered on despotism.

Pride in the Federalist legacy and New England exceptionalism informed the party's stand on national and local issues. In keeping with the exclusionary mood of the Alien and Sedition Acts, they celebrated the ethnic homogeneity of New England that made residents of that region a "superior caste." Federalists, who in their youth had been synonymous with the creation of an American nation, came to view national issues such as the Louisiana Purchase, the Embargo, the War of 1812, western development, and slavery through ascriptive ethnic and regional prisms. The traditional narrative of the early republic pictures New England Federalists following the rest of the nation marching into the Republican tent. Siegel's study of Connecticut, however, demonstrates that Jeffersonian Republicanism never triumphed. With Anglo-American relations settled, peace in Europe, and the structure of American government and development in place, the distinction that separated Federalists and Jeffersonians became irrelevant. In Connecticut, Federalist and Jeffersonian persuasions died simultaneously.

Alan Taylor's "From Fathers to Friends of the People: Political Personae in the Early Republic" analyzes the partisan struggle in the context of the emerging capitalism on the northern frontier. Taylor studies the careers of Henry Knox and William Cooper, two Federalists who owed their rise and fall to these changes. Men of humble origin, they obtained through shady maneuvers large tracts of land confiscated from exiled loyalists. Once established, they adopted paternalistic aristocratic behavior, rejected the market culture they had used to gain their wealth, and became staunch defenders of the status quo. Their efforts "to bring the Revolution to a premature end" were defeated by a new political culture that rejected the aristocratic pretensions of the eighteenth century. Indeed, the difference between Federalist and Jeffersonian leaders came down to the timing and pace with which they rose. Federalists gained power and wealth quickly in the 1770s and 1780s, while Jeffersonians accumulated them later, and more slowly.

Federalists initiated, benefited from, and even celebrated some of the social changes and economic prosperity unleashed in the period following the American Revolution. They welcomed the commercial prosperity that came with the second half of the 1780s and accelerated after the outbreak of the wars of the French Revolution. Wealth, after all, was the prerequisite for gentility. They did not, however, wholeheartedly embrace a "vision of America as an advanced commercial republic."[30] Ever aware of their humble origins and dreading displacement by new and aggressive challengers, Knox and Cooper tried to reinvent themselves as natural aristocrats deserving of their socioeconomic standing. The genteel ideal, Taylor explains, created a paradox: the acquisition of substantial property required traits of cunning that were at odds with aristocratic traits of gentility and disinterested benevolence. Rural Federalists wanted to restore the order of colonial society with themselves on top. They failed because they underestimated "the enduring potential of the American Revolution's legacy to legitimate upstarts unwilling or unable to achieve or to endure genteel authority."

In sum, this volume presents a nuanced, tension-ridden, and paradoxical Federalist legacy. Deriving their social and political position from the American Revolution, whose ideology legitimized perpetual challenges to the established order, the Federalists attempted to write the final act of Revolution and the beginning of normal politics. They proposed a political course, uniquely American, between the two extremes: British monarchic tyranny and French republican despotism. Their successes and failures, together with those of their rivals, formed the foundations of American politics. These chapters question the wisdom of the traditional dichotomies of elitist, reactionary Federalists and democratic, progressive Jeffersonians; of treasonous New Englanders and unionist Jeffersonians; and of the wealthy and the people. We portray an active Federalist coalition that offered a vibrant intellectual and political alternative throughout the era of the early republic. We show Federalism cutting across the boundaries of region, culture, race, gender, and class and struggling with the complex problems of nation building, national identity, and economic development. And as contemporary America struggles with similar issues, we propose the unthinkable—that the Federalists are relevant.

PART I

Age of Federalism

1

CONSTRUCTING AMERICAN NATIONAL IDENTITY

Strategies of the Federalists

Rogers M. Smith

EARLY IN ONE of the most rapidly repudiated Supreme Court decisions in history, *Chisholm v. Georgia* (1793), the Federalist justice James Wilson digressed to complain about the custom of offering toasts to "the United States." "This," he chided, "is not politically correct." Since such toasts purported to praise "the first great object in the Union," they should be given to the "People of the United States." Wilson wished to stress, in republican fashion, that the people, not their government, were sovereign. But he also wanted to insist that Americans were one people who had created their national government as an act of collective sovereignty, rather than seeing it as the work of the sovereign states, as he feared too many Americans did.[1] Like the *Chisholm* ruling itself, Wilson's digression reflected a crucial concern of Federalists: to foster a sense of American national identity conducive to their aims and governance.

Few scholars would deny that this was Wilson's aim. Nonetheless, many have underestimated how necessary this task was for the Federalists, and how their electoral failures reflected their inability to accomplish it. For example, in their magisterial study of the Federalist era, Stanley Elkins and Eric McKitrick fail to mention the *Chisholm* decision and give little attention to other controversies over citizenship rules that sparked Anti-Federalist agitation in the Jeffersonian press. Elkins and McKitrick then have trouble making sense of the measures that so badly discredited the Federalists, the Alien and Sedition Acts.[2]

Their difficulties exemplify two broader deficiencies in the interpretive tendencies of many scholars of American political development. First, many have written as if existing political boundaries, demographic and physical, could largely be taken for granted. They thereby underestimate just how endemic to all politics is one central task confronting would-be political elites. Aspirants to power must recurringly persuade their potential constituents both that they form a "people," and that by rights they are a people who should be led by those elites.

Those needs are especially pressing when a new political regime is being launched, as in the Federalist era. Yet the distinctiveness of the Federalists' nation-building challenges should not be exaggerated. All political leaders face some of the same tasks, for no political community is natural. All contain or confront populations with histories and beliefs that can be stirred on behalf of allegiance to political communities defined very differently than the ones they inhabit. And all communities contain or confront rival aspirants for leadership eager to do the stirring.

Hence elites engage in sometimes intense, sometimes peripheral, but always continuing contestation over how the bounds of political communities should be defined, in terms of both people and land. They seek to bound political communities in ways that strengthen their constituents and causes while disadvantaging their opponents. In republics those measures often take the form of laws assigning or denying the powers of full citizenship. Such struggles over citizenship form a major dimension of the Federalist-Jeffersonian conflict that intensified through the 1790s, a dimension that explains many otherwise puzzling Federalist statutes and judicial rulings.[3]

The second deficiency is visible even in scholars who recognize the severity of the early American tasks of nation building. Most focus on clashes between national and state allegiances, as Wilson did in *Chisholm*. Those issues mattered greatly, but here I stress another type of conflict. It arises from the propensity of American elites to win adherents by invoking not just state and national ties or related republican and liberal discourses but also "ascriptive" notions of American identity. Ascriptive conceptions define identity not as a matter of personal choice but as one of inborn, largely unalterable characteristics that are claimed to determine who a person is. I have previously argued that Americans long defined their national identity not simply in terms of liberal and republican discourses stressing consensual allegiance to a republic dedicated to individual rights and the common good.[4] They also have held that certain unchosen traits, such as place of birth, race, ethnicity, gender, and hereditary religious affiliation, properly defined who could be a first-class American citizen, with full voting rights. They have done so because often such ascriptive versions of "Americanism" offered a more compelling sense of common identity than secularized, deracinated conceptions of American political communities as merely the contingent creations of people attracted to liberal republicanism.

Such ascriptive doctrines have often been valuable resources for elites trying to foster senses of national allegiance conducive to their rule. The Federalists and Jeffersonians were no exceptions. They advanced distinct visions of American nationality that blended contrasting ascriptive elements with liberal and republican features in conflicting ways. The Federalists were the party of national power and commerce but also the champions of almost unalterable hereditary allegiances and nativism. The Jeffersonians were the party of state power and agrarian republicanism but also, paradoxically, the defenders both of citizenship based on mutual consent and of civic racism. Both partisan positions were the results of comprehensible political calculi as well as sincere principles. And if the Jeffersonians pursued their vision with more electoral success, the Federalists did at least as much to shape the kind of nation the United States would become.

Like the nationalistic Wilson, most members of Washington's new administration believed that they had to establish policies, institutions, customs, and traditions that would give flesh to the more perfect union projected in Philadelphia. Officials in all three branches would erupt into high-flown disquisitions on first principles of republican citizenship and American identity to settle issues ranging from import duties to expatriation to how a republican chief executive should dress (plainly but with dignity). They were acutely aware that their fledgling government faced stiff challenges from every direction. Many Americans doubted that the new national institutions were any good, much less deserving of their highest loyalty. Communal attachments were overwhelmingly local, extending at most to state or regional (as well as denominational) identities. Most state and local officials resisted each assertion of new national authority. Most European powers ignored, derided, or bullied the upstart colonials. Moreover, the success of the republic seemed to require displacing many native tribes while exploiting enslaved blacks. Those groups struggled against white domination in ways that challenged the physical security and moral legitimacy of the new regime.[5]

Most salient, however, were the divisions within the national leadership itself. Initially the government was staffed largely by the more nationalistic Federalists who had won adoption of the Constitution, including Hamilton and Washington. Yet in that first blush of elite unity, Secretary of State Thomas Jefferson and House floor leader James

Madison were happy to join in showing the haughty Europeans that Americans could build a successful, enlightened republic.[6] Then, however, the hostile Hamiltonian Federalist and Jeffersonian Republican camps emerged, in part out of differences over the principles, purposes, and participants appropriate to the new American nationality.

Their conflicts drove segments of these competing elites to define their legal conceptions of U.S. citizenship in ever more sharply opposed terms. At first the differences were not vast. Prominent figures in both camps endorsed liberal republican notions of consensual membership, even if some Federalists stressed the value of native birth. Many leaders hoped for peaceful assimilation of the Indians and the eventual demise of slavery, though few championed racial equality. Those agreements muted major disputes. The Federalist vision of a great commercial republic involved a stress on the primacy of national identity and expansive federal powers, blended with desires to gain new immigrant workers for the cities, a quiet wish to curb slavery, and a passive, live-and-let-live policy toward the unconquered western tribes. Conversely, the Jeffersonian vision of a westward-expanding, state-centered agrarian republic always sanctioned slavery and conquest of the tribes, often by alleging their racial inferiority. In the Confederation era Jefferson also had queried the immigration of European workers who might swell the cities and manufacturing enterprises favored by Hamilton.[7] But Jeffersonians quickly realized that immigrants often felt more affinity for the partisans of small farmers and democratization than for mercantile and financial elites. Hence they reversed course on immigration. And just as the need for immigrants kept most Federalists from expressing aversions to the foreign-born, so southern and western Federalists quickly persuaded most of their northern allies to stifle all antislavery measures and to downplay opposition to white settlers encroaching on Indian lands. Hence, though the nascent parties differed over policies concerning the place of blacks, Native Americans, and immigrants, as well as economic policies and national powers, at first all seemed compromisable.

But in a polity where voters were overwhelmingly white men with localistic allegiances, the Federalists' doubts about slavery and westward expansion and their advocacy of national powers aroused suspicions. When their economic and foreign policies spurred Jeffersonian opposition, Federalists came to believe they could not tolerate disloyalty to the national regime or welcome potentially subversive immigrants. Thus Federalist officials in all three branches abandoned their more cosmopolitan, consensual notions of national identity for more restrictive ones, launching the "first great wave" of American nativism.[8] By adopting statutes and judicial rules defining political allegiances heavily in terms of birthplace, they hoped to compel obedience to the U.S. government and to curb the influx of foreign-born Jeffersonian voters.

Correspondingly, the Jeffersonian Republicans came to champion policies encouraging immigration, including expansive expatriation, naturalization, and voting rights. Hence they became more the party of consensually based democratic citizenship, the self-proclaimed party of "the people," though only for whites. Americans would long continue to build the prosperous national commercial republic the Federalists envisioned, but after 1800 they would do so while primarily electing Jeffersonians. To see why, let us first consider the Federalist view of American nationality in more detail, then turn to the electorally fatal strategies it engendered.

Most Federalists shared Hamilton's hopes to build an extended republic internationally recognized as free and great. It was to be the first large nation ultimately, though only indirectly, governed by its people, and it was to win the world's respect as well as a prosperous security through federally assisted mercantile and industrial growth. Hence it represented a bold new kind of national liberal republicanism, but from early on, many Federalists also gave American nationality further meanings. Those were suggested in *Federalist* no. 2 by the man who was later Wilson's chief ally in *Chisholm*, John Jay.

Jay had proposed to Washington in 1787 that the new president be "native born," a requirement the convention adopted with little recorded discussion. Jay's advocacy of that restriction is understandable in light of his oft-quoted claim in his first essay defending the Constitution. There he said, "Providence has been pleased to give this one connected country to one united people—a people descended from the same ancestors, speaking the same language, professing the same religion, attached to the same principles of government, very similar in their manners and customs, and who, by their joint counsels, arms, and efforts . . . have nobly established their general liberty and independence."[9]

As many have noted, Jay lived in the already ethnically and religiously cosmopolitan New York City and was himself three-eighths French and five-eighths Dutch, without any English ancestry. He knew the inaccuracy of his assertions. His exaggerations were aimed in part at countering Anti-Federalist charges that America was too heterogeneous to make a consolidated republic possible. His claim that national unity seemed to be "the design of Providence" leading toward "Greatness" also helped reassure Americans that the path of the new Constitution was the right one to take.

Still, Jay's proposal to restrict the presidency to natives suggests that these arguments were not just rhetoric. For many Federalists, America had indeed been given by God to a "chosen people" of northern European–descended Protestants destined to build a great nation that would be a beacon of political freedom and spiritual truth. Their national vocation might falter, however, if persons not sharing in the "inheritance" of this chosen "band of brethren" exercised too much influence. Hence from the start the national vision of many Federalists had potentially exclusionary ethnic and religious elements.[10]

But at first the need to attract new immigrants for nation building reinforced the more inclusive, cosmopolitan conception of American identity previously articulated by Tom Paine and Crèvecoeur. They held that America's special role in promoting freedom called for providing opportunities to all European newcomers. Washington himself long called for America to be an "asylum" for the "oppressed and persecuted of all Nations and Religions," a view that gave higher moral purpose to Hamilton's arguments for the economic benefits of adding laborers.[11]

The Federalist vision had little place for black chattel slavery, but few thought they could safely challenge it. Congress did reenact the Confederation's antislavery, ethnically inclusive Northwest Ordinance with minor modifications, and it rejected later efforts to open the Northwest to slavery. Federal officials also did not pressure Britain to pay reparations for slaves taken from Americans during the war. Hamilton and Jay dropped that demand, among others, in negotiating the Jay Treaty in 1794, sparking charges of betrayal by slave-owning Jeffersonians. Congress also banned exports of slaves in 1794.[12]

But because even these mild antislavery acts hurt the Federalists politically, they also offered major concessions to slaveholders, unsuccessfully striving for damage control. From 1789 on, Governor Arthur St. Clair interpreted the Northwest Ordinance's ban on slavery as only prospective. Existing property rights in slaves must be respected, he insisted, a dubious statutory reading which Congress tacitly accepted. Under pressure from southern states, particularly North Carolina, Congress also organized first the Southwest Territory and then the Mississippi Territory under provisions allowing slavery. Congress sanctioned slavery in the District of Columbia as well, and in 1792 it passed a Militia Act which called for the enrollment of all "free, able-bodied, white male" citizens because white citizen-soldiers would be needed to put down slave revolts.[13] The most active aid the national government gave to slavery was the Fugitive Slave Act of 1793, passed with little debate and strong support (48–7 in the House). The law abrogated virtually all canons of legal due process, including habeas corpus, trial by jury, assistance of counsel, protection against self-incrimination, and time limitations on vulnerability to arrest, to slaveholders' great benefit.

On balance, then, by silent consent and active legislation, Congress did much to perpetuate slavery in these years and virtually nothing to move blacks toward freedom or citizenship. It accepted a harsh racial caste system as constitutive of the new nation. Federalist concerns to placate the slave states, along with fears raised by the Haitian rebellion in 1791 and religious and scientific arguments mounted by slavery's defenders, easily trumped arguments for equal human rights. Yet northern Federalists only managed to alienate antislavery forces while failing to still southern suspicions.[14]

The Federalists' policies toward Native Americans also were conflicted and counterproductive. The Washington administration tried to treat the tribes with what Secretary of War Henry Knox termed "liberal justice," in part because it was still hard to dictate to them. Governor St. Clair's forces were badly beaten in the Northwest Territories by Shawnees and others in 1791, and federal forces only gained control over these areas after victories in 1794.[15] Hence the United States dealt with the tribes by treaty, instead of claiming that the tribes had been conquered and legislating directly over them. Waving aside such claims, Knox always referred to the tribes as "foreign nations." Federal treaties supposedly were consensual agreements with these sovereign foreigners.

The leaders of the infant U.S. government pursued this course partly to promote national authority versus the states. If the tribes were foreign nations, the Constitution required that they be dealt with only by the United States exercising its exclusive treaty powers. Washington's men knew about the crippling inability of the Confederation Congress to constrain state actions toward the tribes, and they knew that apart from the treaty clause, their constitutional title to exclusive conduct of Native American affairs was ambiguous. Even with his government's new military powers, Washington despaired of its inability to "restrain Land Jobbers, and the Incroachment of Settlers, upon the Indian Territory." Thus it seemed strategic to secure constitutional sanction for federal predominance by treating the tribes as nations.[16]

Strategic, but still risky. Many citizens viewed Indian lands as rightfully part of the United States and denied that the tribes had any rights which white men were bound to respect. As with slavery, the Federalist policy of relative passivity toward Native Americans fueled opposition to the national regime, among both whites seeking tribal lands and supporters of state power. Complaints that the U.S. government was holding back settler "Incroachment" contributed to the Pennsylvania Whiskey Rebellion of 1794. National officials tried to make their loyalty to the interests of white citizens and the states clear by claiming for the United States and the states a "right of preemption." The tribes' property rights in the lands they occupied were said to be limited to occupancy. The American government, state or national, within whose limits a tribe resided had a preemptive right to purchase any lands the tribe might wish to sell and to veto other sales.[17]

The assertion of such preemptive rights reassured whites that the U.S. government did not really regard the tribes as independent nations. Instead it assumed a vague measure of special authority over them that looked much like ultimate sovereignty. Yet this step did not suffice to quell opposition to Federalist policies. Heated disputes arose over whether the states had ceded all their preemptive powers to the federal government. National officials still regularly opposed proponents of white expansion and states' rights, at great cost to Federalist popularity.[18]

The leading sources of partisan conflict over how national identity should be shaped in law came, however, on three further fronts. First were Federalist efforts to declare the legal primacy of national over state citizenship. Second were Federalist judicial rulings insisting on near-perpetual allegiance to the nation. Third were the Federalists' mounting legislative attempts to deny full political privileges to immigrant Jeffersonians. On all three fronts Federalists increasingly expressed a sense of American national identity with harsh nativist elements.

Although nationalist-minded Federalists maintained a strong hold on Congress and the cabinet through the late 1790s, Jeffersonian defenders of state prerogatives often were numerous enough to compel concessions in nationalizing legislation.[19] Thus many of the most controversial actions on citizenship came from Federalists in the judiciary. The constitutional text offered federal judges some tempting bases for expanding their own power as well as the rights of national citizenship. Article III, section 2 (the diversity of citizenship clause), extended federal judicial power to cases "between a State and Citizens of another State" and between "citizens of different States." Article IV, section 2, granted the citizens of "each state" all the "privileges and immunities of citizens in the several States." The diversity clause gave the federal courts opportunities to assert and expand the primacy of national membership by allowing federal judges to rule whenever citizens were involved in interstate conflicts. The terse language of the privileges and immunities clause offered federal jurists an even more open-ended vehicle for giving national content to the rights of the "citizens of the several states." But efforts to read both provisions broadly ran afoul of state-centered republican beliefs.

Even choices to create lower federal courts and grant them any diversity jurisdiction at all were controversial in the First Congress. That body nonetheless adopted the landmark Judiciary Act of 1789, written largely by the Connecticut Federalist Oliver Ellsworth, a chief author of the judiciary article in the Constitution who would follow Jay as chief justice of the Supreme Court. Unsurprisingly, the act mapped out extensive national powers, but Federalists also made concessions to Anti-Federalists. Congress did not give the federal courts the full range of powers that Article III permitted. Civil diversity cases had to involve amounts greater than $500, a large sum. One of the parties had to be a citizen in the state in which the suit was brought, and most significantly, federal courts had to apply state laws in "trials at common law." Thus litigants could not hope to be heard in a federal court far from the state political interests their cases might implicate, nor did the federal courts have much power to craft national common law rules altering state practices. These features meant the states would not be too greatly subordinated to the national courts.[20]

Even so, the Supreme Court appealed to the centrality of national citizenship to read its diversity jurisdiction expansively in *Chisholm*. Alexander Chisholm, a South Carolinian, sued the state of Georgia for payment of a war debt owed to an estate of which he was executor. Georgia denied the Supreme Court had jurisdiction. It insisted that the words of Article III, section 2, granting jurisdiction in controversies "between a State and Citizens of another State" had never been meant to override a sovereign state's venerable common law right not to be sued without its consent. Indeed, Georgia viewed the case as such an affront to its sovereignty that it refused even to appear before the Supreme Court.

The justices were affronted in turn, but Georgia's claim was strong. True, the broad phrasing of Article III did not mention the exception the state asserted. That absence had been both criticized and defended in ratifying debates. Two members of the Constitutional Convention's Committee on Detail, Edmund Randolph and James Wilson, later urged ratification while arguing for the suability of the states. But in Virginia,

Madison had asserted that Article III was not meant to end sovereign immunity. Even Hamilton argued in *Federalist* no. 81 that to read the Constitution as altering this prerogative would be "forced and unwarrantable."[21]

Yet with Wilson on the bench and Randolph representing Chisholm as a private client (though Randolph was now the U.S. attorney general), the Supreme Court ruled that Chisholm could sue Georgia, with only Justice James Iredell in dissent on technical common law grounds.[22] The other justices stressed the absence of any overt recognition of state immunity in the Constitution and the clear vulnerability of the states to suits from other states. Chief Justice John Jay as well as Wilson grandly insisted the true issue was the worth of national citizenship.

Wilson was clearly glad of the occasion to drive that point home. Calling the case one "of uncommon magnitude," he contended it rested on the "radical" question, "do the people of the United States form a Nation?" He dismissed the views of international law writers as irrelevant, claiming that until recently the "great idea" of a true "Nation" had been contemplated by only a "few comprehensive minds," such as those of the nation-building English monarchs Elizabeth and Henry IV. Wilson rejected as "degrading" the "feudal" conception that governments were sovereign and could refuse to be sued if they so chose. In a real nation the "body of the people" held "supreme power." Hence the ancient "Saxon government" had been suable by all comers, Wilson asserted. American state governments, built in this Saxon tradition, should also be suable.[23] Wilson thereby blended a myth of Americans' Anglo-Saxon identity, Tudor notions of nationhood, and the national republican doctrine that all the American people formed one popular sovereign to assert a nationally enforceable citizenship right limiting state power.

Jay's brief opinion carried forth his *Federalist* argument that even before the Declaration of Independence, Americans were one people "already united for general purposes." He dismissed the allegedly sovereign early state governments and the Articles of Confederation as mere "temporary arrangements." Jay also claimed, with the same disregard for facts displayed in *Federalist* no. 2, that American citizens were all "as to civil rights perfectly equal." Since all free citizens could sue all other citizens, Jay said, citizens of one state should be able to sue all the citizens of another state, as represented by their state government. To hold otherwise would be to violate equal justice for all, for "the few against the many, as well as the many against the few."[24]

Jay's insistence on the rights of the "few" in question—public creditors—was true to Hamiltonian economic precepts and to the Federalists' political base among wealthy elites. It was therefore anathema to most believers in republican state sovereignty. Georgia refused to comply with the decision, and others attacked it as fostering "a general consolidation of these confederated republics." In January 1794 opponents introduced the Eleventh Amendment in Congress, aiming to undo *Chisholm.* The Senate quickly approved it 23–2, the House 81–9. Even most Federalists were unwilling to brook such a direct, confrontational assertion of the supremacy of national citizenship and national courts over state prerogatives. State ratifications came quickly. The requisite number was reached by February 1795, though the president did not certify ratification until 1798.[25] The battle reenergized those advocating state-centered republicanism, the backbone of the future Jeffersonian coalition. In its wake the Supreme Court made no effort to give the privileges and immunities clause the great nationalizing significance Hamilton had projected for it.[26]

Though most accounts of the Federalist-Jeffersonian conflicts have stressed their differing constituencies, their clashing economic visions, and their rival allegiances to France and England, some have noted briefly that the two camps also struggled over expatriation and naturalization issues in ways that climaxed with the Alien and Sedition Acts and a new Naturalization Act in 1798. Most scholars, however, agree with Elkins and McKitrick that the 1798 laws were almost unfathomably irrational creations of "Federalist bedlamites." Yet even they concede that the leading advocate of the 1798 Naturalization Act, Harrison Gray Otis, was no extremist but rather a "'moderate' Adams supporter."[27]

A better explanation is needed. Though irremediably counterproductive, the Federalists' expatriation and naturalization judicial rulings and laws are comprehensible once we focus on how their struggles pushed Federalists and Jeffersonians to advocate opposed views of U.S. citizenship. Out of their commitment to the primacy of a national republic, their belief in the superiority of the native American variant of northern European civilization, and their ardent desires to command allegiance to the national government, during the 1790s Federalists in Congress and on federal benches moved toward the position foreshadowed by Jay in *Federalist* no. 2. They maintained American citizenship was rightfully as much a matter of birth, heritage, and natural allegiance as of choice, and that some sorts of "blood" were more truly American than others. The nativistic laws of 1798 were only the final bitter fruit of this more natural-istic and restrictive view of citizenship. Conversely, both principle and partisan advantage fueled the Jeffersonian assault on these doctrines as "feudal" and unrepublican violations of the Revolution's principles. The key point for historical understanding is to see how the Federalists' turn to ascriptive conceptions initially gave them many tools to reinforce their hold on power, while also expressing a vision of common identity many found wise and inspiring. Thus it seemed prudent and right, though in the end it provided only short-term gains.

An illuminating prelude to these developments occurred almost as the first congressmen were taking their seats. Dr. David Ramsay of South Carolina petitioned the House not to accept one of South Carolina's elected representatives, William Smith, on the ground that Smith had not been a naturalized citizen of the United States for the requisite seven years. Smith, born in Charleston, had gone to study in Europe in 1770 at age twelve and was absent from the United States until 1782, missing the entire Revolution. In Ramsay's petition, which he also published as a pamphlet, he maintained that citizenship was more than mere inhabit-ancy. It involved a share of "the common sovereignty," including "the right of voting at elections," which was why "Negroes are inhabitants, but not citizens." Blending Blackstone and Locke, Ramsay said such a share of sovereignty could be acquired in five ways: by being a party to the Declaration of Independence, by taking an oath to a Revolutionary state government, by tacitly consenting to remain in the states as they achieved independence, by being born in such a state after it attained indepen-dence, or by formal naturalization. Smith had done none of these things. His absence meant he had neither explicitly nor tacitly consented to the Revolution. He had been born in South Carolina before its indepen-dence. On return, he had never been formally naturalized.[28]

Smith responded in Congress that he and others had been effectively authorized by the Revolutionary South Carolina legislature to continue their studies abroad, and that his actions showed he had always chosen to be an American citizen. South Carolinians had signaled their agreement by electing him to office. Madison, though speaking on Smith's behalf, took a less consensual view. He contended that people acquired alle-giances at birth primarily to the society in which they were born and only secondarily to the sovereign it had established. When society replaced that sovereign, its members continued to owe allegiance to the society by "ties of nature" and to the new sovereign it designated. Smith was thus "bound by the decision" of the Revolutionary states "with respect to the question of independence and change of Government." It would have been treason for him to have sided with Britain. Others attacked Madison's view because it implied that even American-born children of loyalists could claim U.S. citizenship. They preferred to say that the Revolution had created a state of nature, with children owing allegiance only to their parents. Congress seated Smith without resolving the debate.[29]

Ramsay's, Smith's, and Madison's critics all accepted that though children always owed their parents allegiance and might ordinarily owe allegiance to the society in which they were born, the Revolution had created a situation in which individuals could choose their political membership. But Madison, then still a Federalist nation builder, took the more ascriptive view that birthright citizenship created ongoing duties to one's society. These held even if its people changed governments without one's own participation or choice. Though he called the issue "a question of right, unmixed with the question of expediency," Madison probably was influenced by desires to end this minor controversy quickly, to affirm the duty of allegiance both to the states and to the United States, and to define U.S. citizenship inclusively. The second motive later would prompt ascriptive Federalist doctrines of membership that Madison sided against once he moved into opposition.[30]

Some of the fiercest Federalist and Jeffersonian clashes over citizenship came in regard to expatriation. Though logically implied by views of membership as based on the revocable "consent of the governed," such rights were also convenient for disavowing duties to the new national government. Amid the international conflicts of the 1790s, many Americans engaged in lucrative overseas privateering on behalf of France. Some tried to drop their links to the weak, neutral U.S. government. Hence Anglophilic Federalist congressmen urged restricting expatriation. In the same cause Federalist judges turned away from the consensualism of Locke and the Declaration of Independence to Blackstone's more ascriptive views of membership. The Jeffersonian press responded with paroxysms of polemical outrage.

The impetus to support some sort of expatriation right came not only from Americans' Revolutionary legacies, the common law doctrine that British subjects could be expatriated with parliamentary approval, and international law, but also from needs for more immigrants. Specifying expatriation rights and procedures proved controversial, however. Some high Federalists like Theodore Sedgwick were far more concerned to hold on to the native born than to accept newcomers. They spoke longingly of the advantages of perpetual allegiance and favored Madison's view that there were permanent obligations at birth to one's society, if not its sovereign. Such men thought Americans could not be expatriated without specific legislative approval, as Blackstone had held.

More argued, like William Vans Murray, that American consensual principles compelled the assumption of legislative approval when a citizen in some way indicated his intent to expatriate himself, especially in cases of permanent emigration. Yet few agreed on what indications of intent counted. Murray complained that Virginia's statute, drafted by Jefferson in 1779, wrongly permitted men to expatriate themselves without leaving the country. Congress discussed expatriation provisions in 1794 and in 1797, but divisions over federal versus state powers, judicial versus legislative authority, and the extent of any birthright allegiance were too great for any agreement.[31]

As secretary of state, Jefferson continued to defend expatriation as a natural right. He insisted, however, that neither treason nor any other criminal act counted as a proper indication of intent to relinquish citizenship. This stipulation produced confusion, since some acts, such as violations of neutrality, were criminal only if the individual remained a citizen. In keeping with his more state-centric republicanism, Jefferson also believed that state expatriation acts like Virginia's simultaneously voided U.S. citizenship. Few subsequent secretaries of state agreed, but most endorsed his general defense of expatriation rights. They criticized the British practice of impressing Americans into the Royal Navy, which the British defended by claiming that Americans born under the British crown still owed it perpetual allegiance. Against those claims even Federalist diplomats usually supported expatriation.[32]

The judiciary, however, confronted cases involving unpatriotic Americans, not British high-handedness, so judges were much less warm toward expatriation. Many Federalists tried to restrict the right without denying it completely. In 1793 the Pennsylvania circuit court considered *Henfield's Case*, involving an American, Gideon Henfield, who had joined a French privateer and had been made prize master upon capturing an English vessel.[33] Washington had then declared the United States neutral between France and England, and Henfield was accused of violating the proclamation. He responded in part that he had no obligation to honor it because he had relinquished his citizenship abroad. The case report provides Chief Justice Jay's general charge upon the impaneling of the grand jury as well as the charge of presiding circuit justice Wilson. Again these two centralizing Federalists used the new national republicanism to defend the claims of the national polity, but now they did so against unqualified consensual membership and against efforts to justify service to radical France.

Jay insisted it was part of every individual's "contract with society" to abide by "the will of the people" as expressed in law. The "common good and the welfare of the community" depended on enforcing the contractual "rights of society and one another." Hence individuals could not escape the (national) social contract at will. Wilson elaborated on how the Enlightenment's "spirit of liberty" animated the U.S. system so that it might uphold "the dignity of man." But he, too, stressed that states and individuals had "duties" to provide for human preservation and general happiness. Although men had a "natural right of emigration," it could only be exercised by acts consistent with their civic duties. Wilson implied that even though the United States was not at war nor was Henfield liable for any crime when he left America, he still had unrelinquished civic obligations which required conformity to U.S. foreign policy.

Wilson's argument was a strained effort to preserve consensual doctrines and a right of expatriation while severely constraining them in the name of broad civic duties. Despite these pointed charges the jury acquitted Henfield, accepting that he had not known of the declaration of neutrality.[34] The case thus not only showed Jay and Wilson struggling to define consensual national allegiances that could not easily be altered. It also revealed the jury's lack of zeal for enforcing duties to the new nation. Many Jeffersonians began to suspect all these doctrines of national duties were means for Federalists to compel allegiances they could not inspire.

In later cases Federalist judges displayed even more wariness about expatriation and moved toward yet more binding conceptions of national allegiance. Jeffersonian objections then mounted. In *Talbot v. Jansen*, 1795, the Supreme Court rejected claims of expatriation made by two native Virginians who had commanded a French privateer illegally fitted out in the United States.[35] The justices affirmed a lower court ruling that expatriation did not involve any right to injure the country of one's "native allegiance."[36] The appellants' brief insisted that any such perpetual allegiance perpetuated the "servitude" of feudal subjectship. Citizenship was properly the result of a "compact and could be freely relinquished." Even the appellee brief conceded that on American principles "birth gives no property in the man."[37] Though all justices professed to accept these consensual views to some degree, they ruled that the appellants' acts did not amount to "reasonable" expatriation procedures.

Most interesting are the opinions of Justices William Paterson of New Jersey and Iredell of North Carolina. Paterson focused on the illegalities of the appellants' conduct and called for a federal statute on expatriation to forestall such unorthodox claims. He also argued, like Representative Murray and contrary to Jefferson, that even if appellant Ballard had complied with Virginia's expatriation statute, he had relinquished only his state citizenship, not his U.S. citizenship.[38] Since Ballard had not given up his U.S. residency and acquired another national citizenship, recognition of his alleged national expatriation would render him a denationalized "citizen of the world," a status Paterson dismissed as "a creature of the imagination." Paterson's call for federal legislation, his refusal to subordinate national citizenship to state citizenship, and his denial of full denationalization all suggest that even this former champion of small states now saw a need to assert the claims of U.S. citizenship against the states, other nations, and a dangerously rootless cosmopolitanism.

Justice Iredell ringingly endorsed the Lockean view that birth on "a particular spot" did not mean a man should "be compelled to continue in a society" to which he was thus "accidentally attached, when he can better his situation elsewhere." Even so, the southern Federalist justice was more receptive to national claims than he had been in *Chisholm*. Expatriation was a "reasonable and moral right" but not a "natural right" that could be exercised at will. It was constrained by "principles of patriotism and public good" which "in a Republic" ought to prevail over "private inclination." Persons could accept foreign naturalization, but they did not thereby dislodge all the duties a citizen "owes to his own country."[39]

In their concern to preserve national authority against the anarchical implications of pure consensualism, these justices turned chiefly to assertions of republican civic obligations, now directed to the nation. Some arch-Federalists found this insufficient. As fears of French radicalism rose, such men revived a more traditional defense of national duties: the ascriptive doctrines of English common law. While sitting in Connecticut's circuit court in 1799, Chief Justice Ellsworth considered *Williams' Case*.[40] It involved yet another American employed on a French ship at war with Britain. But Isaac Williams had formally renounced his U.S. citizenship and been legally naturalized in France in 1792, residing on French soil thereafter. His actions might well have seemed sufficient for expatriation. Yet Ellsworth, asserting that "the common law of the country remains the same as it was before the Revolution," rejected

Williams's claim. Like British subjectship, U.S. citizenship could only be dissolved with the "consent of the community." That could not be inferred, since the new nation had "no inhabitants to spare." If Williams had acquired dual allegiance by his own act, that "folly" was "his own." It did not alter his American obligations.[41]

Thus instead of straining to read the social contract as imposing consensually based national duties, Ellsworth flatly reasserted Blackstone's ascriptive view of obligations incurred at birth. The Jeffersonian press denounced the *Williams* decision as abrogating a "natural right" through appeal to an "obsolete . . . feudal" principle. Ellsworth's "birth-duty of allegiance" was termed "a fraud upon infancy" that fastened "chains of slavery" on children. The Republicans' polemics were exaggerated, since Ellsworth had not embraced full perpetual allegiance; but the decision was an attempt to assert almost unshakable claims of national identity. *Williams* thus exemplifies how notions of American membership contradictory to liberal republican consensualism could be invoked to combat threats perceived by the governing elites. Here arch-Federalist judges thought broad rights of expatriation too subversive, so they abandoned consensualism and defined membership in older naturalistic terms. Such rulings gave new vividness to Jeffersonian portraits of Federalists as unrepublican, Anglophilic Tories.

The Federalists gave Republicans even more ammunition by seeking to write other ascriptive features into citizenship laws, especially restrictions on naturalization. In the First Congress these were not controversial. Though the new representatives left immigration and permanent residence open to all, they agreed citizenship should not be. The first Naturalization Act in 1790 provided citizenship to any "free white person" who resided for two years in the United States and for one year in the state in which he sought admission. Applicants also had to prove "good character" and take an oath to "support the Constitution of the United States." Children were included in their parents' naturalization, and foreign-born children of citizens were to be citizens if their fathers had once been resident in the United States.[42]

In these and later naturalization debates, congressmen regularly weighed the benefits of population growth against the dangers to republican institutions that immigrants might pose. Perhaps most revealing were the matters Congress did not discuss. The racial and patriarchal features of naturalization bills received no recorded consideration. Perhaps the propriety of sustaining both of these civic hierarchies was so accepted that none was required, or perhaps the racial issue was too controversial to be debated. At any rate, the promotion of racial homogeneity and patriarchally defined membership became integral parts of naturalization policies suitable for "republican government." They were thus defining components of American national citizenship.

The First Congress did debate whether the nation's view of itself as an "asylum" for all, including "Jews and Roman Catholics," should be altered because the "foreign-born" might lack sufficient knowledge of and attachment to the United States and its free institutions. High Federalists like Sedgwick, who wished to confine citizenship and office essentially to natives, took over Jefferson's argument that those raised under "monarchical and aristocratical governments" might lack a "zest for pure republicanism." Jeffersonians no longer worried about European farmers and mechanics, but they decried the emigration of "merchants" and financiers who would be "leeches" in America. These differences were still compromisable. Most agreed that residency requirements were the answer: time spent in America would foster informed loyalty toward it.[43]

The power of state-centered Jeffersonian views of membership was similarly evident when even many Federalist congressmen accepted that the states would continue to exercise much regulatory authority over naturalization into U.S. citizenship.[44] The judges of the Pennsylvania circuit court, including the nationalistic Wilson, agreed in 1792. *Collet v. Collet* held that states could exercise a "concurrent authority" over naturalization so long as they did not "contravene" national laws by conferring citizenship in a "too narrow," insufficiently "liberal" fashion.[45]

New fears of easy naturalization then rose after the French Revolution fed into international warfare in 1792 and after Toussaint L'Ouverture's black and mulatto rebellion in Haiti. The United States became a haven for European refugees, prompting alarm throughout the nation's elites. Federalists feared an influx of radical French Jacobins. Jeffersonians worried about antirepublican aristocrats. The intermingling of these fears with partisan disputes surfaced in 1794, when the Federalist-controlled Senate refused to seat Albert Gallatin, the Genevan-born Jeffersonian, on the ground that he had not fully complied with state naturalization laws. Compelled to bear the burden of proof, Gallatin noted that the Declaration of Independence had made British barriers to naturalization one of its "principal" complaints, and that "encouraging population" was the wisest policy. In terms of principle, he argued that his "active part" in the Revolution made him "a citizen according to the great laws of reason and of nature," certainly as much so as the absent William Smith. But he could not claim specific compliance with state laws, and with the northeastern Federalists against him, Gallatin was unseated by a 14–12 margin.[46]

The incident strengthened Republican beliefs that the Federalists were using citizenship measures to drive opponents from office. They were suspicious when men like Sedgwick went on later in 1794 to argue for greatly extending residency requirements for naturalization, if the nation did not indeed confine officeholding to natives. Sedgwick maintained that Americans were more "wise and virtuous" and "better qualified" for republican government than any people on earth, but they were so as a result of their "early education." He doubted "republican character" could be formed any way "but by early education." Hence all adult foreigners were a risk. They should not be encouraged to come merely for "accumulation of commercial capital," certainly not when Europe was in Jacobinite upheaval.

Jeffersonians resented the talk of Jacobin threats but equally feared foreign aristocrats and merchants. Thus most accepted some lengthening of residency requirements. William Giles of Virginia also wished to compel newcomers to profess their "attachment to the Republican form of government" or to renounce all hereditary titles and claims to nobility. Federalists derided the "Republican" requirement as too vague. They exploded when Jeffersonians demanded a roll-call vote on renouncing titles, seeing the vote as a device to portray Federalists as the party of aristocracy. Samuel Dexter of Massachusetts responded by proposing that new arrivals be required to free their slaves, thereby raising the temperature in the House even higher. Finally, Congress agreed to extend the residency requirement to five years, while adding requirements that applicants file a declaration of intent three years before naturalization as well as the requirement for renunciation of all hereditary titles of nobility. The intense debate showed how strongly the national government was becoming polarized between parties with very different views of what it meant to be an American citizen.[47]

By a narrow 13–11 vote, with northeastern Federalists again prevailing, Congress also added that aliens were to be naturalized on these conditions "and not otherwise." Many Jeffersonians saw that phrase as imperiously rescinding permission for state naturalizations, at least those claiming to grant U.S. citizenship. And since the requirements pertained to processes making a person "a citizen of the United States, or any of them," any naturalizations purporting merely to confer state citizenship could not be done on easier terms. Congress further buttressed federal control of naturalization by giving federal territorial courts the power to grant foreigners citizenship.[48] Thus Federalists made American citizenship both more nativist and more nationally directed. Both these changes ran counter to Jeffersonian principles and political prospects.

The Northwest Territory's governor Arthur St. Clair also outraged Republicans in the mid-1790s by arguing that even the Anglo-American state citizens who moved there "ceased to be citizens of the United States, and became their subjects." He was disturbed that so many of the inhabitants were "indigent and ignorant" men whom he thought unprepared for full citizenship, especially since they were likely to vote Republican. Jeffersonians denounced St. Clair as "a British nabob" with "princely ideas" that "no man with the blood of an American in his bosom can contemplate with pleasure," criticisms which neatly blended republican and anti-British ascriptive themes. The Washington administration did not endorse St. Clair's position, but it added to Federalist unpopularity.[49]

The political warfare became all-out when the Federalists enacted the Naturalization, Alien Friends, Alien Enemies, and Sedition Acts in 1798 as part of stridently nativist efforts to silence, disfranchise, and deport immigrant Jeffersonians. Voting along partisan lines, Congress first extended the residence requirement for naturalization to fourteen years. Robert Harper of South Carolina then suggested that only the native-born should be citizens, and Otis of Massachusetts proposed that federal offices, at least, be limited to natives. Otis was concerned that the "wild Irish," whom the English had long depicted as a drunken, popishly enslaved lower race, would overrun his state. The Republicans successfully argued that this proposal would create an unconstitutional form of second-class citizenship. Although second-class citizenship for free blacks, women, and some Native Americans already existed, tiers among white men were less tolerable.[50]

Next, on the crest of the anti-French xenophobia churned up by the XYZ affair in France, the Federalists squeaked through the Alien Friends Act, winning 46–40 in the House. It made all "dangerous" aliens subject to arbitrary arrest and deportation in peace and war, even if the United States was not officially an enemy of their homelands. The act expired in 1800, and no one was deported under it; but the Jeffersonians denounced it as tyrannical, almost as much as they did the Sedition Act, which applied to citizens and foreigners alike. Congress also passed the less controversial Alien Enemies Act, giving the president wartime powers to control aliens from countries the United States was opposing. Republicans made sure this law could not apply to citizens, but most supported it.[51]

As they championed these measures, many Federalists openly turned their backs on their earlier view of America as an "asylum" nation and spread harsh denigrations of not only the Irish and the French but the foreign-born in general. Washington had already retreated from his old cosmopolitanism. In his Farewell Address of 1797, he expressed concern that the growing national absorption in the pursuit of "mammon" and partisan conflicts threatened national unity. He sought to persuade Americans, whether citizens "by birth or choice," that they should exalt their national identity over local ones. Like Jay in the *Federalist*, Washington told his fellow citizens that they had "the same religion, manners, beliefs, and political principles," with but "slight shades of difference." And he urged them to cultivate their religiosity as a check on their divisive economic and political ambitions. He did not endorse, but never spoke against, rising Federalist nativism. Hamilton now stated that though foreigners were desirable as workers, they could prove a "Grecian horse" if they were admitted to citizenship too quickly. And more extreme Federalists spoke as if American "freedom" was not, after all, a universal principle of natural right but rather a special feature of native white Americans' unique traditions, education, and inbred character.[52]

The Federalists' nativistic stances on citizenship issues made Republicans out of many voters, such as the German-Americans of Pennsylvania, who previously had been content with Federalist governance. Though the Supreme Court steered clear of the Sedition Act, even moderate Federalists like Justice Iredell enforced it in the notorious treason trial of the German-American rebel John Fries. Iredell admitted that during the Constitution's ratification he had denied Congress would have such powers, but he now saw that view as dangerously "erroneous." Americans not holding national offices as Iredell did instead regarded all these Federalist laws and trials as dangerous.[53]

Furthermore, the Jeffersonians had placed enough loopholes in the statutes so that they could still vote large numbers of immigrants against the Federalists in 1800. That immigrant vote was an important factor in the Jeffersonian victory. Perhaps if the Federalist laws had never been enacted, Adams might not have fallen into such disrepute; but conversely, had these laws been harsher yet and more thoroughly enforced, they might have kept the Federalists in power.[54] At any rate, the Federalists felt they had to stress the restrictive, naturalistic views of American identity that many of them had long favored, because more cosmopolitan, consensual positions seemed to help their political foes.

And even if many Federalists had seen these acts as long-shot measures, they might well still have undertaken them, for their program was ill suited to win popular favor. Since they favored directly helping economic elites, slowing the rapid displacement of the native tribes, and discouraging slavery, they were on the losing side of the systems of inequality that most white American men favored. Resort to a nativistic, restrictive Americanism justifying imprisonments, disfranchisement, and deportations was one of the few options available to them. And though it did not produce electoral success, the Federalists' Americanism helped provide a patriotic language that celebrated their vision of a national republic with expansive powers, a growth-oriented market economy, and a national identity centered on the traits of Anglophone, native-born white men. That political language would remain an important, if morally ambiguous, resource in future struggles to strengthen the nation and define what it should become.[55]

2

ALEXANDER HAMILTON'S ALTERNATIVE

Technology Piracy and the Report on Manufactures

Doron Ben-Atar

ON MARCH 24, 1791, an announcement appeared in the Philadelphia *Federal Gazette*. George Parkinson, of that city, advertised that he had recently obtained a U.S. patent for spinning flax, hemp, and combed wool by methods that represented "improvements upon the mill or machinery of Kendrew and Porthouse of the town of Darlington in Great Britain." Why had Parkinson, an English weaver who later worked for the Society for Establishing Useful Manufactures (SEUM) in Paterson, New Jersey, been granted a patent monopoly even though his version of Richard Arkwright's flax-spinning machine only marginally improved on the original? Parkinson's announcement provided the answer. It was because this "machinery, with the original mechanism . . . [was] of the utmost value to the United States."[1] By granting a patent to an "introducer" of a machine that was protected under Britain's intellectual property laws, the U.S. Patent Office rewarded technology piracy.

Prohibitions on the emigration of artisans and the export of machinery from the British Empire had been in effect throughout the eighteenth century. In the period following American Independence, growing anxiety in Britain over industrial piracy prompted stronger legislation and stricter enforcement. Under the new laws illegal emigrant artisans forfeited their nationality and property and could be convicted of treason. Recruiting agents could be fined £500 and imprisoned for twelve months for each emigrant they enticed. A £200 fine, forfeiture of equipment, and twelve months' imprisonment (or a £500 fine and forfeiture in the case of textile machinery) were laid down for the export or attempted export of industrial machinery. Ships' captains were required to submit lists detailing passenger occupations to customs officials at British ports before departing, and in at least one instance the Royal Navy seized an illegal emigrant on an American ship, the *Union*, as it left Liverpool.

British consular officials in America were instructed to report on British artisans and machinery in the United States.

In 1791 Secretary of State Thomas Jefferson was in charge of American patents. In that official capacity Jefferson approved Parkinson's patent application and helped arrange the migration of Parkinson's family to the United States.[2] He thus sanctioned an overt violation of British restrictions on the diffusion of industrial technology. But Jefferson, staunch foe of Great Britain that he was, held conflicting views about technology piracy. He lent a hand to Parkinson's family but not to Parkinson himself; as Julian P. Boyd writes, he "took no part in aiding the immigration of British artisans because it was forbidden by law." A year earlier Jefferson had been reluctant to support William Pollard's application for a patent monopoly of another version of Arkwright's machine.[3]

Treasury Secretary Alexander Hamilton, on the other hand, wholeheartedly supported technology piracy. Parkinson was a partner of Tench Coxe, Hamilton's trusted assistant, who had contracted with Parkinson to build a mill based on his claim of detailed knowledge of the secret Arkwright machine. Hamilton thought the experiment merited a $48 Treasury subsidy to cover Parkinson's living expenses in the spring of 1791.[4] This episode was one of many instances in which Hamilton's Treasury Department organized and supported raids on Britain's industrial preeminence. Such projects strained Anglo-American relations because, as Anthony F. C. Wallace and David J. Jeremy explain, for "some of the highest officials of the American government to reward the violation of British law by issuing a patent for stolen invention—and thus to encourage similar adventures by other industrial spies—would hardly be considered a friendly act."[5]

Hamilton's efforts to undermine British technological supremacy seem out of character for a statesman whom historians often depict as something between an obsessive Anglophile and a traitor. Boyd long ago charged that Hamilton acted as a British operative in George Washington's cabinet and that his deceptions and betrayals undermined the independent diplomacy Jefferson was trying to orchestrate. Albert Bowman similarly argues that in conceiving American interests "exclusively in terms of a close connection with England," Hamilton's diplomacy grossly misread "the American tradition . . . the American spirit and . . . the American promise." Richard Buel, Jr., holds that throughout the 1790s Hamilton remained "committed to Anglo-American collaboration, even though worsening relations with France eventually made a formal alliance with Britain no longer necessary or even particularly advantageous." Bradford Perkins writes that Hamilton acted as a double agent in the Washington cabinet, "betraying information" to British representatives and subverting American interests by being "indiscreet, or disloyal." Critics of American diplomacy concur. William Appleman Williams sees Hamilton committed to "an American-British empire embracing most of the world." Jerald A. Combs vilifies Hamilton as a ruthless imperialist, obsessed with heroism, glory, and power, who, to serve his personal ambition, mortgaged American independence to Britain's political and economic interests. And Alexander DeConde has portrayed Hamilton as "an ardent Anglophile" intent on frustrating the anti-British initiatives of Jefferson.[6]

Hamilton has always had defenders. From nineteenth-century writers such as Richard Hildreth and John Bach McMaster through twentieth-century analysts such as Samuel Flagg Bemis to Forrest McDonald to Stanley Elkins and Eric McKitrick, scholars have rejected the portrayal of Hamilton as an English dupe and preferred instead a depiction of a highly gifted man who decided it was in the young nation's best interest to throw in its lot with Great Britain. Yet even those who do not rush to condemn Hamilton's policies explain those policies in terms of realistic acquiescence to English superiority. Elkins and McKitrick, for example, declare that an "Anglophile position on virtually everything" is at the core of Hamiltonianism.[7]

Here I take a fresh look at Hamilton's political economy from the perspective of international economic competition. I argue that British and American leaders believed technological competition played a crucial role in the international balance of power and that Hamilton's initiatives in the battle over manufacturing expertise threatened the perceived source of Britain's economic power—its industrial technology. I have stated elsewhere that Hamilton's commercial program "amounted to . . . acquiescence in British restrictions on American commerce."[8] His industrialization plan, on the other hand, challenged Britain's position as the premier industrial power in North America. He was willing, temporarily, to accept his country's skewed balance of trade with England; at the same time he challenged Britain's industrial superiority by pirating British technology. Hamilton was on the mark when he reflected in 1800, "I may at some time have suggested a *temporary* connection [with Great Britain] for the purpose of co-operating against France . . . but . . . I well remember that the expediency of the measure was always problematical in my mind, and that I have occasionally discouraged it."[9]

Contemporaries correctly pointed out, as have historians since, that Hamilton greatly admired Britain's economic and political power and wanted the United States to emulate it. Yet constructing a British-modeled political economy in America did not mean turning the United States into a British satellite. On the contrary. British political economy and economic diplomacy were founded on the assumption of a zero-sum game in which a gain for Britain meant a loss to other countries, and vice versa. Transplanting this vision across the Atlantic did not mean that the United States would become a weakened British crony, but a strong egocentric competing power.

Hamilton's commercial and industrial programs, in spite of their opposing international orientations, complemented one another. Like British neomercantilists of the late eighteenth century, who "combined economic liberalism with economic nationalism," Hamilton, "the preeminent neomercantilist in the United States," favored the liberalization of trade, development of the domestic economy, and government sponsorship of home manufactures.[10] He believed that economic independence was inseparable from political independence and was dismayed by the American addiction to manufactured British imports. After securing the financial stability of the nation, Hamilton outlined his vision of government aid to industry. Close examination of Hamilton's supposed Anglophilia in relation to his practice of technology piracy reveals a sophisticated and subtle plan of government sponsorship of manufactures that would challenge British industrial preeminence without risking U.S. involvement in a trade war it could not win.

THE REPORT ON Manufactures, unlike Hamilton's other two financial papers, did not address a specific or immediate fiscal problem. It dared to project the future, expressing the Hamiltonian vision at its fullest. Hamilton put forward a powerful theoretical argument in favor of the federal government's active promotion of manufacturing. He took on the antistatist political economists of the time, particularly Adam Smith and the Physiocrats, who had argued that "manufactures without the aid of government will grow up as soon and as fast, as the natural state of things and the interest of the community may require."[11] Submitted on December 5, 1791, the report failed to inspire congressional legislation because it contained, as the editors of Hamilton's papers note, "few, if any, specific proposals."[12] The report therefore has been evaluated primarily as a theoretical presentation.

On January 15, 1790, the House of Representatives had asked the secretary of the Treasury to prepare a report on the state of American manufactures and to devise a plan for their encouragement. Hamilton turned to manufacturing societies that had appeared in many cities in the 1780s for information. The responses had much in common. They described growing industrial activities and at the same time elaborated on the obstacles to manufacturing in the United States.

Overcoming technological backwardness was seen as the key to success. Correspondents from states unable to attract foreign workers, such as South Carolina, blamed their industrial underdevelopment on the shortage of skilled labor.[13] One Connecticut industrialist complained that the price of hats had fallen significantly in the past few months because of "bad Work done which goes to Market & has injured the Credit of American Hats very much, & must in time ruin it entirely."[14] Glass manufacturing in Massachusetts was said to be handicapped because entrepreneurs "wait only for Workmen which are engaged & probably on their passage to commence making Sheet and other Glass."[15] Textile manufacturing in Massachusetts was "destitute of the necessary information," as local investors were "misled by every pretender to knowledge."[16]

Naturally, Hamilton consulted manufacturers who had successfully established factories. These men did not hide the fact that their success depended on their ability to pirate British technology primarily by enticing skilled British artisans to emigrate. Button production in New Haven, noted a report from John Mix, Jr., received a boost from the arrival of an English worker who "has the Skill perfectly, who is a Gentleman who is able, and has Engaged to Instruct and teach us every thing Necessary in the making of them."[17] Elisha Colt, manager of the Hartford Woolen Manufactory, emphasized the crucial role played by British artisans in the success of his factory. When the company was first established, "we were at that period not only totally unacquainted with the various parts or subdivisions of the Labour; but equally destitute of every kind of Machinery and Labourers for executing such a project—But the news of this infant attempt to establish so useful a Manufacture soon collected a number of Workmen about us, who had been bred to different branches of the Woolen & Worsted Business in England." Colt boasted that "every part or branch of the Business is managed in the same manner as practised in England."[18] From Providence, Moses Brown wrote that repeated technological failures had halted his attempt to introduce textile manufacturing to Rhode Island until an operator who had worked in English factories came. Brown felt lucky to be approached by "a young

Man then lately Arived at Newyork from Arkwright's works in England."
Brown had to pay a price. The young man, Samuel Slater, demanded and
got complete control of the mill's operation. All the same, the success of
the venture became evident to Brown as early as the summer of 1791.[19]

Among the respondents was the secretary of the Pennsylvania Society
for the Encouragement of Manufactures and the Useful Arts (PSEMUA),
Tench Coxe, who, according to his biographer, was "among the nation's
best-known and most active advocates of manufactures."[20] Coxe had
come out publicly for state and federal support of industrial piracy
as early as 1787. He made sure that the technological deficiencies of
American industry were on the minds of the men who convened in
Philadelphia to frame the new constitution in the summer of that year.
On May 11, three days before the delegates were scheduled to begin
deliberations, Coxe addressed the need for government-sponsored
industrialization in a passionate talk at the home of Benjamin Franklin.
Then, on August 9, while the convention was in session, he called for
importing technology in a public address to the PSEMUA.

The new national government, he told the men gathered at
Franklin's, must support industrialization to provide employment to
the many who "will probably emigrate from Europe, who will chuse
to continue at their trades."[21] Artisans would cross the Atlantic because
tyranny, unemployment, low wages, and civil wars in Europe, contrasted
with freedom and opportunity in America, "will bring many manufacturers to this asylum for mankind. Ours will be their industry, and, what is
of still more consequence, ours will be their skill." America's industrial
virginity would work in its favor for if Europeans continued to improve
their machinery, "their people must be driven to us for want of employment, and if, on the other hand, they should return to manual labour, we
shall underwork them by these invaluable engines." It was time for the
young nation, he declared, to "borrow some of their inventions."[22]

Coxe urged that his listeners and the men who were about to devise
the new form of federal government "carefully examine the conduct of
Other countries in order to possess ourselves of their methods of encouraging manufactories." He made two specific proposals: grant federally
protected exclusive rights over inventions to introducers of technology
and make land grants to skilled Europeans who introduce European
machinery to the United States.[23] Coxe did not confine himself to words.
In the summer of 1787, he recruited Andrew Mitchell to return to
England and pirate English textile technology. The scheme was discov-
ered, British officials seized the trunk containing the illegally obtained

models and drawings, and Mitchell fled to safe haven at Copenhagen. In the same year Coxe entered into partnership with a Philadelphia clockmaker, Robert Leslie, who was known as a collector of "every model, drawing or description" of European machinery.[24] In 1788 Coxe, together with John Kaighan, reported that the process of coloring leather, although attempted in America, "has not yet been obtained here." They published the process "as communicated by Mr. Philippo, a native of Armenia, who received from the society for the encouragements of arts in London, one hundred pounds sterling, and also the gold medal of the society, as a reward for discovering this secret."[25] Americans "heartily rejoice," declared Coxe in Mathew Carey's *American Museum*, "in the early success of our endeavors to obtain" Europe's industrial secrets.[26]

When Coxe wrote of technological rivalry, he had only Great Britain in mind. During the colonial period "it was the unvaried policy of Great Britain, to discourage manufactures," and after the separation Britain continued to block the westward flow of technology.[27] In England, Lord Sheffield's 1783 attack on Anglo-American economic reconciliation showed that Coxe was not off the mark. Sheffield held that it would "be a long time before the Americans can manufacture for themselves." The high cost of labor would discourage investors. Skilled immigrants, tempted by the affordability and availability of land, would abandon their trades: "they will not work at manufactures when they can get double the profit by farming."[28] Sheffield's views were backed by British agents in the United States who labored to retard American technological development. Coxe pointed out that in 1787 the British consul in Philadelphia, Phineas Bond, bought four carding and spinning machines that had been smuggled out of Britain and shipped them back to Liverpool. Such actions, Coxe hoped, would wake American industrialists to the "dictates of national and commercial rivalship" in the all-out battle for technology. He urged the several states to adopt a "prudential spirit of jealousy and circumspection" and imitate Pennsylvania, which, following the Bond incident, had enacted legislation "to prevent the exportation of machines, and enticing away artizans."[29]

Coxe's reply to the Treasury secretary's query in 1790 was upbeat. He expressed enthusiasm about the prospects of industrialization in the Philadelphia area; his main concern was the need for labor and industrial know-how.[30] Hamilton, doubtless impressed by Coxe's knowledge and connections, appointed him assistant secretary of the Treasury and entrusted him with organizing the data of the inquiry and preparing the first draft of the Report on Manufactures. By the end of winter of 1790–91, Coxe had drafted the report.

Coxe repeated the themes he had elaborated in the 1780s. American manufactures were plagued by labor problems. Labor was scarce, wages were high, and the United States did not have competent operators versed in modern techniques. Coxe proposed three remedies. First, the United States should import modern machinery that used fewer workers, thereby reducing competition for laborers and bringing wages under control. Second, women and children, who earned much lower wages, should do the unskilled work. Third, the U.S. government should campaign aggressively to persuade European artisans to emigrate.[31]

Inducing emigration was pivotal to the program's success. Yet how could a nonmanufacturing, capital-starved economy attract skilled workers? Coxe proposed setting apart "five hundred thousand acres, of a good quality and advantageously situated," to grant "first introducers or establishers of new and useful manufactories, arts, machines, & secrets not before possessed, known or carried on in the United States."[32] A fund under the direction of the president was to remunerate introducers of items or ideas that "will not yield an immediate or adequate benefit" in the market.[33] People who brought in "manufacturing Machinery and secrets of great value" should be rewarded with "such exclusive privileges for a term of years as would have been secured by patent had they been the inventors." Coxe concluded the draft by explaining that "those great Instruments of Manufacture in the European Nations, labor-saving Machines," were crucial to American industrial development and that the present state of American manufacturing made governmental efforts to help secure such machines politically and economically prudent.[34]

HAMILTON REWORKED and expanded Coxe's draft five times before submitting his report to Congress almost a year later. He introduced new ideas, expanded some proposals, modified others, and did not endorse Coxe's call for protective tariffs. His additions and subtractions did not affect the anti-British spirit of Coxe's draft. Hamilton's report projected a powerful neomercantilist vision that maintained the challenge to England's industrial preeminence in North America.

Hamilton agreed that technological deficiencies accounted for the great disparity between American and European manufacturing and that the gap would be "diminished in proportion to the use which can be made of machinery."[35] With modern technology, American manufacturing would catch up. The process need not take long. The great techno-

logical advances of the preceding twenty years, for example, were responsible for "the immense progress" of British textile industrial output. The
forward movement was all the more remarkable because it was achieved
without drawing on the agricultural labor supply.[36]

Technology could be acquired by smuggling up-to-date machinery
out of England and by inducing skilled workers to move to the United
States and build the machines they had operated in Europe.[37] Hamilton
believed that "machinery forms an item of great importance in the general mass of national industry."[38] He warned that to "procure all such
machines, as are known in any part of Europe, can only require a proper
provision and due pains." He explained that America had an advantage
over Europe in its abundant supplies of raw materials and energy sources
needed to construct and operate advanced machinery. Moreover, modern machinery required fewer operators, which was appropriate for a
young country with a chronic labor shortage.[39]

Machine importation, however, was problematic. Americans could
not build machines from European manuals because few inventions
were ever published. Even those recorded in magazines were not trans-
latable into actual machines because the descriptions and drawings
lacked specificity and clarity. In theory, patented English inventions
could be examined by the public in the London Patent Office during
the term of the patent, but the knowledge required to conduct an effective search rendered copying specifications all but impossible. Moreover,
seventeenth- and eighteenth-century technical improvements were
"more of a 'knack' than an invention." When a machine was taken apart
and sent to the United States, only those who had operated it in England
could put it back together and make it work. Such was the case with the
carding machines Bond had sent back to England. They sat idle in
America for more than three years because no one knew how to reas-
semble them. Successful acquisition of prohibited English industrial
knowledge thus depended on the emigration of skilled operators and
factory managers.[40]

Hamilton understood this. In order to compete with the British textile
industry, he wrote in the SEUM prospectus, Americans must have a
better-qualified workforce, competitive pricing, and additional capital
for investment. His two reports on public credit addressed the last
two needs. Skilled workers were "an essential ingredient" of American
industrialization, yet thus far efforts "employed have not generally been
adequate to the purpose of procuring them from abroad."[41] In the
Report on Manufactures, Hamilton explained that "progress of particu-

lar manufactures has been much retarded by the want of skilful workmen." Leaving it to individual entrepreneurs to rectify this imbalance would not produce the desired results, because "the capitals employed here are not equal to the purposes of bringing from abroad workmen of superior kind." The federal government through some "auxiliary agency" must manage this "source of valuable acquisition to the country."[42]

There was no difference between Hamilton's and Coxe's views on the centrality of emigration. Both believed that enticing foreign—that is, British—workers to emigrate to the United States was the surest and quickest way to get the knowledge. Coxe came at the issues from the perspective of industrializing Philadelphia. Hamilton understood the larger domestic and international ramifications of an enticement program and used the public pages of the Report on Manufactures to explain and advocate his position.

As Hamilton knew, the dominant agricultural sector would resist government sponsorship of competing employment in manufactures. Former physician-in-chief of the Continental army John Morgan, for example, wrote in 1789 that manufacturing was suited to a country "fully stocked with inhabitants." America's labor shortage meant to Morgan that industrialization would have to come at the expense of agriculture, which was the real source of national wealth.[43] To counter "dearness of labour" objections, Hamilton followed Coxe's lead and played on the national mood favoring population growth. He promised that manufactures "will have the strongest tendency to multiply the inducements" to foreign emigration.[44] He realized, however, that this promise would not alleviate the widespread fears that industrialization would further deplete the already labor-starved agricultural sector. He elaborated: the advantage of manufacturing is its "tendency to draw emigrants from foreign countries." Artisans would not come unless they could find employment in their familiar line of work because "men are commonly reluctant to quit one course of occupation and livelihood for another." And America had much to offer: higher wages, cheaper raw materials, and political liberty. European migrants, Hamilton promised, would industrialize America. They already had become a reliable source of labor and innovation. Go through the towns of America and see the

> large proportion of ingenious and valuable workmen, in different arts and trades, who, by expatriating from Europe, have improved their own condition, and added to the industry and wealth of the United States. It is a natural inference from the experience, we have already had, that as soon as the

United States shall present the countenance of serious prosecution of manufactures—as soon as foreign artists be made sensible that the state of things here affords a moral certainty of employment and encouragement—competent numbers of European workmen will transplant themselves, effectually to ensure the success of the design.

In sum, American manufactures would "in a great measure trade upon a foreign Stock."[45] The agricultural and commercial sectors would also benefit, as this "fruitful mean of augmenting the population"[46] would result in higher prices for agricultural products without "deducting from the hands, which might otherwise be drawn to tillage."[47]

Why would a considerable number of skilled European artisans move to the United States? Hamilton's answer was that artisans would value higher wages, cheaper provisions, lighter taxes, and political and religious freedoms. Yet he did not wish to imply that the disparity, as Americans saw it, would be sufficient inducement. If that were the case, then Congress would not have to promote emigration. This delicate balancing act—predicting that America would naturally attract skilled emigrants yet not lulling Congress into inaction—made its way into the final version of the report, where Hamilton inserted a statement that immigration would flow "as soon as foreign artists shall be made sensible that the state of things here affords a moral certainty of employment and encouragement."[48] On the one hand, the workers would be drawn by objective conditions to cross the Atlantic of their own accord. On the other hand, active dissemination of the news of an aggressive industrialization effort in America was necessary to make sure that European workers would learn of the opportunities and be moved to migrate.

Hamilton endorsed many of Coxe's emigration-inducing proposals such as travel subsidies for artisans and customs exemption for their tools, implements of trade, and household furniture. Most important, he came out strongly in favor of granting an inventor monopoly to introducers of technology. That issue had surfaced the previous year during debate on the Patent Act the Congress passed in 1790. The president had asked Congress in his annual message of January of that year to enact legislation encouraging "the introduction of new and useful invention from abroad."[49] The House of Representatives' version of the bill followed English law in giving to the first importer of technology the monopoly privileges accorded to original inventors. But the Senate amended the bill to grant patent monopolies only to inventors of machines "not before known or used" and deleted the location qualifier "within the United States."[50] In his report Hamilton urged Congress to revise the Patent Act of 1790, explaining that the United States must employ the same methods "which have been employed with success in other Countries."[51]

Yet Hamilton did not actively campaign for modeling U.S. patent law on that of Britain. In his first draft Hamilton revised Coxe's call for awarding patent privileges to introducers with the qualifying clause, "if within the compass of the powers of the government."[52] Far from undergoing a sudden conversion to the doctrine of strict construction, he had realized that the prohibition on patents of importation could be circumvented without changing the language of the law. Applicants could claim the rights of inventors by slightly improving European inventions. Parkinson and Pollard received patents under just such a pretext. And Hamilton supported the patent application of William Pearce, a British textile operator, even though he recognized that the latter's claim to originality was unfounded and that Pearce was merely introducing to America techniques already under monopoly protection in England.[53]

Hamilton also agreed with Coxe that Congress should promote new undertakings and promise rewards to introducers of industrial secrets. Yet his first revision of Coxe's draft eliminated the idea of offering land as an inducement, noting that the manner of inducing such migration "will be submitted hereafter."[54] John R. Nelson, Jr., has argued that Hamilton scrapped the plan because such aggressive recruitment would develop American manufactures at the expense of Great Britain.[55] But the mechanics who might have responded to the promise of land would have been those inclined to change their trades. While threatening to attract skilled artisans from Britain, the proposal actually would have limited American competitiveness by leading them to abandon their trades for agricultural pursuits. If Hamilton really feared offending Great Britain, why did he retain introducer monopoly and travel subsidies? Those programs, after all, directly challenged British industrial supremacy.

Hamilton omitted the land grant proposal because he believed that men were naturally inclined to become farmers. He feared that immigrant artisans would yield to the temptation of bucolic life and not remain in urban centers to develop their trades. "The desire of being a proprietor of lands depends upon such strong principles in the human breast, that where the opportunity of acquiring is so easy as it is in the United States the proportion must be small of those, whose circumstances would otherwise lead to it, that would be diverted from the pursuit toward manufactures."[56]

Population and migration patterns in the second half of the eighteenth century lend some credence to Hamilton's observation. The South and

Southwest were growing so rapidly by immigration that North Carolina, for example, which around 1760 had roughly the same number of people as New York, twenty years later had gone ahead by about sixty thousand. Contemporaries assumed that the trend would continue and that immigrants, even skilled artisans, would become farmers. In eliminating the land grant program Hamilton was not driven by a reluctance to confront Great Britain. Rather, he did not share Coxe's confidence in the natural superiority and attraction of manufacturing, and he feared that skilled immigrants would flow to the fields of the South and Southwest without sharing their precious trade secrets with their new countrymen.

In his fourth draft Hamilton expanded upon another one of Coxe's suggestions. He proposed a federally funded board, similar to the PSEMUA, which would "defray the expenses of the emigration of Artists and Manufacturers in particular branches of extraordinary importance" and promote "the prosecution and introduction of useful discoveries, inventions & improvements by proportionate rewards judiciously held out and applied." American manufacturing, he repeated, was hampered by "the want of skilful workmen," and the federal government should subsidize the numerous "workmen, in every branch, who are prevented from emigrating solely by the want of means." The very same fund also could be used to "procure and import foreign improvements"—that is, machines.[57]

This idea was so central to his vision that Hamilton made it the conclusion of the Report on Manufactures. He explained that societies like the PSEMUA were "truly invaluable"; "there is scarcely any thing," he wrote, "which has been devised, better calculated to excite a general spirit of improvement." But the funds of such local voluntary associations "have been too contracted" to launch an adequate incentive campaign. The United States could not wait for patriotic private entrepreneurs to undertake the costly effort of bringing over machines and artisans from Europe.[58] The "public purse must supply the deficiency of private resources." What is more useful, Hamilton concluded, than "prompting and improving the efforts of industry?"[59]

PROMOTION OF legal and illegal emigration was as old as British New World colonization. As Bernard Bailyn has shown, anxiety over depopulation of the countryside became pronounced in England in the 1760s.[60] But Hamilton's proposed industrialization program went further than the pre-Revolutionary recruiting of farmers and indentured servants. It

targeted the men the British most desired to keep. The British government resented such unabashed, state-sanctioned flouting of British law.
On a less principled level, officials and manufacturers feared the economic consequences of skilled workers' emigration and growing foreign
competition.

The Report on Manufactures was shelved in America, but in Britain
it took on a life of its own. The SEUM founders counted on circulating
the report in England to attract industrial immigrants. Thomas Digges,
accused double agent, embezzler, and industrial spy, had one thousand
copies printed in Dublin in 1792 and circulated among the manufacturing societies of Britain and Ireland. He believed the report would
"induce artists to move toward a Country so likely to very soon give them
ample employ & domestic ease." The Dublin edition was "distributed
and Sold cheap," reported Edinburgh bookseller Samuel Paterson. Yet
the report's encouragement to "the poor distressed Subjects of these
States to flock to America" antagonized "the great people & Landed
Interest [who] discourage Emigrations to America, as Well as governments."[61]

In the 1780s and early 1790s British representatives in the United
States kept their London superiors informed about American appropriation of British technology. Phineas Bond dedicated much of his official
correspondence to it. Major George Beckwith, who discussed the possibility of an Anglo-American alliance with Hamilton in 1790, alarmingly
reported the arrival of a model of Arkwright's machine in America.
When the Report on Manufactures and the SEUM plan became public,
British officials immediately understood their explosiveness. As David
J. Jeremy has explained, if Hamilton's industrialization program had
proved as successful as his stabilization of American finances, Britain
could have lost much of its export trade—worth more than $15 million
in 1791 alone—to the United States.[62] Bond urged vigorous prosecution
of laws "against seducing manufacturers and conveying away implements
of manufacturing."[63] The British minister in Philadelphia, George Hammond, expected the federal government to support fully the proposed
program because "Mr. Hamilton's reputation is so materially involved in
the result of the experiment."[64] England must now energetically enforce the
prohibitions on technology export, he wrote to Grenville, "to prevent the
emigration and exportation of machines necessary to the different
branches of manufactures."[65] Beckwith reported to the governor of Canada, Lord Dorchester, that Americans were copying protected English
machinery. He was particularly alarmed by the report's support of the

SEUM and warned of the enterprise's "ultimate effects upon the interests of The Empire."[66]

During 1791 Hamilton sought introducers of English technology by interviewing immigrants. He sent a Scottish stocking weaver back home to recruit men for a factory in America. English artisans heard of the secretary's interest in English technology and expected assistance upon arrival. Roger Newberry, for example, believed Hamilton should help him find a job in America because he possessed plans for two "most ingenious & very beneficial" new English textile machines.[67] In December, Hamilton reported his understanding with one Mr. Mort, who agreed to "go to Europe, to bring over Workmen, at his own Expense in the first instance; but with the assurance of reimbursement and indemnification." The society's directors approved the agreement unanimously on December 9, 1791, and promised to "carry the same Effect on their part."[68]

European correspondents, such as Samuel Paterson of Edinburgh, aware of Hamilton's support for travel subsidies, reported that thousands of eager-to-emigrate skilled artisans were not coming because "they are Utterly unable to pay for a Passage to America." Paterson begged Hamilton "to procure a Grant of Some Bounty or Relaxation of the Duties, to Europe Shipping bringing over Poor Industrious workmen to America."[69] A year earlier Congress had debated such a subsidy. A House committee recommended loaning John F. Amelung $8,000 to bring hundreds of European glassworkers to America, reasoning that "a manufactory attended with so much difficulty in its commencement, so important in its consequences to the United States, and of such general utility to the whole Union, ought to receive the assistance and protection of the United States." Opponents of this subsidy ultimately prevailed.[70] Hamilton favored reversing the Amelung decision. In planning the SEUM he called for allocation of means "to procure from Europe skilful workmen and such machines and implements as cannot be had here in sufficient perfection."[71]

When Hamilton suggested defraying the expenses of artisans' emigration, he knew he was aiding in the violation of the central codes of English economic policy and hence challenging British power. His European correspondents informed him of both the prohibitions and penalties of such activities. Paterson, for example, reported that in "Britain the Penalties are £500 Str & 6 Mo Imprisonment for every person Indented to goe out of the Kings Dominions." He suggested that bounties for smuggling artisans be given to European shippers because the "Penalties

& Forfeitures, are so very heavy & so easily incurred, that No person
Unacquaint[ed] with the Laws durst Venture upon Such a Measure—But
the European Captain & owners know how to agree with Passengers so as
to Escape the Penalties."[72] Another English correspondent, Thomas
Marshall, who professed to have been trained by Arkwright, explained to
Hamilton that he came to the United States without documentation of
his skill due to the "Laws of England being very severe against the Emigration of Mechanic's." Marshall claimed he was "fully Acquainted with
every modern Improvement"; he had worked with Arkwright since 1786
and had learned the most recent secrets of the trade.[73] Marshall's application earned him a position with the SEUM, which shows that Hamilton
read this letter with sufficient attention to be impressed with Marshall's
qualifications or his name-dropping, or both. He could not have missed
either Marshall's detailed account of the English laws or his defiance.
In the Report on Manufactures, Hamilton acknowledged that most
manufacturing nations "prohibit, under severe penalties, the exportation of implements and machines, which they have either invented or
improved." The U.S. government must circumvent the efforts of industri-
ally advanced nations to frustrate and prohibit the international diffusion of industrial know-how.[74]

Not all eighteenth-century statesmen defined knowledge and skill as
property. Franklin, for example, believed "science must be an international
pursuit" for "the improvement of humanity's estate."[75] He had actively
sponsored the dissemination of European technology in America since
the early 1750s, and he shared his scientific findings and technological
innovations with friends and rivals. He never sought to profit from the
implementations of useful inventions such as the lightning rod and
the Franklin stove. But his position was rapidly becoming anachronistic.
Invention was now taken to be the fruit of the labor of the inventor, and
by the time of the Revolution, the American consensus was that "only an
individual's labor created property, and therefore the individual had sole
right to possession and disposition of that property."[76]

Hamilton did not share Franklin's views, nor did he subscribe to
Enlightenment ideas about universal access to knowledge. He was more
swayed by William Barton's *The True Interest of the United States*, which
declared that nations should "spare no expense in procuring the ablest
masters in every branch of industry, nor any cost in making the first estab-
lishments; providing machines, and every other necessary or useful to
make the undertaking succeed."[77] In the Report on Manufactures, a few
paragraphs after suggesting ways to bring knowledge across the Atlantic,

Hamilton called for prohibiting Europe-bound transmission of American innovations by imposing stiff penalties against export of technology invented or acquired by Americans. While supporting a strong patent protection law in the United States, he openly campaigned for the violation of British patents. On the one hand, he saw nothing improper in stimulating the "introduction of useful improvements" from abroad. On the other, he strongly supported regulations protecting American improvements from foreign competitors so as not to allow "foreign workmen to rival those of the nation."[78] In sum, Hamilton believed that intellectual property, like physical property, was confined to national boundaries. Accordingly, he had no reservations about orchestrating a mass violation of English laws.

Hamilton's position was in line with international law, in the sense that such law was "not ordained by nature, but established through international behavior," most notably in treaties among nations.[79] Prohibitions on technology piracy were not defined in any international agreement until the nineteenth century. English patent law was originally conceived to encourage foreign artisans to come to England and teach apprentices their trade. The policy remained in effect well into the nineteenth century and was highly successful. Britain attracted artisans in sufficient numbers to change from a technologically debtor nation in 1700 to a creditor just half a century later. It continued to draw on Continental technology throughout the industrial revolution. Rival states, in turn, spied on British innovations for their own industrialization efforts. Jacques Necker, Louis XVI's chief adviser, explained that acquisition and exploitation of foreign industrial technology was the surest way to national economic independence. Industrial espionage was practiced "on a very wide scale by all western countries of any industrial significance."[80]

Hamilton's actions, then, contravened English municipal prohibitions, not the law of nations. Other members of Washington's cabinet, however, felt the United States should avoid promoting direct violations of British laws. Jefferson and Attorney General Edmund Randolph advised the president early in 1791 not to support a proposed textile factory in Virginia because it would be equipped with machines feloniously imported from England. Washington agreed, explaining that "it certainly would not carry an aspect very favorable to the dignity of the United States for the President in a clandestine manner to entice the subjects of another Nation to violate its Laws."[81] Hamilton, for his part, denied that the United States was obligated to respect the British restrictions.

Technology piracy, he wrote, did "not violate any positive right of another" country.[82]

Hamilton provided neither constitutional nor moral justification for technology piracy. His argument was utilitarian. "It is the right of every independent nation," he explained, "to pursue its own interest, in its own way."[83] He saw the early 1790s as an excellent time to plunder European technology because the "crisis of the affairs of certain parts of Europe" would dispose "the requisite workmen" to emigrate.[84] By offering inducements and developing opportunities for employment, Hamilton wrote in the Report on Manufactures, the United States could immeasurably increase "the number and extent of valuable acquisitions to the population arts and industry of the Country. To find pleasure in the calamities of other nations, would be criminal; but to benefit ourselves, by opening an asylum to those who suffer, in consequence of them, is as justifiable as it is politic."[85] And Hamilton voiced similar sentiments in his model of American industrialization. The SEUM was to be founded on Europe's distress.

ON MARCH 1, 1792, inspired by the Report on Manufactures, Representative Hugh Williamson of North Carolina introduced a revised patent law that proposed to use fees paid by patent applicants to import useful inventions from abroad. But later that month the Treasury secretary's vigorous efforts on behalf of American technology became an embarrassment. His own favorite creation, the SEUM, did his program in. The Report on Manufactures was the theoretical expression of Hamilton's industrial vision, and the SEUM was its practical application. Hamilton's authorship of the SEUM's plan and his involvement in its operations were public knowledge. The revelations that the SEUM's directors had lost most of the company's funds in the financial crash of March 1792 discredited Hamilton's program. The panic that "helped wreck the SEUM also helped make Congress less inclined to adopt innovative measures" to remedy American technological deficiencies.[86]

As late as June 1793 Hamilton continued to promote efforts to acquire British technology. Partial fulfillment of his prediction that the "disturbed state of Europe" would incline "its citizens to emigration"[87] lessened the need for federal recruitment of industrial workers. In the summer of 1793 James Currie of Liverpool advised Hamilton that the outbreak of war in Europe was "occasioning great emigrations from Britain to America," mostly "manufacturers, the most valuable part of our labourers. How this may affect your schemes for establishing manufactures in America, you will be able to judge."[88]

More generally, France's decision to export its revolution forced Hamilton to move away from programs that could adversely affect Anglo-American relations. The European war made Hamilton "absolutely determined that nothing should be done which might directly benefit France."[89] While Jefferson thought that the "liberty of the whole earth was depending on the issue of the contest" and was willing to sacrifice "half the earth" for the French cause, Hamilton publicly denied that "the cause of France is the cause of liberty." He believed that the revolution brought to power the "most cruel" social order in human history, which annihilated "the foundations of social order and true liberty."[90] When the John Jay mission was launched in 1794, he advised Jay to work for an arrangement that would exempt America-bound industrial immigrants from the British emigration restrictions. Lord Grenville rejected the proposal. Although the Jay Treaty did not address the British restrictions on the movement of machinery and men across the Atlantic, Hamilton ignored this omission and campaigned energetically for the treaty's ratification. The French Revolution had changed his priorities. U.S. technological deficiencies did not justify alienating the nation he believed was America's sole protector from France.

These later developments must not obscure the facts that before the wars of the French Revolution, Hamilton publicly urged the U.S. government to sponsor large-scale violations of Britain's laws and that technology piracy threatened the perceived source of Britain's premier position in the world—its superior industrial base. Hamilton's challenges to British industrial power make him no more an enemy of Britain, however, than his opposition to commercial coercion make him the double agent portrayed by historians from Boyd to Perkins and DeConde. The Report on Manufactures was not an aberration. It was "an integral part of Hamilton's total design."[91] The Treasury secretary, whose career sprang from the American rejection of English colonial rule, had concluded that only through emulation of the English financial system and transfer of industrial expertise could American independence be made secure. Acquiring prohibited technology at the risk of alienating Britain and stabilizing the country's finances at the risk of alienating France were the twin sides of a neomercantilist plan to raise the United States to the rank of a great power.

Believing economic independence was inseparable from political freedom, Hamilton was alarmed by American dependence on British imports. He opposed commercial coercion, fearing that the young nation would be devastated by such a contest. His less confrontational design envisioned ridding the United States of British economic domination by developing American manufacturing. He concluded that American technological backwardness stood in the way of American manufactures and urged the federal government to launch an aggressive campaign to acquire England's protected industrial secrets. Congress and the country refused to go along with this subtle and sophisticated plan, opting instead to make no industrial policy. Inaction proved prophetic. European immigration and American ingenuity combined to overcome the technology gap. By the middle of the nineteenth century, the United States became the industrial model that other nations sought to emulate.

3

HAMILTON'S SECOND THOUGHTS

Federalist Finance Revisited

Herbert E. Sloan

NEVER ONE TO surrender without a struggle, Alexander Hamilton kept lecturing his countrymen on the importance of public credit until almost his final day in office as secretary of the Treasury. His last major report, delivered on January 16, 1795, urged Congress to perfect "*whatsoever may remain unfinished of our System of Public Credit,* in order to place that credit as far as may be practicable *on grounds which cannot be disturbed.*"[1] At first sight, Hamilton's plea seems odd; public credit, we thought, had been vindicated triumphantly in 1790. Yet Hamilton was right: funding and assumption began the process of establishing public credit; they did not complete it. Public credit required more than a solution to the debts inherited from the Confederation, and by 1795 Hamilton was only too aware of what remained to be done. As domestic politics grew in rancor and the situation in Europe deteriorated, he had every reason to press for a permanent system that would ensure the longevity of public credit and immunize it from political attack. What is striking in Hamilton's valedictory, then, is its implicit confession of failure, its recognition that the nation's public credit had yet to be established on a secure and lasting basis. That failure has much to tell us about the limitations of Federalist finance and why, in the end, Hamilton's larger program had so little chance of succeeding.

Assessments of public finance under the Federalists usually focus on the beginning of Hamilton's tenure at the Treasury—more precisely, on the hopes and plans he revealed in 1789–91. Hamilton, it is clear, had an understanding of the potential of the market economy and the role of the state in creating that economy that surpassed anything in the thought of his political contemporaries. Thus the traditional story emphasizes Hamilton the visionary brought down by a combination of self-interest (the "monied men" he depended on failed to live up to his expectations) and Republican ideological intransigence (itself a reflection of the self-interest of Virginia planters and their like).[2] This version has a good deal to recommend it, for it focuses on some of what Hamilton was up against, and it points the finger of blame at identifiable parties. But when stress falls on brilliance frustrated, we are less likely to recall that Federalist finance did not end with Hamilton or to pay attention to the limitations of Hamilton's policies as blueprints for late eighteenth-century America. Both points need consideration if the study of Federalist finance is to move beyond the biographical and become more than simply another strand in the political narrative of the early republic.

It is equally important not to dismiss the charges of Hamilton's Republican opponents as the vaporings of overstimulated imaginations. The Republicans were given to placing Hamilton in the worst possible light, sniffing tyranny in every passing breeze, magnifying and distorting the least of the Treasury's activities into a plot to destroy republican liberty and anglicize and monarchize the new nation. But there was enough in Hamilton's and the Federalists' doings to justify Republican alarms, and if the Republicans erred in thinking that Hamilton sought to overthrow the Constitution by fair means or foul, they were not entirely wrong to see Federalist finance as leading the country in a direction antithetical to their vision of America. Most politically active Americans came to agree with them, and we may take this as powerful evidence that Hamilton's plans were ill suited to late eighteenth-century American realities. For what Hamilton proposed was unworkable, given conditions in the new nation and the worldviews of its inhabitants. Much of what he hoped to create presupposed material and cultural resources unavailable in the early republic; his best efforts could not summon them into being. Given the political consequences of Hamilton's program, we might wonder whether a secretary of the Treasury with less vision and more measured ambition would have served Federalism better in the long run. But it was characteristic of Hamilton to prefer what might be possible to what was practicable.

Some things Hamilton could do, and these he accomplished with considerable and even lasting success. He organized and directed a bureaucracy and established a system depending in large degree on the collection of the most accessible source of revenue—customs duties. He arranged the disordered finances inherited from the Confederation in a modern and comprehensive fashion, simplifying the welter of obligations and putting them on a paying basis. And he established a national bank on the model of the Bank of England to serve as both the government's agent and a support for the merchant community. But if this was the extent of his accomplishment in the realm of public finance, it hardly marked the limit of his ambitions. By measuring the latter against the former, we can see why Hamilton never really had a chance to complete the transformation he intended his program to initiate. The heart of his program, establishing public credit on a firm and permanent foundation, would be frustrated by circumstances beyond his control, and his valedictory report of 1795 can be read as a last, desperate attempt to convince his countrymen of principles they had never been willing to put into practice.

Finally, a note of caution. We do not know everything we should about the workings of Federalist finance. While there is a considerable literature on Hamilton's intentions and the organization of the Treasury Department, we lack studies of practice at the local level. In the case of the excise and the Whiskey Rebellion, we have several good accounts of the impact and consequences of a specific part of the Federalists' financial program.[3] But because the focus is usually on Hamilton himself and the role of his policies in shaping the first party system, we have much less information about a number of other things it would be useful to know. Little attention has been given to the Treasury's operations after Hamilton retired at the beginning of 1795; thus his successor, Oliver Wolcott, the dour Connecticut Federalist who served from 1795 to 1800, remains a cipher, except in narratives of the Adams administration. Wolcott's problems, it might be argued, were more than a matter of his modest talents; they had much to do with the system Hamilton staked out in 1789–91 and the difficulty of keeping it viable in a setting that changed dramatically after the mid-1790s.[4] Most of all, and surprisingly, we have no competent account of the impact of Hamilton's debt program, except, again, in so far as it is connected with the emergence of the Republican opposition. Gaps of this sort make it difficult to speak with confidence about Federalist finance as a whole. These perspectives—suggesting that Hamilton accomplished less than he set out to, that there were real limits on what could be done, and that his critics were not unjustified in raising the alarm—frame the following pages.

HAMILTON'S GOAL was the creation of *public credit*, not simply putting the public debt on a paying basis. Proper management of the existing debt was one of public credit's main components, but it was hardly its only aspect or the one that mattered most. Hamilton was far more successful in dealing with the public debt than in establishing public credit; the distinction between the two will help us to arrive at a sense of how Hamilton failed and why.

Public credit, eighteenth-century writers agreed, was evanescent; opinion mattered greatly. Unless government bonds were believed to be safe, no one would buy or hold them; confidence that interest on old issues would continue to be paid and that new ones could be supported made all the difference. Thus it was never enough to show that current levels of debt could be serviced, for public credit looked to the future and borrowings at distant points of need. The question for investors was whether revenues could be developed to service both old loans and new ones without endangering either. As Hamilton's contemporaries were aware, Britain's ability to command the confidence of the investing public at home and abroad in this respect made all the difference to its public credit. In contrast—in 1789 this was clear to everyone—inability to command that confidence led to bankruptcy and political upheaval in France.

If public credit rested on something so intangible as confidence, that confidence had to manifest itself in concrete ways. In the eighteenth century it was important to be able to draw on the resources of foreign investors as well as those of the domestic public. Above all, this was a matter of the Dutch money market, the great source of loans for European nations and, from the early 1780s, for the United States as well. In addition to loans from foreign investors, public credit also depended on the government's ability to bolster confidence by developing significant resources through domestic taxation. (Again, by 1789, France served as a warning of what would happen in the event of failure on this score.) Customs duties, though important and easily tapped, were never enough. Vulnerable in wartime, there was a point beyond which they could not be raised without encouraging smuggling or substitution and hence diminishing the revenue they yielded. Essential to bolster the revenue flow that maintained investor confidence, a respectable level of domestic taxation was a sine qua non of public credit.[5]

On both counts—foreign loans and domestic taxes—Hamilton's expectations would be disappointed. The wars of the French Revolution, beginning in 1792, brought the armies of France to the Low Countries, where they took the Austrian Netherlands for good in 1794 and, in the winter of 1794–95, successfully invaded the United Provinces. The stadtholder fled to England, and the French gorged on the Dutch wealth.[6] The resources of the Batavian Republic, the puppet state established by the French and their local collaborators, were no longer available to sustain

American finances—this at a time when the United States was drifting rapidly toward conflict with France. It was a disaster of potentially monumental proportions for American public credit. Without a reliable external source of financing, the administration was forced to rely on the domestic market, and experience during the Quasi-War demonstrated that market's limits. Interest rates rose alarmingly, and it was not only Republicans who found them usurious; John Adams was horrified by the cost of the 8 percent loan of 1798.[7] From 1795 on, then, the sole source of money abroad was London, but before the Barings financed the Louisiana Purchase in 1803, there was little serious effort to borrow in England; in any case, Pitt's wars absorbed available capital, and it would have been impossible to float a loan without official British consent.[8]

Moreover, Hamilton was unable to develop significant revenues from domestic sources. His major effort, the excise, was not a success: costly to administer, it raised political hackles, and it never produced much of a return. The results of the other important experiment in domestic taxation, the direct tax of 1798, were equally unimpressive. Nor did the sale of national assets (whether western lands or the government's shares in the Bank of the United States) yield more than a fraction of the income from customs revenue.[9] Yet from the start Hamilton had known that it would be necessary to accustom Americans to paying taxes, if only because he thought that "less dependence can be placed on one species of funds, and that too liable to the vicissitudes of the continuance, or interruption of foreign intercourse, than on a variety of different funds formed by the union of internal with external objects."[10] But, as Secretary of State Thomas Jefferson pointed out to President Washington in 1792, the excise—"of odious character"—could only be enforced "by arbitrary & vexatious means" and so would weaken government rather than strengthen it. Jefferson's outrage two years later at the massive force employed to put down the Whiskey Rebellion—he damned the "excise-law" as "an infernal one"—similarly reflected his fear that enforcement would alienate the people before they had become reconciled to the new government.[11]

Jefferson and the Republicans were right to doubt the wisdom of Hamilton's response to the Whiskey Rebellion. Using 13,000 men to subdue a minor insurrection in western Pennsylvania was a show of force the government could not afford to repeat. Hamilton, of course, thought otherwise. For him, the uprising was a test that had to be met, and in such a way that no one would dare to provoke the government a second time. "Whenever the Government appears in arms," he insisted on a later occasion, "it ought to appear like a *Hercules*," and the cost was "of no moment compared to the advantages of energy."[12] Yet the response was also an admission of the government's inability to run a serious program of domestic taxation. Sending an army to overawe frontier farmers implied—or rather proved—that taxes could not be gathered under normal conditions. Compared to the ease of collecting customs duties, the excise was a nightmare. Administrative costs were higher, and it had the additional, and key, disadvantage of bringing the government into contact with people who were not inclined to pay the kinds of taxes demanded. Yet excises on liquor were among the most traditional forms of taxation in the Anglo-American world. If Americans would not pay this, what would they pay?

That, in a sense, was Hamilton's dilemma, and he was never able to resolve it, either to his satisfaction or to anyone else's. The Republicans had a better notion of what would and would not work, and once in power they dispensed with internal taxes as rapidly as possible, allowing Jefferson to announce in 1805 that it was the "pleasure and pride" of Americans "to ask, what farmer, what mechanic, what laborer, ever sees a tax-gatherer of the United States?"[13] But how could a strong and modern state be created without internal taxation? Every European model available to Hamilton—above all, that of Britain—proved that internal taxation was a necessity. Indeed, by 1800 internal taxes produced 64 percent of the British revenue; in the United States, the comparable figure was slightly over 14 percent.[14] Yet trying to duplicate the British achievement in America would raise insuperable difficulties, if only because the United States was, in comparison, economically underdeveloped, less populous, and more sparsely settled; thus it was harder to find acceptable items to tax and more costly to tax them.

The practical consequences of the Federalists' inability to create an adequate flow of income from domestic sources were exceedingly important. With more than half the federal revenue committed to servicing Hamilton's consolidated debt and no possibility of substantial increases from domestic sources, American policy had to be cautious and pacific. Dependence on customs revenue thus had the great disadvantage of limiting policy choices, especially in foreign relations. It is by now a commonplace to say that Hamilton tied the United States to Britain in order not to disturb relations with its largest trading partner and kill the goose whose golden eggs paid the interest on the national debt. And indeed that was so, though it need not follow, as it sometimes does, that this was a bad thing.[15] What has to be emphasized, however, is that dependence on customs revenues, given the disappearance of Dutch support for American credit and the failure to develop domestic tax resources, made any aggressive foreign policy problematic, whether directed toward Britain or, in the later 1790s, toward France. Here, it can be argued, Hamilton and other Federalists erred badly in seeking a military buildup during the Quasi-War that could only be paid for with expensive loans and dangerous domestic taxes. Capable of supporting cheap government and interest on the current debt, customs duties could not support, for very long, a navy and a vastly expanded army. If there was to be a military so that the United States could act like a European state in the international arena, then the money for it would have to come from other sources. By the time of the Quasi-War, those sources had to include increased domestic taxation certain to cause political trouble.

Against this background, the Republican alternative to Hamilton's program of adopting the techniques of European public finance to support the developing American state—Jefferson's and Madison's program of commercial coercion—begins to seem a good deal more attractive, at least from the domestic angle. Americans, as their representatives in Congress made clear, and as some of them also made clear out of doors, were not prepared to pay taxes to support a powerful military and an aggressive posture in foreign affairs. Republican policymakers seized on that reluctance, creating an alternative that left Americans alone and sought to achieve national goals through commercial coercion. Granted, the underlying premise was just as flawed in the early republic as it had been during the years of boycott before the Revolution, but to some it offered a way around the basic problem. Military forces, Republicans believed, were dangerous to liberty, and taxes were bound to be unpopular; commercial coercion avoided both and at the same time held out the promise of substantial benefits for the United States, thus offering foreign policy on the cheap, always the great Republican desideratum. Once the Republicans had a chance to put these notions into practice, they produced failure after failure in the international arena. But this only underscores the irony: neither the Federalists nor the Republicans were able to find a workable solution to the problem of supporting their ambitious dreams for America.[16]

THOUGH EXAGGERATED, most of the Republican arguments against Hamilton's system had some basis in fact. What contemporaries understood, and historians now recognize, is that Republican fears and Federalist behavior fell into well-established patterns. The Republicans were right: Hamilton's program did bear a strong resemblance to the British model. The country party notions the Republicans inherited from the opposition

in Britain had a good deal of accuracy, provided one accepted the underlying assumptions. The American Treasury was political, and its actions
seemed to favor one part of the community—a small and unrepresenta-
tive group of speculators and merchants—at the expense of the majority,
those honest farmers, planters, and artisans whose merits and just claims,
Republicans believed, received no recognition from the Federalist faction.
As the Republicans saw it, Hamilton's policy was wrong not only because
it promoted the interests of the wrong part of the community, but also
because the system it underwrote was inherently dangerous to liberty.
They were sure that borrowing allowed government to disguise the true
costs of its policy and so encouraged war, that opportunity for speculation
and profiteering. And in the end, there was always the likelihood that
militarism would be the death of liberty—the fate of Rome, the potential
fate of eighteenth-century Britain. Government was dangerous, and power
too likely to corrupt, yet Federalist financial policy seemed hell-bent on
making government stronger and creating power that would sooner
or later be used to oppress the people. This was a potent set of ideas,
and there was enough connection between the images and fears of
Republican publicists and the actual workings of Federalism to suggest
that the Republicans were on to something. By the end of the 1790s,
with military expansion during the Quasi-War financed by heavy government borrowing and domestic taxes, with political repression in full
swing, no Republican doubted for a moment the wisdom of the country
party critique.[17]

Yet there were differences between the arrangements Hamilton over-
saw and their British prototypes, and these have often been overlooked,
not least by Republicans in the 1790s, who focused on the political consequences of Hamilton's system without pausing to observe its other features. The Republicans failed to appreciate how fortunate they were.
Hamilton's system might look British; in fact, it was so only at a very high
level of abstraction. For one thing, Hamilton could start with a fairly
clean slate in arranging his bureaucracy. The results were lean and tight;
British "economical reformers" like Edmund Burke and the younger Pitt
would have envied them. There were no medieval holdovers, no cumber-
some structures, no arcane procedures.[18] In contrast, and despite Republican claims, the system Hamilton put in place was straightforward and
relatively simple. If the "common farmer"—the standard Jefferson
wished to apply—had difficulty understanding the results, it was more
a matter of failure to comprehend what public finance was about than
because it was intentionally wrapped in mystery.[19] And while the Treasury

did have more civilian employees than the other executive branches, and political considerations often guided their selection, otherwise it hardly resembled its British counterpart.[20] American arrangements were mercifully free of the sinecures that pervaded the British system; Hamilton's men earned their money, and there was nothing on this side of the Atlantic to compare with, say, the Grenville family's tellership in the army pay office that brought its holder some £7,000 a year.[21]

But none of that made any difference to Republicans, for whom administrative efficiency in the service of a bad cause had no charms. Efficient administration of an aggressive program only made matters worse, and again, Republicans were right to fear that Federalist "energy" meant favoring the national government at the expense of the people and, in any case, at the expense of the states. Jefferson was alarmed by the legal implications of Hamilton's program, hating the way the creation of the Bank of the United States twisted the necessary and proper clause and invaded states' rights by unilaterally altering the laws relating to property. The Treasury secretary's propensity to act at the states' expense was no Republican myth: Hamilton cared little for the states, especially when they got in the way of things he wanted done. To Republicans, who numbered many of the Anti-Federalists of 1787–88 among their adherents, Federalist willingness to ride roughshod over the rights of the people and the states raised serious issues and brought back memories of predictions uttered during ratification, too many of them, it seemed, now coming true.[22]

BY THE CLOSE of his term in office—he retired on January 31, 1795— Hamilton realized that more was required. At this point—shortly after the expedition to suppress the Whiskey Rebellion in the fall of 1794 and with the growing likelihood that the French would overwhelm Holland—the failure of his initial vision must have been evident to him, and he turned his attention once more to the problem he had raised briefly in 1790 and neither then nor later had been able to resolve: what to do about Americans' reluctance to tax themselves. The debt, it was now clear, was dangerous, for the habit of piling up debts was "the *natural disease* of all Governments" and eventually would "lead to great & convulsive revolutions of Empire." It is almost as though Hamilton had been rethinking the warnings of David Hume and Adam Smith and other orthodox eighteenth-century commentators on the British public debt, so closely does his language track their warnings.[23] But Hamilton wished to "give *immortality* to *public credit*," and thus, because Congress was reluctant to impose taxes and America was unlikely to enjoy further support from the Dutch bankers, he fell back on the tried-and-true eighteenth-century panacea, a sinking fund religiously adhered to. It was clearly second-best, but in the circumstances it was all there was, and Hamilton made what he could of it.[24] Once the sinking fund was in place, he concluded, the country could "guard as far as possible against the dangers . . . , without renouncing the advantages which those systems [of public credit] undoubtedly afford."[25]

Contemporaries had doubts, especially those Republicans worried that Hamilton was stealing their thunder; Jefferson and Madison were predictably skeptical. But Hamilton was genuinely worried; he feared that hostility to the very idea of debt would prove the death of public credit. In the end, it was public credit that mattered, and if preserving it required reducing the debt, Hamilton would do that. That he had come to this is a measure of the nation's failure to respond as he had hoped, a measure of the mistakes he had made in placing his hopes on the "enlightened part of the community" and in failing to anticipate the hostility his propositions would arouse. He now found himself trying to shore up public credit by extinguishing public debt. It was also a measure of what he had learned since 1790 that he sought to insulate the debt from congressional interference as much as possible.

A good deal of the final report was taken up by technicalities. For our purposes, as for contemporaries, what really mattered was the plan to put the debt on the road to extinction. Hamilton offered a remodeled sinking fund secure against raids by the legislature, which, British experience showed, was all too likely to raid using the fund as a painless alternative to borrowing or additional taxation when regular revenue fell short of current needs. Because the government would now promise bondholders that the sinking fund would be used only to retire the debt, and because that promise would be part of the contract between the government and the bondholders, in theory it would no longer be possible for the legislature to divert the sinking fund to other purposes.

What will strike us about this proposal is its rhetoric: Hamilton, for once, appears in the guise of a proponent of the orthodox theory of public finance, arguing that debt was dangerous and led, at least potentially, to social upheaval. Quoting Washington's language in the November 1794 Annual Message—undoubtedly he had inspired it—Hamilton urged Congress to consider "the adoption of a *definitive plan* for the *Redemption* of the public debt, and to the Consummation of *whatever may remain unfinished of our System of Public Credit*, in order to place that credit as far as may be practicable *on grounds which cannot be disturbed,* and to prevent *that progressive accumulation of Debt which must ultimately endanger all Government.*" He returned to the point in the body of the report, urging that "there is no sentiment which can better deserve the serious attention of the Legislators of a Country than the one expressed in the Speech of the President; which indicates the danger to every Government from the progressive accumulation of Debt."[26]

These were widely shared notions, even if largely absent in his previous performances, and so Hamilton pressed quickly on to the practical problem the legislators must confront: the reluctance to match words with deeds by imposing the taxes that would bring about the desired result. Since even those opposed to debt will on occasion advocate more spending, there was, Hamilton said, an "artificial embarrassment in the way of the administrators of Government," who were likely to take the path of least resistance and "conciliate public favor by declining to lay even necessary burthens." Thus, "the public Debt swells 'till its magnitude becomes enormous, and the Burthens of the people gradually increase 'till their weight becomes intolerable." Then—here Hamilton echoed Hume's predictions—the "Natural offspring" of these "great disorders in the whole political oeconomy" will be "convulsions & revolutions of Government." Thus Hamilton urged the legislators to adopt a program of "extinguishing with reasonable celerity the actual debt of the Country, and for laying the foundations of a system which may shield posterity from the consequences of the usual improvidence and selfishness of its ancestors: And which if possible may give *immortality* to *public credit.*" The practical remedy is Hamilton's proposal for a sinking fund beyond the control of the legislature, incorporated into the contract between the creditor and the public, secure from violation under all but the most extraordinary of circumstances.[27] Hence as well Hamilton's argument in favor of tying any future loans to new taxes that will extinguish them. (It is a measure of Hamilton's orthodoxy here that Jefferson would make the same argument during the War of 1812.)[28]

But Hamilton's apparent conversion to the orthodox view was less than complete. He could not let the opportunity pass without remarking that the objections to public credit "have much less support" in the facts of the case than was usually assumed; while those objections were "not wholly unfounded," his proposed system allowed the country "to guard as far as possible against the dangers . . . , without renouncing the advantages which those systems [of public credit] undoubtedly afford."[29] At the same time, though he did not stress this, his sinking fund would make it necessary to maintain taxes at their present level, since the fund would now be part of the contract with investors.

Contemporaries differed widely in their assessment of Hamilton's new plan. Noting that it would require thirty years to extinguish the debt under Hamilton's plan, Republicans like Madison and Jefferson did not take it seriously. It was a sham, they told each other, and Madison strongly doubted that the funds Hamilton proposed to assign to the debt would suffice to retire it. Federalists, on the other hand, found satisfaction in the discomfiture of their political enemies. At last the truth was out. For years the Republicans had denounced the debt and its burdens; now, presented with an opportunity to do something about it, they hung back and created spurious objections, revealing their true colors.[30]

Republicans were right to be suspicious; the Federalists were up to something. By the end of his term of office, Hamilton had concluded that public credit was far too vulnerable to the whims of the legislature and required additional protection from such interference, and he addressed the issues involved at considerable length in his report. Congress had already debated taxing the interest on federal securities, a prospect Hamilton deplored, since he thought it would be an invasion of the contract between the public and the bondholders; having stipulated a given rate of interest, the legislature was now proposing to take back with one hand what it had given with the other. Moreover, there had been moves to sequester the property of alien enemies in the event of war, their property in government securities included, and again Hamilton protested: anything that threatened the sanctity of contract had to be avoided at all costs.[31] Given Hamilton's sense that Congress was likely to go on interfering with the debt, the logical solution was to make the debt as untouchable as possible, and his new sinking fund offered a way of doing this. Not only would it be part of the contract but, by demonstrating the government's determination to extinguish the debt, it would also—this was not its least important aspect—make the debt less prominent as an issue in politics.

Hamilton now appreciated that political controversy over the debt threatened the larger and more important matter of public credit. In 1790 he had been eager to dilate on the advantages of the debt, whether as a substitute for metallic currency or as a resource, a sum of capital, that in the right hands could lead to important improvements. Half a decade later, hostility to debt threatened public credit itself. Forced to choose between the debt and public credit, Hamilton had no hesitation in sacrificing the former to maintain the latter; by making the debt more secure in the hands of those who held it and at the same time reducing it in order to remove it from political contention, Hamilton hoped to secure public credit once and for all.

If none of this had been apparent to Hamilton and his fellow Federalists at the outset in 1790, perhaps it should have been. There were limits on what could be accomplished by financial policy, given the state of the country, the opinions of its citizens, and the underdevelopment of its economy, and Hamilton had tried to stretch those limits further than they would go. In his hands Federalist finance was visionary to a degree we sometimes fail to realize. Federalist finance was, then, a failure by 1795, if judged by the ambitions its founder and presiding genius entertained. But it would be a mistake to see this as a missed opportunity, for it is doubtful that there was ever a chance that Hamilton's larger goals could have been realized in post-Independence America. His reports were sophisticated exercises in eighteenth-century economic thinking, far too sophisticated for the primitive conditions of his country. Had he in fact been able to do more than he did, to continue in the path of state-directed development, we are entitled to ask whether the outcome would have been satisfactory. The particular brand of liberalism espoused by the Jeffersonians was surely more in harmony with the views of most Americans who thought about these matters and voted on them, for the state was precisely what America was not supposed to have.[32]

Congress adopted many of the features of Hamilton's valedictory report. But Hamilton was far too sanguine about the results to be obtained from his new version of public credit insulated from political controversy. Republicans continued to harp on the evils of the debt, and they were aided by the policies of the Adams administration, which added further mountains of debt to the existing sums. Toward the end of his life, Hamilton admitted that his projects had been too bold for his countrymen. Unable to find a place for himself in the post-1800 era, he confessed to Gouverneur Morris that his was "an odd destiny." "Every day," he added, "proves to me more and more that this American world was not made for me."[33] The Treasury he created passed into the hands of Albert Gallatin, a European who had naturalized himself in the new nation and who would carry out a reduction in the debt far more ruthless than Hamilton had envisioned in 1795.

HAMILTON'S SUCCESSOR, Oliver Wolcott, secretary of the Treasury from 1795 to 1800, was a figure of the second rank. Competent but uninspired, Wolcott was the early republic's equivalent of a career administrator, having served in state and lesser federal office before Washington turned to him when Hamilton resigned. Capable of administering a going concern, Wolcott showed less ability when it came to coping with the problems of the Quasi-War. His early letters to Hamilton suggest a man easily given to panic. "I do not see how [the affairs] of the treasury are to be managed," he wrote in the fall of 1795, noting that "our foreign resources are dried up—our domestic are deeply anticipated."[34] But the conditions under which the Adams administration attempted to finance the maritime contest with France probably would have taxed even Hamilton's capacities, for it was now that luck turned sour and the effects of the failure to transform American finances came home to roost. Wolcott's problem was the simple one of where to get the money demanded by the administration's program of naval armament and increased military activity. Unlike his predecessor, and unlike Congress during the Revolution and Confederation, Wolcott could not borrow abroad. French conquest of the Netherlands closed the prime European source of funds to the Americans, and no substitute emerged to take its place. This left the administration dependent on domestic sources, and that was the trouble. Wolcott could not raise money at less than 8 percent, a figure contemporaries deplored, and even then there was difficulty in filling the loans he opened.[35]

Taxation was the obvious other resource, but taxation was a tricky business. Significant increases in the levels of the tariff might be counterproductive, and the administration did not resort to this tactic. Yet if imports were not to be taxed at higher levels, what was left? Excises were problematic, as the Whiskey Rebellion had demonstrated, and even though *Hylton v. United States* in 1796 confirmed the principle that taxes on luxuries were excises, not direct taxes, the administration—wisely, no doubt —did not resort to the taxes on specific items that were so notable a feature of Pitt's wartime finance. Instead, it decided to levy a direct tax on lands, houses, and slaves. The results were less than satisfactory, from either the monetary or the political standpoint, and the tax contributed more than a little to the eventual defeat of the Federalists—just as the Republicans expected it to.

Administering the direct tax was an enormous undertaking, given the scope of national government in the 1790s, comparable only to the administration of the census, and it brought federal agents into an unusual degree of contact with ordinary Americans, especially ordinary Americans who lived in the interior or away from the shipping centers along the Atlantic coast. The results were predictable: murmuring and grousing, and even modest resistance. In Philadelphia's hinterland, German-American farmers with long memories of life in the old country were alarmed by the measure. They frightened away the tax collectors, and then in March 1799 a group of them led by a local veteran, militia officer, and auctioneer, John Fries, forced a federal marshal to release prisoners he had taken.

In the capital the administration went into overdrive. Fries and his band had just enough similarity to the Shaysites of 1786–87 and the Whiskey Rebels of 1794 to convince Adams's cabinet that the sternest measures were called for. Once again troops were dispatched to put down this challenge to authority. In hindsight, the episode seems more farce than anything else, but that was not how Wolcott and his colleagues saw matters, and it was certainly not so for Fries and the other men tried with him, two of them, like Fries, found guilty of treason and sentenced to hang. Though pardoned by President Adams, Fries and his followers were a powerful lesson in what happened when the United States resorted to European methods and principles.[36] The Fries episode was an indication, and an important one, of what was going wrong with Federalism, particularly in the sphere of government finance. "The taxgatherer has already excited discontent," Jefferson reported early in 1799, and that discontent during the Quasi-War played a significant part in the popular reaction against Federalism that culminated in the election of 1800; taxes, as Jefferson confidently predicted, were high among the causes of the Federalists' undoing.[37]

The Federalists' belated attempt to impose a program of internal taxation required far too much interference with Americans' preferred way of doing things and so was doomed from the start. Rarely popular, taxes traditionally had rested on the sanction of the political nation, as in eighteenth-century Britain (and even then they were often contested), or, as was more usual in eighteenth-century Europe, on the strong arm of the state. In the new nation there was neither a political consensus solid enough to impose internal taxes on an unwilling populace nor a developed state to administer and enforce them. Both the Whiskey Rebellion and the Fries episode demonstrated that the government had only one answer to refusal to pay: military force in overwhelming measure. By its very nature, however, such force could not be used on a regular and consistent basis. What was required was a modern, permanent, efficient body of internal revenue collectors, the sort of thing that had been created in the customs service. But such a service would have challenged some of the Americans' cherished notions. An army of excisemen was exactly the army Americans did not want. And there was a further problem: as long as internal taxes were hit-or-miss affairs, imposed only occasionally in response to pressing necessities, it would be hard to justify a standing corps capable of instilling the habits of obedience necessary to make the system work without friction and at a reasonable cost of collection. On these and other counts, therefore, internal taxes did not recommend themselves.

Nor were the Federalists the only ones to come to grief over such issues. It says a good deal about the difficulties the Federalists faced, I think, that they did not disappear once the Republicans took office in 1801. Pledged to repeal internal taxes, boasting, as Jefferson did, that no farmer ever saw a tax collector of the United States, the Republicans, too, would find themselves confronted with the difficulties of revenue enforcement. When the Embargo barred trade with Britain and Britain's possessions, Americans routinely ignored it, and smuggling on the northern frontier reached epidemic proportions. The militia had to be called out, and even that was not enough. Moreover, and this was entirely predictable, all of the Adams administration's problems with financing the Quasi-War returned to haunt the Madison administration during the War of 1812; then, too, there would be the failure of the domestic loan market to support the government, an unsuccessful resort to direct taxes, and a drastic collapse of finances.[38]

THE EARLY REPUBLIC survived the Federalist episode. As Stanley Elkins and Eric McKitrick have reminded us, it was Federalism's fate to be the road not taken. So, too, the individual parts of the Federalist program—above all, Hamilton's effort to establish a British-style system of public credit—represent alternatives with little chance of success in the early republic. Too bold, too ambitious, too much at odds with American realities, whether political or economic, Hamilton's grand designs foundered on the unwillingness of Americans to subject themselves to a European system of discipline and taxation. The Republican alternative was all too seductive, promising gain without pain and satisfying the pervasive American desire to be left alone and escape the attentions of the state. By rights it should have come to grief. Yet—through no merit of their own—in the end the Republicans succeeded where the Federalists did not, managing to hold onto the luck that deserted Hamilton. They ought to have failed, for the string of policy disasters from the Embargo through the War of 1812 surely should have discredited them. But matters turned out otherwise, and the end of the Napoleonic Wars allowed Americans to put off for another hundred years the lessons Hamilton tried to teach. God, Bismarck is supposed to have said, looks after fools and the United States.

4

RADICALS IN THE "WESTERN WORLD"

The Federalist Conquest of Trans-Appalachian North America

Andrew R. L. Cayton

THE MOST DECISIVE development in the early American republic was the conquest of the trans-Appalachian West. In a few decades European Americans invaded the Ohio and Mississippi valleys, defeated American Indians, plowed fields, erected homes, constructed towns, established political and legal systems, and initiated commerce that eventually would link them to peoples throughout the world. In the 1770s Anglo Americans west of the Appalachians numbered only a few hundred, most of them in Kentucky. By 1820 there were hundreds of thousands of citizens of the United States living in the states of Ohio, Indiana, Illinois, Missouri, Kentucky, Tennessee, Mississippi, and Alabama. By any measure, what contemporaries called the "western world" was a vastly different place in the 1820s from what it had been in the 1780s.

This rapid transformation would not have occurred as it did without the effective use of national political and military power. In the critical years of the 1780s and the 1790s, supporters of a strong national government ensured the supremacy of the nation-state in the expansion of the American republic. They made certain that the development of the United States would be more than a laissez-faire enterprise, that it would involve a coordinated national policy as well as the actions of thousands of individual households.

While Federalists generally managed to establish what they would have called the "tone" of American expansion, their impact in trans-Appalachia was decidedly uneven. Their legacy would encompass a broad spectrum of success, ranging from considerable in Ohio to minimal in Kentucky. In part because of the resistance of frontier peoples and in part because of the national government's inability to bring to bear substantial resources in the 1790s in order to implement designs largely

77

devised in the 1780s, Federalists were unable to transform the West in a uniform fashion.

Still, they did succeed in making loyalty to the United States a primary ingredient of social identity. A significant number of white men began to consider themselves citizens of the United States as well as members of households and local communities. Not all of them would be happy with that fact. But most would increasingly appeal to the impersonal principle of the sovereignty of the people, which, for better or worse, they equated with the national government created by the federal Constitution, as the ultimate authority in their lives.

We may take this development for granted. (After all, most trans-Appalachian settlers were from one of the original thirteen American states.) But very few people did so in the late eighteenth century. Indeed, many saw the efforts of nationally oriented men to attach people to the new republic as essentially radical innovations designed to undermine traditional social relationships. Not only were Federalists elevating imperial authority above local authority. By privileging abstract impersonal principles above particular personal ties, they were redefining the nature of social and political relationships.

Confronted by opposition from both European American and American Indian frontier peoples and defeated politically, many Federalists would conclude in the early 1800s that the West was a permanent obstacle to American political unity and social coherence. They would agree with former Massachusetts congressman Fisher Ames's 1805 contention that patriotism—or shared principles—was impossible in a country as large as the United States. "Safe in their solitudes, alike from the annoyance of enemies and of government," Ames wrote of the residents of the "straggling" western settlements, "it is infinitely more probable that they will sink into barbarism than rise to the dignity of national sentiments and character." The "capacious wilderness" was the home of "men who remain ignorant, or learn only from the newspapers that they are countrymen, who think it their right to be exempted from all tax, restraint, or control, but to make rulers for it."[1]

Ames was far from alone in suggesting that the trans-Appalachian West was the antithesis of the Federalist vision of the good society—a world of regular settlements, schools, churches, and orderly economic development suffused by a shared respect for national authority and social obligations. It would be wrong, however, to accept such fatalistic resignation as the sum total of Federalist interest in the West.

Such a judgment ignores the dynamic and evolutionary nature of their attitudes toward the region. In the 1780s whatever fears many future Federalists had about trans-Appalachia were more than counterbalanced by dreams of personal fortune and national glory. The opposition they soon provoked and the lamentations of self-pity in which they eventually indulged must not obscure their substantial achievement: the establishment of the foundations of a radical political and social order west of the Appalachian Mountains.

ORIGINS, 1783–88

In the 1780s nationalist land speculators, promoters, and congressmen laid the foundations of national power west of the Appalachians. These men, many of whom became ardent Federalists in the 1790s, assumed a fundamentally symbiotic relationship between national power and western development. One could not exist without the other. To survive, the United States would have to demonstrate its ability to control the disposition of trans-Appalachian lands and guide the development of political and social structures in the region. Its officials had to persuade the people west of the Appalachians that it was in their best interest to recognize the sovereignty of the United States.

The proto-Federalist western policy that emerged by the end of the 1780s was largely an elaborate refinement of old ideas, a continuation of speculative schemes for a coordinated development of the trans-Appalachian region whose implementation had been interrupted by the American Revolution. Powerful men had been dreaming about the future of the North American interior for decades. Now they had a chance to realize some of those dreams, which were personal as well as public.

Virtually every American military officer and territorial official in the late eighteenth century was a land speculator who hoped to make a fortune from western lands. Most of them saw private gain as a legitimate reward for public service. How else could a government as underfinanced as that of the United States win the services of ambitious and talented men, unless it allowed them to share in potential profits? Moreover, giving scope to the operation of economic self-interest was a useful way to "attach" men to the national government. They would work for the government's survival more enthusiastically if their prosperity directly depended on it.

The reciprocal relationship that developed between the Continental officers who organized the Ohio Company of Associates in 1786 and the national government in settling the Northwest Territory exemplified the ways in which the Federalists would govern the United States as a whole in the 1790s. Congress not only sold the Ohio Company hundreds of thousands of acres at the cost of about one dollar an acre in 1787, assuming the associates would reap financial rewards from future land sales, it also entrusted the development of the Ohio Valley to the company. In return, Congress expected that the associates would establish, maintain, and extend the authority of the United States.

George Washington believed in 1783 that the West could not "be so advantageously settled by any other Class of men, as by the disbanded Officers and Soldiers of the Army." They would "connect our governments with the frontiers, extend our Settlements progressively, and plant a brave, a hardy and respectable Race of People, . . . [who] would give security to our frontiers."[2] The associates of the Ohio Company could be trusted because their service during the War for Independence had demonstrated that their loyalty to the United States ultimately took precedence over all other public and private obligations. The government turned to veterans of the Revolutionary War because it needed all the help it could get in trans-Appalachia in the 1780s and early 1790s. Before the ratification of the federal Constitution, western lands ceded by the various states to the United States in the 1770s and 1780s were the most promising source of revenue for a national government that lacked the power to tax. These lands, located north and (later) south of Kentucky (the only substantial area in trans-Appalachia to remain under the control of a state), produced little income in the 1780s. But, as James Madison noted in *Federalist* no. 38, "the Western territory" was potentially "a mine of vast wealth to the United States."[3]

If the United States could secure it. The republic was most vulnerable to attacks from European nations and American Indians on its western frontier. Great Britain in Canada and Spain in Florida and Louisiana surrounded the new nation on its flanks. Few in number, the Europeans were strategically located. They controlled the major waterways that allowed access to trans-Appalachia. The British had posts throughout the Great Lakes, continuing to occupy several—Detroit, for example—in defiance of the terms of the 1783 Treaty of Paris. Meanwhile, the Spanish controlled the Mississippi River and the coast of the Gulf of Mexico.

Above all, British and Spanish alliances with Indians made them commercial rivals as well as strategic threats to the United States. The Spanish signed treaties of alliance with leaders of the Creek, Alabama, Choctaw, and Chickasaw in 1784, promising mutual trade, tolerance, and protection. By 1794 annual gifts to these Indians constituted 10 percent of the budgets of West Florida and Louisiana.[4] To the north, the British continued to cultivate relationships with the Miami, Shawnee, and Delaware. The Indians were thus in the enviable position of playing Europeans off against each other while the Spanish and the British got what amounted to borderland buffers between themselves and the Americans.

The British and especially the Spanish also tried to entice Americans into settling in their territory or, at the very least, making special commercial arrangements with them. Unable to stop migration, they tried to control it. In 1784 the Spanish closed the lower Mississippi to foreigners, thereby effectively bottling up Kentucky commerce and infuriating Americans. The Spanish were gambling that this assertion of their authority would make their offers of economic and political concessions more enticing to American citizens.

Ambitious Americans in Kentucky, anxious for free access to the Mississippi River and New Orleans, were willing to listen to Spanish offers. They found that small payments opened legally closed waterways and markets. Others found offers of land and access to the Mississippi impossible to resist. Americans helped the population of Louisiana more than double in the 1780s while the Natchez area attracted so many people that the Spanish appointed a governor there in 1789 who required little more of American immigrants than that they swear allegiance to the crown of Spain.

In short, Spain and Great Britain posed serious challenges to the United States in the 1780s. Eventually, the sheer numbers of Americans, combined with the higher quality of their goods, would overwhelm the British and the Spanish (and later the French). But in the 1780s the authority of the United States was at stake. Could the new republic secure the West? Could it prove its value to the people pouring into the Ohio and Tennessee river valleys?

The inability of the Confederation to force Spain to open the Mississippi River to free trade was not a good omen. Indeed, the fact that a majority of Congress (although not the two-thirds needed to pass) were willing in 1785 to give up navigation of the Mississippi for thirty years positively enraged the residents of trans-Appalachia.

Courted by the Spanish and the British, rebuffed by an ineffective United States, trans-Appalachian settlers in the 1780s could justifiably ask: Of what earthly good was a government that could not solve the fundamental problems of its people? Why would not the people of the West turn their attention elsewhere? Warned Washington in 1784: "If this country . . . are suffered to form commercial intercourses (which lead we know to others) with the Spaniards on their right and rear, or the British on their left, they will become a distinct people from us, have different views, different interests, and instead of adding strength to the Union, may in case of a rupture with either of those powers, be a formidable and dangerous neighbour."[5]

The future president's description of the Spanish on their "rear" emphasizes the extent to which proto-Federalists saw the expansion of their republic as literally backing into what contemporaries called the "backcountry," making it safe for future development. Demonstrating the authority and value of the new national government created by the Constitution was critical in any effort to counteract the attractions of other political attachments. Nationalists had to establish a political order in the West which simultaneously depended on and supported the national government.

The Land Ordinance of 1785 and the Northwest Ordinance of 1787 outlined the parameters of national authority and established the framework of political discussion for decades. Together they ensured that the distribution of public lands and the formation of new states would be under the control of the United States. The Land Ordinance provided for the surveying of federal lands into rectangular ranges. Not only would these facilitate the sale of land at distant locations, they would make it easier for distant authority to exercise some control over its distribution. Whether land was good or bad, it would be subject to uniform development. This system represented a rejection of the common system of surveying in greater Virginia, which followed the lay of the land rather than artificial boundaries.

Two years later the Northwest Ordinance outlined the procedure by which a region (specifically that north of the Ohio River) outside of the original thirteen states might become a state. It provided for a territorial government, appointed by national officials, which would eventually give way to an intermediate stage in which an elected legislature would govern in conjunction with a nationally appointed governor and executive council. When the territory had a population of 60,000 people, it could apply for admission to the United States as an equal partner. The ordinance sought to guide the development of political and economic structures in trans-Appalachia by requiring that all governments be "republican" and by recommending the encouragement of schools, religion, and orderly behavior.

Although men of different political persuasions supported these ordinances, the Northwest Ordinance in particular outlined what would become an essentially Federalist vision of the West. The basic assumption was that a prosperous and stable social order would have to be artificially created in the West. Settlers could not be left to their own devices; they had to be guided by institutions–schools, churches, and especially the national government created by the federal Constitution of 1787.

The 1787 ordinance further attempted to dictate the future of the Northwest Territory by forbidding slavery and arguing that Native Americans be dealt with in good faith. These provisions, which easily win the approbation of modern Americans, were radical notions in the Ohio Valley in the 1780s. And while most trans-Appalachian Americans ignored them, they did not think well of the notion that a national, indeed imperial, government would dare to tell them how to handle their property or deal with their sworn enemies.

Essentially elitists, national-minded officials and speculators wanted to concentrate power and opportunity in the hands of gentlemen like themselves. But they were hardly nostalgic conservatives. Their vision of trans-Appalachia's future was not a replication of the East but an improvement on it. They wanted to create an orderly, prosperous, regular world dominated by gentlemen and founded on the pillars of education, Protestantism, and government.

There was an important gendered dimension to this new world. Territorial officials often had to plead with their wives to accompany them to the Ohio Valley. In October 1788 Northwest Territory judge Samuel Holden Parsons reassured his wife in Connecticut "that however much I may most ardently wish your company in my future walks of life . . . I will never compel your choice." But, Parsons explained, "duty," by which he meant public service, and "the interests of my children keep me here."[6] Like other proto-Federalists in the West, Parsons was willing to sacrifice domestic happiness in order to realize national and long-term goals.

However reluctant, women were nonetheless essential to the fulfillment of the Federalists' social vision. In addition to anchoring household and community economies, they also were expected to lead in civilizing the West. In Marietta (the principal Ohio Company settlement at the confluence of the Ohio and Muskingum rivers) in the late 1780s and 1790s, women encouraged activities that eighteenth-century Americans associated with a highly developed society. Parsons noted that "fifteen ladies as well accomplished in the manners of polite circles as any I have ever seen in the old States" attended "the first Ball in our country" in December 1788.[7] Years later, people recalled Rebecca Ives Gilman as "excelled" by few "men of classical education . . . in matters of history, pure English literature, poetry, or belles-lettres."[8]

These were not idle attributes, for the unspoken assumption of Federalist planners was that refined women were both evidence and bulwarks of a highly developed society. While they would attend to the business of household production and reproduction, wives and daughters also would form social circles that would contribute to the stability of the West. Whether male or female, people must cultivate associations beyond their individual households. Family ties were important, but they alone could not guarantee social stability.

In general, nationalists wanted people in the West to think of themselves as citizens of a great republican empire, as voluntary participants in a radical experiment in political and social organization. They envisioned their empire as a grand, extensive nation dominated by republican principles in all aspects of life. Today we associate the word *empire* with the conquest and domination of other peoples, a definition that accurately describes what happened to Indians as well as many Americans in the early American republic. Still, what most Federalists had in mind when they used the word *empire* was a matter of sovereignty, the power to define the future of frontier regions, the conquest of which they essentially took for granted. Ignoring the consequences of their vision, they thought in terms of creation rather than destruction. Their goal was to create and to develop not only the wilderness but society, to cultivate both fields and human relationships in order to create a world in which people acted as if they were parts of something larger than families and local communities.

We tend to characterize Federalist towns such as Marietta as transplanted New England communities. In the last decade, however, scholars have demonstrated that the ideal New England town was largely created in the late eighteenth century. The cluster of well-maintained, substantial dwellings clustered around a well-tended green with a white, steepled church was a novelty in the early 1800s. Bourgeois citizens now had the money to spend on architectural refinements and decorative improvements. They made dispersed and somewhat shaggy settlements into decorated models of social decorum. According to John Brooke in his study of Worcester County, Massachusetts, this "post-Revolutionary reshaping of public space" involved subtle "efforts to transform the sounds and shapes of the countryside" in order "to impose order and regularity upon all townspeople."[9]

This spirit of improvement was not limited to either New England or Federalists. What was distinctively Federalist about it was the notion that the national government would direct development. If many Virginians dreamed of canals linking the Potomac and Ohio rivers, only nationalists such as Washington talked in terms of a system of internal improvements which would link western and eastern waterways and facilitate commerce, social intercourse, and national unity.[10]

It was this new world of commerce and improvement, of schools and churches, that proto-Federalists were talking about expanding or creating in the West. Indeed, far from being conservative, territorial officials and land speculators had a more dynamic and coherent vision of American expansion than most ordinary settlers, who were primarily concerned with the challenges of daily existence and the preservation of their households.

None was more visionary than the Congregational minister, Federalist politician, botanist, and relentless promoter Manasseh Cutler, one of the directors of the Ohio Company. For him, Marietta was more than a commercial or political colony. It had to become "a wise model for the future settlement of all the federal lands." Through education, religion, and industry, its settlers would bring to the West the "habits of government and allegiance to the United States" that the "lawless banditti" of distant frontiers lacked.[11]

According to Cutler, the development of this "American Empire" was something more than the transplantation of New England to the Ohio Valley. It was "a new thing under the sun." In addition to its commitment to "principles of equal liberty and justice," it had "a constitution of government [meaning the federal Constitution of 1787] for an extensive consolidated body." With regard to education, Cutler urged people to remember Lycurgus's "grand principle . . . that children belonged to the state rather than to the parents." In sum, the first settlers of Marietta were the advance guard of the American Empire. They "ought to consider [them]selves as members of one family, united by the bonds of one common interest." They were, above all, citizens of the United States.[12]

THE EMERGENCE OF THE UNITED STATES, 1787–95

Once the Constitution was ratified and the Washington administration was installed in office, national officials and speculators were able to create a context in which many of the plans of the 1780s eventually would come to fruition. The new federal government had power and resources well beyond those of the Confederation. Congress moved quickly to confirm the ordinances passed by the Confederation Congresses, to continue the appointment of federal officers west of the Appalachians, and to create the Southwest Territory in 1790.

But the Federalists' achievement in the West was something more than the sum of their policies and appointments. In order to achieve their goals of establishing national authority and setting the terms of future development, they had to win (or coerce) the cooperation of at least two powerful groups of diverse peoples whom some men tended to lump together as "lawless banditti" or "white Indians."

The first was the thousands of American Indians who ringed the expanding American settlements. The second included the tens of thousands of Americans who were settling trans-Appalachia, moving into and through Kentucky, the majority of whom were either from or associated with the largest state in the new republic—Virginia. None of these peoples would long doubt either the radical agenda of Federalists or their ultimate strength in implementing it. For Federalist success depended on either their transformation into model citizens of the United States or their elimination.

In the 1780s the United States had dealt with people west of the Appalachians with a relatively weak hand. The Confederation dispatched hundreds of troops under the Pennsylvanian Josiah Harmar to the Ohio Valley in the middle of the decade. Their mission was to establish a national presence in the region. More specifically, they were to stop whites from migrating into the Ohio Country and to attempt to mediate with Native Americans.

Harmar and his men built forts along the Ohio and Wabash rivers and attempted to do their duty. In an immediate sense, they were singularly unsuccessful. After all, both the British and the Spanish continued to exercise influence in the area; the former continued to hold posts in the Great Lakes region that they had promised to evacuate under the terms of the 1783 Treaty of Paris. Meanwhile, families of "squatters" from Pennsylvania and Kentucky continued to move across the Ohio River into federal territory.

South of the Ohio River, the federal presence was even weaker. Until 1791 Kentucky was part of Virginia; in that year it became a sovereign state, completely skipping the territorial stage so vital to the establishment of national authority. Meanwhile, in the Southwest Territory (created in 1790 when North Carolina ceded what is now Tennessee to the federal government) and in what would become the Mississippi Territory in 1798, the United States was not a formidable concern. Not only was the military presence smaller, the commitment of territorial officials to national authority was weaker.

The greatest immediate challenge to the Federalists in the West was American Indians. If they were to establish national authority, they would have to demonstrate its value to settlers west of the Appalachians; they would have to earn the respect of ordinary people. After all, as Secretary of War Henry Knox noted in 1792, "To obtain protection against lawless violence, was a main object for which the present government was instituted. . . . A frontier citizen possesses as strong claims to protection as any other citizen."[13]

In retrospect, the outcome of the struggles between whites (mainly in Kentucky) and American Indians to the north and south may seem inevitable. But in the early 1790s no one knew what was going to happen. The United States in the 1790s had few troops and resources. Fighting a war cost money, an expense neither President Washington nor Secretary of the Treasury Alexander Hamilton was eager to incur. While federal officials were genuinely committed to the proposition that some men could deal with each other in civilized ways, they were equally sure that frontier peoples were not among that select group. Explained Knox in 1787, "The deep rooted prejudices, and malignity of heart, and conduct, reciprocally entertained and practiced on all occasions by the Whites and Savages will ever prevent their being good neighbours." They acted out of personal and local motives. If they would not move away from each other, "government must keep them both in awe by a strong hand, and compel them to be moderate and just."[14]

Questions of economy dictated an initial strategy of making common cause with settlers against the Indians. But the blending of national authority and frontier resources proved an unmitigated disaster. In the fall of 1790 the Shawnee and Miami humiliated an American army under the command of Brigadier General Josiah Harmar at the site of present-day Fort Wayne, Indiana. The Indians outmaneuvered and outfought the Americans, who retreated to Fort Washington (Cincinnati, Ohio) in disgrace. More devastating for the Americans was the utter rout of an expedition commanded by Major General Arthur St. Clair, governor of the Northwest Territory, on November 4, 1791. In one of the worst defeats ever suffered by an American army, a coalition of Indian warriors, including Miami, Shawnee, and Delaware, surprised and routed sleeping American soldiers and hundreds of women accompanying them in their camp about twenty-nine miles northwest of Fort Jefferson (in east-central Ohio).

These defeats were not auspicious beginnings for the Federalists in the West. They forced the Washington administration to take a more forceful approach to trans-Appalachia. While officials worked for a negotiated settlement with American Indians, they also prepared for a major

demonstration of the majesty of the United States, following what the
historian Richard Kohn has called a "dual policy of negotiation and esca-
lation."[15] In 1792 Congress created the Legion of the United States, and
the president appointed Major General Anthony Wayne to command it.
In August 1794, after opportunities for negotiation had been squan-
dered, Wayne and his 3,000-man Legion defeated a coalition of perhaps
1,300 Indians in the brief battle of Fallen Timbers.

A month later some 500 Kentucky and Tennessee militia attacked and
destroyed the Chickamauga villages of Nickajack and Running Water.
Combined with the suppression of the Whiskey Rebellion in western
Pennsylvania in the fall, the events of 1794 constituted a turning point in
Federalist fortunes in the West. The displays of military power in western
Pennsylvania and northern Ohio essentially made the same point: they
were tangible demonstrations of the seriousness with which the Washing-
ton administration approached the business of securing the West. Regard-
less of race, "lawless banditti" would learn to respect the majesty of the
United States.

No less important than military success was Federalist diplomatic
triumph. For reasons that had less to do with negotiating skill than the
complicated politics of the wars of the French Revolution, the United
States signed treaties with both Great Britain and Spain in 1795. The
Jay Treaty, which excited opposition in Kentucky because it seemed to
subordinate Americans to British interests, nonetheless meant the end of
British occupation of posts in the Northwest Territory. In the Treaty of
San Lorenzo del Escorial (Pinckney's Treaty), Spain surrendered its
claims to land north of West Florida, including Natchez; it also conceded
to Americans the rights to free navigation of the Mississippi and to use
the port of New Orleans.

Abandoned by the British and confronted by a well-organized and
determined American force, most Indians agreed to terms. The Chero-
kee essentially stopped fighting. In the Treaty of Greenville (1795), the
Shawnee, the Miami, the Delaware, and other Indians surrendered all
claims to the southern two-thirds of Ohio. More than that, the Indians
"acknowledged the fifteen United States of America to be [their] father."
After all, as General Wayne, resplendent in his buff and blue uniform,
had explained to the assembled Indians, "the Great Spirit seems disposed to incline us all, to repose, for the future, under [the American
Eagle's] grateful shade, and wisely enjoy the blessings which attend it."[16]

American Indian resistance to the expansion of the American Empire,
while dormant for a decade after 1795, was hardly at an end. It is easy to

read too much significance into the events of 1794 and 1795. The fact remains, however, that the United States had resolved decades of conflict with Indians in both the North and the South and successfully called the bluff of both the British and the Spanish. Wayne's Legion, like the army that marched westward across Pennsylvania to crush the Whiskey Rebellion, brought to bear in a coordinated and public fashion the power and majesty of the government of the United States. Flags, forts, uniforms, and cannon were visible and welcome manifestations of federal authority in the Northwest Territory. Fallen Timbers and Greenville demonstrated to all the world who the dominant power in the region was. Settlers and Indians alike might disparage, but they could hardly ignore, the Federalists' impact on the West.

This military triumph, however, had an uneven impact on the expanding American Empire. It made possible the development of the Northwest Territory along the lines laid out in the late 1780s. The region north of the Ohio River would become a place of commercial farms and small towns, of public schools and Protestantism. Federal money, moreover, helped transform places like Cincinnati into major commercial centers that would dominate the region for centuries. On the other hand, the fact that the Washington administration committed most of its limited resources to the Northwest Territory necessarily led to feelings of resentment in the Southwest Territory. Governor William Blount, irritated by the failure of the United States to send him troops, grew alienated from the Washington administration. To a considerable extent the Federalist achievement of legitimacy in the Northwest cost the national government legitimacy in the Southwest.[17]

Still, the emergence of the United States as the hegemonic power in trans-Appalachia provoked strong reactions from white settlers from Ohio to Tennessee. It was not that they objected to the subjugation of Indians or the establishment of a political order west of the Appalachians. Rather, they objected mightily to the notion that these deeds were being accomplished by and for the national government.

THE UNITED STATES VERSUS VIRGINIA, 1794–1801

The tens of thousands of people who poured into the Northwest Territory, Kentucky, and Tennessee in the 1790s were in a hurry. They had little interest in the grandiose schemes and careful development the Federalists had in mind for the West. Of far greater importance to them was the protection of households and families. Above all, they were interested in local control of their affairs; many came from places in and around Virginia with long traditions of local government. In general, they were concerned with perpetuating those traditions rather than improving them.

Many settlers saw Federalists, both at the national and territorial levels, as threats to the security of their world. Sometimes the specific threat came in the form of higher taxes, sometimes as increased regulation, sometimes as restrictions on participation in political affairs. Whatever the specific issue, in any case, in the second half of the 1790s Federalist officials throughout the West found themselves under increasing attack as arrogant, aristocratic, and corrupt.

We tend to think of these movements as populist in character, in no small part because they were directed at the Federalists, whom we expect to be reactionary elitists. The rhetoric, moreover, like that of most men who became Jeffersonian Republicans, was often democratic in substance as well as spirit. Whether in Mississippi, Ohio, or Tennessee, critics of Federalist territorial governments demanded statehood, called for popular sovereignty, and denounced appointments in the language of classical politics. In their cries for more representation, more respect for local wishes, more open governments, they echoed colonial critics of British imperial policy in the 1760s and 1770s. And, more often than not, they celebrated their eventual victories as triumphs of the people over corrupt would-be aristocrats, as a revolution in government, as minor reenactments of the American Revolution.

Without disparaging their democratic rhetoric and policies, however, it is fair to say that Jeffersonian critics had a far less radical vision of the future of trans-Appalachia than Federalist territorial officials. Most were interested in the perpetuation of a somewhat idealized version of eighteenth-century Virginia in the interior of the United States. Their vision of the future, while it involved a great deal of motion, was essentially a static one. In the words of Drew McCoy, they wanted the nation to develop through space rather than time.[18]

By 1850 there were more than 388,000 native Virginians living in other states. In order of the number of Virginia immigrants, they were Ohio, Kentucky, Tennessee, Indiana, Missouri, and Illinois. Virginia also exported enslaved African Americans. Indeed, it was the largest slave-exporting state in the Union. Perhaps 40 percent of the tens of thousands went with their masters; the rest were sold.[19]

Most of these Virginians were critics of territorial governments; most became Jeffersonian Republicans. Their world was a familiar one. It was a society in which everyone's basic frame of reference was the patriarchal household rather than national citizenship. It was a society in which the independence of white males rested squarely on the dependent condition of enslaved African Americans as well as women. It was a society of large-scale commercial agriculture, involving the cultivation of tobacco, cotton, hemp, and grains on plantation-like farms. It was a society in which towns figured only tangentially, in which men gathered in urban areas primarily for political, legal, and temporary economic purposes. Above all, it was a society in which people thought of power and patronage primarily in local terms, in which the county was more important than the nation.[20]

From the Scioto Valley of Ohio to the hills of southern Indiana to the bluegrass of Kentucky and the fields of Tennessee, Virginians attempted to replicate this world west of the Appalachians. Even north of the Ohio, where slavery was illegal, they either lobbied for a repeal of the Northwest Ordinance's prohibition or found ways to make blacks into permanent indentured servants.

The Federalists, with their emphasis on national loyalty and their notions of ordered development, threatened this relatively static and local world. In each territory officials had an agenda united by a commitment to national authority: they promoted regular land sales, uniform laws and regulations, territorial control over elections and appointments, diversified commercial development, and improvements in transportation and communication.

With the support of ambitious farmers and entrepreneurs, who preferred an open to a regulated system, Virginia-born patriarchs led assaults on the Federalist hierarchy throughout trans-Appalachia in the late 1790s and early 1800s. They wanted local sovereignty, which amounted to the power to preserve traditional society from the assault of radical Federalists, who wanted to weaken household ties, abolish slavery in certain areas, deal with the Indians in a more dignified fashion, and make national citizenship the supreme loyalty.

In the Southwest Territory, where the Washington administration had never established a firm presence, Governor Blount, recognizing widespread alienation from the United States and disappointed by the failure of the Washington administration to deliver on its promises, eventually supported statehood in 1796. Tennessee's early leaders, from John Sevier to Andrew Jackson, remained staunch supporters of state or local sovereignty.

In the Northwest Territory a group of Virginians centered on the town of Chillicothe spearheaded the campaign against Governor St. Clair. Led by gentlemen-farmers with the support of urban artisans, they fell out with the inflexible St. Clair over issues such as the location of county seats and the appointment of local sheriffs and other officials. Minor as these issues may seem today, they were of paramount importance to Virginians. Gentry governance depended on their domination of local governments. With the election of Thomas Jefferson as president in 1801, these budding Jeffersonians were able to get Congress to create the state of Ohio and the president to fire St. Clair.[21]

Another Virginian, William Henry Harrison, was appointed governor of the Indiana Territory when it was established in 1800. He built himself a house, Grouseland, to rival the homes of his ancestors on the James River, and he ignored the Northwest Ordinance's prohibition against slavery personally as well as publicly. Nonetheless, Harrison, perhaps because he had served as an army officer in the Northwest Territory in the 1790s, was as committed to the establishment of national authority as he was to the world in which he had grown up. He tried to consolidate government and patronage in his hands, thereby offending large numbers of Virginians and Kentuckians who vehemently denounced him as an aristocrat. Actually, many of them wanted to be aristocrats, too; the question was whether the source of such high status was national or local, political or economic.[22]

In the Mississippi Territory, created in 1798, another group of interrelated planters, farmers, small merchants, and Natchez mechanics fought with the high-handed and personally unpleasant Governor Winthrop Sargent, formerly secretary of both the Ohio Company of Associates and the Northwest Territory. They objected that land titles were uncertain; that they had to pay higher taxes; that Sargent's Code, a detailed series of statutes that attempted to prescribe and regulate almost all commercial and personal relationships, was unconstitutionally promulgated; that they could not import slaves as freely as before; and that they did not get their share of local appointments, which tended to go to Sargent's allies among the wealthier merchants in Natchez. In other words, they testified to the strength of the territorial regime by protesting its successful interference in their efforts to perpetuate a traditional social and political order.

The Mississippi critics, most of whom became Jeffersonians, did not like Sargent's innovative government. But they had no intention of challenging the authority of the United States. To the contrary, they intended to use that authority to get rid of the arrogant executive. "It is not with the [federal] Government we are sour'd" but with the administration of the territory, wrote a group of petitioners in October 1799. Their larger purpose, they wrote with some disingenuousness, was "to draw to the salient point of the Constitution and Government of the United States, every congenial particle that exists in the Country." As much as they talked about their rights and denounced the oppressive tyranny of Sargent's regime, they deferred to the majesty of the United States. "We therefore pray," they concluded, "that the Honorable Congress will be pleased to take our situation into serious consideration" and allow them more say in their government.[23] They got their wish in 1800, when Congress established a territorial legislature, and in 1801, when President Jefferson replaced Sargent with the Virginia-born William C. C. Claiborne.

Throughout trans-Appalachia, Federalist territorial officials eventually gave way to Jeffersonian Republicans espousing democratic government. Their defeats had less to do with massive public outcry than with the change in national politics that accompanied the election of Thomas Jefferson as president in 1801. The transformation of national politics made possible the transformation of territorial politics in Ohio and Mississippi, vindicated Tennessee's leaders, and emboldened opposition to Harrison in Indiana. In fact, the way in which critics of territorial governments achieved victory—appealing to the sovereignty of the United States rather than the people of their territory and working within the guidelines established by the Northwest Ordinance—solidified the Federalist achievement in making national authority the political arbiter west of the Appalachians. It was as citizens of the United States that the people of the West sought redress from unpopular territorial regimes.

Similarly, when Congress liberalized the land laws in 1800, making it easier for men to buy land, it did so within the context created by the ordinances of the 1780s. Numerous land offices became visible symbols of federal authority as federal lands became something more than a potential gold mine. By the first decade of the nineteenth century, the government was averaging over $500,000 per year in income from the public lands; by the early 1830s the figure was over $2,500,000.[24]

The great exception to this pattern of Federalist influence in the West was Kentucky, the only state in trans-Appalachia that was not first a federal territory. When Kentucky became a state in 1792, it did so at the sufferance of Virginia and with a constitution that solidified the positions of gentlemen-planters. Only through the federal courts did the national government affect Kentucky's development and politics in the 1790s.

The state's handful of Federalists were almost always on the periphery. The most prominent, Humphrey Marshall, did win election as a U.S. senator in 1794. But he soon became so unpopular with his constituents that he was stoned in Frankfort and nearly thrown into the Kentucky River.

Many Kentuckians, resenting the federal excise tax on whiskey and flirting with the Spanish, took a long time to reconcile themselves to the national government created by the Constitution of 1787. Ironically, they cursed the incredible quagmire of overlapping land claims in Kentucky without recognizing the superiority of the rules and predictability of the land ordinances of the 1780s. According to Mary K. Bonsteel Tachau, "Many Kentuckians did not come unequivocally into the Union until after the election of Jefferson."[25]

In sum, the extent of Federalists' influence on society in trans-Appalachia was in direct proportion to the amount of time they held positions of political power and their success in demonstrating the utility of the United States. Ohio most completely fulfilled the Federalist vision, and long before New England immigration had become a significant counterpoint to that from Virginia. There the national government had proved its worth, and there emerged most fully the world of bustling towns and cities, churches and schools, diverse agriculture and far-flung commerce, that the promoters of the late 1780s had imagined. Meanwhile, Kentucky, where federal influence was the weakest, was in many ways the most complete replica of Virginia west of the mountains, with its great plantations, enslaved African Americans, and reliance on local county governments as the basic units of society.

LEGACY

With the defeat of the Federalists on the national level in the election of 1800, virtually all of the men appointed to implement the Federalist vision of the West soon lost their jobs. Trying to absorb the enormous scale of their political rejection, Federalists produced dozens of self-pitying jeremiads, many offering the West as evidence of the decline of the United States and implicitly lamenting the triumph of Virginia, home of the despised Jefferson and other hypocritical slaveholding, liberty-talking aristocrats.

In defeat, the naive optimism and boundless energy of the nationalist vision of the 1780s and early 1790s gave way to crabby and constricted fears of national disintegration. The Manasseh Cutler who celebrated the possibilities of the Ohio Valley in 1788 worried that the admission of the state of Ohio in 1803 posed a threat to the stability of the republic.[26]

Federalists' fears climaxed in their reaction to the Louisiana Purchase in 1803. Behind their objections to the constitutionality and cost of the purchase lay their terror at the prospect of an even larger West supporting the anarchic and immoral activities of the reprehensible Jefferson. Inevitably, it seemed, the United States must break apart into smaller nations. The country was too extensive to sustain a republican form of government and loyalty to the United States, the wilderness too much a hothouse of selfishness to nurture the ties of commerce and affection so necessary to the maintenance of a solid social order. Cutler lamented that the purchase was "a finishing stroke" to New England's "influence in government." Once Louisiana became part of the Union, he concluded, "the seeds of separation are planted."[27]

Not all Federalists quailed at the prospects of doubling the size of the United States. Those actually in trans-Appalachia could hardly ignore the commercial advantages of the purchase. And Alexander Hamilton offered a measured, thoughtful appraisal. While refusing to give the Jefferson administration any credit for the action, Hamilton reasoned that the purchase was "an important acquisition, not, indeed, as territory, but as being essential to the peace and prosperity of our Western country, and as opening a free and valuable market to our commercial states." Yet even he, a longtime friend of western development, was pessimistic as he contemplated the political implications of the purchase. Hamilton feared that if Americans hastened to settle the trans-Mississippi West, they would encounter "all the injuries of a too widely dispersed population" and add to "the great weight of the western part of our territory," thus hastening "the dismemberment of a large portion of our country, or a dissolution of the Government."[28]

Even the most cursory student of eighteenth-century Anglo-America knows that the use of national power in order to secure loyalty to a national government was not a popular policy. But we err if we equate unpopularity and political defeat with historical failure. After all, if people were reliable judges of their own significance, we would not need historians. Defeat rarely is as complete or cataclysmic as the defeated imagine while nursing their wounds.

Jeffersonian critics could not—and in some cases, did not—want to undo all the Federalists had achieved. Like all people who perceive themselves as losers, Federalists described their unhappy fate in apocalyptic terms. They exaggerated. For in a decade and a half, they had transformed trans-Appalachia from a potential source of revenue, disunion, and chaos into a region of genuine revenue, growing external security, and increasing loyalty to the United States of America. They also had established the structures of a national political and social order, which would endure for decades and eventually produce elaborate government commitments to public education and private morality, at least north of the Ohio River.

During the past two centuries, historians have tended to characterize Federalists as conservative bulwarks of the standing order who inevitably gave way to the forces of democracy, largely because they also have tended to associate laissez-faire democracy with progress. Sometimes Federalists are the villains of the story, sometimes noble anachronisms resisting the tides of history with pathetic irony. But Federalists' policy in the West suggests that their agenda was less reactionary or anachronistic than different from that of most Americans. Indeed, with their elaborate plans and their willingness to use national power to implement them, Federalists were the most thoroughgoing radicals in the "western world" in the late eighteenth century.

PART II

Federalism and the Origins of American Political Culture

5

FEDERALISM, THE STYLES OF POLITICS, AND THE POLITICS OF STYLE

David Waldstreicher

WHAT IS THE relationship between style and substance in politics? Journalists, biographers, and political scientists often attribute presidential triumphs (and tragedies) to rhetorical and personal style; perhaps for this very reason professional historians rarely investigate the styles of political speech and action—or what, given their controversial nature, we should call "the politics of style." For all of the attention that has been bestowed upon the ideas that informed late eighteenth-century politics (what some scholars call political thought), and for all of the books that describe cultural styles as political, there has been rather little attention paid to the overlap of what we see as distinct realms: politics and style.[1]

But it has not always been so. During the era of the American Revolution, styles of speech and political action themselves became the subject of controversy: the very nature of the political persona—when she acts, how he speaks, who she or he may be—occupied the center of political contest. Loyalists decried "rebels" as vulgar rabble-rousers or as crowds of "boys" and "negroes"; Patriots denounced "Tories" as effeminate would-be aristocrats. It is crucial to note that such depictions, which filled a rapidly expanding press, referred to both modes of action (the what and how of politics) and to particular groups of people, including different classes, genders, ages, and races (the who of politics). As such, they help us see that when we investigate the styles of politics and the politics of style together, we gain insight into the social codings of what might seem to be merely partisan commitments. We begin to see how even after the end of the war against Britain, matters of state, conducted in the context of an ongoing discussion over the very definition of "the people," continued to bring more and more people—including women and "ordinary" folk—into the streets and into the new national polity.

If heated, often violent controversy over the modes of political action and the identities of political actors can be said to have characterized the Revolution, in a certain sense America during the 1790s was still within the revolutionary process. Political actions such as group meetings, public celebrations, oratory, and publication were seen as having liberatory or cataclysmic implications for the future of the United States. Debates about style wholly permeated controversies over policy. Outrageous examples of rhetoric and spectacle were dissected endlessly in the papers, whether because they seemed too fashionably new or rather unfashionably old. In short, style was substance, and rhetoric was action. This politicization of such things as dress, mannerisms, modes of public gathering, and communication was a legacy of the Revolutionary movement, during which the distinctions between Tory and Patriot were drawn in precisely these ways.[2] To toast the king on his birthday, for example, was to subscribe to monarchy and the British imperial way of doing things. Those who drank tea or dressed in imported finery despite the boycott chose material comforts (and their associations with gentility) over allegiance to a hard-pressed Patriot community. Manners made the political man and woman. Little wonder that elites made the reform of manners—the politics of style—one of their first goals for fashioning a successful American republic.

This chapter examines the Federalist style of politics, and politics of style, during the 1790s. It inquires into the relationship between Federalist rhetoric and political practice during the period of Federalism's national ascendancy. While following the Federalists through their tumultuous decade in power, I argue that Federalism was every bit as much a politics of style as the "Jacobinical" brand of republicanism that Federalists denounced as an imported fashion. At the same time, we also must consider Federalists' lamentations over their opponents' style as an integral part of their own developing style: indeed, as itself a style—a stylized antistyle. Indeed, Federalism's fatal flaw may have been its disingenuousness. Federalists wanted so dearly to naturalize (and nationalize) their orderly and respectable style of leadership that they denied that this, too, was a style. And in denying style they denied the new forms of political activity, and the new political actors, that the Revolution had brought into being— that had brought them into being.

Often—all too often—historians have acquiesced in this denial. Emphasizing the course of high politics from the perspective of national statesmen, they have missed how much of politics and public life in the 1790s consisted of toasting rituals, parades, public meetings, songs, oratory, political festivals, and debates over these and other modes of public address. To see such developments as so many distractions or impurities that prevented the pursuit of true "interests" or the discussion of the real "issues" is to unwittingly take the side of the Federalists—the party in power whose position made it in their interest to proclaim certain sorts of innovative political speech and action to be illegitimate, "fashionable," or merely rhetorical. It is itself to adopt a particular style: a "realist" style that "gives us a real world by contrasting it to a textual world and denigrates opposing perspectives by associating them with their means of expression."[3]

Realism too is a style: it only seems to do away with style. Moreover, realism's rhetoric of antistyle, in its modern liberal version, often has served as a way of naturalizing certain class and gender norms under the post-Enlightenment guise of reason or common sense.[4] In Federalism as later, this was done in a conservative, backward-looking mode; but in the way it was done during the late 1790s—by mobilizing a version of "the people" and by denigrating the opposition's activities as mere rhetoric—Federalism looked forward to modern politics (and modern scholarship). We may find that our own inability to come to grips with style has roots in the Federalists' rhetorical denials of what they had so effectively, and stylishly, done.

ORIGINAL COMPROMISES: A REPUBLICAN COURT?

The Federalists' disavowal of popular and partisan activity draws attention away from their originating acts: the building of a movement, state by state, to ratify the federal Constitution. As demonstrated by their effective yet unacknowledged "selling of the Constitutional Convention," this was the kind of movement that could not appear to be a movement if it was to succeed. The movement, like the Constitution itself, invented a national people who convened to ratify the document that, by its own bold proclamation, had itself brought them into existence.[5] The national populace thus called into being was supposed to be three things that Americans in the Revolutionary movement often were not. They were to be orderly; they were to be unified; and they should appear, and ultimatley become, "respectable," or of middling social class.

This much can be seen in the widespread celebrations that Federalists held when the various states ratified the Constitution (and then again in the summer of 1788, when ratification by the crucial ninth state, New Hampshire, and subsequent ratifications by Virginia and New York sealed acceptance of the new governmental structure). These festivals, from the early, spontaneous ones to the more famous, planned Grand Federal Processions, aimed to demonstrate the popularity of the Constitution and simultaneously to create that popularity. In mounting such spectacles, the Federalists significantly increased the numbers and types of people who usually participated in such civic parades and festive dinners. In Charleston, an observer noted, mechanics sat down next to men of great wealth. Women of the upper classes marched in some of the parades. There was no better way to demonstrate that the American people—not just politicians, or elites, or a self-interested faction—were behind the creation of a new national governmental structure.

Historians have rightly cited the Philadelphia and New York Grand Processions as tableaux of the compromises that went into the making of the Constitution. The nationalistic perspective of the continental elite is foregrounded in the symbols utilized by participants and commentators. At the same time, the parades also showcased the local artisans, the rank and file of the urban Revolutionary movements. Here they carried their own banners representing their local trade groups, banners whose artisanal metaphors referred to the artisans' own roles in the making of the new political, as well as material, world. "Both buildings and rulers are the work of our hands," insisted the Philadelphia bricklayers. The butchers in the procession at York, Pennsylvania, proclaimed: "As the marrow is connected to the bone, or one joint with another, so let us be united, and may no cleaver ever disjoin us." We know nevertheless that the leaders of the Federalist (that is, pro-Constitution) forces took the lead in planning, executing, and then describing these festivals for the newspapers, in which these lengthy accounts were printed locally and then reprinted elsewhere. In an official capacity Francis Hopkinson and Richard Platt, chairmen, respectively, of the Philadelphia and New York processions, thanked the artisans for maintaining "order." They stressed the respectability of all the participants—a respectability that, to be sure, had been enlarged by the presence of the artisans, but which still was a mark of cultural style, a badge of social class. Aristocracy made natural was still aristocracy, and according to this version of the American present and future, everyone (who mattered) could take part. In this sense, July 4, 1788, in Philadelphia was the apotheosis of all that the new nationalists desired. Hopkinson looked around the festive throng and saw in the crowd of thousands "every countenance . . . the index of a heart glowing with urbanity and rational joy."[6]

We might dismiss this reportage as merely an eighteenth-century way of saying that despite the huge crowds, nobody got hurt and a good time was had by all. But it was not only the unprecedented urban Grand Federal Processions that were described in this manner. At the Fourth of July celebration in New Haven the next year, according to the printed account, "the greatest decency and decorum was observable through all the transactions, and happiness [was] visible in every countenance." These paeans to public order came in the wake of the Revolutionary disorder of the 1770s and the post-Revolutionary political turbulence of the 1780s. The new nation might be a parade, but it would not be a crowd, any more than the American Revolution—in its finished, constitutional version—had been class warfare. The women and young people who had been so necessarily (and at times embarrassingly) present in Revolutionary crowds had been incorporated into the parade or neutralized as "the people"—the delighted, passive spectators.[7] This is what the editor of the *Salem Gazette* had in mind when, after the local July 4 celebration in 1793, he pronounced himself "happy to observe that nothing like riot and confusion took place during the day, which have so often, in societies less refined, disgraced public festivities, designed to celebrate great national blessings." Or a report from New Brunswick, New Jersey, that related how July 4, 1796, "was celebrated in this city, neither by the ringing of bells, the discharge of cannon, nor by the noisy bustle of a promiscuous crowd; but in social mirth and pleasantry."[8] The printed reportage, like the festivals themselves, attempts to create the very order that it ostensibly describes. Indeed, the very language of action in the reportage, its objective accounting of real activities, permits its rhetorical injunctions to order.

How to keep Americans urbane, how to keep them "social" without becoming "promiscuous" or crowdlike, how to keep their joy "rational," was a political and cultural problem of immense magnitude, and one that had overlapping local and national dimensions. It spurred a number of proposals for educational and linguistic reform during the immediate post-Revolutionary era. The problem, from the elite point of view, was the same as the problem of republican self-government. Having done away with the reign of compulsion and tyranny known as monarchy, how would republicans be educated to govern themselves? How could self-discipline be internalized? How might the people of the new nation be made to make themselves happy, orderly, and "respectable"?[9]

After ratification, the inauguration of George Washington, braced by his triumphal progress from Mount Vernon to New York, his tour of New England later that year, and his journey south in 1791, provided further occasions to test and at the same time to create the happiness and respectability of the American people. Upon Washington's arrival in New

York for his inauguration, just as in the earlier constitutional celebrations, "every heart," including those of women and young people, was said to expand with "universal joy": "The Aged sire—the venerable matron, the blooming virgin, and the ruddy Youth were all emulous in their plaudits —nay, the lisping infant did not withhold its innocent smile of praise and approbation." The editor of the arch-Federalist *Gazette of the United States*, revealingly, devoted as much attention to the audience as to Washington himself: "How *sincere*—and how *expressive* the sentiments of respect and veneration!"[10] Nearing the end of his southern tour, Washington himself revealed the ends of these displays of patriotic sentiment, writing that "the attachment of all classes of citizens to the general government seems to be a pleasing prospect of their future happiness and respectability." Deliberately conflating his own popularity with attachment to the federal state and seeking in that conflation evidence of future "respectability," Washington placed a great burden upon manners, appearances, even spectacles in determining the state of the nation (*determining* in both the creative and the evaluative senses of the word). It was a move that would be characteristic of Federalist political culture and its institutions.

One of these institutions was the "Republican Court." As recovered from the dustbin of history by David S. Shields and Fredrika J. Teute, the Republican Court was a loose grouping of salons, or weekly gatherings, that coalesced around Martha Washington, Abigail Adams, and their friends in the capital of Philadelphia. Modeled upon the courts of Europe but significantly republicanized, the court functioned as a space for polite conversation about matters of state, society, and culture. Crucially, it was a heterosocial space, a public space upon which both men and women had claims.[11]

The court quickly came under fire by the opposition for its "monarchical" trappings and its apparent exclusivity. But the larger cultural significance of the court lay beyond its political role in the new capital. The court was in fact the apex of genteel culture, of the educating institutions, parlors, and dancing parties (revealingly called "assemblies") in which upper-class men and women were made into persons of refinement and respectability, to use the contemporary terms. These social spaces, or rather the behaviors and attitudes they promoted, epitomized the Federal style, at least when they did not partake too much of unrepublican "luxury." They typified what the Federalist editors and commentators were looking for when they anxiously searched the faces of people celebrating the Fourth of July. And not incidentally, they were places in which women could participate, both as talented individuals and as women, something they could not do in the designated political process. The most genteel woman in Hannah Webster Foster's 1797 novel, *The Coquette*, insists that women too can talk politics—in the parlor. She asks: "Why, then, should the love of our country be a masculine passion only? Why should government, which involves the peace and order of the society of which we are a part, be wholly excluded from our observation?" Observation is a key word here, as are love, peace, order, and country. Mrs. Richman, the revealingly named wife of a Revolutionary War officer, is describing the kind of social order in which the acts of observation, simultaneously sentimental and rational, bind all the members together to make an orderly whole. Observation is a form of participation in this order, as well as a kind of education. The government or country thus described works not unlike a dress ball, a lively tea party, or a well-orchestrated parade. Little wonder that the gentlemen at the festive gathering can applaud Mrs. Richman's "truly republican" sentiments.[12]

RESPONSES: STYLE AND COUNTERSTYLE

This "court" view of the 1790s cultural scene described something very real. But it did not describe everything. The Revolution had given energy to many other, not so orderly or genteel ways of participating in public life. This is what Gordon S. Wood means when he refers to public discourse having "ballooned out to hitherto unmanageable proportions" in the Revolutionary era. "It is scarcely possible for a dozen Americans to sit together without quarreling about politics," wrote the British visitor Isaac Weld after quaffing in a number of American taverns. Another traveler noticed the farmers of New England spending their Sundays reading "the public laws, and the newspapers" as well as religious books. Republicans and Federalists alike devoted their efforts to getting their increasingly partisan newspapers out to the widest possible audiences. Political controversy, given life by exposés and pithy satires, contributed greatly to this reading revolution.[13]

The administration's foreign and domestic policies fostered the heated debate. They also led to the formation of an opposition party. This new party coalesced around a series of innovative political practices, including opposition newspapers and the Democratic-Republican societies. In sympathy with the French revolutionaries, the opposition developed a style of its own, building upon three basic principles: the critique of aristocracy, an emphasis upon the primacy of "the people," and a demand for openness in public life. Taken alone, any one of these emphases might not seem distinctive, for each developed themes and emphases that had appeared during the American Revolution. Taken together, however, they issued a potent challenge to the cultural politics of Federalism.

Just at the time when critics of the administration's policies were groping for a standard around which to rally, the French Revolution began to look more and more like a radical departure in human history, destroying aristocracy, uplifting "the people," and demanding that politics—indeed, the entire life of the nation—be open to plain view and candid reconsideration. For several years most Americans interpreted the French Revolution as the logical fulfillment of America's own struggle against monarchical tyranny. At the same time, revolutionary France and still-monarchical Britain had gone to war, upsetting Hamilton's plans for a close commercial partnership between Britain and the United States but opening up the possibility that Britain too might be transformed into a republic. By 1793 international events had contributed to the sense among both Federalists and the opposition that the fate of the American republic and the fate of republicanism worldwide would be determined in the course of the Anglo-French conflict.[14]

It was not merely a question of what kind of foreign or commercial policy—pro-British, pro-French, or neutral—one would support. Any such statement, any such rationale, had implications for domestic politics; foreign and domestic policy could hardly be separated. Democratic-Republicans seized upon the French Revolution as the culmination of their cause at home. They held public celebrations, Fourth of July style, for the anniversaries of that revolution's great events. Like the Federalists of 1788 with their Grand Federal Processions (not to mention the Patriot movement during the American Revolution), these "democrats" made "civic feasts" into effective interventions in public life between elections. But the Democratic-Republicans' feasts were more than attacks on the Washington administration's "neutral" policy. Their very existence challenged Federalism's new world order.

Democratic-Republicans caustically criticized the pomp of the new national state, the seeming worship of Washington on his birthday, and the parties of the "Republican Court." One insisted that Washington should visit taverns in order to hear the true opinions of the people. In many places they formed the Democratic-Republican societies in order to call this public opinion into being and to publicize it to the nation. All this was conceived as a battle against an aristocracy that had crystallized around the Washington administration. A Vermont militia company wished in one of its July 4 toasts: "May the American states be long defended from the inundation which is threatened by the increase in aristocrats, who wish for a rich metropolis and a poor peasantry; want a great personage's head on the current coin; and are advocates for keeping shut the doors of the Senate." This last accusation referred to a debate over whether the deliberations of the U.S. Senate should be open to the public. The Republicans urged more attention, more public vigilance; they asserted that Federalists and the institutions they controlled exhibited a closed, hierarchical, and exclusive style. To point out the contrast, Democratic-Republicans began to call each other "citizen" and to wear badges of their affiliation—the revolutionary cockade—on their hats. They held meeting after meeting, festive dinner after dinner, filling the newspapers with celebratory toasts that expressed the sentiments of "the people."[15]

But my concern here is less the character of this challenge to Federalism than Federalism's response to the challenge and what it can tell us about the Federalists' own developing politics of style. The Federalists' first move was to express outrage at the Republicans' supposed politicization of style. They accused their opponents of being too French, of being foreign. According to this logic, Democratic-Republicans were the real style mongers: they were even trying to introduce a new language, a "new party dictionary" that reversed the true meanings of words. Like proponents of the early 1990s backlash against so-called political correctness, they bemoaned the foreign (French!) "philosophy" supposedly being used to transform American culture. As John Lowell recalled in 1797, Democratic-Republicans had introduced French "bombastic and tragical expressions: they affected also the republican rudeness (in France termed simplicity)—in their manners, their conduct, and their conversation. Like them too, they attempted to influence the public opinion, by raree shows, by civic feasts, by republican symbols, by revolutionary *music.*"[16] Outrage at the Democratic-Republicans' "gallic" style suffused Federalist discourse for the rest of the decade. Naturalizing their own style allowed the Federalists to expose their opponents' as mere style.[17]

Portraying their opponents as introducers of a foreign style and as demagogues who were trying to make "the people" into something that they patently were not enabled Federalists to claim that they themselves were the true patriots, the real Americans. "There is in our country so much Nonsense, so much affectation, so much *Fashion* and so much Insincerity, about the French *Republic. . . .* The sobriety and Stability of the American character have never been so much impaired," wrote Peter Van Schaack to a fellow Federalist.[18] If the consumers of "French" sentiments could be portrayed as hysterical, foppish, and insincere to boot, they—and not those who favored strong diplomatic and commercial ties with England—would be seen as the real threat to a stable, independent (and presumably male) national "character." Style itself here becomes effeminate, a sign of weakness associated wholly with the opposition.

This strategy worked better and better after the administration pushed the Jay Treaty, widely interpreted as very friendly to England, through Congress in 1795. By 1796 the previous situation had been reversed: now, if there was any threat to bring America into international warfare, it was French—not British—resentment and intransigence. French vessels attacked American neutral shipping, and French diplomats proved themselves to be even more venal than their British counterparts. When war appeared imminent two years later, the combination of wartime Francophobia and 100 percent Americanism coalesced in the United States' first great episode of nativism and antiradical persecution. Foreigners and the foreign-born were denied the rights of citizenship; legislation targeted those who seemed to support "French" principles. Looking back a few years to an earlier Fourth of July, when Francophilic Democratic-Republicans had joined the symbols of French and American liberty, Cyrus King noted that "no political carmagnoles are [now] bellowed in the streets; no societies are self-created to cherish and preserve the darling influence of France, or superintend the operations of our government; no tri-coloured ribbons grace the fair daughters of America." "Great God!," he wondered, "could [this] have been a true picture of America, of free, independent, neutral America? No, never— never—those who have thus conducted, must have been soul fiends of darkness, who assumed the glorious appelation of Americans." The opposition had become fiends, political demons, "disseminators of *anti-American* sentiments." Federalism, to Federalists, became Americanism.[19]

This much looks familiar—all too familiar. Yet it would be too easy to say that Federalists dressed up their conservative, Anglophilic ideology in nationalist rhetoric in order to crush their opponents. Nationalist rhetoric and ritual was not window dressing: it was integral to the evolving style of both partisan subcultures, Federalist and Democratic-Republican. Equally so its nativistic strain, since the Jeffersonians followed the Revolutionary Patriots in damning all things British. Patriotic Americanism was central to the Federal style, but since both sides claimed "the revolutionary center," what was particular to the evolving Federal style must be sought elsewhere, in how the changing international context gave new resonances to their flag-waving Francophobia and prompted them to push aspects of their stylized battle against style further still.[20] Federalism was an Americanism of a particular strain, one that held particular associations, some of which help explain its peculiar brand of repression.

Most of all, it should be remembered that the Federalist attack on the Jeffersonians' French style was first and foremost an attack upon popular mobilization. Jesse Appleton, a school instructor who later became president of Bowdoin College, fulminated over all the popular activity against the Jay Treaty: "Who gave to common farmers, blacksmiths and ta[i]lors, sufficient knowledge to prove that two thirds of the senate are knaves, or fools[?]" Respectable public meetings were composed of respectable people—not ordinary workingmen. In arguing against such activity, Federalists faced the paradox of appealing to the people to stay out of politics.[21]

How did the Federalists fashion such an appeal? First, they attempted to replace the opposition's public criticism with public praise for the administration. They made support of the "constituted authorities" a virtue in and of itself. Mass participation was completely acceptable, it seems, as long as it supported the existing order. A group of female Independence Day revelers in York, Pennsylvania, for example, toasted "The constituted authorities—may they be reverenced in place of equality." Since celebrations of President Washington's birthday were not legally compelled, as leaders' birthdays were in the monarchies of Europe, they must be "the *free* and *sincere* effusions of respect and gratitude"—themselves marks of virtue, patriotism, and Federalism. As Oliver Fiske explained in 1797, "A deference to our rulers, is no other than a respect for ourselves. . . . the rulers and the people are but the different modifications of the same mass." By this reasoning, "ingratitude" was the worst vice of republics. Federalists proposed a cult of leadership that rested upon a presumption that America's leaders and its people were one and the same, indivisible. Political jealousy, then, was no longer a virtue, as it had been during the 1760s and 1770s. Since the authorities had been chosen by the people, opposition to them was opposition to the people—or treason.[22]

The oppositional activities of the Democratic-Republican societies—such as holding public meetings that passed resolutions against the Jay Treaty and then publishing those resolutions—assumed that the people and their government were two different entities, and that the process of democratic and republican government consisted in some measure of negotiations between elected officials and their constituents. Federalists responded by mobilizing their supporters in displays of concert, or identification, with the federal government. Washington's Birthday and Fourth of July dinners served these functions, as public officials could be toasted and praised in ways that buttressed their claims to authority. But the Federalists' elite dinners, along with their nervous warnings about the licentious side of liberty, could work at cross-purposes to the more inclusive aspects of their partisan spectacles. How could the entire nation plausibly be mobilized to ratify its deference to Federalist leadership and its standards of "respectable" public activity? How could the link between the (right) leaders and followers be reestablished?

Washington himself provided the beginning of a solution to this problem in his proclamation for a national Day of Thanksgiving on February 19, 1795. Citing the need to offer thanks to God, "the Great Ruler of Nations," the president described the current prospects of international and domestic peace, linking the forthcoming Jay Treaty to the suppression of the backcountry tax revolts known as the Whiskey Rebellion. Flanked in many cities by Democratic-Republican celebrations of the old French alliance (February 6) and the mainly Federalist fetes in honor of Washington's birthday (February 22), the Thanksgiving's most lasting effect was to restore the clergy, and religion itself, to an important role in Federalist politics. In their sermons established clergy posited a national duty to honor God. The clergy of 1795 sought to reverse what they perceived as an erosion of clerical authority. In doing so they linked sacred and secular order. By giving thanks, the good Protestant would simultaneously serve God and nation, while supporting the government. The nation was one big congregation that would, they hoped, sit contentedly in the pews.[23]

Federalists' efforts to bolster their politics with religion grew more aggressive during the Quasi-War with France. President Adams appointed two national fast days—May 9, 1798, and April 25, 1799—and his second declaration was even more explicitly Christian than the first. For the 1798 fast Boston's *Columbian Centinel* suggested that lest the political importance of the fast be missed, ministers might read aloud from the reports of the American diplomats in France "between the [church] services."[24] The fasts also became the venue for members of the New England clergy to advance their theory of a French-inspired conspiracy against Christianity. The fasts of 1798 and 1799 produced a great deal of bitterness throughout the country because they were part and parcel of an attempt by Federalists to purge an opposition that they portrayed as unrespectable, blasphemous, and disloyal. The cultural politics of that attempt can tell us much about Federalism's stylized mobilization against style. For the moment, however, it should be noted that for all their seeming abhorrence of popular activity, of feasting and fasting, of public meetings and publication, the Federalists of 1798 either had learned a great deal from their opponents or had remembered something about the Revolution and about constitutional ratification. They had come to understand that their dream of a deferential populace had to be modified. Indeed, the Federalists were already mobilizing supporters in the streets as well as in the churches. The fight of '98 was a fight over what form that activity would take, over who would be active and how. The attack upon popular mobilization had clarified its goals and strategy: it was an attack upon certain people and certain styles of mobilization, executed in no small measure as an attack upon style itself.

FEDERALISM IN ARMS: THE STYLE OF '98

Our overriding, at times obsessive, concern with statesmen like Hamilton, Jefferson, and Washington has blinded us to what contemporaries experienced as the cutting-edge political phenomenon of the late 1790s. This was the mobilization of "young men." According to Republican newspapers, young men who sported the black "American" cockade were among the most hawkish of Federalists, "continually brawling about their patriotism, and crying out for war."[25] With war looming in June 1798, Congress had passed a law calling for a 10,000-man reserve army and the mobilization of an 80,000-man militia. But eager young men who had spare time and money for uniforms had already begun to form private volunteer militia companies that met regularly and paraded on festival days.

In a certain sense, young men in uniform had been highly visible throughout the decade. Many militia units had formed in response to the diplomatic crisis with England in 1794–95. Others were called out to suppress the Whiskey Rebellion. At such times of crisis, more and more accounts of these military groups' dinners and toasts appeared in the newspapers. Given the traditional American hostility to standing armies, local militia companies had certain advantages over other groups that gave voice to public opinion—for example, the Society of the Cincinnati, whose all-star cast of characters had been officers in the disbanded Continental army. Privately initiated volunteer companies, however, wore their refinement literally on their sleeves. The difference between the ragtag regulars of the state militia and the stylish expertise of the elite private corps was a commonplace of the day. The "lady" who presented a flag to the new Volunteer Greens of Philadelphia in 1794, for example, praised the respectable soldiers "whose valour has every excitement that the most intimate relations with the common community, honor, duty, connections, birth, education, and property can inspire."[26]

Until 1797, calls for the formation of militia companies could still carry a decidedly anti-British political message. But when President Adams released the documents proving that French diplomats had demanded a cash tribute (the XYZ affair), the resonances of these patriotic exercises shifted dramatically. Federalists seized their chance, organizing meetings to express approval of the chief executive's actions. And young men took the lead by affirming their willingness to defend the nation.

During the late spring and summer of 1798, public messages sent to the president and his responses to them filled the pages of all but the most Jeffersonian newspapers. They came from all over the country— from cities, towns, and rural counties; state legislatures, groups of clergy-men, and Masonic lodges. Many claimed to represent the voice of the people from those places, though not all succeeded in this task. At a public meeting in Newark, the young men of the town voted down a resolution to send Adams such a message; the Federalists among them regrouped and sent one anyway. More remarkable than the messages themselves, however, is the entire ritual process they initiated. President Adams responded to each and every address with a personal letter; when it arrived via post, a second meeting—one that women could attend—was held to receive it formally.

These letters, their reception, and their publication joined president to citizens through direct forms of address. A prolific correspondent, Adams found in the epistolary arts all the charisma he otherwise lacked. On paper, in print, he looked like a president. In the letters Adams took on the role of arbiter of American identity, but in doing so he recog-nized—even thanked—his addressees for affirming his own patriotic services. To the Maryland Freemasons, Adams wrote, "Your appeal to my own breast, and your declaration that I shall *there* find your sentiments, I consider as a high compliment." Revelations of refined sentiments—his own and his correspondents'—invited every feeling citizen to participate with the commander in chief in the affective field of patriotism, or what the celebrants of 1788 had called "federal feeling."[27]

Federalists noted approvingly—and their opponents disparagingly— that the propertied were more than well represented among the signees of these patriotic addresses. Yet the particular identities of those who ac-tually attended the meetings and who actually signed the petition-letters is usually washed out in the printed versions that appeared in the papers. The vagueness invited the reader to join in and rise with the occasion. In practice, it seems, these Federalist rites of "gratitude" to the president enacted their rhetorical invocation of an identity between the people (or the people that counted) and the government. This helps explain why Federalists did not see the addresses as implying undue deference or as warmed-over monarchy, as Republicans did. Having gratitude for their leaders did not make them servile; it made them like their leaders, full of virtuous sentiments revealed in their words as well as by their actions.

Nowhere was this more true than in the sentimental exchanges between Adams and the groups of self-identified "young men" that in some cases first formed in order to address him. In Philadelphia fifteen hundred of them marched to the executive mansion to deliver their message. Adams met them in full military dress and proclaimed that "no prospect or spectacle could excite a stronger sensibility in my bosom than this which now presents itself before me." Expressing appreciation for the sacrifices of their fathers, the young men promised allegiance to "the religion and the laws" that made up their inheritance. The president complimented them on the respect they showed for the older generation, but if his words included anything about public order, it was lost on these young Federalists. After leaving the president's house, they proceeded to attack the print shop of the city's foremost Francophile, Benjamin Franklin Bache.[28]

In 1798 young men demonstrated their patriotism through Federalist rituals of prodigal reunion. At Federalist celebrations of July 4 in 1798, old and young patriots explicitly toasted each other. These well-heeled young males rose to maturity by demonstrating to the French "that we are NOT 'a divided People.'" In Newburyport they sang out that there was no need for any other kind of noise:

> Our Constitution and laws, by our fathers designed
> To render us happy—and useful and kind;
> We'll freely support with our lives and estates,
> Without hesitation or lengthy debates.[29]

Yet given the sudden ubiquity of "young men" in 1798 and their apparent effectiveness in shunting aside the specter of "a divided people," we can perhaps see the elevation of youth to centrality in Federalist rhetoric and practice as more than an overdue recognition of a natural constituency. To identify the leaders of public meetings as "young men" (rather than, say, as "merchants" like those who initiated the memorials in favor of the Jay Treaty) shifted attention from one kind of difference (class) to another (age or generation). Like the mobilization of churchmen and Christians generally to celebrate pro-administration fast days, the young men's festive and martial gatherings blunted the Jeffersonians' class-inflected campaign against "aristocrats."

Moreover, the acts of identification that sealed those of age and religion, truly demonizing the sources of class and partisan division, were utterly and significantly gendered. The intergenerational rites that brought "fathers" and the "young men" together had complementary places for women. Indeed, women played a particularly prominent role in many towns' 1798 July Fourth celebrations. The ladies of New Mills, New Jersey, proved "not less patriotic and federal than their husbands." Deerfield women gave a fiery toast: "May each Columbian Sister *perceive* and pursue the *unfallible* system of *extinguishing* Jacobinism." The "Patriotic Fair" women of Middletown, Connecticut, added six of their own toasts to those of the men and then led them in procession to the liberty tree, atop of which flew the pre-Independence serpent flag, "Unite or Die." In Philadelphia women ignored William Cobbett's strictures against those unfeminine women who had participated in the French Revolution or had celebrated it in America: they wore the Federalist "American Cockade," with metal eagle pins, in public. At the New Jersey State House in Trenton, women sang "Hail, Columbia," the pro-Adams war song, just as the city's three militia companies had earlier in the day.[30]

That summer also saw a remarkable revival of the still older female practice of presenting handwoven standards to militia companies. Women's pleas for men to protect them and their homes were hardly new: in urging their young men to enlist and parade rather than accompany them to July 4 balls, a group of Stockbridge ladies cited the women of ancient Carthage, who cut off their hair to make ropes for the hanging of their enemies. What does appear innovative here are the sentimental exchanges between the officers and the ladies at these flag ceremonials. The presenters were usually young, unmarried women, dressed in white, and their speeches to the militias were often reprinted in the newspapers. As if to complete an alliance, female speakers connected the protection of the nation to the guarding of their hearts and their religion. As one young woman told a militia captain, "Our love can only be obtained by bravely defending our liberties, the Independence, and the Religion of our Country." "As Christians and as Americans," Charleston's Federalist artillery promised Mary Legaré that they would defend the flag of their fathers and the "religious liberty" threatened by the French.[31]

Federal style brought these ladies to the center of public attention in defense of the Christian nation. In doing so they represented not just their social group or constituency—women—but also womanhood itself.[32] This is not to play down the very important contributions of these women to the Federalist cause, or their implications for the emerging ideal of separate spheres. Rather, these women's actions need to be seen in the context of male Federalist commentary about the threats to American womanhood—and manhood—represented by the French. Francophilic democracy, according to William Cobbett, would subvert traditional gender roles. Even without a war, Federalists were counseled to "remove your wives far from the Infernal Fraternal embrace, or you may prove witnesses of their violation and their expiring agonies, or if reserved for future infamy, may increase your families not only with a spurious, but with a colored breed" (fathered, presumably, by the Haitian blacks who would give up their own fight against the French to join them in the deflowering of America). "What would be your sensations, O husbands!" asked William J. Hobbey, speaking before the Augusta, Georgia's Volunteer Corps of Artillery and Light Infantry, "to see your wives—what your reflections, O fathers! to see your daughters—what your feelings, O brave American youth, to see your amiable and beloved female companions . . . subjected to a foreign foe, placed within the power of those lawless hordes who have reduced iniquity to a system, sanctioned immorality, and openly denied the influence of religion?" The sentimental joining of men in uniform with women in white, by contrast, expressed the balance of a true American marriage, in which the gendered virtues of male and female make the nation, like the family, whole.[33]

As the initiative in public festivals shifted to Federalist young men in 1798–99, they made their own manhood central to their Federalism. In Boston, Hartford, New York, Portsmouth, and other cities they held widely publicized celebrations of Adams's birthday in October and of the dissolution of the old French treaty on July 17. If July 4 and the Declaration of Independence signified America's birth, July 17 marked "the day of our nation's *manhood*." "*Freedom's* sons were born again," a "second birth" on "the *day* that rent proud Gallia's chains." Rather than overthrowing bad parents, these young men declared their liberation from the arms of a French coquette of tellingly ambiguous gender, "whose *touch* is *pollution*—whose *friendship* is *poison*—whose *embrace* is *death.*"[34]

Most of the time, the gender of those who engaged in the dreaded French "fraternal embrace" was not ambiguous at all. Edmond-Charles Genet, the discredited French minister, was said to have brought these indiscriminate affections overseas to America in 1793. Years later Federalists still recoiled at the "hugging and rugging," the "addressing and caressing," that had marked Genet's joyous reception by their political opponents. In the mid to late eighteenth century, French men were characterized by Anglophiles as foppish and effeminate, and syphilis was known as the "French disease." Moreover, the practice of sodomy among men had long been associated with atheism and radical republicanism—precisely those trends that Federalists feared most in the French Revolution. Thus it is not at all anachronistic to suggest that the Federalists' own nationalist male bonding took place over the metaphorical bodies of these French and Frenchified effeminate, homosexual men. William Cobbett was not alone in calling for war to "cut off the cankering, poisonous sans culottes connexion."[35]

Eve Kosofsky Sedgwick has observed that normative relations between men are often transacted, metaphorically as well as literally, through the physical bodies of women. Such an understanding helps explain the political importance of the women—often explicitly identified as mothers and daughters—who appeared in public dressed in white: they not only established an American national family of men and women but also helped stabilize relations among older and younger men. Sedgwick also observes that such transactions among men have often been cemented, at least since the nineteenth century, against the closeted possibility of perverted, illicit male-male relations. The rhetoric of the young men of '98 was replete with jokes, conscious or not, that invented a homosexual threat to their heterosexual manhood. For Thomas (later Robert Treat) Paine, "America had been nearly suffocated in the extatic rapture of the 'hug fraternal.'" One toast ran, "The Fair Sex: the only human beings to whom we will bend the knee." A variation on "Yankee Doodle" included a chorus, "If Frenchmen come with naked bum / We'll spank 'em hard and handy." An alternate refrain linked military to male-male sexual domination: "'Their 'fernal hugs may squeeze Dutch bugs, / But we will have no master; / And while the Swiss, Sans Culottes kiss, / We'll spread a blister plaister."[36] Real men would act, militarily, against the contagion of style.

The issue here is less whether Federalists consciously tried to gay-bait the French and their political opponents at home than what this evidence tells us about Federalism itself as a political style. Federalists were no less scurrilous than the opposition they tried to silence. The corollary is that in mobilizing against the Democratic-Republican threat, they were no less creative, and perhaps even more so, than the "democrats" themselves. Federalists did successfully mobilize, and the secret to their admittedly temporary success was that they got particular groups to dominate the streets and the press without violating their own overriding concern with respectability. Once again, as in 1788, they had reconstituted the people against an antifederal, un-American, low-class enemy. Now, as in 1776, these enemies were ungodly and effeminate as well. Federalists gave substance to their quite intolerant Americanism with specifically religious and gendered spectacles, such as the fast days, the addresses to the president, and the rhetorical denunciations of all things French. They made their antirhetorical rhetoric real by effectively revising their own newly oppositional style.

In Federalist practice style was substance; but in Federalist rhetoric style was foreign, effeminate, "cankering." When we understand that, the repression of 1798 seems less a question of nativistic "fear," or even an issue of press freedom, than a chapter in the ongoing struggle over the meanings and modes—the styles, and thus the substance—of American politics. The results of this struggle can only be considered ambiguous. The Federalists won some battles but lost power nationally in 1800. They launched an effective attack on style that only confused the issue further by depending upon its own standards for political correctness. They lost their larger gambit against the continuing politicization of the populace yet learned that they could subtly change the whole playing field by encouraging certain players, like the clergy, the young men, and the women in white. And they proved for all time that spectacular exchanges of patriotic sentiments, however mobilizing and potentially democratic, could work to profoundly conservative, even repressive, ends.

6

Gender and the First Party System

Rosemarie Zagarri

ON THE FOURTH of July in 1815, various groups gathered at Dickinson College in Pennsylvania to celebrate the thirty-ninth anniversary of the nation's independence. Once on the college grounds, individuals went their separate ways to attend functions sponsored by several different organizations: the Republican party, the Federal Republican party (Federalists), and the nonpartisan Belles-Lettres Society. Each group followed roughly the same order of events for the day. A speaker addressed the audience in a formal presentation, highlighting patriotic themes and events particularly geared to the audience's partisan sentiments. Afterward, assembled guests enjoyed alcoholic beverages and engaged in series of spirited toasts to honor celebrated causes and national heroes. Citizens from nearby Carlisle as well as male students from the college attended the festivities.

Given the social and legal restrictions excluding women from politics in the early republic, one might reasonably expect these functions to have been all-male affairs. Yet as it turned out, men did not have a monopoly on the day. The printed version of events reveals a surprising circumstance: women were present, and their presence was acknowledged, at both the Federalist gathering and the meeting of the Belles-Lettres Society. The Federalists, in particular, made a point of welcoming women to their meeting. As a group they offered an emphatic toast to "The ladies who this day honored *our party* with their presence.—May we ever continue to deserve their favours." Yet the third group, the Republicans, said little about women. Although in their postspeech activities they gave a halfhearted toast to "The Fair," they neither addressed women directly nor acknowledged their presence in the audience. It is impossible to tell whether women attended the Republican celebration or not, though the difference between Federalist and Republican toasts suggests they did not. Clearly, the feminine presence did not possess the same significance to the two political parties.[1]

One might view this incident as merely a curious anecdote or an isolated artifact of the intense partisan struggles of the early national era. Evidence, however, suggests that the episode was not unique; it was part of a larger pattern. In the early republic one party proved to be more receptive than the other to incorporating women into the political process and articulating women's role in the polity. That party proved to be the Federalists.

On the face of it, one might assume that the Democratic-Republicans would be more open to women than the Federalists. Yet this was not the case. In making their demands for equality, Republicans meant equality for all white males. In their efforts to expand the franchise and open up the political process to all levels of society, they reconfigured—though did not abolish—social hierarchy. The broadening of political privileges for white males rested on—and in a sense depended on—the subordination of women, as well as blacks and Indians.

Federalists, however, possessed a certain flexibility to innovate. They welcomed women to their public gatherings and honored women's contributions to the polity. Differences in ideas about liberty and the social order gave rise to each party's approach to women. Whereas Republican ideology challenged social privilege and attacked invidious class distinctions, Federalist theory accepted such divisions as inevitable and embraced the existing social hierarchy. Within the limits of their system, Federalists thus felt free to explore the possibility of an informal role for women—especially elite white women—in politics. Far more than their competitors, they acknowledged and encouraged women's political potential. Paradoxically, the social conservatives of the early republic proved to be more progressive concerning women than their putatively more liberal rivals.

IN THE WAKE of the American Revolution, many Americans had come to recognize that women played a more significant role in politics than they had previously believed. During the Revolution women had demonstrated their commitment to the Patriot cause in a variety of ways—through boycotting British goods, relinquishing their loved ones to the war effort, and running farms and businesses while their husbands were away. In their own fashion women had suffered and sacrificed as much as men. Now, it was understood, women as well as men would help build the new nation. As wives and mothers, women shaped the character, morals, and patriotism of their sons and husbands. They were men's first teachers and educators; they had both the privilege and the responsibility of encouraging men to become virtuous citizens, informed voters, and willing soldiers. While few people claimed that women should vote or hold public office, many were ready to acknowledge that women had an important, though indirect, influence on politics. Historian Linda Kerber has labeled this cluster of ideas "Republican Motherhood."[2]

As the partisan struggles of the early republic intensified, women became more directly involved in politics. In the early 1790s women wore tricolored or black cockades to demonstrate their support for or opposition to the French Revolution. Federalist women regularly participated in an elaborate ceremony in which they presented their home militia troops with flags they had embroidered themselves.[3] A foreign visitor to New York during Jefferson's Embargo thought that women wore certain clothes to indicate their party affiliation. "Methought I could discern a pretty *Democrat* à la mode Françoise, and a sweet little *Federalist* à la mode Angloise," observed John Lambert.[4] Several decades later, one orator recalled, "Even the fair sex lent their aid to the general uproar, and with their delicate fingers framed the emblems of contending parties—men and boys wore them."[5]

The leaders of the first political parties, however, did not support women's involvement in politics, or Republican Motherhood in general, with equal enthusiasm. Federalists seem to have been more favorably disposed toward women in politics than their Republican adversaries. A case in point is Thomas Jefferson and John Adams.

Even before assuming the leadership of the Democratic-Republican party, Thomas Jefferson probably had thought more about educational matters than any other member of the founding generation. Yet he never turned his attention to the education of women. Except for his daughters, he admitted, "a plan of female education has never been a subject of systematic contemplation with me."[6] For his daughters he essentially wanted a traditional feminine education, heavily weighted toward dancing, drawing, and music. He abhorred their reading of novels and urged them to learn French, the language of refinement and gentility. Disregarding the tenets of Republican Motherhood, Jefferson believed his daughters would play little role in educating their sons; only if the "fathers be lost, or incapable, or inattentive" should the mothers become involved in the process.[7]

More generally, he scorned women's interest in politics. Commenting on the tumult leading up to the French Revolution, he remarked: "Gay and thoughtless Paris is now become a furnace of Politics. All the world is run politically mad. Men, women, children talk of nothing else." Obviously disapproving, he hoped that was not the case in America. "Our good ladies,

I trust, have been too wise to wrinkle their foreheads with politics. They are contented to soothe and calm the minds of their husbands returning ruffled from political debate. They have the good sense to value domestic happiness above all other, and the art to cultivate it beyond all others."[8] As president, he abruptly dismissed a woman's request for a position as postmistress. This was not, he said, an "innovation for which the public is prepared, nor am I."[9]

Jefferson's friend and political antagonist Federalist John Adams was himself no feminist. His famous dismissal of Abigail's plea in 1776 to "Remember the Ladies" and his extended altercation with Mercy Otis Warren over her portrayal of him in her *History of the American Revolution* are well known. Yet in many ways he was much more open to women's potential than Jefferson. Unlike his foe, Adams had imbibed the implications of Republican Motherhood. In reply to Abigail's comment, "If we mean to have Heroes, Statesmen and Philosophers, we should have learned women," he remarked, "Your Sentiments on the Importance of Education in Women, are exactly agreeable to my own."[10] He encouraged his wife in her efforts at self-education and treated her as an intellectual equal. He urged his daughters and granddaughters to read widely in philosophy, literature, and history, including works from learned authors such as Locke, Berkeley, and Hume. He supported Emma Willard's efforts in 1819 (though she was a known "friend of Mr. Jefferson") to establish a school of higher education that would provide a classical college curriculum for women.[11]

He also welcomed women's involvement in political matters in a way Jefferson did not. Long before his falling-out with Mercy Warren, Adams had been her mentor and friend. He encouraged her to write political works, helped arrange for their publication, and praised her "genius."[12] He sought out her opinion on political matters during the Revolution. In 1776 he had told her husband that he had never thought "either Politicks or War, or any other Art or Science beyond the Line of her Sex: on the contrary I have ever been convinced that Politicks and War, have in every age, been influenced, and in many, guided and controuled by her Sex."[13] While constrained by the assumptions of his time, Adams nonetheless explored the boundaries of women's participation in the political process.

This was not simply Adams's personal preference. Evidence suggests that the Federalists acknowledged the presence of women in their midst and honored their political contributions, while Republicans tended to ignore or slight them. The Federalists' attitudes appear most explicitly in their Fourth of July orations. One major organization that attracted a Federalist membership was the Society of the Cincinnati. Formed in 1783 by French and American officers who had served in the Revolutionary War, the Cincinnati aimed to foster continuing friendships among the men and provide financial assistance to needy members and their families. As party loyalties solidified in the 1790s, it was clear that the society harbored many prominent Federalist leaders such as George Washington, Alexander Hamilton, Benjamin Lincoln, Henry Knox, Timothy Pickering, and James Wilson. Yet even the rank-and-file members leaned toward the Federalists. A study of the New Jersey Cincinnati concluded that only 2 of the 101 original members in that state identified themselves as Republicans. Especially before 1800, the Society of the Cincinnati was regarded as an "auxiliary arm" of the Federalist party.[14]

Despite the quintessentially male, martial character of the Cincinnati, the organization welcomed women to its gatherings. Printed speeches from 1786 to 1815 reveal numerous occasions in which Federalist orators directly addressed women sitting in the audience. In his 1790 speech to the Delaware Cincinnati, for example, James Tilton noted, "I shall be pardoned in deviating so far from ordinary form, as to address this head of my discourse to my fair audience."[15] In another venue, during one of his "Lectures on the Study of the Law in the United States," James Wilson observed: "Methinks I hear one of the female part of my audience exclaim—What is all this to us? We have heard much of societies, of states, of governments, of laws, and of a law education. Is every thing made for your sex? Why should not we have a share? Is our sex less honest, or less virtuous, or less wise than yours?"[16] He then proceeded to elucidate the women's contributions.

Comments directed specifically toward women were significant for several reasons. First of all, they indicate that women were in attendance at a variety of political gatherings, especially, though not exclusively, at Independence Day celebrations. Members seem to have regarded the women's presence as both useful and appropriate. Moreover, by speaking to women in the audience, Federalist orators transformed the females from passive bystanders into active participants in the day's events. They acknowledged women to be thinking, sentient beings who had a stake in the polity. In effect, they affirmed women's role as Republican Wives and mothers.

In many more speeches Federalist orators spoke about women even when they did not speak directly to them. They honored women's contributions to the Revolutionary cause, exhorted them to support the country in its present crises, or celebrated women's distinctive brand of patriotism. Many speakers used the Independence Day celebrations, for example, to remind audiences of women's role in winning the Revolutionary War. "To the fair of our country," observed Keating L. Simon in 1806, "are we as much indebted for that glorious achievement, as to the generous souls, who endured the toils of the camp, and withstood the shocks of battle. Warmed by the same honorable feelings, they maintained, throughout, the same devotion to the cause. Their patriotism became the more noble, as it was of a kind entirely suited to their sex."[17] Other Federalists commented on women's continuing service to American society. In 1788, during the ratification of the federal Constitution, William Hull observed, "With gratitude and admiration, we here likewise pay the tribute of applause to the fair daughters of America—for their unexampled exertions at this critical season; denying themselves the luxuries and delicacies of life and ornament, and practising the duties of industry and oeconomy, they animated youth by the splendour of their example and inspired them with manly pride, to defend the beauties of innocence and the violated rights of their country."[18]

Federalist speakers also pleaded with their female audience to provide continuing support for the nation in its present struggles. Women, it was assumed, shaped the county's morals and manners; men controlled government and the lawmaking process. This was not an insignificant contribution. As James Tilton noted, "In a republic, manners are of equal importance with laws."[19] In forming manners, women influenced men to perform the civic functions essential to the republic's survival—to volunteer for battle, serve in the statehouse, or vote at the polls. Federalist speakers emphasized women's ability to sway, even manipulate, men into doing their duty. "You, my fair friends," said David Daggett to the New Haven Cincinnati in 1787, "are possessed of a kind of magic influence over the other sex. . . . It is with you to promote oeconomy and industry, or luxury and extravagances at your pleasure. By attending to the former, you will yield an essential service to your country."[20] During the War of 1812 speakers exhorted women to support the war effort. "To you fair daughters of my country," proclaimed Philip Mathews, "I fly for auxiliary. Assist I beseech you . . . by your electrifying influence. . . . Urge then your husbands, your brothers, your sons, and your lovers, to those scenes where danger calls, and glory invites."[21] Or as John Grimké exclaimed, "Whilst the daughters of Carolina shall remain virtuous, her sons will ever prove valorous."[22] Whether speaking directly to women or about them, Federalist orators went out of their way to show that women had a crucial place in the new republic—different from that of men, but equally valuable.

Yet the Federalists did not push their ideas too far. Although supporters of women in politics, Federalists never advocated a more direct role for women in the political process. Women, they believed, could be political—but only within the bounds of their traditional role as wives and mothers. The problem, as Linda Kerber explains, lay within the concept of Republican Motherhood itself. Republican Motherhood, she says, was a "Janus-faced" notion,[23] an idea that represented "one of a series of conservative choices that Americans made in the postwar years . . . [which] avoided the full implications of their own revolutionary radicalism."[24] Federalists thus acknowledged women's participation in politics but at same time refused to consider the further expansion of that role. The paradoxical nature of Republican Motherhood also explains why certain Federalists, such as Timothy Dwight and Benjamin Silliman, could celebrate women's political contributions and at the same time launch vicious and vituperative attacks on the idea of women's political rights.[25] Whatever their blind spots, Federalists—both as individuals and as a group— became the most systematic and coherent supporters of Republican Motherhood in the early republic.

In contrast, Democratic-Republicans seemed less supportive of women's potential as political beings. They made very little room for women, either in their organizations or their rhetoric. From the beginning, lower- to middle-class white men began joining different organizations from the Federalists. They especially gravitated toward the Tammany Society, named after a mythological Indian chief. Founded in New York in the 1780s, the Tammany attracted former enlisted veterans, craftsmen, artisans, and skilled laborers. The Tammany and its affiliated organizations—the Mechanic, Cooper, and Hibernian societies—were Democratic-Republican in orientation.[26] Though committed to liberty, equality, and fraternity, these organizations clearly understood "equality" to mean the equality of all white males.

Unlike the Federalists, Republican orators seldom spoke directly to women at their gatherings.[27] On one such rare occasion, a Springfield, Massachusetts, Independence Day celebration in 1800, a Republican speaker addressed women as "*female citizens.*"[28] In 1806 Republican Elias Glover of Ohio appealed to the "Columbian Fair."[29] Given the male-dominated nature of the political system, the paucity of appeals to women hardly seems surprising. But the contrast with the Federalists' not infrequent allusions to the female sex makes the absence of Republican references significant. Unlike Federalists, Republicans may not have chosen to invite women to attend their meetings. Or perhaps Republican gatherings were less hospitable to women. Even if women were there, Republican speakers may have been less willing to acknowledge the women's presence in their midst.

Beyond the quantitative difference, there was also a qualitative difference in the way Republicans depicted women when they mentioned them. Republicans tended to underscore the secondary, or auxiliary, nature of women's political achievements. Hailing women's "*virtuous liberty*," for example, Elias Glover urged his female listeners to "accept the station nature intended for you, and double the knowledge and happiness of mankind."[30] Women's place was subordinate to men. In 1804 Richard Dinsmore of Alexandria noted approvingly that female Patriots during the Revolution had, in his words, "emulated the decisive patriotism of their husbands and brothers."[31] Female patriotism was portrayed as derivative rather than primary. In a similar vein, the Reverend Solomon Aiken of New Hampshire praised what he called women's "patriotic concurrence. . . . Our heroines, in their place, were not a whit behind our foremost heroes."[32] The Reverend Joseph Pilmore's comments, made in 1794 to the New York Tammany Society, seem to be typical of the Republicans. "See on this joyful Festival of our country's Independence, a multitude of *free men* met to commemorate your valiant acts, while the fair daughters of our nation strew your graves with flowers."[33] While the Tammany Society was meeting to celebrate its collective male valor, women were putting flowers—either literally or metaphorically—on the graves of fallen heroes.

Rather than stressing an active brand of female patriotism, Pilmore and the other Republicans emphasized a more marginal, passive patriotism for women. In their version, women were clearly subordinate to men. The Federalists, on the other hand, concentrated on the importance, if not equality, of women's contributions to the polity. Pilmore, however, at least said something about women. Most other Republican commentators did not.

This is not to say that the Republicans totally ignored women. During the 1790s Republicans, like their Federalist counterparts, sometimes mobilized women for public processions and partisan rallies, as visible demonstrations of popular support for their cause. Also like the Federalists, Republicans often drank toasts to "the American Fair" or to "the improvement of Female Education."[34] In 1799 the New York Tammany honored "*American Mothers*—May they teach their sons to love liberty, and their daughters to hate tyranny and adore virtue."[35] Similarly, the Democratic Association of Gloucester, New Jersey, made a toast in 1801 to "The Fair Sex—May they, like the ladies of the Roman Republic, esteem the instruction of their offspring in virtue, literature, and the liberties of their country, as their duty and highest honor."[36] In addition, certain individual Republicans worked out the implications of their egalitarian political philosophy for its effect on women. In courtrooms and newspapers men such as James Sullivan and Philip Freneau began to press for broader civil rights and legal privileges for women. In making such arguments, they anticipated the later direction of feminist thought. Yet their arguments fell on deaf ears, even among members of their own party. As a whole, the Republican party of the early republic was not as receptive to women as the Federalists, either in institutional or rhetorical terms.[37]

One event underscores this point. In New Jersey women did come to occupy a central role in the conflict between Federalists and Democratic-Republicans. The New Jersey constitution of 1776 included a broadly worded provision that enfranchised all free adult inhabitants in the state who owned property worth £50. Because of the language in the provision, single women with property were eligible to vote—a capacity they enjoyed in no other state in the Union. (By law, married women could not own property and thus were not eligible to vote, even in New Jersey.) As historians Judith Apter Klinghoffer and Lois Elkis have demonstrated, this language was not the result of carelessness or imprecision; it seems to have been the New Jersey Assembly's deliberate choice.[38]

Enfranchisement, however, did not politicize the women of New Jersey—at least not immediately. Women's politicization at this time existed largely outside official governmental institutions and formal legal channels. Male party leaders, however, recognized the women's electoral potential long before they themselves did. Although the Federalists took the initiative in mobilizing female voters, both parties soon realized that women could provide the margin of victory, especially in a closely contested election. Although the precise number of women voters is not known, some historians estimate that as many as 10,000 women may have been eligible, though probably fewer than 100 voted in any given election. As one commentator wrote in 1802, "Each party will of course muster all its female champions, from apprehension its antagonists will do the same."[39] Yet neither party ever completely reconciled itself to the situation. In 1807 Republicans introduced a bill, of dubious constitutionality, that limited the franchise to white taxpaying male citizens. Operating strictly on the basis of a partisan calculus, the Federalists acceded to the law, believing that the number of black and women supporters they would lose would be less than the poor and naturalized voters lost to their opponents.

Despite the outcome, the New Jersey episode refines our understanding of the role of women in the first party system. Perhaps not surprisingly, the women of New Jersey, who had not fought for the franchise in the first place, did not object to its loss. Most did not yearn for formal incorporation into the political process and quickly reverted to their extra-institutional roles in the system. Yet among women who voted, a clear pattern of partisan allegiance had emerged. Females overwhelmingly preferred the Federalist party to the Republican. The reasons are not obscure. Class imperatives as much as principled support of Federalist policies seem to have been at work. The relatively high property qualification ensured that only well-off women would be eligible to vote. Because Federalists found their traditional base of support among the upper classes, the women's social class determined their partisan affiliation. Commenting on the New Jersey situation, a contemporary English observer remarked, "Ladies have the reputation of hating democracy as well as demogogues."[40] The class-based nature of Federalist support had other consequences as well. Unlike Republicans, Federalists had the advantage of knowing who their women constituents were: propertied members of society, like themselves. Furthermore, as the minority party struggling to regain their dominance, Federalists had more incentive than Republicans to seek out their female supporters. A variety of factors, then, led Federalists to be more open to the inclusion of women than their Republican rivals.

For a fuller understanding of this phenomenon, however, we must examine the ideas of the two most prominent women political writers of the early republic, Mercy Otis Warren and Judith Sargent Murray. Despite many similarities, the two women supported rival political parties. Warren of Plymouth, Massachusetts, was the author of several pre-Revolutionary political satires against the crown, a stinging diatribe against the Constitution signed "A Columbian Patriot," and a volume of politically charged poetry and plays. A strong believer in the centrality of civic virtue in republican government, she had by the early 1790s become an avowed opponent of the Federalists and a supporter of the Democratic-Republican party. In 1805 she issued her magnum opus, a three-volume *History of the American Revolution*, which interpreted the country's political development from the Stamp Act Crisis through the presidency of John Adams from a decidedly Republican perspective.[41]

Warren's partisan sentiments contrasted sharply with those of Murray. Also from Massachusetts, Murray began in the 1780s to publish poetry, political essays, and fictional stories in various periodicals, especially the *Massachusetts Magazine*. In 1795 she wrote two plays; three years later she released a collection of her writings under the title *The Gleaner*. An advocate of the U.S. Constitution and a supporter of strong centralized government, she quickly became a firm adherent of Federalist policies and ideas.[42] The juxtaposition of these authors' beliefs about women, in the context of their larger political thinking, helps show why the Federalist Murray could envision a broader role for women than the Republican Warren.

Neither Warren nor Murray can be called a feminist in the modern sense of the term. While both believed in the intellectual equality of the sexes, neither advocated the political enfranchisement of women. Both believed in separate spheres for men and women and in the necessity of women's subordination to men—"perhaps," as Warren put it, "for the sake of order in families."[43] Women thus made their primary contribution to society in their traditional domestic roles. Better education, Murray noted, would enable women "when they become wives and mothers" to "fill with honour the parts allotted them. . . . They will be primarily solicitous to fulfill, *in every instance*, whatever can *justly* be denominated *duty*; and those intervals, which have heretofore been devoted to frivolity, will be appropriated to pursuits, calculated to inform, enlarge, and sublime the soul."[44] Both regarded biology as destiny.

Whatever attitudes they shared about women's nature, Warren and Murray had notably different opinions about the role of women in politics. The Reoublican Warren retained a much more conventional understanding of woman's position. Though at times she seemed to chafe at the "narrow bounds prescrib'd to female life,"[45] she never publicly challenged the structure of gender relations. In her *History of the American Revolution*, she defended her own right to write about "masculine" matters, such as war and politics, but she never argued that her privilege was a right that should be extended to other women.[46] Neither in her published writings nor in her private correspondence did she advocate a broader political or economic role for women.

Even on the one occasion when she had a chance to take a decisive stand on the issue, Warren remained silent. In 1776 Abigail Adams wrote to Mercy about her husband's patronizing dismissal of her plea to "Remember the Ladies" in writing a new code of laws for the nation.[47] "I thought it was very probable," Adams told her friend, that "our wise

Statesmen would enact a New Government and form a new code of Laws. I ventured to speak a word in behalf of our Sex, who are rather hardly dealt with by the Laws of England which gives such unlimitted power to the Husband to use his wife Ill." She mentioned her "threat," partly serious and partly jocular in nature, that women would stage a rebellion if their demands were not addressed. She noted John's infuriatingly "sausy" response and urged that Mercy join her in submitting "a petition to Congress."[48]

Warren, however, was not interested in petitioning Congress for women's rights. She never replied to the issues raised in Adams's letter. Although a crisis in Mercy's personal life may have precluded an immediate response, even when she resumed the correspondence Warren chose to ignore her friend's political protests. She showed no desire to foment a female "rebellion." Through her literary career Warren had found a way around the constraints of the gender status quo. Having made her own private accommodation, she saw no need for a broader alteration of sex roles.[49]

In contrast, the Federalist Murray was a vocal supporter of women's rights, as she defined the term. She believed the Revolution had opened up a whole new array of opportunities for American women. "Such is my confidence in THE SEX," she wrote, "that I expect to see our young women forming a new era in female history."[50] In her writings she forcefully and directly asserted the intellectual equality of men and women, promoted the expansion of educational opportunities for women, and advocated women's economic independence from men. In several published essays she celebrated the achievements of women from the past, including Semiramis of Nineveh, Zenobia, Sappho, Lady Astell, and many others. "Our object," she claimed, "is to prove, by examples, that the minds of women are *naturally* as susceptible of every improvement, as those of men."[51] Although accepting of women's subordination, she was much more critical than Warren of the limitations on women's role. "From the conspicuous rewards of merit, the female world seem injudiciously excluded," she wrote in the *Gleaner* essays. "To man, the road of preferment is thrown open—glory crowns the military hero—the bar, the pulpit, the medical career, the husbandman, the merchant, the statesman, these all have their *points* of *eminence*. . . . But the sex, agreeably to existing regulations, can enjoy but *secondary* or *reflected* fame."[52] Her intent was openly radical. Arguing that women were as heroic, patriotic, ingenious, energetic, and eloquent as men, she demanded "the female right to that *equality with their brethren, which, it is conceived, is assigned them in the Order of Nature.*"[53] Murray saw women's equality with men as a right rather than a privilege, necessitating a general reform of sex roles.

The divergence between Warren's and Murray's attitudes toward women in politics was no accident, neither a function of geography (since both were from Massachusetts) nor of gender (since both were women). The key to their differences resides in their larger political philosophies, particularly their ideas about liberty and the nature of the social structure. Whereas Warren's Republican sentiments diverted her from considering a broader role for women, Murray's Federalism created a context that enabled her to entertain such ideas.

The women voiced essentially the same views on political issues as the male members of their parties. As an adherent of the Republican party, Warren supported the French Revolution (at least in its early phases), opposed a concentration of power in the executive (which she deemed "a partiality for monarchy"),[54] and despised Hamilton's financial schemes. She regarded Jefferson's election in 1800 as a triumph for her brand of republicanism. Over and over in her *History of the American Revolution,* she stressed the centrality of individual rights and personal freedom as the basis of American society. Rejecting invidious class distinctions, she supported the reconstitution of American society based on certain key principles—"the natural equality of man, their right of adopting their own modes of government, the dignity of the people, and that sovereignty which cannot be ceded either to representatives or to kings."[55] Americans had a natural affinity for these ideas. "It was obvious to every one," she said, "that dignified ranks, ostentatious titles, splendid governments, and supernumerary expensive offices, to be supported by the labor of the poor, or the taxation of all the conveniences, were not the objects of the patriot. . . . The views of the virtuous of every class in those exertions, were for the purchase of freedom, independence, and competence, to themselves and their posterity."[56] She, like Jefferson, was a "friend of the people."[57]

Although a friend of the people, Warren clearly did not include herself or any other woman as part of "the people." When she discussed "the rights of men," for example, she literally meant, the rights of all males. "Natural equality" referred to a state existing among males, not females. She could not even conceive that political rights might be extended to women. While "virtue," as she wrote in her play *The Ladies of Castile,* "must spring from the maternal line,"[58] citizenship did not. Warren appeared neither to resent nor to object to women's exclusion from the polity.

Murray, however, came to quite different conclusions. Like other Federalists, Murray was an ardent supporter of President Washington. Unlike some other Federalists, she even championed John Adams, dedicating her book to him at the height of his unpopularity in the late 1790s. She also cast a skeptical eye toward the French Revolution and was repulsed, though not necessarily surprised, by its bloody excesses. More philosophically, Murray and other Federalists believed that freedom could be found within the constraints of a traditional hierarchical society, not outside of it. Her Federalist principles, she said, rested on the identification of her party with "the lovers of Peace, Order, and good Government."[59] She distrusted the masses and insisted that liberty depended on nature's "systems, her laws, and her regular chain of subordination."[60] Tampering with the established social order might lead to chaos, or even anarchy. "Custom," she claimed, "has judiciously affixed to the various ranks in society its ascertaining marks, and we cannot see her barriers thrown down, or the rushing together of the different classes of mankind, without regret."[61] Disparaging the possibility of an egalitarian social order, she quoted Dr. Samuel Johnson: "Your *levellers* . . . wish to *level down* as far as themselves, but they cannot bear levelling *up* to themselves; they would all have some people under them; why not then have *some people* above them?"[62] Whereas Warren's watchwords were "rights" and "equality," Murray's were "subordination" and "order." Her ideal was, as Federalist Samuel Stone put it, "a *speaking* aristocracy *in the face of a silent* democracy."[63]

The political views of Murray and Warren provide insight into the larger philosophical differences that underlay Federalist and Republican attitudes toward women. The Republicans' assault on the traditional social hierarchy precluded the possibility of their thinking creatively (or perhaps even thinking very much at all) about gender issues. In their efforts to expand the electorate, Republicans attacked the established order of society, especially the deferential notions of political authority and governance. Equality of rights, they claimed, provided a valid justification for more widespread, if not universal, participation in the electoral process. Merit and virtue should determine who should vote as well as who should be elected. Political life should be freed of the constricting restraints that had limited participation in the past and should be opened up to all men on a voluntary basis, without regard to wealth or property. To their credit, Republicans expounded a far more inclusive definition of political participation than any previous American political group. As historian Joyce Appleby has noted, Republican ideas did not simply "take aim at a class of men but rather at a concept of class itself— at the belief in inherent, ineradicable differences among men."[64] The threat of these ideas to the established order should not be minimized. Arguably, the Republicans' social vision was so radical for its time that any attempt to include other dispossessed groups would have doomed the party's efforts at reform for white males.

Yet as Warren's views demonstrate, the Democratic-Republican ideal possessed real limitations. Contrary to their rhetoric, Republicans did not seek to destroy social hierarchy altogether; they aimed to replace one hierarchy with another. In expanding the compass of political participation, they were not extending citizenship to all people—only to white males. In rejecting wealth as the basis of political privilege, they devised a social order in which supposed biological differences, as defined by gender, race, and age, determined relative status. Subordination would be for those for whom, as Pauline Maier put it, "dependency seemed right and natural."[65] To paraphrase Samuel Johnson, all white males could be leveled up because women, children, blacks, and Indians were leveled down. Ironically, Republican radicalism with regard to white males necessitated—at least in the short run—the exclusion of other dispossessed groups, including women, from political consideration.

Conversely, it was the Federalists' social conservatism that enabled them to be more receptive to women in both their institutions and their rhetoric. This is not to say that conservatism necessarily or regularly predisposes a group to more openness on women's issues. But at this particular time and place, Federalists, because they were not contesting the precedence of social distinctions, had a certain freedom to acknowledge, and even welcome, the political contributions of women. Obviously, the kind of participation they welcomed was extremely circumscribed in nature. Yet Federalists such as Murray showed greater willingness than the Republicans to see women's political potential and incorporate them into the process.

There was another dynamic at work as well. J. H. Hexter and others have pointed out that eighteenth-century Anglo-American society inherited both a negative and a positive tradition of liberty.[66] Republicans espoused the negative, or liberal, tradition that defined rights largely in terms of freedom from state intervention. Assuming the existence of a society composed of atomistic individuals separately pursuing their own private interests, they conceived of freedom in a narrow legalistic sense that protected the individual's rights from intrusions by the state. The

Republicans' liberal ideal did not presuppose any particular vision of the social order; rather, as Hexter noted, it presumed "that liberty was a collection of rights belonging to free men regardless of the structure of society." Federalists, on the other hand, adhered to a positive rights tradition that depended on an organic, hierarchical conception of society. Liberty consisted of the freedom to participate in the polity, such that each person or group could, through the practice of civic virtue, make a contribution to the general welfare. The Federalists' positive rights tradition thus possessed a "sociological dimension"[67] that the Republican tradition lacked.

These differing notions of liberty affected the parties' ability to appreciate what women had to offer. Drawing on negative ideas of liberty, the Republicans defined political participation narrowly. They saw legal rights and privileges in terms of voting or holding public office. As a result, they tended to overlook or ignore the contributions of those who were not officially incorporated into the system—most especially women, but also blacks and Indians. Federalists, on the other hand, understood that political participation extended well beyond the possession of certain legal privileges. "Politics" encompassed a variety of informal activities, such as attendance at political functions, the presentation of flags to the militia, and the rearing of republican sons—all of which women were able to do within the existing political system.

Thus it was the Federalists' continuing embrace of what the Republicans had rejected—a hierarchical society and a positive rights tradition—that allowed them to think more expansively about women's political contributions than their adversaries. The Federalists articulated a kind of archaic feminism founded on a nonliberal, anti-individualistic basis. Their theory stands in stark contrast to later ideas of women's rights, such as the Seneca Falls Declaration, which were grounded in the same sources as the Republicans' egalitarian individualism. Although the Federalist idea represented a kind of intellectual dead end, in that it did not lead to a collective movement for the expansion of women's rights, Federalist feminism is worthy of note—not least because it reveals the necessary, if temporary, costs of Jeffersonian ideology to the dispossessed.

Perhaps in the end it matters less which party took greater notice of women and more that both parties acknowledged women's existence as political entities, to a greater or lesser extent. Women were far more in evidence in the era of the first party system than historians have realized. Nonetheless, it seems no accident that the decline of the Federalist party coincided with the diminution of women's role in the nation's political life. The triumph of Republicanism meant that women were excluded from politics primarily, and not incidentally, because of their sex. The political assumptions and institutional mechanisms that had allowed women a small but significant place in the nation's political life disappeared. It took a later generation of social conservatives—the Whigs—to revive that possibility.[6]

7

THE PROBLEM OF SLAVERY IN
THE AGE OF FEDERALISM

Paul Finkelman

HISTORIANS OF the Founding often have difficulty dealing with slavery. It is an uncomfortable subject. William Wiecek brilliantly compared discussions of slavery at the Constitutional Convention to the "Witch at the Christening" in a fairy tale—the uninvited evil guest who comes to curse the whole society. Scholars of the Age of Federalism prefer to discuss the creation of democratic political institutions, the adoption of the Bill of Rights, the rise of a great nation. Thus, Stanley Elkins and Eric McKitrick wrote that after the Revolution, Americans "possessed—or imagined they did—the one essential element, hitherto lacking, for releasing the creative energies of an already favored people. This was individual liberty. An all-but-miraculous force, liberty would give wings to every conceivable endeavor."[1]

While personal liberty and constitutional government were surely the great accomplishments of the Revolution, slavery is nevertheless a striking reminder of the incompleteness of that Revolution. Sadly many scholars who focus on the early national period deal with slavery by ignoring it or explaining it away.[2] For example, in their 900-page book *The Age of Federalism* Elkins and McKitrick barely acknowledged the existence of slavery. It comes up nine times in the index, and all of the references are to passing mentions of slavery as part of some larger discussion.[3] It is as though slavery was epiphenomenal—an institution existing outside of the political, economic, constitutional, legal, diplomatic, and social structures of the society.

This is peculiar because the United States began as a slaveholding nation. In 1776 slavery was legal in all of the American states, although its importance as an economic and social institution varied tremendously. By 1787 Massachusetts and New Hampshire had abolished the institution, and Pennsylvania, Connecticut, and Rhode Island had adopted gradual emancipation statutes, guaranteeing its eventual end. New York and New Jersey joined this "first emancipation" before the end of Jefferson's first presidential term. By the end of the Age of Federalism, new states, slave and free, had entered the Union, and the nation had become, in language Abraham Lincoln would coin a half century later, "half slave and half free."[4] The emergence of the free North during the Age of Federalism was in itself a tremendous accomplishment. Rarely has a master class so peacefully voted itself out of existence.

The virtual absence of slavery from *The Age of Federalism* is also odd because the authors call this period an "Age of Passion."[5] But nothing stirred passions greater than slavery, both for Americans who found it abhorrent and those who vehemently defended it. Slavery was one of the key issues debated at the Constitutional Convention, which was the birthplace of the Age of Federalism.[6] Some of the most passionate opposition to the Constitution came from Anti-Federalists opposed to slavery. Similarly, during the Age of Federalism southerners began to passionately defend slavery on racial and pseudoscientific grounds and to argue for the necessity of a permanent system of racially based bondage in the new nation. The Age of Federalism spawned a firming of resolve on the part of southerners and the emergence of a pro-slavery ideology to defend bondage.

Coming to terms with the importance of slavery in the Age of Federalism requires setting some parameters for both the age and the term itself. Elkins and McKitrick have a weirdly constricted notion of the Age of Federalism. Like John Adams climbing into a stagecoach to start his long trek back to Boston at 4:00 A.M. on the morning of Jefferson's inauguration, the Age of Federalism, as Elkins and McKitrick imagine it, disappeared into the night air sometime between sundown on March 3, 1801, and sunrise on March 4. Implicitly, they define the "age" to coincide with the time the political party controlled the presidency.

This is a curious notion of an "Age." At the national level the Federalist party had the potential of regaining national power at least until 1812.[7] Moreover, the Federalist party continued to be a factor in national and state politics until at least 1820. In New York, for example, Federalists sometimes held power after 1801 and "remained a substantial electoral threat to their opponents until 1820."[8] In New England the party remained in power even longer. Josiah Quincy was the Federalist speaker of the Massachusetts House of Representatives in 1822 and mayor of Boston from 1823 to 1829.

During the Missouri debates of 1819–21, Federalists for the last time acted as a recognizable national political force, marshaling most northerners in Congress to support at least some restriction on slavery in the western territories. While the Missouri debates were the last gasp of organized Federalist political activity, Federalism lived on. Federalist politicians were successful without their party. John Quincy Adams, for example, was a Federalist in his policies and ideas, despite his rejection of the party in 1812.

Finally, it is worth remembering that, especially after John Marshall's decision in *Marbury v. Madison* (1803), the Supreme Court constituted a third, if not quite equal, branch of the national government. That branch remained firmly in Federalist hands until the 1830s.

Indeed, one might argue that the final coup de grâce to Federalism came not at the hands of Thomas Jefferson but rather at the hands of Andrew Jackson. The destruction of the Bank of the United States, an end to federally supported internal improvements, a sea change on the Supreme Court, the Indian removal, the belligerent western expansion culminating in a war of aggression again Mexico, and the disfranchisement of blacks where they had previously voted—this was the Jacksonian agenda that destroyed Federalism. Well after 1801, when Federalists ceased to dominate politics, many of their ideas—Marshall's vision of the commerce clause, Hamilton's concept of a national bank and a uniform system of currency, Washington's notion of reasonably fair treatment for Native Americans—remained viable. However, Jacksonian Democracy finished off all of these notions.

SLAVERY AND POLITICS IN THE AGE OF FEDERALISM

Throughout the Age of Federalism slavery was a significant factor in politics. We conventionally date the emergence of slavery as a central political issue with the Missouri Compromise controversy, but as James Roger Sharp correctly notes, during the early national period "sectionalism, as it had been since the Revolution, . . . was the main catalyst inciting political conflict."[9] Slavery was at the center of that sectionalism.

Moreover, Federalism affected the debate over slavery beyond 1820. Although their party was no more, a number of prominent Federalists and ex-Federalists took strong stands against slavery and the emerging "slave power." John Quincy Adams of Massachusetts, Joseph C. Hornblower of New Jersey, Samuel Fessenden of Maine, and William Jay of New York are striking examples of neo-Federalist opponents to slavery. In addition to prominent political leaders, many abolitionists, such as William Lloyd Garrison, Wendell Phillips, and the Tappan brothers, were the cultural (and often the biological) descendants of the Federalists. "That so many sons of Federalist fathers assumed leading roles in the abolitionist crusade after 1815 was certainly not coincidental."[10]

These second- and third-generation Federalists resurrected ideas about slavery that their Federalist parents had used. For example, Federalists understood that the three-fifths clause gave the South—especially Virginia—undue power in the national government. Had slaves not been counted for purposes of representation and the electoral college, John Adams, not Thomas Jefferson, would have been elected president in 1800. Opposition to the three-fifths clause was a major component of demands of the Hartford Convention. Abolitionists later made similar points. In *The Constitution a Pro-Slavery Compact*, Wendell Phillips, the scion of a Massachusetts Federalist family, analyzed "that 'compromise,' . . . between slavery and freedom, in 1787" which among other things, gave the South extra political muscle through the three-fifths clause.[11]

Thus Federalists and Federalist ideas persisted past the demise of the Adams administration and the dissolution of the party itself. In some ways the Federalists helped lay the groundwork for what would become the abolitionist critique of American politics. Moreover, the Federalists set a tone for some measure of racial equality in opposition to the Jeffersonians, who fostered the emerging racially based pro-slavery argument.

From the Constitutional Convention to the Missouri Compromise, Federalists often opposed the pro-slavery racism of the Jeffersonians. As Linda Kerber demonstrated, Federalists "in dissent" were antislavery.[12]

The Northwest Ordinance

While the Constitutional Convention was in session in Philadelphia, the Congress operating under the Articles of Confederation adopted the Northwest Ordinance, with its famous, although not immediately successful, ban on slavery in the western territories north of the Ohio River.[13] It is of course anachronistic to ascribe the Northwest Ordinance to "federalists," since there were none at the time of its passage. However, the two men most responsible for the prohibition of slavery in the ordinance, Manassah Cutler and Nathan Dane, soon became Federalist politicians of "the old school."[14]

Furthermore, the slavery prohibition in the ordinance may be seen as a proto-Federalist measure in that it embodied three themes the Federalists later embraced: the notion that the central government should have the power to set economic policy for the nation, the idea that commerce (in this case land sales) was important to the nation, and opposition to slavery. When the Federalists did take power under the new Constitution, they reenacted the ordinance.

The Constitution and Its Adoption

While the Confederation Congress was adopting the ordinance, the Constitutional Convention was deeply involved in a debate over the place of slavery in the new republic. The record of the convention on slavery is not terribly admirable. Most delegates, whatever their subsequent political affiliations, were willing to make pro-slavery compromises. But what little opposition to slavery was found in the convention generally came from future Federalists like Rufus King, Alexander Hamilton, Gouverneur Morris, and William Paterson. Frustrated by persistent southern demands for special considerations for slavery, Morris wondered if the Union was worth it: "Either this distinction is fictitious or real: if fictitious let it be dismissed and let us proceed with due confidence. If it be real, instead of attempting to blend incompatible things, let us at once take a friendly leave of each other. There can be no end of demands for security if every particular interest is to be entitled to it."[15] Morris later argued that counting slaves for representation "when fairly explained comes to this: that the inhabitant of Georgia and South Carolina who goes to the Coast of Africa, and in defiance of the most sacred laws of humanity tears away his fellow creatures from their dearest connections and damns them to the most cruel bondages, shall have more votes in a Government instituted for protection of the rights of mankind, than the Citizen of Pennsylvania or New Jersey who views with a laudable horror, so nefarious a practice."[16]

The document that emerged accommodated the needs and demands of slavery at almost every turn. Slavery affected the makeup of Congress, the method of choosing the president, interstate relations, and the regulation of commerce. The document that launched the Age of Federalism was subsequently called a "Covenant With Death" by the Garrisonian abolitionists.

Many northerners opposed the Constitution because of its pro-slavery provisions: the three-fifths clause, the prohibition on ending the slave trade until at least 1808, and the guarantee that the national government would suppress slave rebellions. "A Countryman from Dutchess County" thought that Americans might become "a happy and respectable people" if under the Constitution the states were forced into "relinquishing every idea of drenching the bowels of Africa in gore, for the sake of enslaving its free-born innocent inhabitants." In New Hampshire, Joshua Atherton told his fellow delegates to that state's ratifying convention: "We will not lend the aid of our ratification to this cruel and inhuman merchandise, not even for a day. There is a great distinction in not taking a part in the most barbarous violation of the sacred laws of God and humanity, and our becoming guaranties for its exercise for a term of years." "A Friend of the Rights of People" asked: "Can we then hold up our hands for a Constitution that licences this bloody practice? Can we who have fought so hard for Liberty give our consent to have it taken away from others? May the powers above forbid."[17]

This critique forced northern supporters of the Constitution—the original Federalists—to offer less than candid answers on how the document dealt with slavery. James Wilson, who surely knew better, told the Pennsylvania ratifying convention that the clause would allow Congress to end all slavery in the United States. Wilson argued that after "the lapse of a few years, . . . Congress will have power to exterminate Slavery within our borders."[18] This of course was decidedly not the case.

Wilson, Hamilton, Jay, King, and other supporters of the Constitution overlooked, talked around, or ignored the pro-slavery implications of the Constitution. This was politically smart. Having made compromises over slavery, they now wanted to get the document ratified. Once it was ratified, however, Federalists were more likely than Republicans to oppose slavery in state and national politics. After ratification, some Federalists would devote a good deal of their energy to undoing or modifying the very compromises over slavery they had helped make.

Slavery in Politics: The 1790s

Hardly had the new government begun when slavery threatened sectional harmony. "Some of the sharpest remarks heard by the first Congress" followed a proposal that the national government tax slaves imported from Africa. In this short debate South Carolinians and Georgians vociferously defended slavery with arguments anticipating the "positive good" defense of slavery that became common a generation later. Georgia's James Jackson, who became a stalwart Jeffersonian, also attacked the idea of allowing free blacks in the United States, declaring "he was opposed to the 'liberty of negroes' under any circumstances."[19] A year later Congress erupted over a petition signed by Benjamin Franklin urging action to curb slavery and the slave trade. The most virulent opposition to this proposal came from Thomas Tudor Tucker, who would later become the treasurer of the United States under Jefferson. Aedanus Burke, who later emerged as a Jeffersonian, threatened an end to the new Union if Congress considered any limitation on the African trade.[20]

Although slavery had the potential to disrupt politics and national harmony, sectional cooperation also smoothed over some slavery-related issues. Thus in 1793 Congress passed the first criminal extradition statute because Virginia refused to return to Pennsylvania three men charged with kidnapping a free black. The act also included the first fugitive slave law.[21]

In this period party affiliation was uncertain, and the connection between party affiliation and slavery was tenuous. It is probable that a careful analysis of all roll-call votes in Congress on slavery—something beyond the scope of this essay—would reveal a pattern that shows Federalists or future Federalists were more inclined to oppose slavery than Republicans or future Republicans. More significant than the party affiliation is the understanding that in this early period slavery was already a divisive issue with a potential to cause sectional disharmony.

Slavery and the Growth of the Nation

Slavery was also part of the story of the growth of the nation in the Age of Federalism. At the Constitutional Convention most delegates assumed (incorrectly, as it turned out) that the South would grow faster than the North. Vermont (1791), Ohio (1803), and Indiana (1816) entered the Union with constitutions that flatly prohibited slavery. Illinois, less emphatic in its opposition to slavery, allowed some forms of bondage to continue in what was clearly not yet "the Land of Lincoln." In 1799 New York passed its gradual emancipation statute, putting that state on the road to freedom. New Jersey followed suit in 1804. By 1819 the North had emerged as a region free of slavery. Meanwhile, new southern states —Kentucky (1793), Tennessee (1796), Louisiana (1812), Mississippi (1817), and Alabama (1819)—strengthened the South. By the time Congress debated the admission of Missouri, sectionalism, and the need for a sectional balance in the Senate, was obvious to anyone who cared to notice it.

The Missouri debate is often seen as the opening salvo in the sectional war, as northern Federalists—or politicians who had once been Federalists—took the high ground in attacking slavery. Jeffersonian Republicans, who had so successfully vanquished the Federalists in the preceding two decades, fought hard to allow slavery to spread into the empire that their hero had acquired from France. This was consistent with the Republican emphasis on westward expansion. Federalists viewed trade and commerce as the way to make the nation grow; Republicans wanted more land and westward settlement, including the spread of slavery.[22]

At his home outside Charlottesville, the leader of the Republicans brooded over this debate, because the Federalists seemed to have come alive once again and were threatening to curtail both the settlement of the West and the growth of slavery. Congressman John Holmes, who had drifted into the Republican party when his own Federalist party began to collapse, asked the Sage of Monticello to endorse a restriction on slavery. Jefferson responded that the Missouri crisis had, "like a fire bell in the night, awakened and filled" him "with terror." Jefferson feared the crisis would destroy the nation he had worked so hard to build. Rebuffing Holmes, Jefferson wrote, "I regret, that I am now to die in the belief, that the useless sacrifice of themselves by the generation of 1776, to acquire self-government and happiness to their country, is to be thrown away by the unwise and unworthy passions of their sons." Jefferson bemoaned that his countrymen, misled by Federalists like Rufus King, Daniel Webster, and even Justice Joseph Story,[23] were willing to risk national harmony over slavery. Jefferson despaired that his fellow white citizens could "perpetrate this act of suicide on themselves, and of treason against the hopes of the world," over, of all things, the place in society of a people Jefferson believed were inferior.[24]

Slavery and Foreign Policy in the Age of Federalism

Slavery was also an important aspect of early national foreign policy, but Federalist foreign policy was ambivalent or hostile to slavery. The Treaty of Paris (1783) obligated Great Britain to return slaves who had escaped with the British army, but Federalists never pushed hard for the actual return of such slaves. Hamilton argued that the British should "make indemnification for, not restoration of, Negroes carried away." John Jay understood the treaty to require the actual restoration of the American slaves, but in his negotiations with England in the 1790s that led to the treaty which bore his name, Jay, "in a strongly humanitarian way," was willing to accept monetary compensation. Washington "discouraged his fellow Virginians from their efforts to regain slaves freed by the British."[25]

Jefferson, on the other hand, wanted the British to return the former slaves who had gained their freedom by entering British lines. In 1794 the newly organized Republicans managed to secure House (but not Senate) passage of a nonintercourse resolution calling for a boycott of British trade until, among other things, the British returned slaves who had escaped with them at the end of the war.[26] When debating the Jay

Treaty, Republicans attempted to force the issue of compensation for slaves. This may have simply been a ploy to defeat the treaty by splitting off southern Federalists who otherwise supported the treaty. The move failed by a vote of 15 to 12. After the treaty had passed by the necessary two-thirds majority, the Republicans "in a last gasp of protest" once again "moved to renew discussion on compensation for the Negroes." In 1795 a Democratic-Republican Society in South Carolina asserted that the failure to gain full "compensation for the value of the Negroes" who gained their freedom by leaving with the British army was an "insurmountable objection" to the treaty "were there no others."[27]

The contrast between Jay and Jefferson on this issue illustrates the difference between Federalists and Republicans on issues involving slavery. Jay ultimately refused to press for the return of slaves because there was obviously something horrible about demanding that people who escaped to find liberty should be returned to bondage. Furthermore, Jay "believed that satisfaction for the Negroes had been obtained, 'though not in express words,'" when he gained the northwest posts and won privileges for his country's vessels in the British West Indies."[28] For the Federalists trade was clearly a higher priority than regaining custody of escaped slaves.

For the Jeffersonians, regaining their slaves, or at least obtaining direct compensation for them, seemed to be a matter of principle. It became an inordinately high priority for them. Even after the ratification of the treaty, the Jeffersonian press "recurrently reminded" Americans "that England continued to violate the treaty of 1783 by withholding compensation for kidnapped negro slaves. "These papers attacked the Jay Treaty in part because "the carrying of Negro slaves" was "not even mentioned." Ironically, in the aftermath of the XYZ affair Jeffersonians complained that a defeat of the French, which Federalist policy might lead to, would "insure slavery to man for centuries to come."[29] Presumably, if the Federalists supported France, the Jeffersonians would have been free to continue to enslave their own blacks for "centuries to come."

EXPLAINING THE FEDERALISTS

Most opponents of slavery in the early national period were motivated by religion, Revolutionary sentiments, or both.[30] There was no such thing as an antislavery party until the emergence of the Liberty party in 1840. The first political parties were surely uninterested in discussing the issue at all. It was a divisive issue at the Constitutional Convention and had the potential to rip apart the fragile bonds of Union in the early years. Nevertheless, as Donald Robinson has demonstrated, slavery was a constant and pervasive issue in American politics from the Revolution until the Missouri debates.[31]

Slavery led to sectional conflict. The North emerged as a free section; the South as a slave section. Where tobacco, rice, and cotton grew, slavery flourished. It did less well where fishing, commerce, wheat, and cattle were more common and where manufacturing was taking hold. Federalists, as we know, were more powerful in the North, especially New England and parts of New York.

But beyond the economic and geographic aspects of slavery, was there also a political or ideological dimension to Federalists' opposition to slavery? Why were northern Federalists more hostile to slavery than their Republican neighbors? Why were southern Republicans more rabid in defense of slavery than their Federalist neighbors? Why were Federalists somehow different from the Republicans when it came to thinking and legislating about slavery and race?

Federalists and Opposition to Slavery

Although the political parties did not take a position against slavery, many politicians did. Republicans were severely constrained in their opposition to slavery because their party was so dominated by the slaveholding elite of Virginia. After 1800 any criticism of slavery was an implicit criticism of Jefferson and his cohorts. Those northern Republicans opposed to slavery were "by and large, embarrassed by their partisan connections with Southern slaveholders."[32]

Federalists, on the other hand, were in a strong position to attack slavery. Not only was the party more solidly based in the North, but its slaveholding president, George Washington, voluntarily freed his slaves in his will. Thus some Federalists opposed slavery through private actions; others did so through state and local politics or through participation in manumission societies; still others tried to shape national policies to challenge the institution. Although there are some important exceptions to this, generally speaking Federalists were more likely to oppose slavery than Republicans. Similarly, on the related question of the rights of free blacks, Federalists tended to be less racist and more accommodating than their Republican opponents. Indeed, after the Revolution "what remained of the antislavery cause in the North therefore passed into the Federalist Party."[33]

The most obvious example of this can be seen in the three Federalist presidents of the nation's early years, George Washington, John Adams, and John Quincy Adams.[34] Two of these—John Adams and John Quincy Adams—were the only presidents elected before 1836 who had never owned slaves. Moreover, both Adamses, but especially John Quincy, were the only northern presidents before Lincoln who actually opposed slavery.[35]

George Washington, although a slave owner, was never committed to slavery and was the only president to manumit his slaves. At the Constitutional Convention he was a strong nationalist, ready to sacrifice slavery to strengthen the Union.[36] His opposition to the institution stands out, especially when compared to Jefferson. "As President, Washington was sensitive to the scandal of a national leader holding slaves, and he hired white servants to do the publicly visible work at his residence." Jefferson, of course, brought his choice slaves with him to the new presidential mansion in the District of Columbia.[37]

Leading northern Federalists—Alexander Hamilton, John Jay, Gouverneur Morris, Jared Ingersoll, Joseph Bloomfield, Francis Hopkinson, Elias Boudinot, and Josiah Quincy—joined abolition societies or worked against slavery in some other way. These men, and their children, continued to fight slavery after the early national period. "Most of the great American philanthropists in 1819 were Federalists, and these had opposed slavery all their lives, regardless of whether they had a political ax to grind."[38]

Starting with the election of 1800, northern Federalists constantly reminded voters of the connection between Jeffersonianism and slavery. Sometimes the connection was personal. In 1800 there were allegations of "Mr. Jefferson's Congo Harem." After 1802 there was the story of Sally Hemings, "The African Venus."[39]

Scholars and others have been so caught up in the debate over Jefferson's personal morality that they have failed to adequately explore why the Federalists would have raised such an issue, and why it should have mattered. The allegations about Jefferson and Hemings go to the heart of part of the emerging Federalist critique of slavery, upon which abolitionists would later expand. The Federalists pointed out—with the Master of Monticello as their prime evidence—that slavery was fundamentally immoral and led to exploitation of blacks, personal sinfulness among whites, and naturally corrupted American politics. It was the essence of hypocrisy to be a slave owner and call oneself a democrat. Federalists zeroed in on the "domestic monarch [who] writes and spouts incessantly about . . . the *danger of power*" but of course abused others with his power. Josiah Quincy "mocked Jefferson's first inaugural: 'Intimacy . . . with all women—matrimonial alliance with none.'"[40] Whatever his relationship with Sally Hemings, Jefferson provided a convenient proxy for all southern white men who did father children with their slaves, in violation of Federalist notions of morality and religious teachings.[41]

Federalists also pointed out that slavery produced a dissolute society filled with lazy, pompous, domineering planters. Josiah Quincy suggested that "Democracy" was really "an Indian word, signifying '*a great tobacco planter, who had herds of black slaves.*'" "They starve their Negroes," Roger Griswold complained, while Thomas Boylston Adams argued that "there is a spirit of domination engrafted on the character of the southern people" which made them the "most imperious" "inhabitants of this continent."[42]

Free Blacks and Federalists

During the Age of Federalism blacks who were enfranchised generally supported the Federalists. Massachusetts changed its suffrage laws in 1811 by opening "the vote for town officers to all adult males except paupers." This led to increased voter participation in 1812. In Salem blacks who had previously not voted did so, resulting in Federalists taking over what previously had been a Republican-controlled town meeting.[43] Given an opportunity to cast a ballot against the party of slaveholding Virginians and the Embargo,[44] the blacks in Salem naturally gravitated to the Federalists.

In Pennsylvania the majority of the Quaker abolitionists openly affiliated with the Federalists, as did most black voters. In Philadelphia it was "almost an oddity" to find a Jeffersonian involved with the Pennsylvania Abolition Society. "Among several hundred members of the Democratic-Republican Society of Philadelphia . . . only two belonged to the PAS."[45] By the 1790s the Jeffersonian newspapers, including William Duane's *Aurora,* were among the few in the city that continued to run advertisements for slave sales. Such advertisements suggest that people interested in buying and selling slaves were most likely to be Jeffersonians and that Federalist editors may have refused to accept advertisements for sale of human beings. By 1800, as Gary Nash and Jean Soderlund have concluded, "the antislavery impulse" in Philadelphia was in the hands of Quakers and "those who subscribed to a failing Federalist political persuasion." The Republicans, meanwhile, began to war against black rights. In 1813 a Republican paper declared free blacks were "useless," while that same year a Republican politician proposed legislation to prohibit free blacks from entering the state and to sell into servitude any black convicted of a crime.[46]

In most cities the Jeffersonians appealed to the white working class. In the seventeenth century blacks and whites had worked side by side, and "the two despised groups initially saw each other as sharing the same predicament."[47] But by the 1790s this was a forgotten past. In northern cities white workers, particularly Irish immigrants, already were pitted against blacks. In Philadelphia the Republicans appealed to the Irish while at the same time "becoming overtly hostile to the city's growing black population."[48]

New York provides a good case study. Many important and wealthy New Yorkers owned slaves. It would not have been out of character for an aristocrat like Jay or a parvenu like Hamilton to accept slavery and perhaps even own slaves themselves, as Jay did. Instead, Jay helped organize the New York Manumission Society. Leading New York Federalists, like Jay, Hamilton, Gouverneur Morris, James Duane, and Philip Schuyler, were early and active opponents of slavery in the state. They lived in a state that was late in moving toward abolition. In 1799 New York became the penultimate state to adopt a gradual abolition law. The vote on the 1799 law, "enacted by a Federalist legislature and signed by" Jay, "a Federalist governor," appears to have been somewhat partisan, with Federalists more likely to support gradual emancipation than Republicans.[49] Jay's antislavery legacy was later carried on by his son, Judge William Jay, and his grandson John Jay, Jr. In the antebellum period both of the younger Jays were active abolitionists who viewed their opposition to slavery as a continuation of Chief Justice Jay's Federalist ideology.

In comparison to Jay and Hamilton, with the exception of Chancellor Robert R. Livingston, there is no evidence that leaders of the Republicans in New York like George Clinton and DeWitt Clinton cared much about slavery or the plight of free blacks.[50] As governor DeWitt Clinton sought the repeal of a portion of the gradual emancipation law that encouraged masters to free their slaves. By 1820 Clinton's faction of the New York Republicans at least openly opposed the extension of slavery in the West. However, Martin Van Buren, who came to control the Democrats in New York, supported the interests of slavery at the end of the Federalist period and beyond. The Fox of Kinderhook refused even to take a public stand on the Missouri Compromise, while many in his faction, the Bucktails, "were generally lukewarm" in support of any antislavery measures and "opposed" to any restrictions on slavery in Missouri or the West. According to Rufus King, the Federalist senator from New York, Van Buren's ally, Senator Daniel D. Tomkins, "fled the field . . . of battle" on the day of the vote in Congress over restricting slavery in Missouri and the West.

In the mid-1820s Van Buren tried to resurrect the old Jeffersonian alliance of "the planters of the South and the plain Republicans of the North."[51]

New York blacks voted overwhelmingly Federalist. The traditional explanation for this is that free blacks had been owned by kindly Federalist masters, and that these blacks "who had been well treated, stood by the 'families' after freedom almost as faithfully as before."[52] More likely, however, free blacks in New York and elsewhere were Federalists for three concrete reasons. First, blacks agreed with Federalist policies supporting emancipation in the North, Haitian independence, and an end to the slave trade. Federalists filled the ranks of the emancipation societies from Virginia to New England. Second, Federalist economic policy, including expanded trade, dovetailed with the heavy concentration of free blacks in the maritime industry. Third, blacks saw no alternative: Jefferson's was the party of slavery. The Republican leaders were Virginia masters. In the North the Republicans supported slavery and opposed black rights. "Anti-Negro prejudice eventually became a test of party regularity for the New York Republican party."[53] Jefferson and his party wanted to destroy the "black Republic" in Haiti. Thus for quite logical reasons, having nothing to do with the kindness of their former owners, black voters gravitated to the Federalist party, which accepted them, and moved away from the Republican party, which in fact wanted nothing to do with them. In the 1790s, for example, the Philadelphia Democratic-Republican Society rejected a black who wished to join.[54]

In the 1808 election New York Republicans attacked Federalists with a campaign song that included the verse, "Federalists with blacks unite." Black voters, meanwhile, endorsed the Federalists and attacked Jefferson's Embargo, which probably hurt northern free blacks harder than any other single group because so many of the men in that community were sailors, shipyard workers, or sailmakers.[55] When Republicans gained control of the New York state legislature in 1811, they attempted to restrict black voters by requiring that they show proof of their status as freemen. Federalists who controlled the Council of Revision defeated this "humiliating" and "wanton insult . . . on account of their complexion."[56]

Not surprisingly, free blacks in New York continued to vote Federalist. So did other easily identifiable groups. However, the followers of Jefferson only singled out blacks, in an attempt to stigmatize them and then disfranchise them. Republicans, even in the North, opposed free blacks and, by extension, supported slavery. In New York and elsewhere in the North, Federalists stood for emancipation and black rights.

In 1821, when the New York Constitutional Convention debated revising the requirements for suffrage in the state, Republicans pushed for the removal of property requirements for white male voters and the full disfranchisement of blacks. This was the essence of Jeffersonian "democracy." Federalists supported the right of black men to vote. Noting that blacks with property could already vote, Chancellor James Kent, one of the last of the New York Federalist leaders, argued that the goal of the convention was not "to *disfranchise* any portion of the community or to take away their rights." Peter Augustus Jay, Judge Jonas Platt, and other Federalists joined Kent in arguing against racial discrimination in the franchise. Leading the charge against black suffrage were the Republicans who had supported Jefferson and soon would follow Andrew Jackson. Here ideology and political strategy went hand in hand: blacks in New York generally supported the Federalists, so disfranchising them made good sense to the Republicans.[57]

Haiti as a Test Case for Federalist and Republican Attitudes toward Race

The most profound example of the difference between Federalists and Jeffersonians over slavery can be found in American relations with St. Domingue, or Haiti as it is now called. In the 1790s a series of slave revolts destroyed the system of human bondage on the island. John Adams and his Federalist administration viewed this revolution with great sympathy. For many Federalists, Toussaint L'Ouverture was the Haitian Washington, leading his people out of colonial domination. Adams encouraged the new regime and quickly developed a strong economic relationship with Haiti. While not according Haiti full diplomatic recognition, the Adams administration was moving in that direction.

Although not directly affecting the United States, the image of slaves emulating the American Revolutionaries was enough to send shivers of fear through the South. Some Republicans opposed the new regime in Haiti because of their close ties to France. Southern Republicans, fearful that their own slaves might follow the lead of Toussaint L'Ouverture, naturally opposed the Haitian Revolution. As one scholar sympathetic to the Republicans and the liberation of Haiti noted, "Although there were scores of resolutions adopted by the popular societies hailing and supporting the French Revolution, not one was passed supporting another revolution occurring at the same time—the black revolution of slaves in the French West Indies."[58] Federalists were more friendly to the liberation of Haiti. The revolt against French rule dovetailed with their Francophobia. Federalists opposed to slavery were naturally sympathetic to ending slavery there. Federalist support for Haiti seems to have been even stronger than the Anglophile streak in that party. The Federalists "lent little aid or comfort to the British while His Majesty's forces mounted a savage four-year-long assault on the island, though American interests in trade lay manifestly more with monarchical Britain than with incendiary St. Domingue."[59] In 1799 the United States was actively trading with Haiti and, more importantly, providing arms and supplies to Toussaint. The normally Anglophile Federalists rejected concerns of the British who looked upon this support of Toussaint with "horror." In February 1799 a new law, passed by the Federalist-dominated Congress, authorized President Adams to lift the embargo on Haiti. Secretary of State Pickering immediately sent Edward Stevens to the island for face-to-face negotiations with L'Ouverture. Stevens traveled "in a ship loaded with provisions for Toussaint, escorted by an American warship."[60] Quickly Stevens negotiated an agreement that allowed British and American merchants access to the Haitian markets.

A variety of circumstances—including the Quasi-War with France and the interests of New England merchants—led Federalists to support the revolution of Toussaint L'Ouverture. As early as June 1798 Secretary of State Timothy Pickering indicated that Americans would look kindly on an independent black republic in Haiti with L'Ouverture at the top. It is impossible to imagine Secretary of State Jefferson taking such a position. Indeed, at the very time his nation was aiding L'Ouverture, Jefferson was fretting about the possibility that the example of Haiti would spread to the United States. Commenting on Haiti, Jefferson wrote a friend, "If something is not done & soon done, we shall be the murderers of our own children."[61]

By 1800 Haiti was in the throes of a civil war, not between the master class and the slaves but between an army of mulattoes—*gens de couleur*—led by General André Rigaud and L'Ouverture's army of ex-slaves. In the final battle of this war an American frigate "stood off the port, cutting out Rigaud's supply vessels, and in the final assault used her artillery to bombard Rigaud's harbor forts and compel their evacuation." Some months later another American ship captured Rigaud at sea.[62]

Under the Federalist regime of John Adams and Secretary of State Pickering, the United States urged the Haitians to declare their independence; under Jefferson and Secretary of State Madison, the nation offered France help to suppress the slave rebellion. For Republicans, Haiti was a frightening prospect. Jefferson was obsessed with Haiti, fearful that the slave revolt would become a model for slave unrest in the South. Republican policies reflected the fears of their leaders and of the slaveholding elite of the South.

The results of these differences are clear. When Federalists were in power, trade with Haiti ballooned. "Before Jefferson became president, the value of the American exchange with St. Domingue was perhaps seven times the value of the French commerce on the Island." This ended with the end of Federalist rule, as Jefferson and his colleagues in the House and Senate imposed an embargo on the black republic. As historian Rayford Logan observed, "In 1799 a strong Federalist majority had been in favor of reopening trade with Haiti. In 1806 an overwhelming Democratic majority closed that trade."[63]

When Jefferson became president, he recalled Edward Stevens and replaced him with Tobias Lear, a cipher of limited abilities. When Lear arrived at St. Domingue he carried no letter or other official greeting from the new president. Toussaint L'Ouverture "complained bitterly" about this, and Lear lamely replied that because he was merely a commercial agent it was not "customary" to present such a letter or other commission from the president. L'Ouverture knew better. He declared to Lear that "his colour was the cause of his being neglected."[64] More precisely, it was the color prejudices of President Jefferson and his party. Thus, "in St. Domingue it was the Federalists who held far more closely to the faith of the founders and the Jeffersonian Republicans who tried far more tenaciously to tether and traduce the will of the people. It was the Federalists who were keen to aid the oppressed in their effort at independence and the Republicans who resisted that effort. It was the Federalists who fostered freedom and the Republicans who attempted the restoration of a colonial regime and, indeed, the reimposition of slavery itself."[65]

The debate over the embargo on St. Domingue illustrates the distinction between Federalists and Republicans on questions of race and slavery. This embargo both preceded and lasted longer than Jefferson's general Embargo on all foreign trade. Once in power, the Jeffersonians tried mightily to destroy the black republic. In 1805 and 1806 the Congress debated an absolute embargo on trade with the island. During this period Republicans raved about the need to undermine Haiti. Albert Gallatin believed that any American trade with Haiti was "illicit" and "contrary to the law of nations." Senator James Jackson argued that the black government "must be destroyed." Congressman John Wayles Eppes, Jefferson's son-in-law, denied that Haiti was free and declared he would "pledge the Treasury of the United States that the Negro government should be destroyed."[66] By this time even the French had written off the island. The United States could gain nothing from the embargo, except to harm its own economic interests. Nevertheless, Jefferson insisted on the embargo.[67]

In the Senate, Samuel White, a Federalist from the slave state of Delaware, called the bill a "disgrace." White argued at great length that Haiti's ex-slaves were free under French law and that they were "de facto the governors of the country, and in every respect act as an independent people." The Senate voted 21 to 8 in favor of the embargo. The opposition came from Federalists. In the House, Congressman Eppes was so anxious to embargo Haiti that he declared he "violently opposed" a motion to delay consideration of the bill by even a day. On the final vote almost all of the opponents of the measure were Federalists. Some southern Federalists, like Joseph Lewis of Virginia, who dared not vote against the measure, managed to be absent and thus avoid the roll call.[68]

In this debate the Republicans could not countenance the possibility of free black people having their own country and trading with the United States. The Federalists, while certainly not racial egalitarians, were willing to accept the reality of Haiti, recognize the nation, and trade with the black republic. As Michael Zuckerman has observed about Haiti, "In the realm of race, the Federalists clung to the ideological inheritance of the Revolution far more than the Jeffersonians."[69]

GEOGRAPHY, ECONOMICS, AND MORAL CULTURE

Clearly Federalists and Republicans had a different approach to slavery. While there are a few exceptions, generally opponents of slavery were more likely to be Federalists than Republicans; the Republicans were more likely to support slavery than Federalists. In the North, Federalists were more likely to support gradual abolition programs, and Republicans were more likely to oppose them, although sometimes such laws seem to have had substantial support from both groups. On black rights the division is more clear. Federalists were far more likely to support the rights of free blacks, and Republicans were clearly more likely to oppose them. Not surprisingly, where they were enfranchised, blacks voted for Federalists.

While these divisions are most obvious in the North, it is also clear that southern Federalists were more likely to oppose slavery and favor free blacks than were Republicans. While most southern Federalists were supporters of slavery and opponents of black rights, this was not always the case. North Carolina provides some evidence of this.[70] Blacks voted in

North Carolina until 1835. While "it is difficult to ascertain the extent to which free Negroes were a factor in politics during the national period," evidence suggests they were Federalists. John Chavis, one of the few politically active blacks in North Carolina, complained about the possibility of the reelection of Andrew Jackson, noting that the nation "would require a Hamilton, a Jay, or an old Adams bottomed upon G. Washington." In 1835, when North Carolina disfranchised all blacks, supporters of disfranchisement included not only the new Jacksonian Democrats but longtime Jeffersonians, like Nathaniel Macon. Old-line Federalists like William Gaston fought this racist change. Gaston and the Federalist Archibald Henderson, both justices on the North Carolina Supreme Court, often wrote decisions favorable to slaves and free blacks. John Culpepper, an active Federalist and a Baptist minister, signed a published resolution urging that a black minister be allowed to preach. Similarly, the Federalist William Boylan signed a petition to the legislature urging that a free black family be allowed to remain in the state.[71]

On the big issues—like the extension of slavery into the West or allowing Missouri to enter the Union as a slave state—the issues were clearly drawn. Northern Federalists led the charge against slavery; Republicans from the North and the South defended against that charge. Why was there such a split in the two parties? Why were the Republicans so proslavery; why were the Federalists less pro-slavery and even antislavery? Four answers seem to emerge.

Pro-Slavery Republicans

In the 1790s the Republicans emerged as the party of Virginia and Thomas Jefferson. While undoubtedly uncomfortable with slavery and fearful of the dangers that slaves posed to white society, "Jefferson had only a theoretical interest in promoting the cause of abolition." From the time he returned from France until his death in 1826, Jefferson never publicly opposed slavery, while often supporting the institution. Jefferson's position on race was extreme, even by the standards of his own age, and, as Winthrop Jordan has noted, "constituted, for all its qualifications, the most intense, extensive, and extreme formulation of anti-Negro 'thought' offered by any American in the thirty years after the Revolution."[72] While Madison and Monroe may have been less Negrophobic, they never gave any support to opponents of slavery or supporters of black rights. It should not surprise us, then, that a party led by such men would have been pro-slavery and anti-black. To support the Republicans meant to support slave owners at the top of the ticket. In northern cities the Republicans appealed to working-class whites and recent immigrants, who seem to have quickly come to believe that free blacks threatened their economic status. One of the "wages" that white urban workers earned, as early as the 1790s, was their privilege of being white.[73] Republicans openly played the race card early on in American history. Their party would continue to play it, in the Jacksonian era, the antebellum period, during the Civil War, and well into the twentieth century.

Elitism and Racial Acceptance

Thus blacks rejected the Republicans. The dishonorable attempts of New York Republicans to disfranchise blacks illustrates why African-Americans supported the Federalists. The pro-slavery, Negrophobic policies of the Republicans left them no choice.

But why were the northern (and some southern) Federalists both receptive to free blacks and hostile to slavery? Why didn't Federalists also play the race card? Or, to put it another way, why were they less concerned about paying themselves and their constituents in the wages of whiteness?

Part of the answer has to do with the elitist views of so many Federalists. Their social position and aristocratic nature also allowed Federalists to grant blacks political rights without thinking of them as their equals. They did not see or want equality among all Americans; thus they had less need to relegate one group of people—blacks—to a permanent underclass status in order to uplift themselves.[74]

In the South the master class had long understood the necessity of keeping blacks and whites separated. As Edmund Morgan has so eloquently argued, in the American South freedom was dependent on American slavery.[75] Slavery made all whites equal by creating what James Henry Hammond later would call the "mudsill" for American society. The Republicans easily carried this idea to the North where it was used to organize whites. Jeffersonian democracy led to racism, elevating all whites to equality on the backs of slaves and free blacks. Federalists did not need the wages of whiteness to feel secure in their social place; Republicans, North and South, needed to suppress blacks to feel better about themselves.

Economic Interests

Economic ideology went hand-in-hand with Federalist notions of racial accommodation and a hostility to slavery. As supporters of property, they were able to reward property-owning free blacks with the franchise as easily as they would have denied the franchise to propertyless whites. Similarly, as men of commerce, they were more interested in economic efficiency than race. Selling goods to the British West Indies was far more important than compensation for slaves who escaped to freedom with the British army; selling goods to Haiti was far more important than worrying about the color of their trading partners. New England Federalists went to China, India, and Polynesia to trade. Haiti was just one more port to the New York, Philadelphia, or New England trader, who was likely to have had black crewmen, had his ship repaired by black workers, or even to have purchased his sails from a black sailmaker.

Both Federalists and Republicans had notions of manifest destiny in this early period. They both wanted to make America a great nation. But for Federalists this would come through free trade and economic expansion across the oceans, in ships manned by integrated crews in ports where the people were of many colors. Republicans, and later the Jacksonians, wanted to move west, eliminating the nonwhites in their way and bringing their slaves with them.

Religion, Culture, and Morality

The final explanation of the Federalists comes back to concepts of morality and justice. Federalists were elitists with a sense of noblesse oblige. Washington, the greatest Federalist of all, was the embodiment of moral rectitude. Washington believed slavery was morally wrong, and he acted on this belief in many ways, including refusing to buy and sell slaves and providing for the ultimate manumission of his slaves. The contrast with Jefferson on both counts is striking. As a slave owner Jefferson sold scores of bondspeople—at least fifty in the early 1790s alone—all the while protesting that he had "scruples about selling negroes but for delinquency or on their own request." Washington refused "either to buy or sell slaves, 'as you would do cattle at a market.'"[76]

In the North and parts of the Upper South, Federalists joined manumission societies and other philanthropic endeavors that made them sympathetic to the least fortunate in American society. "The New Englanders' version of republicanism was bound up with the Northerners' piety and morality and their belief that the United States was a national organic community striving to build a 'Christian Sparta.'"[77] Such ideas were also common among some New Yorkers, Pennsylvanians, and other northerners. Such ideas naturally led them to oppose—even hate—slavery.

Slavery was the opposite of all that the Federalists stood for. It was also immoral, in fundamental ways that bothered the inheritors of Puritan,

Huguenot, and the Quaker traditions. To explain why some northerners continued these traditions, and others did not, is beyond the scope of this chapter. But clearly the difference was there for the early national period, just as it would be for the antebellum period. We need not thoroughly understand why Lincoln found slavery morally wrong and Stephen Douglas did not to understand that the difference was real. Similarly, while we await a fuller explanation of what motivated Washington or John Jay and Jefferson or Martin Van Buren to act as they did, it is nevertheless important to understand that their approaches to slavery and race were quite different. Thus, in the Age of Jefferson, the Federalists were the people most committed to liberty and racial fairness, if not necessarily equality and fraternity.

8

Ministers, Misanthropes, and Mandarins

The Federalists and the Culture of Capitalism, 1790–1820

Steven Watts

THE PHRASE "American conservatism" has always appeared something of an oxymoron along the lines of, say, Democratic party, modern art, or academic life. The reason for this seems fairly clear. The preservative and static sensibility of conservatism has never quite fit the expansive, growth-oriented, ambitious nature of American society. Some two hundred years ago Edmund Burke established the tenets of modern conservatism and unintentionally made this contrast clear. The "spirit of freedom," he insisted, "should be tempered with an awful gravity." The civilized citizen should cultivate a reverence for tradition and inheritance, for family and community. He should distrust abstract speculation and innovation, political perfectionism, and selfish individualism. Burke's conservatives cherished a timeless "contract of eternal society" that enshrined social and cultural order, personal restraint, and organic rootedness.[1]

But what figure could be further from this ideal than the typical American described several decades later by Alexis de Tocqueville? According to his observation, in the society of the young republic "the woof of time is ever being broken and the track of past generations lost." This atmosphere nurtured a population defined by restlessness and ambition rather than community stability: "An American will build a house in which to pass his old age and sell it before the roof is on; he will plant a garden and rent it just as the trees are coming into bearing; he will clear a field and leave others to reap the harvest; he will take up a profession and leave it; settle in one place and go off elsewhere as his changing desires [dictate]. . . . Death steps in in the end and stops him before he has grown tired of this futile pursuit of that complete felicity which always escapes him." This conundrum has given rise to a peculiar ambiguity within conservative thought which has lasted up to the present. Misty-eyed homages to family and community attachment, social stability and political responsibility, personal self-control and moral rectitude exist side-by-side with equally passionate espousals of ruthless competition, unflinching self-interest, and a market winnowing of the weak. The result has been an awkward juxtaposition of contrary impulses—toward organic connection on the one hand, toward self-regarding ambition on the other—at the heart of American conservatism.[2]

The origins of this situation can be traced to the late eighteenth century and the era of the nation's founding. Following the ratification of the Constitution in 1788, the Federalist faction emerged to define the conservative movement of that age. These defenders of order, stability, and property in the early republic, as most scholars have argued, were engaged in a reactionary effort to hold back the tides of change. Historians looking at political, social, cultural, and intellectual developments of the age have created an interpretive consensus that broadly pictures early national conservatives moving through two stages. First, the Federalists appear to have been staunch opponents of sweeping changes in the post-Revolutionary republic. At their apex of influence in the 1790s, they stubbornly defended a traditional, hierarchical model of society structured by fixed relationships of mutual obligation. Culturally, they upheld an Augustan ethic of discourse focusing on intellectual order, morally restrained reason, and a civilized opposition to experimentation in the arts and sciences. Politically, they opposed a popularized politics of participation while advocating a traditional republic dominated by deference, animated by virtue, and fueled by an elite-directed economy. In a second stage that followed the Jeffersonian "revolution of 1800," Federalists seemed to retain their social traditionalism while adopting increasingly desperate political tactics to regain political power. Federalist conservatism thus has taken shape in the historical literature as a stubborn rearguard action against the historical changes unleashed by the American Revolution.[3]

While certainly valid and insightful in many respects, this interpretive consensus glides by a central problem in the Federalist position: its peculiarly ambiguous, and thoroughly American, view of the social, economic, and political trends it purported to oppose. In fact, much evidence suggests that Federalist conservatism is best understood in terms of a profound, wrenching ambivalence toward liberalizing change in the late 1700s and early 1800s that evoked intense guilt as well as fear. Federalists were not simply traditional, antidemocratic reactionaries. Indeed, they had played a large role in the early republic promoting various innovations—commercial expansion, entrepreneurial individualism, political organization, and factionalism—that gradually proved unsusceptible to control. Then like Dr. Frankenstein overwhelmed by a monster of his own creation, these figures struggled mightily, and unsuccessfully, to restrain the liberalizing impulses they had helped liberate. Thus the shrillness of Federalist jeremiads came from an emotion born of culpability as well as horror. The Federalists performed the first act of a long-running drama of American conservatism where the leading roles have been compounds not just of fear and loathing but of guilt and ideological tension as well.

THE CONTEXT FOR the emergence of the Federalists' ambivalent, guilt-ridden conservatism was created by one of the great transformations in the sweep of American history. In the three or four decades after the War for Independence, a social and economic revolution of massive proportions slowly gathered momentum to transform the life of the young republic. The severing of political ties with Great Britain seemed to intensify an erosion of long-standing restraints on the scope of individual action. Traditional colonial ideals of paternalism in social organization, moral economy and mercantilism in economic activity, and a virtuous republicanism in public affairs began to wither under the intense heat of a historical "release of energy." Trends that had been only dimly evident earlier in the eighteenth century—geographic mobility, challenges to social deference, the search for profit in the marketplace, popular political participation—flourished and intermingled in the hothouse atmosphere of the early republic. Benjamin Franklin, a prophet before his time in the mid-1700s with his message of personal ambition, thrift, investment, and utilitarian work, became by the 1790s the prototype of the American citizen in the early republic.[4]

Several dramatic developments gave glimpses of this shift. By the mid-1790s, with British imperial restraints abolished, Americans had begun to flood into the trans-Appalachian West, a trend culminating in the Louisiana Purchase of 1803 which extended American territorial claims across the continent to the Rocky Mountains. This explosive migration of land-hungry, ambitious Americans was mirrored in an unprecedented overseas commercial boom stretching from 1793 to 1808. The advent of the Napoleonic Wars on the Continent during these years created military preoccupations among the combatants, and American merchants leaped into the commercial void. Moving quickly into Atlantic, Mediterranean, South American, and West Indies markets, U.S. ships became the leading commercial carriers and reexporters in the Western world by the turn of the century. An unprecedented flow of wealth flooded the young republic and raised the general level of prosperity, promoted an entrepreneurial spirit, and created large accumulations of capital for further reinvestment. Merchant millionaires like Stephen Girard of Philadelphia, Robert Oliver of Baltimore, and John Jacob Astor of New York City became living symbols of an emerging new world of profit, commodities, and personal ambition in this expanding and energetic society.[5]

Other far-reaching trends operated in the domestic economy. Growing European demand for foodstuffs, for instance, encouraged an increasing commercialization of agriculture in a great commodity-producing belt stretching from Virginia northward to New York. The old household economy of colonial America began a precipitous decline as regional markets spread their tentacles outward from eastern port cities ever farther into the interior. Moreover, after 1790 the steady development of both household and extensive manufactures slowly systematized a broad thrust toward efficiency, productivity, and profit. This broad, multifaceted commercialization of American life prompted a "business revolution" that gave rise to swelling incorporation, complex bookkeeping techniques, and growing numbers of banks, insurance companies, and commission houses in the late eighteenth century. Such changing patterns of economic endeavor comprised the consolidation of a market economy in the early American republic.[6]

The political culture of the young nation also reverberated and shifted in concert with this rapid market development. In the older world of eighteenth-century politics, an ideology of republicanism had shaped political discourse and practice. Its guiding principles—a creed of "civic virtue" demanding the subordination of self-interest to the public good, a commitment to citizen "independence" free from corrupting dependence on the wealthy, an organic vision of society where ordinary farmers and laborers deferred to the political leadership of an educated, prosperous aristocracy of talent—never created, of course, an actual republican polity in pristine form. Nonetheless, an idealization of civic values and a constant fear of their corruption helped apotheosize republicanism and fuel the revolt against Great Britain.

Within a decade of independence, however, this traditional ideology was beginning to change shape under the enormous pressures of historical change. A growing ethic of popular politics emerging from the Revolution, in concert with the swelling market transformation of social and economic life, created a destructive tension within republican political culture. A struggle between "virtue and commerce," as one historian has put it, pitted an older ideal of self-sacrifice and civic community against a growing instinct for individual ambition, advancement, and expression. By the 1790s—a decade that put political flesh on the skeletal framework created by the Constitution—a new kind of politics had begun to emerge. Modes of economic growth increasingly defined the agenda for debate while party competition provided the means. And a pluralist mind-set, which held that the sifting of many private interests created the public good, increasingly shaped its discourse. In other words, as a liberal model of political formulation slowly displaced a republican one, a market politics was born.[7]

Perhaps even more significant than shifting political and socioeconomic structures, however, was an accompanying transformation of cultural values and assumptions. The American *mentalité* assumed a different shape and color in the decades after the Revolutionary struggle. Traditional cultural definitions of human perception, volition, and acceptable behavior began to take on unfamiliar new meanings as part of a broad crisis of authority. A vigorous "spirit of enterprise," as one historian has termed it, arose from the wreckage of colonial paternalism as entrepreneurialism, geographic mobility, and political participation undermined the traditional authority of ministers and magistrates, courthouse and church. A related epistemological crisis at elite levels of culture raised similiar issues. The demise of patriarchal authority raised questions in many areas—politics, theology, literature, pedagogy—about how we know and learn, of how we understand and internalize morality. From John Locke's exposition of "sensationalist psychology" to Immanuel Kant's claim that the motto of the Enlightenment was "Have the courage to use your own understanding," intellectual trends helped shape an age of increasing personal independence and self-sufficiency.[8]

From this swirling maelstrom of ambition and sensation, mobility and self-reliance, gradually emerged a broad thrust toward individualism in the culture of the early American republic. It became clearly evident in several ways. First, by the 1790s secular advice literature with titles like *The Way to Grow Rich, The Youth's Guide to Wisdom,* and *An Instructive History of Industry and Sloth* was promoting an ethic of self-made success. Second, initial stirrings of the Second Great Awakening at the very end of the eighteenth century promoted the notion of "moral free agency," with its insistence that individual sinners had a God-given choice to pursue salvation or damnation. Third, Scottish moral philosophy invaded the realms of education and moral theory to encourage the cultivation of an innate moral sense as a guide to individual conduct. Finally, in the realm of popular culture in the late 1700s, the newfangled novel had begun to explore the vagaries of individual experience, in both practical and moral terms, in a fluid marketplace society.[9]

This historical transformation brought mixed results. On the one hand, the moral and material possibilities of possessive individualism created an atmosphere of excited anticipation. On the other, the assault on traditions of paternalism, civic humanism, and gentry authority created anxiety over vocation, identity, and authority. The fluid new individualist world of the American early republic simultaneously thrilled and frightened many of its citizens. Not surprisingly, the Federalist response to this watershed proved highly complex as well. Rather than digging in ideologically and emotionally to defend a vanishing worldview, their response comprised an amalgam of collusion and uneasiness, participation and rejection with regard to the tidal wave of change that seemed to engulf them.

The experience of several individuals suggests some of the primary features of this response. Three architects of Federalism who struggled to define and control the transformations of their age—an "Old Federalist" minister, intellectual, and educator; a political theorist and prominent national politician; and a "Young Federalist" golden boy of the early nineteenth century—illustrate the troubled conservative response to the culture of capitalism in the decades 1790–1820. They demonstrate the intensely ambiguous, guilt-ridden relationship between Federalism and the ascending liberal capitalism in the early republic. Their fierce, well-documented struggles to come to terms with a startling new world embodied the central Federalist ambiguity: a desire both to release and to control liberal individualism and a cold fear that it might be uncontrollable. The truth of the tale, however, lies in the telling. As an appropriate act of conservative propriety, let us begin with the minister.

IN THE EARLY nineteenth century, Timothy Dwight, the famous New England Federalist, appeared a deeply divided man in his assessment of the young American republic. On the one hand, as he announced in a sermon preached several times, Europe's Age of Revolution threatened to bring on the "general convulsion of the world," or apocalypse, prophesied in the Book of Revelation. But on the other hand, as Dwight announced in the same text, the upsurge of evangelical Protestantism with the Second Great Awakening marked a glorious "new era in the history of Christianity" and promised the salvation of the American republic.

Such jarring sentiments regarding the American condition were nothing new for this New Englander. His erratic swings between visions of doom and glory stretched back decades to his encounters with the American Revolution. In 1781, for instance, Dwight described the Revolution as the summation of progress in the eighteenth century and noted that its success would invite citizens "to venture far in every path of science and refinement." Yet the struggle for independence, he insisted, also had produced darker effects—"a dissipation of thought, a prostitution of reason, a contempt of religion, a disdain of virtue, a deliberation in vice, and a universal levity and corruption of soul before unseen and unimagined." These contrary images—the evident promise of an American Canaan, the looming threat of national damnation—remained juxtaposed for the next four decades of Dwight's life. Like many other Federalists, at the heart of this unresolved tension lay an anxious, problematic attempt to simultaneously promote and restrain liberalizing change.[10]

Dwight was born in 1752 in Northampton, Massachusetts, the son of a local magistrate and grandson of the famous theologian and philosopher Jonathan Edwards. After matriculation at Yale College, the young man graduated in 1765 and eventually became a licensed minister. During a twelve-year pastorship at Greenfield, Connecticut, Dwight received a Doctor of Divinity degree from Princeton and then assumed the presidency of Yale in 1795 upon the retirement of Ezra Stiles. Serving in that position until his death in 1817, he made Yale a leading American college by expanding its size, curriculum, and faculty.

While at Yale this distinguished New Englander earned the epithet "Pope Dwight," a derisive term coined by opponents of Connecticut's Federalist-Congregationalist establishment. In many ways the title fit because of its holder's immense prestige. Dwight had emerged as a major spokesman for cultural and political conservatism by the turn of the century. A leading figure in the intellectual circle labeled the "Hartford Wits," he wrote several epic poems such as the *Conquest of Canaan* (1785), which proclaimed the glorious rise of the American republic, and *The Triumph of Infidelity* (1788), a passionate attack on anti-Christian doctrines. Another long poem, *Greenfield Hill* (1794), celebrated the virtues of an idyllic New England community based on piety, industrious habits, small rural freeholds, and deference. All the while, Dwight wrote numerous political tracts for Federalist newspapers and served as a leading organizer of missionary and Bible societies in New England. His last major work, *Travels in New England and New York* (1821–22), combined travel documentary with a running condemnation of an American society succumbing to social mobility, political democracy, and personal avarice.[11]

Such efforts made Timothy Dwight the prototype of Federalist conservatism: stern, unbending, moralistic in his opposition to an emerging liberal world of ambitious individual enterprise. Beginning in the late 1780s and continuing throughout the next decade and beyond, he chastised post-Revolutionary American society for its destructive attraction to profit and social advancement. As he wrote typically in 1795, "Honesty is no longer [just] counterfeited, but laughed at. Conscience is not silenced, but discarded. . . . and truth, justice, and the public welfare, are vendued to the highest bidder. . . . Stimulated by avarice . . . every man makes gold his god. To acquire riches becomes the only object, honour, or duty. By his wealth every man's worth is sealed. . . . Extortion, fraud, gaming, and speculation steal into character under the imposing names of industry and prudence." For this indignant Federalist critic, the French Revolution provided a horrifying image of unfettered individualism. The release of human passions, ambition, and avarice during this upheaval had created a panorama of violence, despotism, and moral degradation where social stability fell victim to "the general license to plunder, to defraud, to deceive, and to pollute." The course of events in France, Dwight intoned, described the future of liberalizing America with its promise of a "world of fiends."[12]

The only social salvation, this minister insisted, lay in the maintenance of virtuous, traditional republican communities. Dwight distilled much of his thinking into a single dictum: "Nothing is necessary to make good men harmonious and friendly but that they should live near to each other, and converse often, kindly, and freely with one another." He described this idealized community most fully in *Greenfield Hill.* Dwight's long poem comprised a paean to New England village life where competence, deference, a rough equality of wealth, and virtue—or that which "always seeks the common welfare"—dominated a stable social structure. As one admiring stanza described this "meek good-neighborhood,"

> Here every class (if classes those we call,
> Where one extended class embraces all,
> All mingling, as the rainbow's beauty blends,
> Unknown where every hue begins or ends)
> Each following, each, with uninvidious strife,
> Wears every feature of improving life.

A society of many Greenfield Hills, this Federalist minister argued, provided the only blueprint for the survival of the American republic.[13]

Yet Dwight's analysis of the early republic was not quite the picture of stark alternatives—deference or ambition, community or selfishness, stability or chaos, Greenfield or France—he wanted his audience to see. Like many other Federalists, in sundry and subtle ways he encouraged an ethos of individual achievement and material advancement in the post-Revolutionary decades. But these impulses then resisted confinement after their release. The real problem for this intellectual minister was not so much liberal individualism but the more complicated issue of how to keep it under control.

This subtle but crucial ambivalence influenced Dwight's attitudes on a number of issues. With economic development, for example, he consistently praised the ambitious "enterprise of Americans" and approved their pursuit of "commercial prosperity" in agricultural, mercantile, and manufacturing enterprises in the post-Revolutionary decades. Yet Dwight fretted about the reckless loaning of capital and feared that profit might take "entire possession of the minds" of Americans. In terms of personal volition, a parallel position emerged. The New Englander preached sermons such as *Life a Race*—presented to his charges at Yale in 1799, 1806, and 1812—suggesting that without personal "vigour" and "industry," one "slides down . . . through one gradation of life after another." Yet he demanded that striving individuals should head off excessive "ambition," "avarice," and the "ardent pursuit of property." Even in the realm of social authority, where Dwight's traditionalism might seem impeccable, his belief in hierarchy and paternalism stood on shaky ground. In 1789, for instance, he had sounded a clarion call for a "new system of science and politics" in America. In his words, "It is to be ardently hoped, that so much independence of mind will be assumed by us, as to induce us to shake off these rusty shackles, examine things on the plan of nature and evidence, and laugh at the grey-bearded decisions of doting authority." Such sentiments hardly provided a firm foundation for the edifice of a stable, patriarchal republic.[14]

Dwight's struggle with liberalizing change eventually turned him toward a repressive ethic of personal conduct. With social and political institutions seeming to crumble around him by the late 1790s—and with at least a half-conscious awareness of his own complicity in the process—the New Englander increasingly retreated to the private realm to shape public stability. There he constructed a character ethic of self-control as a kind of social ballast in the turbulent waters of a liberalizing society. In sermons with titles such as *On the Love of Distinction* and *On Independence of Mind*, he earnestly exhorted American individuals to shape an "energy of character" that combined firmness and vigor with "conscience," a faculty that was "patient, sober, watchful, awake to every sin, and guarded against every sin." Only by controlling ambition close to its source, Dwight suggested, could social chaos be averted.[15]

Correctly gauging the trajectory of liberalizing trends and harboring an awareness of his own contribution to the restless spirit of ambition, this Old Federalist ideologue thus would spend much of his mature life struggling to channel that spirit's energy and restrain its excesses. It was no accident that Dwight ended his ideological journey by embracing the evangelical Protestantism that was beginning to reshape American culture around the dawn of the new century. "The Revivals of religion," he concluded, "are a decisive proof that God has not forgotten to be gracious to this land." At the same time, however, they served an even more satisfying purpose. Protestant evangelicalism promised to direct the kinetic energy of his countrymen toward the goals of the character ethic, or in his words "the promotion of useful industry and well directed enterprise . . . ; of frugality and moderation in living." Under the religious auspices of a "moral free agency" that demanded an individual decision for salvation and an avowal of personal responsibility for moral conduct, the revivals thus encouraged both self-assertion and self-control. For Federalist Timothy Dwight nothing could have better solved his long-standing ideological dilemma over the troubling transformation of the early American republic.[16]

IN 1812 JOHN ADAMS wrote a scathing indictment of his countrymen and their restless pursuit of opportunity. In a letter to correspondent William B. Giles of Virginia, he noted the brazen self-interest that promoted an ethic of advancement. "This country and our forms of government which must have their course, opens vast views of ambition to every eye and fascinating temptations to every passion. The aged & experienced & the middle-aged too, find younger generations rising after them ardently coveting their places and not very delicate in the choice of measures to supplant them and shove them off the stage." Such sentiments typified the ideological pronouncements of this distinguished Massachusetts political figure. Adams, of course, was a leading Federalist intellectual and social theorist and a bitter opponent of the Jeffersonian Republicans throughout the 1790s. After serving as second president of the United States, he had been unceremoniously turned out of office with the "revolution of 1800" and slunk home to his farm near Boston to lament the fate of his country.[17]

The Adams image has never quite recovered its luster. He appears a cranky, contentious, long-winded political misanthrope whose overblown sense of dignity earned him the epithet "His Rotundity." While he served as president in the late 1790s, his support of Federalist measures like the Alien and Sedition Acts made him appear a friend of authoritarianism, while his splenetic denunciations of Enlightenment notions of progress put him out of step with the spirit of his age. In all, Adams's unpredictability and moodiness never quite fit the larger-than-life mold of the Founding Fathers, and he usually appears on the second tier, in the shadows of more eminent figures like George Washington, Thomas Jefferson, Alexander Hamilton, Benjamin Franklin, and James Madison.

The facts of his career belie this unfortunate reputation. Probably no American except Thomas Jefferson served his country at such length and with such distinction over the last third of the eighteenth century. From his leading role in the Revolutionary Continental Congress as the "Atlas of Independence" to his overseas diplomacy in the 1780s, from his authorship of the Massachusetts state constitution to his service as vice-president and then president under the new national Constitution, Adams remained at the center of the young republic's political life. Moreover, amid this flurry of public activity, he published a steady flow of writings on government and social theory. Several series of long essays —the *Dissertation on the Canon and Feudal Law* (1765), the *Novanglus* pieces (1775), the *Thoughts on Government* (1776)—helped mobilize New England opinion on behalf of the Revolution, while his three-volume *Defense of the Constitutions of Government of the United States of America* (1787–88) and *Discourses on Davila* (1790) provided learned commentary on republican principles of government. But these published works shrank before a mountainous private correspondence with scores of fellow politicians and intellectuals over some six decades. There Adams explored every topic imaginable—history, science, philosophy, religion, economics, literature, politics, and the future of the American republic.

A central endeavor preoccupied this intensely curious but cautious Federalist intellectual throughout much of his life. Adams consistently probed the transformations remaking the American republic in the post-Revolutionary decades, and he gradually evolved into one of its most sophisticated conservative critics of emerging liberal capitalism. His torrent of observations on everything imaginable in public and private life was largely an attempt to define, understand, and come to terms with this unfamiliar world. The New Englander's life was above all a life of the mind, and his passionate reflections on American society comprised a sustained intellectual confrontation with the transforming early republic.

Throughout his formal and informal writings, Adams offered an unsystematic but often brilliant series of social, psychological, and economic insights into the new polity emerging in the United States by the 1790s. He became convinced, contrary to Enlightenment principles, that human "passions and Interests generally prevail over their Reason and consciences," and the former impulses must be subject to restraint, or chaos would result. Yet Adams did not harp on man's viciousness or greed. Instead he focused on a more complex emotion: the desire for esteem. He concluded that "the passion for distinction" was the mainspring of human action, and that it could follow many paths in the human psyche:

> This passion, while it is simply a desire to excel another, by fair industry in the search of truth, and the practice of virtue, is properly called Emulation. When it aims at power, as a means of distinction, it is *Ambition*. When it is in a situation to suggest the sentiments of fear and apprehension, that another, who is not inferior, will become superior, it is denominated *Jealousy*. When it is a state of mortification, at the superiority of another, and desires to bring him down to our level, or to depress him below us, it is properly called *Envy*. When it deceives a man into a belief of false professions of esteem or admiration, or into a false opinion of his importance in the judgement of the world, it is *Vanity*.[18]

The passion for distinction, Adams believed, loomed particularly important for Americans in two of its manifestations. First, a yearning for social status seemed to prevail among the poor as well as the rich as even the most insignificant of men tried to procure "a kind of little grandeur or respect . . . in the small circle of their acquaintances." Second, an obsessive pursuit of riches resulted not so much from the desire for money itself as from "the attention, consideration, and congratulations of mankind. . . . There is more respectability, in the eyes of the greater part of mankind, in the gaudy trappings of wealth, than there is in genius or learning, wisdom and virtue."[19]

The social consequences of the passion for distinction, Adams insisted, could not be summarized simply. The complex craving for esteem prompted both good and evil consequences. On the one hand, it drove individuals to a "love of knowledge and desire of fame," traits that produced achievement and honor. It produced "the most heroic actions in war, the sublimest virtues in peace, and the most useful industry in agriculture, arts, manufactures, and commerce." It provided "a constant incentive to activity and industry" while also working to soften greed and temper crude self-interest. On the other hand, however, the passion for distinction also tended to intensify "avarice and ambition, vanity and pride, jealousy and envy, hatred and revenge." At worst, according to this Federalist thinker, it could excite rivalries, factionalism, quarrels, and even wars if allowed to run its course. Thus the quest for distinction involved a complex mixture of selfishness and altruism, honor and materialism. For Adams, a social and political conclusion seemed unavoidable. Since the wise polity recognized the futility of changing this fundamental human impulse, it sought to balance its various manifestations and "direct it to right objects."[20]

The myriad cultural and social realignments of post-Revolutionary America—the converging streams of liberal capitalism—lent hidden power and import to Adams's analysis. The emergence of a market society in the early modern Anglo-American world, as C. B. MacPherson has argued, pushed forward the notion of "possessive individualism." According to this formulation, the solitary person came to be seen "neither as a moral whole, nor as part of a larger social whole, but as an owner of himself," and society became "a lot of free equal individuals related to each other as proprietors of their own capacities and what they have acquired by their exercise." The development of possessive individualism played a large role in the consolidation of American liberal capitalism in the late 1700s and early 1800s, and in many ways it defined precisely the broad object of John Adams's concern. Digging beneath the superficial desire for material gain, he uncovered a deeper yearning for distinction that not only tinted pecuniary impulses but colored a whole range of complex social relations. This Federalist's observations on the desperate search for esteem illuminated both the anxious individual thrown back on his own resources and the fluid liberalizing society in which he struggled. As a social psychologist of possessive individualism, Adams was unsurpassed in his own time.[21]

Adams's social analysis of liberal individualism led him to observe, not surprisingly, that some inevitably emerged more successful than others. The emergence of antagonistic social groups was a fact of life for this Massachusetts Federalist, and labor lay at the bottom of such divisions. As he noted frankly, "The great question will forever remain, who shall work? . . . [Those] who labor little will always be envied by those who labor much." In the liberalizing society of the young republic, growing ambitions and resentments among various interests and groups promised serious social factionalism, and possibly anarchy. The greatest problem, however, lay at the top of society, not the bottom. Achievers of distinction, he insisted, threatened American society as but another kind of "aristocracy" who coveted power and profit.[22]

Thus Adams evinced no reverence for elites in the American republic and issued no injunctions of deference. A "natural aristocracy" based on talent and achievement rather than heredity, he believed, was little better than the hereditary version. As he wrote to Thomas Jefferson in 1813, "artificial Aristocracy, and Monarchy, and civil, military, political, and hierarchical Despotism, have all grown out of the natural Aristocracy of 'Virtues and Talents.'" In fact, Adams's prevailing fear of this group led him to condemn innovative versions of republican theory that sought to meld aristocracy into the body of the people and cover the whole with the slogan of "popular sovereignty." This would only produce oligarchy in the long run, he believed, because "the natural Inequalities, intellectual, moral, and corporeal will produce other inequalities of Wealth and Power." For Adams, the key was to isolate the "few" who fulfilled the passion for distinction and give them a branch of government, along with the "many," and set up a strong, independent executive authority to mediate between them. In such fashion, the New Englander's version of Federalism ran across the grain of conservative demands for deference and elite guidance of the American republic.[23]

The complexity of Adams's Federalist conservatism also emerged in his views on the political economy of the young republic. Looking about at liberalizing change in the United States near the turn of the eighteenth century, Adams feared that "the pursuit of gain" was sweeping all before it. Yet he refused to condemn this trend outright. The expansion of "commerce and manufactures" was not without merit because of its connection to industry, temperance, frugality, and the general prosperity of independent republican producers. At the same time, however, Adams loathed the inevitable implications of market expansion. As he burst out in a private letter, "Will you tell me how to prevent riches from becoming the effects of temperance and industry? Will you tell me how to prevent riches from producing luxury? Will you tell me how to prevent luxury from producing effeminacy, intoxication, extravagance, Vice and folly?" An explosion of profit-seeking activity, he feared, had infected the post-Revolutionary republic with "the universal gangrene of avarice in commercial countries" that has "destroyed every republican government."[24]

John Adams's critique of America's swelling liberal society, market economy, and psychology of possessive individualism led him to an ambivalent conservatism. The impulses of ambition and avarice, he noted darkly in 1813, had swept up elites and common citizens alike in a surge of distinction seeking. "When I consider the weakness, the folly, the Pride, the Vanity, the Selfishness, the Artifice, the low craft and mean cunning, the want of Principle, the Avarice, the unbounded Ambition, the unfeeling cruelty of a majority of those . . . who are allowed an aristocratical influence; and on the other hand, the Stupidity with which the more numerous multitude, not only become their Dupes, but even love to be taken in by their Tricks: I feel a stronger disposition to weep at their destiny, than to laugh at their folly." Here was vintage Adams. In the liberalizing republic all social groups were suspect and needed to be represented yet controlled in the structure of government. This prickly, independent Federalist thinker, well aware of the ambiguity of historical change and suffering no delusions about progress, had never shrunk from hard conclusions. He had approved, even encouraged, the trends that had brought about the transformation of the American early republic, and he knew it. For Adams, the only hope lay in controlling the worst excesses of the process. Like many other Federalists, but in his own unique fashion, he confronted the central dilemma of the age: distinction-seeking Americans may have been agents of the young republic's prosperity and prospects, but if allowed to run rampant they would serve as their own worst enemies.[25]

IF FEDERALISM had a future in American politics in the early nineteenth century, it seemed to rest on the shoulders of the handsome, eloquent, and forceful young New Englander Josiah Quincy. Born in 1772 to one of Massachusetts's oldest and most distinguished families, the young Bostonian received his education at Philips Academy and Andover College. A talented student of classical literature, history, and natural science, he entered the bar in 1793 and quickly channeled his energy into politics. A number of attributes—his venerable family heritage, striking good looks, a talent for oratory—quickly pushed him to the forefront of Federalist politics. Winning a seat in the House of Representatives in 1804, he soon became a leading spokesman for the Federalists in their new role as the opposition party. This brilliant young congressman dedicated his early political career to revitalizing the Federalist party in the aftermath of the Jeffersonian "revolution of 1800."

In Quincy's assessment the Jeffersonian Republicans had ushered in a frightening new age of corruption and degeneracy. That party, he argued, had gathered under its banner "the factious, the desperate, the intriguing, the licentious, and the wickedly aspiring." Its irresponsible currying of popular favor, however, was but symptomatic of much deeper ills in American society. The infant United States, according to Quincy's critique, was well on its way to decay and dissolution by the early 1800s. The signs were everywhere. Uncontrolled western expansion, for example, as with the Louisiana Purchase, was threatening the republic's social unity by incorporating groups who lacked "the wisdom and habits of regular life." The scramble for material gain in a booming market society also promised the destruction of public morality as "private interests and personal projects" were advanced at the expense of the public good. Ambition and profit seeking, according to Quincy, had begun "to obliterate the principles of our forefathers, to corrupt their simple and pure manners, and to weaken that attachment to country which was their distinguishing virtue." In such a society it was little wonder that traditions of classical learning were falling into disrepute as every whim of public opinion and every popular fad gained quick credence.[26]

Such degradations had a predictable effect in politics. Public affairs, according to the young Federalist, had fallen into the hands of "chameleon calculators . . . changing at every varying hue of party and every wayward view of interest, worshipping and wallowing before any idol, which can support their selfish advancement." The modern victory of interests over restraint, Quincy observed sarcastically, had come with the ultimate "triumphs of democracy" in the French Revolution, where the "scaffolds of Paris" displayed the "filth and falsehood and rapine and wretchedness" accruing to unrestrained liberty. Unburdening himself in an 1811 letter to John Adams, the young New Englander eloquently denounced the effects of liberalizing change in the American republic: "Since there are no guides which are infallible, whom shall we follow? Since there are no principles which seem absolutely settled, what foothold has reason? . . . The wisdom, which our fathers taught us, is defiled. And the liberty with which they . . . made us free, is little else than a cloak for licentiousness."[27]

Quincy's espousal of the Federalist alternative followed the traditional ideological guidelines of that persuasion. In contrast to Jeffersonian electioneering, Federalists followed the deferential practice of leaving political guidance to men of "talent and integrity . . . reflection, judgment and information." They also encouraged, the young New Englander reminded his fellow congressmen, a scrupulous private character of "exemplary piety," "benevolent conduct," and "exercise of all the social and domestic virtues." Culturally, Federalism promoted respect for classical learning in literature, history, and the sciences, and it sought to restrain reason with the dictates of Christian morality. Overall, Quincy's Federalism was a conservative doctrine encouraging "calmness, concord and respect," and it promised to create a stable American republic of mutual obligation where "virtue and talents . . . shall provide over its destiny." By returning to Federalist principles, he believed, America could yet "cast anchor upon long established principles" and secure its future.[28]

These ideological positions—fear of social change, concern with maintaining cultural stability, deep distrust of popular Jeffersonian politics—suggest that Josiah Quincy practiced politics as a young champion of tradition. In many ways he did. But a focus on this young Federalist's conservative rhetoric obliterates another dimension of his public life, one which greatly complicated his ideological positioning. The youthful congressman, however great his regard for a traditional republican polity, was also encouraging many social and political changes that were overturning it.

Josiah Quincy's ambivalence, which usually remained well hidden in the recesses of his ideological constructions, surfaced in several significant ways. It became visible, for instance, in the arena of party politics. For all his denunciation of Jeffersonian electioneering, the New Englander consistently urged his fellow Federalists to organize and campaign rather than to rely upon deference. As he bluntly put it in 1803, "Our opponents are better politicians . . . [and we must] learn to contend like them, more upon party principles than many of us seem willing to do." As a compatriot once observed, Quincy was one of the few Federalists eager "to pursue politics as a profession." His political malleability and ambition became evident in a revealing episode. This Federalist leader, who denounced Jeffersonians for their factionalism and cunning manipulation of the political process, engaged in one of the most cynical political maneuvers in the history of the early republic. In the early months of 1812, Quincy and his allies secretly met with the British ambassador to concoct a common anti-Jeffersonian strategy in foreign affairs. Skirting the edge of treason, this plan was designed to force the Madison administration into an ill-advised war that would turn it out of office in disgrace and return the Federalists to a position of national power. Although it eventually fizzled, the plan demonstrated the lengths to which Quincy would go to achieve political dominance for his party.[29]

In like fashion, Quincy's frequent denunciations of growing social mobility and materialism in the young republic fit rather uneasily with his enthusiastic endorsement of dynamic commercial capitalism. He publicly defined Americans as a people "commercial in all aspects, in all their relations, in all their prospects . . . in the most exquisite perception of commercial prosperity." In Congress he habitually praised the spirit of trading enterprise that motivated Americans, creating "that profit which makes a great part of their happiness." Moreover, Quincy personally made a fortune by investing in Boston real estate and transportation projects beginning in the 1790s.[30]

In other words, Josiah Quincy, like many other Federalist conservatives, betrayed an underlying attraction to the emerging liberal society he claimed to loathe. His position became a tense and complicated one, part muted approval and part anxious dissent. Thus the man who condemned Americans for their selfish ambition could offer at the same time this tribute to the spirit of possessive individualism that was fueling liberalizing change. The best guarantee of American vitality, Quincy insisted in 1808, "lay in the industry, intelligence, and enterprise of the individual proprietors [of the United States], strengthened as they always are by the knowledge of business and quickened by that which gives the keenest edge to human ingenuity—self-interest."[31]

ULTIMATELY THESE three articulate figures suggest the peculiar nature and limitations of the conservative Federalist critique of liberalizing change. In contrast to Edmund Burke's great English oaks with their deep connections to family, community, and history, Federalist ideology in the early republic offered only shallow sources of social nourishment. By upholding an ethic of commercial growth, entrepreneurial achievement, and individual independence, this conservative cadre unwittingly helped to undermine the deferential, virtuous, and stable polity they rhetorically upheld with such emotion. They did not articulate an organic ideology that offered a comforting "sense of continuity with generations gone before . . . like a lifeline across the scary present," as John Dos Passos once defined the conservative impulse. Instead, they articulated an anxious, venturous conservatism, a deeply troubled creed of ambivalence, despair, and guilt that encouraged the ascendancy of liberal capitalism while lamenting its consequences.[32]

The Federalist dilemma suggests, somewhat unfashionably, that much truth still resides in Richard Hofstadter's description of America as "a democracy in cupidity rather than a democracy of fraternity." A broad perspective also suggests that while the Federalists lost the political battle with their Jeffersonian opponents in 1800, they probably won the cultural war over the long haul. The Federalists' tense mediation between individual assertion and repression became, in fact, the basis of a Victorian culture that moved into the ascendancy in the United States by the 1830s. Drawing inspiration from their Federalist forebears, bourgeois Victorian ideologues demanded self-control in a double sense: direction of destiny and command over the baser instincts. Thus the tensile quality of Federalist social thought became central to the whole structure of America's modern culture of capitalism.[33]

In a narrower political sense, however, the situation of the Federalists in the early republic comprised a revealing early chapter in the longer story of American conservatism, where deference and ambition, stability and growth, community and egoism have remained uneasily linked in a volatile, even schizophrenic combination. By the late twentieth century, this trend has produced some rather curious conservative heroes. They are no longer stern ministers, misanthropic social critics, or expectant mandarins promoting community, tradition, and stability. Instead, they are television preachers, real estate developers, radio talk show hosts, and actors whose calls for old-fashioned values emerge from a fluid atmosphere of endless social and personal growth, corporate image manipulation, and mass material consumption. In the symphony of American conservatism—and here Timothy Dwight, John Adams, and Josiah Quincy are but a step removed from contemporary players— laments for a bygone world provide a dissonant accompaniment to a dominant melody of economic growth, social ambition, and possessive individualism. It has not been a harmonious sound, either then or now.

PART III

Varieties of Federalism

9

BENJAMIN FRANKLIN AS WEIRD SISTER

William Cobbett and Federalist
Philadelphia's Fears of Democracy

Keith Arbour

"Time was," says Macbeth, "when the breath was out, men ceased to exist; but now they rise from their graves . . . and push us from our stools."
—Peter Porcupine [William Cobbett], *A Prospect from the Congress-Gallery* (Philadelphia, 1796)

WHILE TOURING THE United States from 1818 to 1820, Fanny Wright spoke with politically interested citizens wherever she went. She concluded from these conversations that "a coldness of manner in pronouncing the name of Jefferson, and I have observed, of *Franklin*, is what may sometimes enable you to detect a *ci-devant* member of the fallen party."[1] That Jefferson's name annoyed "members of the fallen party" a decade after his second term ended is perhaps unremarkable. But Franklin had been dead for thirty years, buried before the Federalist party was born. The response to his name that Wright detected, therefore, was (as her italics indicated) as remarkable then as it seems today. Why had Franklin figured so significantly in political fights fought after his death as to trouble "fallen" Federalists more than a generation later?[2]

Geographical coincidence is part of the answer. From 1790 to 1799 the new federal government sat in Philadelphia, where Franklin had lived, worked, and—despite absences totaling approximately twenty-two years during his last three decades—died. Had the government remained in New York or moved directly to the Potomac, John Adams and a few congressmen doubtless would have continued to besmirch Franklin's name whenever circumstances permitted. But the problem was aggravated by Philadelphia itself.

To certain fashionable Philadelphians, Franklin for decades had seemed a threat to their culture of pseudo-aristocratic paternalism. To their minds

Franklin had worked his way up to unmerited influence from plebeian origins in a stinking soap shop. Having done this, he had committed a number of crimes against his betters-by-birth, who considered the offenses characteristic. In the 1760s and early 1770s, for instance, he had schemed to have Pennsylvania confiscated from the Penn family and in the process led the antiproprietary Quaker party to defeat. Abandoning his party, he then—as they saw it—had helped cause the Revolutionary War, which (among other things) wrecked the finances of wealthy Quakers' dearest charity, the Pennsylvania Hospital. And he had chaired the convention that drafted the Pennsylvania constitution of 1776, which some considered excessively democratic.

In 1785 he returned to Philadelphia after his decade-long French embassy. Looking back upon his return years later, Franklin's friend Deborah Norris Logan recorded, "I well remember the remark of a fool, though a fashionable party-man at the time, that it was by no means 'fashionable' to visit Dr. Franklin."[3] In his final years Franklin did little that countered the prejudices of Philadelphians who had not welcomed his return. In 1787 he counseled journeymen printers as they struck against their employers' attempt to cut wages. He tangled with the University of Pennsylvania's trustees, whom he charged with having countenanced, to the detriment of the community, its academy's overly aristocratic curriculum.[4] His words led the Library Company's directors to assume that he was going to bequeath them over four thousand books. In anticipation, they ordered a marble statue of Franklin to be placed in a niche over their front door, only to discover when Franklin died in 1790 that he had left them just one work (albeit in eighteen volumes). To the Pennsylvania Hospital he left over £5,000 in debts he had found impossible to collect from fellow Philadelphians and others in his final years. Embarrassed in their own attempt to investigate collection, the hospital's patrons declined the curious bequest.[5] On the other hand, to the cities of Boston and Philadelphia, Franklin left trust funds to benefit young tradesmen.

These were perceived to be serious offenses; but with Franklin's death, the tide was turning. The university trustees pushed proposals for Franklinian reform permanently aside. And wealthy Pennsylvanians rewrote the state's constitution, eliminating its most democratic provisions. Yet while the federal government sat in Philadelphia, and for decades after it left, some well-heeled Philadelphians grumbled that Franklin had deceived them about his library bequest. When they passed or entered the Library Company, Franklin's statue reminded them of the deception (fig. 1).[6] The victories, however, outweighed that loss; and with their vic-

1. *Library and Surgeons Hall in Fifth Street, Philadelphia,* engraving by William Birch & Son, 1799, with Francesco Lazzarini's marble statue of Franklin above the front door. Inscribed below it are the words "The Statue of Benjamin Franklin was presented by WILLIAM BINGHAM Esqr MDCCXCII." (Courtesy of the American Philosophical Society)

tories and his death, Franklin ceased to threaten the established order. For several years thereafter, those who felt they lived high in that order could afford to be relatively easy on Franklin.

But however much Philadelphians of the sort Deborah Logan called "fashionable" temporarily muted their criticism, their behavior continued to embody dislike. There was, for instance, trouble with his funeral arrangements: Pennsylvania's Supreme Executive Council told Franklin's family that it would carry his body to the grave but then reneged at the last moment. The Library Company's directors neglected to pass any resolutions marking Franklin's death, and the available evidence suggests that they did not attend the funeral qua directors, unlike officers of other organizations that Franklin had helped found. The official eulogy was delayed for almost a year. When finally delivered by one of Franklin's lifelong opponents, it included several backhanded compliments.[7]

Yet before long, some fashionable Philadelphians sensed that the established order was again in serious danger. They feared the revolutionary virus, original to America in its modern form but redoubled in virulence since it had been transmitted to France. And from France, as the 1790s advanced, some thought the deadliest strain more and more likely to return. William Cobbett, the most caustic Federalist pamphleteer of the period, embodied these Philadelphians' fears in a series of best-selling pamphlets that attacked the French Revolution, democracy, powerful women, spelling reform, and Franklin together. The combination of these ingredients helps us cut to the core of aristocratic and Federalist Philadelphians' fears of Franklin and democracy. It also helps explain why democracy's opponents introduced gossip and wisecracks about a dead man's sexual activity into the political debates of the late 1790s, and why some of their fears were too deeply rooted to die before Fanny Wright had a chance to see them spring up again in conversations as late as 1820.

IT MAY NOW seem strange that Franklin's image figured at all in American debates about the French Revolution and democracy in the post-Franklin era. Franklin, by dying, might be thought to have done all he could to disassociate himself from posthumous events. But he had followed one of his own maxims: "If you would not be forgotten, / as soon as you are dead and rotten, / either write things worth reading, / or do things worth the writing." He had ensured that his example and writings would remain useful and enticingly readable after his death. His partisans completed the formula by keeping him in print—and cheap enough for wide consumption. So Franklin always remained current. As a result, no one thought to object that the man was dead before almost all the events on which the debate focused took place.[8]

After his death friends of Franklin's memory immediately associated him with the French Revolution. A memorial broadside included the quatrain:

> A life of spotless fame, in Freedom clos'd,
> The Patriot soar'd to Immortality:
>   Anno Domini M.DCC.XC.
> Th'auspicious Dawn of Gallic Liberty.[9]

Another poem noted that the connection was causal, not merely coincidental:

> Each patriot bard throughout these realms shall sing
> The sage's praise who did to Gallia bring
> Those sacred sparks which have not dormant lain,
> And now are kindled to a noble flame.[10]

Of course Philadelphians had long known that Franklin's public affections had lain with France during the last fourteen years of his life. And two months before he died, the *American Museum* had published his 1784 letter to Samuel Mather, in which he warned that a break with France "would infalibly bring the English again upon our backs." Democratic newspapers regularly reprinted this letter, as did twelve editions of Franklin's *Life* and *Works* printed in the United States from 1794 to 1800.[11]

During the 1790s democratically inclined citizens for whom Franklin's rise in life was an inspiring example and for whom his writings glowed with authority were increasingly solicitous that all white men who had participated in the Revolution should have emerged from the convulsion the better for it, materially and politically. They thought that privileges of birth should have been replaced by equality and that aristocratic patronage should have no place in the new nation.

Pseudo-aristocratic Americans were afraid of precisely these possibilities and of the chance that women and African Americans would, with democrats' help, successfully apply the Revolutionary ideology of inalienable equal rights to themselves.[12] With a sureness deeper than reason they feared that these other Americans' gains would be carved from their own political power—and that as a result they would never again be able to behave as they pleased. This was a frightening thought, and as such, one of the easier (if ultimately insufficient) ways of dealing with it was to render it absurd—and to laugh. Two early examples of this strategy will suffice.

In March 1790 (shortly before Franklin died, but after the French Revolution had begun), Philadelphia's *Columbian Magazine* yoked American anxieties about status and power, French culture, and masculinity in an article entitled "Modern Spelling *Humorously Exposed.*" Because spelling reforms attempted to make uniform spelling easier to learn, democrats linked them to the wider dispersion of education, upon which the proliferation of republican virtue depended. For the same reason, the people Deborah Logan derisively labeled "fashionable" associated these schemes with what they considered characteristics of democracy: tendencies to level down and to topple the established order. Within the article, the author impersonated a schoolmaster:

> In agreement with modern elegance, I was determined to strike out *k*, as an useless letter . . . [but] I turned about and what should I see but the ghost of *k*, six feet perpendicular, with a monstrous hand and a prodigious foot. Thou wretch, he cried, how durst thou expel me from my natural right.

> Indeed Mr. *K*, I replied, it is not my fault: it is the public writers who have cut you off from the public*k*. He said, O innovators! ignorant of the genius of the English language, they tear from its foundations, its strengtheners, its props, and bold supports; and emasculate poor words, like Italians, in hopes of gaining an elegant sweetness.[13]

This coupling of spelling reform, banishment from public life, and castration in a single paragraph is uncommon but symptomatic.

In January 1791 (when the French National Assembly's adoption of the Declaration of the Rights of Man and of Citizens was old news, but its abolition of hereditary titles was not), Franklin's grandson published in his Philadelphia newspaper a satirical letter connecting congressional rejection of the administration's excise and militia acts with nationwide gender role-reversal. The letter was so timely an administration plant that John Fenno promptly reprinted it in his Federalist *Gazette*. The letter writer professed to report a conversation overheard between several young ladies, in which one Charlotte noted that if the militia act were to fail, "I suppose that we young women must learn militia duty, and turn out with both musquet and bayonet." To this, Thalestris responded: "Upon my word, I long for this happy change of affairs. We shall then expunge the odious *obey* from the wedding ceremony. Should I be unlucky enough to get a husband . . . I'll keep him quiet as a mouse, by flashing my gun in his face. Then, my girls, we shall first be absolute mistresses of our houses, and then in a very short time govern the state also. We shall in this western hemisphere set up a FEMALE EMPIRE, that shall laugh at all the male governments in the world."[14] A follow-up article printed a mock petition by TEN THOUSAND FEDERAL MAIDS, who opposed Thalestris. The petition closed with the maids' request for "a few small privileges," including "an *absolute command over non-paying and non-fighting husbands*."[15]

These stories are two of many indications that Philadelphians were troubled that their world was still politically unsettled—and that some men feared that this unsettlement threatened both their political roles and their masculinity, which they could not imagine enduring undiminished a diminution of political power. As news from France became more startling—the king's beheading, mass forced de-Christianization—polite satires like these became insufficient to vent aristocratic anxieties.

Those who opposed the French Revolution seized on the connection between Franklin, France, and democracy and maligned the revolution and the dead Franklin together. To them, French violence exemplified the ultimate fruits of the democratical philosophy they and generations of fashionable Philadelphians had attributed to Franklin—a philosophy kept current through inexpensive editions of his *Life* and *Works.*

John Adams claimed in 1817 that he had known before anyone else that the French Revolution would be disastrous for mankind: "I could forsee nothing but calamities to France and to the world, and the French constitution of 1789 confirmed all my fears."[16] By "constitution" Adams meant the Declaration of the Rights of Man and of Citizens, which affirmed that "men are born and always continue, free, and equal in respect to their rights."[17] The first revision of the Declaration, published as the Declaration of the Rights of Man, promulgated even more frightening doctrine. When France adopted a new constitution in 1795, it annexed the Declaration in a third form that "stripped the principle of equality of the . . . 'levelling-down' mentality."[18] But by then Adams could point to years of bloodshed that he considered the result not of generations of despotism but of French revolutionaries' idée fixe: equality. The concept always made him uneasy.[19] Insisting on equality of obligations, he never granted equality of "natural and acquired abilities."[20] As Esther Brown pointed out long ago, "Adams's exactitude was pedantic because the point he labored—that men actually are in many ways unequal—was neither debatable nor debated. . . . He did not see that the real issue was not natural equality but artificial inequality." Whatever blinded Adams to the real issue, he worried about a connection between democratic equality and "a community [i.e., collective use] of wives and women."[21]

Americans who embraced the French Revolution as a desirable continuation of the American struggle increasingly distrusted Adams and the party (Tories they called them) that considered France's revolutionary violence unwarranted. In turn, the so-called Tories feared those of their countrymen whom they considered demophiles, and whom they called Jacobins, thinking them part and parcel of the bloodthirsty French crew.

Both sides' fears were grounded in facts. Democrats were afraid that important federal officials had monarchical tendencies, which manifested themselves in words and manners. In 1791, for instance, Robert Morris, senator from Pennsylvania, was overheard to "say possibly that he would rather have the President elected for 21 years than for four and for life rather than for 21 years."[22] Pennsylvania's other senator, the democrat William Maclay, recorded that during the Revolution

> The abolishing of Royalty [the] extinguishment of servility patronage and dependance attached to that form of government. Were among the Exalted Motives of Many Revolutionaries. . . . In fin[e] the Amelioration of Government and bettering the Condit[ion] of mankind. These Ends and none

other were publick[ly] avowed. . . . Yet there were n[ot] wanting a party Whose Motives were different. The[y] . . . cared for nothing Else but a Translation of the diadem and Sceptre from London to Boston N. Yor[k] or Phila. or in other Words the creation of a Ne[w] Monarchy in America and to form ~~nott~~ Nitches for themselves in the Temple of Royalty.[23]

Early in the 1790s Maclay became convinced that the American Revolution had enabled these monarchists to begin to realize their secret wishes. Then in 1795 the Jay Treaty, which reestablished the young republic's connection to the very monarchy that Revolutionary soldiers had been crippled and killed while breaking, seemed a frighteningly plain step toward the ultimate aristocratic goal.

On the other hand, the aristocratically inclined saw their opponents form the Democratic societies, which embraced the French Revolution and were thought to be behind the Whiskey Rebellion.[24] They also read of the decapitations of highly positioned Frenchmen, with whom they identified. They trembled when American democrats excused this violence as part of a warranted cure for the diseased French state. If printed news of "Madame Guillotine's" daily work did not sufficiently shake aristocratic Philadelphians, someone set up in the city a full-scale working model of the contraption. For a small fee its operator would decapitate a stuffed Louis XVI.[25]

Such violence upset Americans who remained sympathetic to monarchy. Right through the American Revolution, part of Philadelphia had clung to the institution as the stool that supported the aristocratic pose. Largely separated by war from vicarious association with British royalty, aristocratic Philadelphians had embraced the French royal family as their own. Their participation in the French minister's celebration of the dauphin's birthday in 1782 made the elaborate affair one of the most richly attended of the period. In the middle of a two-thousand-word sketch of the festivities, Benjamin Rush commented: "How great the revolution in the mind of an American! to rejoice in the birth of a prince whose religion he has been taught to consider as unfriendly to humanity. And above all, how new the phenomenon for republicans and freemen to rejoice in the birth of a prince who must one day be the support of monarchy and slavery!"[26]

As some of Rush's fellow guests also appreciated, this was indeed strange of post–*Common Sense* Americans. But of course the dauphin's father was (equally strangely) backing the American cause. Less wealthy Revolutionaries of the sort fenced out of the elaborate party were also grateful to the French nation. But as some of them began to believe that their war had disproportionately benefited their well-heeled leaders, their trust in these leaders ebbed. Their gratitude to the French nation then ceased to include French aristocrats and began to manifest itself as a desire for the emancipation of the working people of France, whom they now recognized as their own analogues.[27]

For these Americans, implementation of the federal Constitution—enforced despite the thirteenth Article of Confederation—had previously exacerbated the domestic side of the problem, and it still rankled. As Agricola explained: "Such a *monster of a government* has seldom ever been known on earth. We are obliged to maintain two governments, with their full number of officers from head to foot. Some of them receive such wages as never were heard of before in any government upon earth; and all this bestowed on *Aristocrats* for doing next to nothing. A blessed revolution! a blessed revolution indeed! but farmers, mechanics and labourers have no share in it."[28]

In July 1794 William Cobbett, a recent immigrant from England, rebutted Agricola's complaints. Cobbett's background made his position surprising. Born the son of a tavern keeper in 1763, he had been a soldier in the British army from 1784 to 1791. He ended his military career by publicizing peculation by officers that resulted in daily hardships for common soldiers. In 1792 he published *The Soldier's Friend*, the motto of which was hardly an aristocratic sentiment: "Laws grind the Poor, and Rich Men Rule the Law." Having offended the authorities, Cobbett fled England for France, where the revolution made America seem a safer refuge. He emigrated to the United States in October 1792 and moved to Philadelphia in February 1794.[29]

Cobbett rejected Agricola's position in his second American pamphlet, *Observations on the Emigration of Dr. Joseph Priestley*, published in Philadelphia several months after Cobbett moved there. The *Observations* (the first edition of which does not mention Franklin) reveals Cobbett to have refashioned himself in America into a virulent antidemocrat indifferent to the corruption of English institutions and an enemy of all Frenchman except the king and his defenders, whom he championed because they opposed their base, frog-eating countrymen.[30] Cobbett, in short, had donned high Federalism. For the rest of the century, writing as Peter Porcupine, he fiercely criticized democracy—and Benjamin Franklin, whom he had never met, but of whom he learned much during his first year in Philadelphia.

Cobbett fired his first pamphlet shot at Franklin after reading James Thomson Callender's *Political Progress of Britain: or, An Impartial History of*

Abuses in the Government of the British Empire. Callender quoted Franklin's writings twice to support anti-British arguments.[31] Cobbett responded sharply in *A Bone to Gnaw for the Democrats,* which he completed in January 1795 with a preface denouncing women's involvement in politics. Asserting he would rather see all copies of his pamphlet burned than risk its perusal ruining even one female smile, Cobbett attempted to frighten American women away from political thinking by reporting that when Mary Wollstonecraft "began *The Rights of Women,* she had as fine black hair as you would wish to see," but "before the second sheet of her work went to the press, it was turned as white, and a great deal whiter than her skin."[32]

Cobbett maligned Franklin twice in *A Bone.* The abuse suggests that he sensed a need to damage Franklin's popular *Life* and understood that anti-Franklin jibes would increase pamphlet sales. Because many printers had a friendly interest in Franklin's reputation, Cobbett could count on them to encourage counterattacks. The process kept Cobbett's fame (which Samuel Johnson had likened to a shuttlecock, needing to be struck both pro and con to be kept aloft) and work in the air. Foremost among the printers whose energy Cobbett thus exploited was Franklin's grandson Benjamin Franklin Bache, editor-publisher of the Philadelphia *Aurora.* Modern readers might imagine that if Cobbett needed to attack Bache, he could have done so by portraying him as a disappointment to an upright grandfather. But local aristocratic gossip against Franklin did not permit that construction. So in *A Bone* Cobbett baited Bache for "having, like a second Phaeton, driven the blazing car of democratic fury, till it was within an inch of burning us all up to cinders . . . [then assuming] the gentle gait and modest veil of the Goddess of the morning [i.e., Aurora]: 'A right chip of the *Old Block*;' as *poor Richard* says."[33] In other words, the editor of the *Aurora* behaved just like the father of the Pennsylvania constitution of 1776, who later endorsed the federal Constitution of 1787.

Demagoguery and hypocrisy are the principal charges here, iced with a Franklinian aphorism. But of course "A right chip of the Old Block" is no more Poor Richard's creation than "No pain, no gain,"and that is part of Cobbett's irony: Franklin received popular credit for writing aphorisms he had not coined (however much he may have refurbished them), and for much else that fashionable Philadelphians contended he had not done. Cobbett also appreciated that the attribution "as Poor Richard says," lifted from Franklin's steadily read *Way to Wealth,* was the epitome of self-deprecatory authority to some American readers, a distillation of the perversion of authority to others, and useful both ways. So he wittily introduced it here to deauthorize Franklin while authorizing the suggestion that Franklin himself had been as bold a democrat as contemporary readers knew his grandson was. And just as criticism of Franklin was used to malign Bache, so Bache's thus-smeared conduct was adduced as heightened proof of Franklin's by aristocratic Philadelphians who disliked both. By criticizing them together, Cobbett hit two birds with one stone and ensured that the bird that was not already dead would squawk when hit, thus increasing his own readership and fame.

In *A Bone* Cobbett also took on the Library Company's white marble statue of Franklin. An incident that began in the summer of 1794 provided the form over which Cobbett hammered his imaginative iconoclasm. In August some young Philadelphians sent to the officers of Christ's Church a request that they remove a wooden bas-relief bust of George II (defender of the faith when the church was built) from the church's façade. The petitioners claimed this symbol was preventing "young and virtuous men from attending public worship" and should be removed because "it has nothing to do with the worship of the most high God, nor the government under which we exist." Nonsense, Cobbett responded: "I look upon the destruction of this image and crown as an event, of about as much consequence to the citizens of Philadelphia as the destruction of the *Swiss, at the door of their Library*, would be. The Church is full as well without it as with it."

Cobbett added a footnote elucidating "the Swiss" drawn from criticism that aristocratic passers-by aimed at the library's Franklin: "This image has obtained the name of the *Swiss* for two reasons: First, because the citizens of Switzerland are generally employed by other nations in the capacity of *Porters*; and, secondly, because their motto is . . . 'No pay, no Swiss.' I leave the reader to determine whether the name be applicable or not to the image in question."[34] The note transforms Franklin from philanthropic sage to a base, self-seeking, and treacherous mercenary—a reprise of criticisms Philadelphians had leveled against Franklin as far back as 1764. Benjamin Davies reported similar aspersions on the library's statue in *Tit for Tat*, his defense of Cobbett: "Dr. FRANKLIN chose to keep up the farce to the last. . . . To the Philadelphia Library, where his statue stands in the front, like the pale monument of Guilt, or like a Swiss at the door of an hotel, he gave one old sett of French works of little value."[35]

The statue carried more baggage than library business encumbered it with. When in 1797 Cobbett charged Franklin with craftiness, lechery, and hypocrisy, he added, "[his] very statue seems to gloat on the wenches as they walk the state-house yard, and [his] OPINIONS RESPECTING

ADULTERY can be proved, not by vague assertions, but by LIVING WIT-
NESSES." In Peter Porcupine's *Life and Adventures* Cobbett connected
the observation that Philadelphians "daily accused [Franklin] of having
been a whoremaster, a hypocrite and an infidel" to another reference to
the statue.[36] Cobbett coupled these attacks to the library's statue, prominently displayed above a city thoroughfare, in order to further promote
the profitable controversy his writings were creating. He knew this would
work because he knew Pennsylvanians were as sensitive to publicly displayed images as any Americans of the period.[37] He also did it because
the aristocratic gossip that Franklin's figure excited perfectly suited his
style of argumentation.

Within a year of his arrival in Philadelphia, Cobbett had thus adopted
local aristocratic criticism of Franklin en bloc. He had also conned the
larger, complex web of local aristocratic fears. He reproduced this web in
A Bone, which after finishing with Franklin strikes out in a single two-page
string of paragraphs at spelling reform, powerful and promiscuous
women, and Pennsylvania's Democratic societies.

The specific spelling reform proposal that Cobbett attacked was Dr.
William Thornton's *Cadmus: or, A Treatise on the Elements of Written Language*, which had won the American Philosophical Society's Magellanic
gold medal in 1792. In his preface "To the Citizens of North America,"
Thornton observed, "You have corrected the dangerous doctrines of European powers," and urged, "Now correct the languages you have imported,
for the oppressed of various nations knock at your gates, and desire to be
received as your brethren." Thornton knew of Franklin's proposals for a
reformed alphabet and Noah Webster's adoption of "some of [Frank-
lin's] judicious and forcible reasons" for reform. His plan resembled
Franklin's in that it introduced some new symbols for particular sounds
and advanced for its adoption democratic arguments, among which he
included the following point, which *"alone ought to silence all the objections
that can be brought"* (the emphasis is Thornton's): "Children, as well as all
the poorer classes of people, would learn to read in so short a time, and
with so little trouble, having only to acquire the thirty letters."[38]

Cobbett despised Thornton's plan because of its democratic aims. He
further despised it because it had received the imprimatur of the Philosophical Society—which he attacked as "that club of illiterate Jacobins"
because of its connections with deists, suspected atheists, and the local
Democratic Society (eruptions all of what he called the *mania reformatio*)
and because Franklin had been involved in its founding.[39] Of the ridicu-
lousness of the scheme itself, Cobbett noted, "it will be sufficient to tell,

that the *i* was to be turned upside down, and the point placed under the line, thus ¡."

In fact, it was *j*, not *i*, that Thornton's plan upended,[40] but Cobbett's thoughts upon the inversion of the letter that is also the most personal pronoun led him quickly to a discussion of powerful women via "that Democrat Brissot": "[Brissot] tells us," wrote Cobbett,[41] "that our women are more subject to the consumption than men, 'because they want (as they do in England) *a will* or *a civil existence:* the submission which women are habituated to, causes *obstructions!* deadens the *vital* principle and impedes circulation.' As a remedy for this, he produces us, quack like, his infallible nostrum, *Liberty and Equality!*" From these exclamations Cobbett leaped to his next thought: "Yes, let him persuade us, if he can, that our wives and daughters die of the consumption, because they do not, like his execrably patriotic *concitoyennes*, change gallants as often as they do their *chemises*." Cobbett then asked American women if they were ashamed of their mothers' example—if they would "accept of Mr. Brissot's nostrum?" He answered for them: "No; you are too mild, too lovely, to become the tribune of a Democratic Club: your lilly hands were never made to wield a dagger: you want no rights, no power but what you possess: your empire is much better guarded by a bosom of snow, than it would be by the rusty battered breast plates, worn by those terrible termagants, the 'heroines of Paris.'"[42]

Because Cobbett's work sold well, his local publisher issued an expanded edition of his *Observations* against Priestley shortly after *A Bone* appeared. Cobbett added to this edition anti-Franklin sentiments wholly absent from the first edition. Noting Priestley had disclosed that in 1774 he had written a pamphlet on the American problem for English Dissenters "at the *request* of *Doctor Franklin*," Cobbett added, "He does not tell us whether he was paid in sterling or continental money." Having thus introduced Franklin's name, Cobbett dragged it around by ridiculing Priestley's invocation of his friendships with Franklin and Richard Price as "a drole way of proving the peaceableness of his disposition, and his attachment to his country":

> Franklin, Price and Priestly! A precious trio! . . . Methinks I see them now in one of their dark consultations, like the three Weird Sisters round their cauldron, brewing
>
> > "Double, double, toil and trouble;
> > "Fire burn and cauldron bubble."
>
> As for Benjamin Franklin, Esqr. and Soap Boiler, his character for *peaceableness* is as well known as his character for *gratitude* and *integrity*.[43]

These charges impute pernicious characteristics that aristocratic Philadelphians had perceived in Franklin's political career and his late-life
involvement in university and Library Company affairs: the fondness for
subverting society betrayed in his democratical proposals for the university curriculum, the deviousness betrayed in his dealings with the Library
Company's directors, the ingratitude betrayed in his last will and testament's
salient bequests: for the Library Company, one book; for the Pennsylvania Hospital, uncollectible debts; for young tradesmen, community trust
funds.

In March 1795 an unidentified Philadelphian amicably used Franklin's
name as pseudonym while criticizing the Federalists' Jay Treaty. Fourteen
letters signed "FRANKLIN"—but without other references to him; the
name was enough—appeared in Eleazer Oswald's *Independent Gazetteer*
over three months beginning March 9, 1795. Late in June they were published together as *Letters of Franklin, on the Conduct of the Executive, and the
Treaty Negociated, by the Chief Justice of the United States with the Court of Great
Britain.* Thus the reading public saw the dead Franklin's name associated
with fresh anti-British, pro-French-revolutionary newspaper and pamphlet
literature throughout the spring of 1795.

In August 1795 Cobbett responded to *Letters of Franklin* in *A Little Plain
English*, almost every page of which repeats Franklin's name or the substitute "our Demagogue." In one passage Cobbett called Franklin "this
fawning mob orator." Given that the real Franklin—whom his contemporaries thought unsettlingly silent on most occasions—hardly seems
eligible for this description, it might appear that Cobbett here attacked
only the pseudonymous Franklin. But another passage indicates that
"Franklin" represents pseudonymous author and deceased philosopher
simultaneously and that Cobbett did mean to portray the real Franklin
so.[44] The Federalist literary critic Joseph Dennie (who, like Cobbett, had
never heard Franklin) would later repeat the characterization along with
criticism that Franklin's prose served an analogous literary purpose: to
"degrade literature to the level of vulgar capacities."[45]

Shortly before Cobbett answered *Letters of Franklin*, he had attacked
Franklin again, in part 2 of *A Bone to Gnaw*. In the original *Bone* Cobbett
tied attacks against Franklin up willy-nilly with criticisms of newfangled
spelling schemes, promiscuous women, the Democratic societies, and
revolutionary France.[46] Now in part 2 he attacked Franklin alongside the
democratic notion of equal rights, which he asserted "must ever end, as
in France, in the ruin of the rich, and its inevitable consequence, universal poverty." If democrats, he added, "were to speak the language of their

hearts; they would not say to their rulers: 'You are vicious corrupt men; you are the curses of your country.' No; they would say: 'You are rich rogues while we are poor ones, change situations, and all will be right.'"[47] This articulates one facet of aristocratic fears. But ever contiguous to the fear of economic inversion was the fear of political inversion—and ever lurking darkly beneath both lay the fear of gender inversion.

A single couplet from Susanna Rowson's play *Slaves in Algiers* (Philadelphia, 1794) set Cobbett off on a whirlwind expression of gender anxiety in the pamphlet *A Kick for a Bite*. In her epilogue Rowson's lines posited the reaction of female theatergoers to her play: "methinks you say; / 'Women were born for universal sway, / Men to adore, be silent, and obey.'"[48] Cobbett responded: "Sentiments like these could not be otherwise than well received in a country, where the authority of the wife is so unequivocally acknowledged, that the *reformers* of the *reformed* church, have been obliged . . . to raze the odious word *obey* from their marriage service. I almost wonder they had not imposed it upon the husbands; or . . . [that] they had not dispensed with the ceremony altogether; for most of us know, that in this enlightened age, the work of generation goes hummingly on; whether people are married or not." Cobbett then suggested that his readers should expect from such democrats moral and political revolutions. He instanced as a combination of the two a takeover of the House of Representatives by women—perhaps even pregnant ones.[49] In the context of the times, this prediction rivaled the marquis de Sade's reduction of democracy to absurdity, recently explicated in these terms by Lynn Hunt.[50] Yet it exceeded de Sade in effectiveness, for the Philadelphia diarist Elizabeth Drinker (1734–1807) and her peers could read and approve Cobbett, whereas de Sade remained beyond the pale.

With so much about democracy's lascivious women in the air, it was perhaps inevitable that Cobbett would bring tales of supposed episodes in Franklin's love or sex life again into print. In his *Life and Adventures of Peter Porcupine* (1796) Cobbett countered a charge by calling it a "*bastard*, as abundant in falsehood as any one that ever sprang from the loins of *Poor Richard.*" In *The Democratiad* Lemuel Hopkins lampooned Benjamin Bache and his grandfather together, noting that Franklin had left behind "A Love of science—and a love of fun— / Witness our lightning rods and many a hopeless son." And in the *History of American Jacobins* Cobbett placed at the head of a cabal of "Democratic news-printers" Benjamin Franklin Bache, "a grand-son (whether in a *straight or crooked line*, I know not) of Old Doctor Franklin."[51]

Cobbett's attacks against Franklin constitute a small part of his Philadelphia prose. But his Franklin was not merely one of many details in the large campaign. Franklin was, rather, the historical figure who in aristocratic eyes stood for democracy itself, a bundle of ideas that threatened aristocratic power and potency, pocketbooks, neckcloths, and fore-flaps. In short, to his detractors during this period of intense party conflict, Franklin and his writings stood for continuing revolution and—beneath it—a novel power structure that threatened their masculinity. In this contest Franklin loomed as a representative of superior political skill and sexual potency. Aristocratic Philadelphians coped with the potency of Franklin's image by converting it into a low sexual irregularity of the sort they condemned in their construction of democracy's domineeringly promiscuous women. This line of thought Cobbett distilled in his depiction of Franklin as "Weird Sister"—one of the witches behind the gender-bending, establishment-toppling action of Shakespeare's *Macbeth.* (Profoundly misogynous rhetoric like this indicates how sharply Federalists could turn, as soon as crossed, from the smooth, pro-lady rhetoric with which they flattered wholly loyal audiences.)

Of all the details in Cobbett's writings and his actions as a bookseller in Second Street (where he baited democrats by prominently displaying "Worthies of the Revolution in pairs," viz., Franklin and Marat, and Thomas McKean and Jacob Anckarström),[52] Cobbett's opponents agreed on the significance of his references to Franklin. John Swanwick considered Cobbett's "demonlike" slandering of Franklin "without any additional proof . . . sufficient to blast [Cobbett] in the estimation of every patriotic and virtuous man."[53] Samuel Bradford concurred: "The abusive and contemptuous manner in which this reptile speaks of Doctor Franklin . . . is a key which will unlock the whole secret of his employment." Bradford turned the key and disclosed "an epitome of the design" of Cobbett and his party: "All . . . will not be secure until the late Revolution which gave independence and republicanism to our country can be brought into disgrace, until sunshine patriots, old tories, and proscribed traitors shall have superseded the patriots of 76; hence the traduction of Dr. Franklin, Mr. Paine and others—If the agents of the Revolution can be covered with opprobrium, the Revolution itself will be implicated; for when the props are knocked away the fabric must fall." Once the fabric fell, the social system that Cobbett and his adherents approved of, within which they grouped citizens into "orders," would be restored. Bradford objected: "Did this ruffian ever read the Constitution of the U.S.? He cer-

2. Anonymous engraved cartoon, "Porcupine in Colours just Portray'd" [1795]. William Cobbett referred to this attack on him in his *Political Censor for September, 1796*. (Courtesy of the Historical Society of Pennsylvania)

tainly did not, or he never would have classed the freemen of the U.S. into orders.—Where are *the lower orders of people* among us?"[54]

A contemporary cartoonist depicted this conflation of Franklin and liberty in an attack on Peter Porcupine as British hireling (fig. 2). In the print Porcupine scribbles in favor of the Jay Treaty while Liberty weeps over a monument to the single entity Franklin-and-American-Independence. Two years later Mathew Carey (who admired Franklin) commissioned a title-page illustration for his sarcastic *A Plumb Pudding for the Humane, Chaste, Valiant, Enlightened Peter Porcupine* (Philadelphia, 1798). A local artist supplied an engraving showing Porcupine lynched from a lamppost on an urban plaza that resembles Philadelphia's State House Square (fig. 3). Carey insulated Franklin from this exchange by leaving him out of his anti-Cobbett prose. But the target of Cobbett's ire was never entirely absent from the mind of Carey's Philadelphia audience. Nor was he entirely absent from the *Plumb Pudding* title page.

Franklin's best-selling *Life* and *Works* informed the age's political discourse with explicit exposition of his contributions to American life.[55]
The man was thereby embedded in every allusion to the contributions, as
were the contributions in every allusion to the man. Thus well-disposed
readers knew that the torn paper labeled "Treaty with France 1778" near
the lower left of "Porcupine, in Colours just Portray'd" represented one
of Franklin's crucial diplomatic contributions to independence. These
readers also knew of the lamps that Franklin had improved for incorporation in John Clifton's plan for the nighttime illumination of Philadelphia. Thus for them the streetlamp from which Carey's artist hanged
Porcupine was Franklin's streetlamp. Together, lamp and treaty represent the range of contributions to city, state, and country associated with
Franklin.[56]

Throughout this period and well into the next century, men and
women who opposed whatever they thought Franklin stood for gainsaid
Franklin's authorship of these contributions. Franklin, they asserted, had
not founded the Library Company or the Philadelphia Contributionship,
nor had he originated the electrical experiments attributed to him, and
so on.[57] In 1795–97 the English tourist Isaac Weld, Jr., captured the tone
of the circle in which Franklin's opponents moved: "Pride, haughtiness,
and ostentation are conspicuous; and it seems as if nothing could make
them happier than that an order of mobility should be established, by
which they might be exalted above their fellow citizens, as much as they
are in their own conceit."[58]

As the election of 1800 approached, Federalists who had countenanced
Cobbett's rhetoric (while worrying its opponents with the Alien and
Sedition Acts) had to face its counterproductivity. Abigail Adams opined
in 1798 that Cobbett "frequently injures the cause he means to advocate
for want of"—not opinions or principles acceptable to her husband's
party but—"prudence and discretion." And although John Adams had
acted against Cobbett's opponents, shortly before the election he asserted
that Cobbett's writings and Fenno's *Gazette* "countenanced, and encouraged by *soi-disant* Federalists . . . have done more to shuffle the cards
into the hands of the jacobin leaders, than all the acts of administration,
and all the policy of opposition, from the commencement of the government."[59] What Cobbett and his allies originally had considered effective
attacks against the popular, dead Franklin did not end up helping
the chosen party of those Philadelphians who had snubbed the old
man upon his final return from France. Yet if ultimately ineffective in
one of its principal aims, the rhetoric survived in print to influence read-

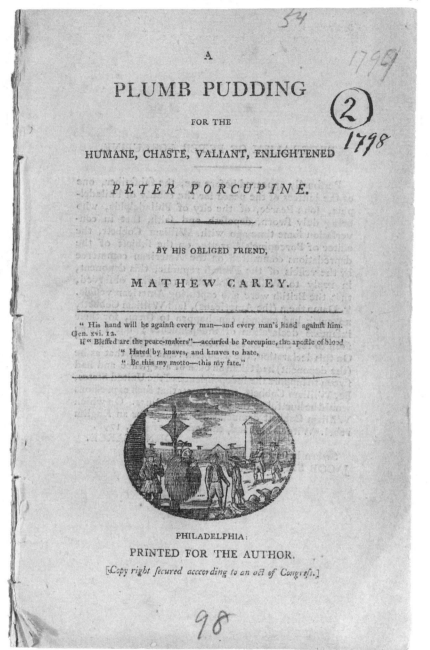

A

PLUMB PUDDING

FOR THE

HUMANE, CHASTE, VALIANT, ENLIGHTENED

PETER PORCUPINE.

BY HIS OBLIGED FRIEND,

MATHEW CAREY.

" His hand will be against every man—and every man's hand against him.
Gen. xvi. 12.
If " Bleſſed are the peace-makers"—accurſed be Porcupine, the apoſtle of blood
" Hated by knaves, and knaves to hate,
" Be this my motto—this my fate."

PHILADELPHIA:

PRINTED FOR THE AUTHOR.

[Copy right ſecured accccrding to an oct of Congreſs.]

3. Title page of Mathew Carey's *A Plumb Pudding for the Humane, Chaste, Valiant, Enlightened Peter Porcupine* (Philadelphia, [1798]), with an anonymous cut of Porcupine hanged. (Courtesy of the American Philosophical Society)

ers of Franklin's works who otherwise would have been beyond the reach of the table talk of those Philadelphians who fed Cobbett's best-selling pen with allegations of social treachery and sexual promiscuity. The rhetoric also survived—with its twisted strands of demophobia, misogyny, and Franklinophobia—to evince the deepest fears of some of the Federalist party's more hysterical supporters and, variously, of the politicians who for a while commanded their votes.

10

"STEADY HABITS" UNDER SIEGE

The Defense of Federalism in Jeffersonian Connecticut

Andrew Siegel

"That the Republicans are all *angels*, and the federalists are all *devils* are notions as false as they are criminal, and as stupid as they are false; and such prejudices are as dishonourable to our nature as they are degrading to our nation. The federalists love their country as well as the republicans. And why should they not? Have they not the same interests at stake, and have they not been nurtured in the same school of republican freedom?"

—William Charles White, *Avowals of a Republican* (1813)

DURING THE LAST years of the eighteenth century and the first two decades of the nineteenth, American politics reached unexpected and unprecedented levels of partisanship and rancor. In the words of one historian, "corrosive mutual distrust" was the dominant political reality of the early national period. The struggle for political control of and ideological dominance within the new republic destroyed old friendships and spurred partisans to acts of violence. The well-known tales of the Adams-Jefferson feud and the Hamilton-Burr duel draw their poignancy from the fact that they are not unique events but representative anecdotes. William Charles White's virulent criticism of the partisan excesses of his Republican colleagues in 1813 reveals the anger and frustration of the rare contemporary observer who was able to transcend this cycle of "corrosive distrust."[1]

While White's words originally were intended to rebuke the narrow partisan perspective of his contemporaries, historians of the first party system are subject to censure on similar grounds. Surveying the historical literature on American politics between 1800 and 1820, one gets the impression that many historians are operating on the very assumption, as White put it, "that the Republicans are all *angels* and the Federalists are all *devils*." Leading scholars have applied a double standard to the Federalists. While traitorous or cantankerous Republicans are seen as anomalous, the entire Federalist party is held accountable for the "insular secessionist schemes of Timothy Pickering and the sulphurous jottings of Fisher Ames." While the Democratic-Republican societies that helped elect Jefferson in 1800 are portrayed as innovative attempts to further participatory democracy, their Federalist counterpart, the Washington Benevolent Society, is dismissed as "a Federalist front organization."[2]

The lack of respect that contemporary historians accord to the Federalist party is also reflected in the ways in which scholars define their research topics. The most recent efforts to explain the transformation of political culture that took place between the Revolution and the Jacksonian period trace this transformation through the eyes of the Republicans. Reading history backwards, scholars such as Stephen Watts, Lance Banning, and Drew McCoy have written off the complex social and political philosophy of Federalism with a few pithy lines and focused their attention on the ideology and political economy of the leading Jeffersonians. The failure to examine the ideas and aspirations of defeated political movements artificially homogenizes the American political tradition by obscuring important sites of conflict.[3]

Connecticut Federalism presents an excellent subject for a case study of Federalist political argument.[4] First, no state was more resolute in its support of Federalist candidates. No Connecticut Republican sat on the Governor's Council or in the U.S. House of Representatives until 1818. Connecticut cast all of its electoral votes for every Federalist presidential candidate. This support was not accidental but the predictable result of Connecticut's peculiar social and political history.

Before the Revolution, Connecticut already possessed a long history of elected government. According to the colony's charter, the governor, lieutenant governor, state treasurer, secretary of state, and both houses of the legislature were elected directly by the people. All officials were elected annually with the exception of assemblymen, who went before the voters twice a year. Every town was represented in the assembly by one or two members, making a total body of approximately two hundred and establishing one of the largest ratios of representatives to constituents in British North America. The governor lacked the power to serve as an effective check against the popular will, possessing neither a veto on legislation nor the right to adjourn or prorogue the legislature. Judges were also dependent on the electorate, though less directly so, as the courts were filled annually by the legislature.[5]

In one of the great paradoxes of colonial politics, Connecticut's government of representative institutions and frequent elections produced a record of extraordinary political stability. In comparison with its fellow colonies, colonial Connecticut had comparatively little partisanship and turnover in officeholding. Elected officials were routinely reelected, and seriously contested elections were rare. Once elected, a judge could assume that his position was secure until he chose to step down. Only the most tumultuous issues could rouse the citizenry to concerted partisan behavior. Only one governor was denied renomination for political reasons during the eighteenth century.[6]

Structural factors contributed to the conservatism of Connecticut's electorate. Suffrage qualifications disenfranchised a substantial number of the colony's residents (though the suffrage was gradually liberalized through a combination of inflation and legislative indifference). Elections were long, ritualized community gatherings that often stretched from dawn to dusk, discouraging those with little at stake from attendance. Voting was by secret ballot for governor and assembly, by public proclamation for the council. Even supposedly secret ballots were subject to inspection by local election officials. Popular preferences were filtered in elections for the council by an ingenious system whereby voters "nominated" candidates for these offices in September and chose among their own nominees in April. By listing the incumbent candidates before their newly nominated rivals on the April ballot, Connecticut's leaders stacked the deck in favor of stability.

Connecticut's religious establishment also contributed to the colony's political and cultural stability. Religion was woven deep into the fabric of Connecticut's politics. The Congregational Church was the established church, liberally supported by the state's tax dollars. Throughout the eighteenth century Congregationalist ministers opened every session of the state legislature with a profoundly political oration and did the same at most local election day gatherings. A resoundingly conservative Puritanism thundered from Connecticut's pulpits, affirming hierarchical social organization as God's design and portraying faction and discord as grave sins. Congregationalism's power was further enhanced by its control of the colony's leading college, Yale. The Great Awakening temporarily shook the state's religious establishment, but the Congregationalist elite responded pragmatically, allowing dissenters limited exemptions from taxation and forming a political partnership with the equally conservative Episcopalian Church.

The coming of the Revolution did little to alter Connecticut's political system. In a move matched only by Rhode Island, newly independent Connecticut did not draft a state constitution. The legislature simply

affirmed the colonial charter as the fundamental law of the land, delet-
ing all references to the crown and substituting oaths of loyalty to the
state for those of allegiance to the monarch. The conditions that led to
internecine political warfare in many of the new states were absent in
Connecticut. Ethnically, Connecticut was the most homogeneous state
in the nation.[7] By the Revolution, Connecticut also lacked a significant
unsettled backcountry. The absence of an internal frontier spared the
state the kind of east-west tensions that racked Pennsylvania, Massachusetts, and the Carolinas.

The state's dominant elite retained its power through the period of
national Confederation and wholeheartedly endorsed the federal Constitution. Elections to national office were integrated into the state's traditional electoral system, with congressional candidates selected through
the same process as councilors (full slate election rather than districts,
a two-stage electoral procedure, and public voting). Connecticut's pre-
Revolutionary leaders retained their positions of power, supplemented
by a new generation of their offspring and protégés.

Throughout the 1790s Connecticut politics retained its extraordinary
stability and homogeneity. The state spoke with a unified voice in the
halls of Congress, supporting the Federalist administrations of Washington and Adams. The French Revolution met with nearly universal approval
in its earliest phases and with equally strenuous condemnation once it
took a more radical turn. An occasional advocate of greater democracy,
religious disestablishment, or the French Revolution found his way into
the assembly, but most elections continued to result in an uncontested
victory by an arch-Federalist. The nascent ideological opposition first
proposed candidates for high office in 1796, but council candidates
Gideon Granger and Ephraim Kirby captured only a handful of votes.
Before 1800 no Federalist candidate for statewide or national office
faced serious opposition.

However, with a suddenness that stunned nearly every political observer
in the Land of Steady Habits, Connecticut's Jeffersonians established an
efficient and energetic political organization to contest the election of
1800. Campaigning with vigor and making unprecedentedly explicit
appeals for popular support, the Republicans succeeded in placing two
of their number on the list of nominees for Congress. When the fall election arrived, over a third of the voters sided with the party of Jefferson.
From that date forward, every election for statewide or national office
was openly contested by a Republican candidate. For the next fifteen
years the Jeffersonians remained a strong minority party, never winning a

statewide election or capturing control of the assembly but often garnering as much as 35 to 40 percent of the popular vote.

The rise of the Connecticut Republican party did more than offer a challenge to the hegemony of the state's Standing Order; it also fundamentally reworked the nature of politics in the Land of Steady Habits. Within a few years Connecticut went from a colonial electoral system, in which election day served as a ritualistic reaffirmation of communal solidarity and deference, to a nineteenth-century structure in which organized groups of men propagandized for rival slates of candidates and dragged unprecedented numbers of voters to the polls. Federalists and Jeffersonians published rabidly partisan newspapers and pamphlets. Both parties organized statewide networks to distribute information, manage strategy, and ensure a large voter turnout. The Republicans went so far as to hold mass rallies, patterned on revival meetings, in the closing days of campaigns. Statewide vote totals, which had lingered around 4,000 during the 1790s, surpassed 22,000 by 1803.

Both the electoral success of the Jeffersonians and the rising tide of popular politics left Connecticut's Federalist elite feeling isolated. Defeated at the polls, neither comfortable with nor proficient at the new politics, and worried that the specific policies of the Jeffersonians promised doom for the republic, Federalism's mood was bleak. The ability of the Connecticut Federalists to retain control of their state had a paradoxical effect on the psyche of the party's leading members; rather than taking comfort from their success, Connecticut Federalists portrayed their state as the last bastion of rational liberty, isolated from the nation and besieged by an alien Jeffersonian culture.

During the interval between Jefferson's election in 1800 and Oliver Wolcott's ascension to the governor's chair in 1818, Connecticut Federalists viewed themselves as politically and ideologically under attack. Their pamphlets, speeches, sermons, and proclamations were the attempts of an entrenched elite to defend a worldview which had once been hegemonic but was now under constant attack. Federalist pamphleteers and electioneers drew on their staple ideological strains—classical republicanism, reverence for tradition, inchoate caution, New England provincialism, and paternalism—with great skill and fervor during these two tumultuous decades. While their efforts ultimately failed, they left behind a literary testimonial to the public philosophy of the Federalist party.

THE LAST THREE decades have seen the rise of the "republican synthesis." Though *republicanism* has meant something different to every historian who has employed the term, a few broad concepts convey its essence. Republicanism focuses on the fragility of civil society, especially participatory government. It posits a cycle of growth and decay which every republic is likely to travel. If the people do not vigilantely protect their government, the ambitious and avaricious will pervert the institutions of the state to serve their particularistic purposes. Civic virtue is the best protection against such corruption; hence, virtue is the sinew of a republic. The term *virtue* stands for a variety of concepts in the republican lexicon. Virtuous individuals are independent, honest, and frugal. Most importantly, they value the common good over their individual interests and are willing to make sacrifices to serve the republic.

Just months before the "revolution of 1800," a Philadelphia publisher released an anonymous treatise entitled *Essay on Political Society*. The author, Connecticut Federalist congressman Samuel Whittlesey Dana, defined the political task facing his contemporaries in classical republican terms. At the beginning of the text, he announced, "In the present eventful crisis of human affairs, the grand question . . . is *how shall humanity be protected against despotism?*" Sixty pages later he expanded upon these sentiments: "How shall the constitutional order of the whole be protected against the despotism of the administrative authorities? How can the social body be saved from the death which has long since desolated the countries so famous in Grecian, and in Roman, story? In a word, how is the system to be conserved?" Dana's essay, the most thorough work of political philosophy written by a Connecticut Federalist, revealed the concerns motivating Federalist thinkers. The questions that they sought to answer concerned the fragility of republican government and the persistent threat of despotism.[8]

Nearly every Federalist writer or orator emphasized the importance of republican virtues such as "frugal tempers, simple habits, and industrious, active spirit." David Daggett, a Yale law professor who held virtually every office of honor in the state except governor, made repeated references to these virtues in his influential tracts. David Humphreys, former minister to Spain, spoke in the richest detail: "It is not fickle fortune, but calculated effort, that makes and keeps men free and happy. When they become habitually sluggish, immoral, ignorant, or indifferent to their interests, they are far advanced to the brink of perdition and ready to fall, an easy prey to a crafty Demagogue or a daring Despot."[9]

Public-spiritedness lies at the heart of the Federalist conception of virtue. For a republic to survive and thrive, both voters and officeholders must value the general welfare over particularistic aims. As Yale president

Timothy Dwight argued, "The public good should be the supreme object of every man." To that end, other leading Federalists emphasized that the suffrage is "the only fountain of Republicanism." Voters have a sacred duty "to vote for the best man." If they do so, "the country can be in no danger." If, however, they use their ballots to further their individual interests or if they fail to vote at all, the republic is doomed.[10]

Connecticut Federalists saw government as "the ministry of the good." As the Reverend Benjamin Trumbull explained, "Civil government is arduous work. . . . It is of the highest importance that civil rulers be men, displaying that knowledge, prudence, fortitude, and magnanimity which are the glory of men." Whether these men of talent answered the call of public service was the ultimate test of their moral worth. "For men of great dignity and consideration . . . to prefer private to public good, the honors, wealth, and pleasure of time, to those of eternity, [is] inconsistent with the reason and dignity of man."[11]

Many Connecticut Federalists saw their party's defeat in the 1800 presidential election as a harbinger of the demise of the American republic. They observed the policies of the ensuing Republican administrations through a skeptical republican lens. The Federalists styled themselves as protectors of liberty and watched vigilantly for the first signs of tyranny. Jefferson's decision to remove the Federalist collector of the port of New Haven was greeted with particular horror. The new president was accused of *political intolerance no less despotic than wicked"* and of "a species of mental tyranny." The failure of the new administration to fulfill its campaign promises was taken as an indication that the Republicans only sought office in order to gratify their ambition. Seen through a classical republican lens, the Louisiana Purchase was decried as a usurpation of power.[12]

The Federalists believed they were the real republicans; the Republicans were democrats. As one Federalist pamphleteer explained, both republicanism and democracy view the people as sovereign. However, in a republic, once a government is legitimately formed, sovereignty resides in the government, unless it is forfeited through egregious and repeated acts of tyranny. On the other hand, in a democracy, the populace retains sovereignty even after a government is formed; government caters to its every whim.[13] A republic is a well-ordered political community, carefully designed to filter out the passions and jealousies of the mob before allowing popular opinion to affect decisions of state. Daggett portrayed the democratic alternative with his characteristic sarcasm: "Mobs never talk of any authority except that of the *sovereign people.—*To the *sovereign people* they go, and to the *sovereign people* they appeal until a *sovereign people* are cruelly insulted, cajoled, and enslaved."[14]

After the Republican Congress acceded to President Jefferson's request and imposed an embargo on American shipping in 1807, the virulence of Federalist attacks on the administration increased markedly. In February 1809 Governor Jonathan Trumbull, Jr., refused to employ state officials to squelch the "scandalous insubordination" of those who defied the Embargo.[15] Trumbull's action marked the beginning of a six-year battle between the state of Connecticut and the federal government. When Congress finally voted for war on June 4, 1812, the entire Connecticut delegation, all Federalists, voted against the declaration.

The vocabulary of resistance to the administration's foreign policy drew upon classical republican language and themes. The Connecticut General Assembly declared the Embargo "arbitrary, oppressive, and unconstitutional," while Governor Roger Griswold rejected a federal requisition of the state militia because it is "the duty of Freemen" to watch for and warn against "any system of policy which seeks personal elevation or aggrandizement, or which is calculated to promote the projects of foreign or domestic tyrants, or to aid combinations of enemies at home or abroad against the peace, liberty, and prosperity of the nation."[16]

As the war dragged on, Federalist ire continued to mount. Two British attacks upon the coast of Connecticut fanned the flames of anger and sparked new fears. Like the Massachusetts Federalists described by Banner, by 1814 Connecticut's leaders "had come to view the government in Washington much as the colonists had earlier come to envisage the ministry at Whitehall: distant, alien, determined upon obedience, and heedless of the public will." George Washington Stanley detailed the "calamities" of the war by citing seven grievances from the Declaration of Independence that were applicable to the current situation. Another Connecticut Federalist drew a parallel between the first Republican president and the leading republican villains of antiquity: "Cataline, Cromwell, and Jefferson were very similar characters."[17]

While greatly disturbed by the turn of events, Connecticut Federalists expressed little surprise. For fifteen years they had warned the American people that their nation would one day face such a calamity. To a Federalist the course of events was crystal clear. The people had not been vigilant. The rulers had not been virtuous. Hence, the republic was in decline. One Federalist orator delineated the decay of the republic: "To the slow but certain acquirements of honest industry have succeeded the mercenary and capricious gains of speculation. The interests of the many have been sacrificed to the interests of the few. . . . To peace was succeeded war. . . . To these miseries is to be added the accumulation of taxes of various descriptions." Federalists watched with appropriate republican horror as "war, armies, and taxes with all their train of concomitant evils" dragged the republic toward the abyss. The report of the Hartford Convention can be read as an indictment against the federal government, charging it with crimes against the classical republican creed: "lust and caprice of power, corruption of patronage, the oppression of the weaker interests of the community by the stronger, heavy taxes, and wasteful expenditures."[18]

There has always been a tension between optimism and pessimism implicit in classical republicanism. On one hand, republicanism laid out the road map to an idyllic future. On the other hand, the road to this utopia was replete with danger. At most times republican thinkers could live with such a tension. However, in moments of crisis working out the long-term ramifications of republicanism became an obsession. The year 1814 and the first months of 1815 were just such a time of crisis for Connecticut Federalists. Federalist orators began to broach the possibility that the republic might be mortally ill; they warned their audiences: "You stand on the borders of a frightful precipice—upon the very verge of political destruction. Another step in advance may produce the fatal leap, which succeeding generations can never recal[l], nor future repentance remedy."[19]

No single document reveals more about the republicanism of Connecticut Federalists than a letter which Calvin Goddard wrote David Daggett in November 1814. Goddard, a former congressman and Speaker of the Connecticut assembly about to be named a delegate to the Hartford Convention, would two years later become the first Connecticut Federalist to be defeated in a campaign for statewide office. In this letter he made explicit the republican basis of his opposition to the war: "We must not—*will* not submit to despotism. I am a republican—truly—absolutely and strongly so—born—bred—educated to be so.—I am willing for the sake of repose to make sacrifices, but not to become a slave or to entail slavery upon *six* dear little ones who are to come after me." In a twisting paragraph he expresses the tortured tension that many Federalists felt: "I am no rebel—have no scheme of severing the Union.—I should consider it an act of no small magnitude if accomplished by *compact* in the most peaceable way—As horrible if accomplished by force. . . . But New Englanders are not yet taught to be slaves. . . . We do not mean to threaten. . . . We have not done much yet."[20]

THAT THE FEDERALISTS were conservatives is a matter of little dispute. David Hackett Fischer entitled his work on the development of the Federalist party *The Revolution of American Conservatism*. The standard general history of Connecticut subtitles its chapter on the period of Federalist rule "Conservatism and Then Some."[21] Few historians, however, have explored the nature and basis of the conservatism that is so closely associated with the Federalist party.

When Connecticut Federalists called themselves "conservatives," they meant the term to be read literally. They sought to preserve, to conserve, the state's traditional institutions. They swore eternal hostility against those who attempted to desecrate these sacred institutions with "innovations and schemes." Their powerful traditionalism drew its inspiration from two distinct sources. One was an inchoate sense of caution or prudence. They were skeptical of new ideas, quick to discover the dangers implicit in any proposal. Equally importantly, however, Connecticut Federalists sincerely believed that the institutions that they had inherited were "a specimen of republican institutions." Their ancestors had constructed a system of institutions "envied by many other portions of men, but enjoyed by few, if any." Their reverence for the particular institutions of their state combined with their cautious temperaments to breed a fierce traditionalism.[22]

Connecticut was known as the "Land of Steady Habits," and the state's Federalists wore that designation as a badge of honor. In a pamphlet aptly entitled *Steady Habits Vindicated*, Daggett explained the importance of stability in the realm of public affairs: "Political institutions and systems of laws to which the people have been long accustomed, become natural, and are much more likely to fit easily upon them, than other regulations, equally good, to which they have not been used." Even if they are salutary, new laws for "a longtime fit awkwardly and unpleasantly upon the people." If the innovations are mistaken, the potential damage is extraordinary: "Experiments upon the natural body are dangerous, and on the body politic, they are equally dangerous.—When people are led to make the wrong step in their public concerns, and especially in the arrangement of their government, their first error may lead to a second, and that again to a third—till at length they will have travelled so far astray, as to find it impossible to get back to the plain and safe road that they left." In Daggett's eyes only one conclusion can be drawn from his observations: "Be not in haste to embrace novelties. Sober consideration is the daughter of wisdom."[23]

The Federalists reserved particular antipathy for innovations that grew out of abstract philosophical speculation. Revolutionary France was the paradigmatic example of what can happen when political theory guides political practice. Federalists rejected rationalist challenges to "maxims in politics, morals, and religion which have been sanctioned by the wisdom of the ages" and portrayed "the testimony of long experience" as "testimony that never deceives." One Litchfield Federalist expressed similar sentiments with particular verve: "Jacobins may bark and Revolutionizers redouble their curses at Salutary Laws and Steady Habits. Old fashioned David shall still be found firm to his Post, neither slumbering nor going astray."[24]

Connecticut Federalists believed that their institutions represented the accumulated wisdom of generations. They saw themselves as guardians of these institutions, benefiting from the wisdom and exertion of their ancestors and working to pass on similar benefits to their descendants. As Daggett explained: "We have an inheritance fairer than merchandize, farms, and 'cattle on a thousand hills'—an inheritance of institutions, civil, social, and religious, calculated to make us wiser and better. This inheritance was purchased by some of the best blood of the best men;—it is consecrated by the tears and prayers of our fathers. This inheritance is committed to you—it is a precious deposit. . . . I conjure you to defend and transmit to your children, inviolate, this glorious inheritance." Theodore Dwight argued that "Connecticut exhibits the only instance in the history of nations, of a government purely [r]epublican, which has stood the test of experience for more than a century and a half, with firmness to withstand the shocks of faction and revolution." Paying his state the highest Burkean compliment, he concluded, "Our government, is a government of practice, and not of theory."[25]

Federalist orators and writers described in great detail the institutions that "formed and maintained a state of peace, order, and happiness." In particular, they heaped lavish praise on the structure of the state's government. Connecticut was "purely [r]epublican." "The electoral franchise" served as the basis for selecting the state's leaders. Elections were "free and frequent." However, elaborate steps were taken to insulate the government from the whims of the electorate and the machinations of factions.[26]

When the Federalists praised Connecticut's "institutions," they referred to more than its government. Like other Burkean conservatives, they believed that the social fabric is held together by extragovernmental institutions which bind individual to individual and generation to generation. A well-functioning family is the most effective of such institutions; religion and education are also vitally important. Other institutions—the militia, town meetings, debating societies, even taverns—can, on occasion, perform such a function, but none have the same influence as the family, the church, or the school. Federalists venerated their churches and schools as the "bulwarks of society" and as "our strong fortress of defence." One pamphleteer employed a particularly effective metaphor: "These excellent institutions are the *salt* that has hitherto preserved the body politic from putrification."[27]

Schools and churches developed the characteristics that were necessary for the maintenance of a stable republican society: wisdom, virtue, piety, and respect for authority. Benjamin Trumbull defended an extensive school system on the grounds that "men must understand the great principles of rational liberty, that they may contend and maintain them." Similarly, S. W. Dana depicted "institutions for the general diffusion of knowledge" as indispensable weapons in the struggle to "conserve" a republic. Praising the status quo, Timothy Dwight observed that in Connecticut "four thousand schools receive your children to their bosom, and nurse them to wisdom and piety" and "a thousand churches are vocal with the praise of your creator." Tapping Reeve spoke for his Federalist colleagues when he dubbed the clergy "unshaken friends of peace and good order."[28]

The Connecticut Federalists' praise of their society encompassed not only esteem for its "institutions" but also reverence for its "habits" and "manners." They spoke of the collective character of the people and believed that the relationship between society's institutions and its "system of habits, of manners, and of principles" was symbiotic. Dana described "manners, over which the public administration has such plastic powers, and which in return have such influence on the public administration." Daggett wrote about the "cycle" whereby "habits, manners, and opinions" influence "institutions" and are then reshaped by them. The Reverend Mr. Trumbull spoke of the "mutual influence" of pious habits and republican institutions.[29] Society was an organic entity; any little change in either manners or institutions might severely damage the homeostatic balance.

The public philosophy of Connecticut Federalism during the first decade of the nineteenth century was marked by the comfortable coexistence of caution and reverence for the status quo. These two impulses, the twin pillars of Federalist conservatism, led to similar conclusions on the great majority of public policy issues. Both advised against drafting a new constitution, altering the suffrage qualifications, or limiting public support for religion. At times Federalist pamphleteers appealed to these impulses sequentially. For example, Daggett defended the property qualification for voting in terms both of wisdom and of caution. In *Facts Are Stubborn Things*, he appealed first to the wisdom of the law: "It will be found a sound maxim that the right of suffrage should principally rest in the great body of landholders. They have too much self-respect to endure the slightest approach to slavery—they have too much at stake to tolerate anarchy—equally opposed to these dreadful extremes and bound to their country by a strong tie, they should have a commanding influence in the choice of rulers." A few lines later he emphasized caution: "It should also be noted that on an experiment of nearly two centuries, Connecticut has been happy without universal suffrage—an experiment thus sanctioned should not be abandoned upon the arguments of interested partizans."[30]

More often, however, Connecticut Federalists wove the two arguments together. Writers and orators skillfully combined the language of prudence with self-congratulation to produce a powerful conservative rhetoric. As they would soon discover, this persuasive rhetoric was purchased at a price. The amalgamation of the two conservative impulses into one idiom obscured the philosophical basis of the Federalist persuasion. Long after the twin impulses suggested different policy courses, Federalist pamphleteers were still employing amalgamated rhetoric in their propaganda. For example, one pamphlet, written during the pivotal campaign of 1817, attacked the wisdom of changing course: "Why should this mighty good be put in jeopardy at the call of pretended reformers— why unsettle the foundations, laid with so much skill and wisdom by our ancestors?—why demolish in a few days what was attained by the labor and toil, the anxiety and fortitude of many years—why throw away in sport, or in passion, blessings which good men obtained with their blood?"[31] Words such as "jeopardy," "unsettle," "demolish," and "throw away" suggest an argument premised on prudence, while "good," "skill," "wisdom," and "blessings" imply reverence for the particular institutions of the state.

The twin crises of the Embargo and the war exposed the contradiction between a conservatism based on caution and one premised on reverence for traditional institutions. Before, criticism of the administration had called principally for pro-active behavior. Even the most hated policies of the Jefferson administration were despised more for the despotism they foreshadowed than for their direct consequences. The Embargo and the war, however, were different. They were portents not of distant danger but of imminent disaster. In the eyes of New England Federalists, "want

and beggary" were the most likely fruit of an embargo, while war promised only "fire and desolation."[32] Abstract fears of standing armies, heavy
taxes, and draconian conscription became concrete realities. Speculation
and profiteering ran rampant. The status quo had become unacceptable.

Connecticut Federalists were left without a philosophical compass.
The two impulses that undergirded their conservatism pointed them in
different directions. For the first time they were forced to choose between their cautious temperaments and the institutions and habits that
they valued so deeply. If they were to save their institutions, they would
have to fight. Vigilance was no longer enough. They would be forced to
challenge the national authorities, to provoke discord, to take steps that
might end in the dissolution of the young nation. They faced the same
dilemma that confronts all conservatives when they no longer approve of
the status quo: do they remain true to their conservative temperaments
and retreat into a defensive posture, or do they transform themselves
into reactionaries and battle tenaciously to restore some glorious past?

Connecticut Federalists struggled with this quandary throughout the
war. While they opposed federal efforts to requisition the state militia,
refused to lend money to the war effort, and dissuaded the state's citizens
from volunteering for service, Connecticut's leading citizens consistently
delayed any direct challenge to the authority of the federal government.
In the words of the Connecticut General Assembly, they "felt themselves
constrained by . . . their sacred regard to the constitutional union of the
states." The assembly reminded its constituents, agitating for more forceful action, that "intemperate, rash, disorderly proceedings injure the
reputation of a people, as to wisdom, valour, and virtue without procuring them the least benefit."[33]

In the fall of 1814, with the British menacing the region's shores, the
New England states convened at Hartford to decide upon a common
course of action. The leaders of the Hartford Convention were cautious
men, unwilling to drive a dagger into the heart of the ailing republic.
As one Connecticut delegate explained on the eve of the convention, the
people were "more ardent" than their representatives; another leading
Federalist advised his son that "the object is not to dismember the union,
but to obtain relief from the pressures of intolerable burdens."[34] The
convention's final recommendations were relatively innocuous; the "infamous" Hartford Convention merely issued a denunciation of the war,
requested that the New England states be allowed to coordinate their
own defense, and called for a series of constitutional amendments to protect New England's interests within the national confederation. When

forced to decide between the two pillars of conservatism, the Federalists chose to err on the side of caution.

The Federalists faced a similar philosophical conundrum in the years immediately following the war. As Steven Watts has argued, "The gratifying denouement of the War of 1812 brought the history of the American early republic to a close."[35] The world that the Federalists faced in the immediate aftermath of the war bore only limited resemblance to the idyllic organic community of their dreams. The forces that had affected these changes had been in operation long before the war. However, the war let loose energies and passions that sped up the process of change. By 1815 many Connecticut Federalists acknowledged that support for the old institutions and habits of the state was a restorationist sentiment, not a conservative one.

Once again, the Federalists struggled to chose between the two principles that had jointly shaped their conservatism. As historians have traditionally portrayed the ensuing events, the Federalists quickly embraced caution and grudgingly acquiesced to the loss of their ordered world. While the majority of Federalists did choose caution, a sizable minority preferred to battle to reestablish traditional institutions and habits. This battle took place on two fronts. On the political front Connecticut Federalists organized societies with the avowed purpose of "restoring in the administration of the government, those principles which were regarded in our better days." These avowedly restorationist institutions actively contested for the support of the mass of voters. As George Washington Stanley commented in an oration before the Washington Benevolent Society, his goal was "to hasten the downfall of error, and to rebuild on its ruins, that glorious temple of civil liberty, which in the days of Washington received the admiration and revere of the world."[36]

Other Federalists chose to view the struggle to reestablish traditional institutions and habits as a moral, rather than a political, battle. Lyman Beecher's 1812 sermon *A Reformation of Morals*, in which he first developed many of the themes that would make him a leader of the Second Great Awakening, is the angry product of a Federalist dismayed by the path chosen by the majority of his party. Throughout the text he decries the "timid" who "lament bitterly, the prevailing evils of the day, and multiply predictions of divine judgments and speedy ruin—But if a voice be raised or a finger lifted to attempt a reformation, they are in a tremor, lest the peace of society be invaded." He reserves particular enmity for those who opposed efforts at reformation due to their novelty: "'What new thing is this? Did our fathers ever do this?' . . . But because they did not make special efforts to repel an enemy which did not assail them, shall we neglect by appropriate means to resist an enemy which is pouring in like a flood, and threatens to sweep us away?" Beecher's reformation was actually a restoration: "Our fathers established, and for a great while preserved the most perfect state of society probably that has ever existed in this fallen world. . . . The same causes will still produce the same effects, and no other causes will produce them. New England can retain her preeminence only by upholding those institutions and habits which produced it."[37]

The Federalists sought to conserve the traditional institutions of their state both because they revered the particular institutions that they had inherited and because they were cautious people who despised the tumult that accompanies change. When these two impulses drew them in the same direction, they provided a firm foundation on which to construct a conservative public philosophy. However, when the impulses pulled the Federalists in different directions, as they increasingly did during and after the War of 1812, they tore the party apart. Ideological fissures soon became political fissures. When no Federalist could remain true to both of the conservative impulses upon which their public philosophy had drawn, the party's days were numbered.

WHILE REPUBLICANISM and conservatism provided much of the content of Connecticut Federalism, regional patriotism also played a crucial role in shaping the party's rhetoric and ideology. Federalist reaction to issues of ethnicity, regionalism, and race was shaped by a condescending yet sincerely philanthropic Yankee provincialism. Uniformly male, cocksure in their opinions, unwilling to share authority, prone to moralizing, yet ultimately benevolent, the leaders of Connecticut Federalism were archetypal paternalists.

New England Federalists believed that their region was "the birthplace of the American Union." They saw the jealous defense of liberty as the nation's defining characteristic. This principle was brought to America by Puritans fleeing religious persecution and was maintained and disseminated by hardy New Englanders. Dana was repeating one of the first lessons a young Federalist learned when he noted that "a zeal for civil and religious liberty planted the first settlements." Uriah Tracy described the citizens of Connecticut as "the descendants of parents who braved the dangers of the ocean, and the wilderness howling with beasts and with savages, for the sake of securing themselves and descendants the right of thinking and acting independent of every man and every thing, the laws of their country and their God excepted." Connecticut Federalists were certain that these early efforts had borne extraordinary fruit. As Beecher smugly commented, "Our fathers established, and for a great while preserved, the most perfect state of society probably that has ever existed in this fallen world." Benjamin Trumbull ended his litany of praise for the institutions and customs of his region with the rhetorical question, "Where is the community upon earth which rivals her?"[38]

Federalists believed that New England's homogeneity had facilitated the success of their society. David Humphreys reminded his audience that "few districts with equal population, in any part of the world are more homogenous . . . than New-England." Dana prefaced his essay lauding the institutions of Connecticut with the comment, "The inhabitants of New-England are known to be, almost universally, descended from a common ancestry." Timothy Dwight commented more extensively: "In this country you all sprang from one flock, speak one language, have one system of manners, profess one religion, and wear one character. Your laws, your institutions, your interests are one. No mixture weakens, no stranger divides you."[39]

The emphasis in these orations is upon the homogeneity of the population, not on its particular racial or ethnic origin. The Federalists believed that a homogeneous population provided for a unified society. The more similar the members of a community were, the easier it was to divine the general interest and base policy upon it. In a society divided along racial, ethnic, or religious lines, individuals might place their loyalty to a particular group over their loyalty to the society as a whole, dooming the polity.

New Englanders saw themselves as "a superior caste." Federalist rhetoric consistently emphasized the environmental roots of this superiority; Connecticut Federalists understood that republican citizens are made, not born. References to New Englanders' "manners," "habits," and "character" were consistently conjoined with praise for the region's parents, teachers, ministers, and magistrates. When Daggett wrote, "There is virtue and intelligence in the people of Connecticut," he was complimenting the state's churches and schools, not its gene pool.[40]

Antipathy for outsiders was the negative flip side of provincialist pride. The Federalists were critical of immigrants, whom they feared carried with them dangerous political and religious ideas. They were particularly fearful that the dreaded Jacobinism of the French Revolution would contaminate the shores of their young nation. The leading role that immigrants played in the Republican party (seen by many Federalists as the

American Jacobin party) confirmed their fears. Congressman Matthew Lyon was vilified as an "*imported* bear in human shape"; Albert Gallatin was dismissed as an "*imported* Secretary of the Treasury." While New Englanders had been "nurtured in the . . . school of republican freedom," the majority of their European counterparts were not yet prepared for republican citizenship. Immigrants were the dregs of European society, those least qualified for the rigors of civic participation. For Daggett, they were "foreigners. . . who fled from the justice of their own countries, with characters as black as mid-night darkness." That many of them were Catholic further terrified the Federalist clergy. Making a charge which Catholics would continue to face for the next century and a half, Timothy Dwight questioned whether Catholic citizens would place their duty to the republic over their loyalty to the "Romanish Empire." These fears and prejudices were at the root of the Hartford Convention's proposed constitutional amendment to ban naturalized citizens from holding national office.[41]

The provincialism of New England Federalism both encouraged the growth of antislavery sentiment and limited Federalist commitment to American blacks. Following Revolutionary War pamphleteers, Federalists used words such as "slavery" and "bondage" to describe a political condition characterized by the loss of self-determination and the tyrannous rule of a despot or oligarchy. Daggett praised his ancestors for possessing "the intrepidy of freemen who despised even the appearance of slavery" and argued that landowners "have too much self respect to endure even the slightest approach to slavery." Writing about the relative merits of a standing army and a navy, Noah Webster suggested that an army is more likely "to reduce the people to bondage." Expressing opposition to the War of 1812, Calvin Goddard spoke for most Federalists when he wrote, "New Englanders are not yet taught to be slaves."[42]

While both political parties condemned political slavery in early nineteenth-century Connecticut, Federalists were much more likely to draw a connection between the political slavery that they feared and the continuing slavery of African Americans. In the immediate aftermath of the Revolution, Connecticut's "Standing Order," the leaders who would one day form the backbone of the Federalist party, had taken steps to eradicate slavery in their own state.[43] Federalist leaders often pointed to the abolition of the slave trade as a rare exception to their principled aversion to "reforms." Orations before the Society of the Cincinnati and the Washington Benevolent Society routinely attacked the evils of chattel slavery. One orator turned opposition to slavery into a moral litmus test: "Let not that man call himself a friend to his species who can see with indifference even the humbled African reduced to slavery." Another concluded his speech with a poem which included the question, "Oh! gracious Heaven, must the shackles be yet riveted on endless generations?"[44]

Bernard Bailyn has described liberty as a "contagion" which, upon entering the body politic, attacks forms of oppression never before acknowledged or challenged. During their struggle against the Republicans, New England Federalists received a second dose of this contagion. Sensing the common nature of their oppression and the common identity of their oppressor, New England Federalists became more receptive to the antislavery implications of their republican thought. The Federalists noted the disproportionate representation of Virginians in the councils of power with trepidation. They disparagingly labeled their opponents the "Virginia Party." One circular letter complained that nearly "the whole country . . . lies bound hand and foot at the feet of the proud Lords of Virginia." Several Federalists made explicit connections between the political slavery that they feared and the physical slavery of African Americans in the South. One orator argued that the draconian conscription laws of the War of 1812 could only have been "engendered in a mind familiarized to the horrors of oppression, by an habitual acquaintance with slavery, [and] could not have been harbored in a heart not already dead to every manly and social feeling." In a powerful passage, another Federalist wrote: "The truth is, my countrymen, your interests have been sacrificed to gratify the domineering spirit of Virginia. The lordly planter of the Old Dominion, and of Kentucky, in all the rank pride of a haughty aristocrat, have so long exercised an uncontrolled tyranny over thousands and tens of thousands of their fellow men, whom they hold in cruel and ignominious bondage, that they imagine the interests of all men ought to yield to them. Of what importance are you, my countrymen, in the eyes of a Virginia nabob with a hundred slaves at his heels[?]"[45]

The Louisiana Purchase threatened to breathe new vigor into the institution of bondage, spelling political doom for the North and prolonged indignities for African-American slaves. These two concerns melded in the minds and arguments of Federalists. Humphreys commented critically, "Let those who wish for the increase of slaves, rejoice in this new nursery for them." Connecticut senator James Hillhouse led the congressional opposition to the admission of new slave states carved from the new territory. His argument was forthright: "I consider slavery as a serious evil and wish to check it wherever I have authority." In a passage dripping with irony and outrage, another Federalist wrote: "It may be added that Louisiana is to be a field of blood before it is a cultured field; and indeed a field of blood while it is cultivated. The natives of the soil, a numerous race, who have never injured us, and never will until encroached upon, must be driven out; and a still more numerous race from Africa must be violently brought in, to toil and bleed under the lath. It is for such an extension of human liberty and of human happiness that we are called upon for such sacrifice?" The Federalists had come to see southern chattel slavery and Republican political domination as thoroughly interwoven phenomena.[46]

Slave Representation, a fascinating pamphlet by a well-connected young Connecticut Federalist, provides insight into the party's attitudes toward slavery. Sereno Dwight, a son of the Yale president married to Daggett's daughter, attacked the Republicans as "the Virginia faction," portrayed the Louisiana Purchase as an attempt to "perpetuate the slave country," expressed his sympathy for those living under "the curse of slavery," and bitterly condemned the infamous "three-fifths clause."

But Dwight was not entirely supportive of the oppressed blacks toiling in southern fields. The raging provincialism of his essay tarred the slaves as well as the slaveholders. He referred to the representatives apportioned to the southern states on the basis of their slave population as "Representatives of the Blacks" and observed that "those very Yankees . . . whose necks were too stiff to bend beneath the weight of *Ministerial* or even of *Royal* power . . . have bent them beneath the authority of the *Representatives of Negro Slaves!*" His analysis of the election of 1800 would lead an uninformed reader to surmise that the slaves cast ballots in the election: "*The negroes turned the majority, and actually put in the President.*" Dwight concluded his appeal with a reference to "the deep disgrace of stooping to become *the slaves of slaves.*"

Dwight's comments serve as a reminder that despite any implications to the contrary, the Federalists were not supporters of an egalitarian, biracial republic. In their eyes African-American slaves were even less suited for republican citizenship than European immigrants. Slaves lacked the traditional prerequisites for such a role: virtue and independence. Most had neither significant schooling nor a substantial stake in the community. Their habits and manners had been shaped by generations of dependence, subservience, and toil. To Connecticut Federalists, advocates of a deferential political order and supporters of property qualifications for voting, the idea that people bred and raised to serve as beasts of burden were prepared to participate in the civic life of the republic was laughable. As Dwight mockingly queried, "Shall [such] beings . . . direct when the men of the North *shall go forth into battle?* Appoint the *successors of Washington?*"[47]

The Federalists drew a sharp distinction between the abstract moral community composed of all human beings and the concrete political community whose membership was strictly limited. Hence, they saw no inconsistency between their condemnation of southern chattel slavery and their unwillingness to accord full political rights to anyone but white male property owners. In theory, republicanism drew the boundaries of the political community; participation in the civic life of the republic would be limited to those of demonstrated financial independence and moral virtue. However, as New Englanders grew more isolated and more threatened during the 1790s and the early nineteenth century, they began to believe that the people of their region were uniquely virtuous. Provincialism joined republicanism as an arbiter of the boundaries of the Federalist political community. This shift in attitude manifested itself in the proposed constitutional amendment that would have barred natural-ized citizens from holding office, in efforts to limit the power of Virginia in the national government, and in an 1814 statute which explicitly lim-ited the suffrage to whites.[48]

To early nineteenth-century men, there was nothing unique about treating a group benevolently while at the same time denying its mem-bers participation in the civic life of the republic. Their wives, mothers, and sisters belonged to just such a group. As Kerber has observed, the leading figures of Revolutionary and early national America operated under "the assumption that women were not a central part of the politi-cal community." Federalists portrayed republican virtues in a gendered manner, simultaneously reacting to and reinforcing women's exclusion from the public sphere. Benjamin Trumbull argued that "the dangers attending government call for vigilance, manly wisdom, and exertion." Stanley criticized the despotic behavior of southern slaveholders by accusing them of lacking "manly feeling." John Hall emphasized the importance of "manly integrity." Theodore Dwight's call for republican vigilance employed similar rhetoric, "I call on you then, my fellow citizens, to unite your strength, and activity manfully to resist a foe." In the lexicon of republicanism, virtue and independence were "manly"; weakness and dependence were "womanly." As Stephanie McCurry explains, gendered language "served in political tracts and speeches to construct, legitimize, and patrol the boundaries of the republican political community."[49]

The limited evidence available about the private lives of leading Feder-alists offers a necessary corrective to their public pronouncements. For example, the letters exchanged between Federalist prodigy Roger Sherman Baldwin and his future wife Elizabeth Perkins during their long courtship are filled with serious discussions of the political events of the day.[50] The couple, whose fathers were longtime political and business associates, engaged in a running political dialogue marked by the sophistication of both parties. Even in the letter that ended with his marriage proposal, Baldwin provided several pages of pithy political analysis.[51] As later events confirmed, these two young people, born into leading Federalist families and recipients of the best educations available, were destined for a political and intellectual partnership unfathomable to republican theorists.[52]

However, such a relationship was well within the norm for the couple's Federalist elders. Baldwin's own mother engaged in a serious dialogue on economic issues with Calvin Goddard, an event notable only because Goddard found Baldwin's ideas so provocative that he continued their conversation in print. Goddard's letter begins with the prescient observation, "When your biography shall be written it may create surprise that you and I should have corresponded at all and that surprise may well be increased, when it shall be known that the subject was *trade and manufactures*."[53] The arch-Federalist cabal that dominated politics and society in Litchfield, where young Baldwin attended law school, was particularly progressive on gender issues, playing important roles in the development of women's academies and the expansion of married women's property rights.[54] However inegalitarian it may have been, the paternalism that these Federalists employed toward women should never be confused with raw patriarchalism.

In sum, Federalist orators and pamphleteers combined sincere concern for the welfare of women and minorities with a belief that these groups lacked the ability to fend for themselves in the economic and political realms. This paternalism was the product of the union of a republican heritage, which viewed participation in civic affairs as the privilege and responsibility of the virtuous, and provincialist pride, which viewed the people of New England as a "superior caste." Republicanism required those who lacked "reason and virtue" to "live under the care and supervision of wise citizens." New England provincialism defined those "wise citizens" in gendered, racial, and ethnic terms.[55]

IN APRIL 1817 the world looked very different than it had for the previous quarter century. Most of the leading figures of the first party system were no longer involved in politics. Alexander Hamilton and Fisher Ames were long dead. Aaron Burr and James Madison had exited the political scene, one in disgrace and the other in glory. Albert Gallatin was traveling in Europe. Thomas Jefferson and John Adams, in frequent contact after finally putting their bitter feud behind them, were making the most of their well-earned retirement. Peace reigned in Europe. A new spirit of confidence swept an American nation which had emerged unscathed from its "second war for independence." For the first time in the young nation's history, the republic's immediate future was secure. In this new atmosphere of peace and promise, Connecticut electors did what once seemed unfathomable: they ejected the Federalist party from the seat of power.

For nearly two decades Connecticut Federalists had maintained political hegemony in the Land of Steady Habits. They won every election for governor, lieutenant governor, council, and Congress between the foundation of the Connecticut Republican party in 1800 and the elections of 1816. During that period the Republicans never captured more than 40 percent of the seats in the General Assembly or 43 percent of the vote for any statewide office, and rarely even approached those figures.

In the aftermath of the War of 1812, the electorate initially divided in similar proportions as they had before the Embargo. Fifty-seven Republicans were elected to the assembly in 1815, four less than in April 1808. Republican Elijah Boardman received 37 percent of the vote for governor; the Republican candidate had captured 38 percent in 1808.[56] However, the Republicans soon made a concerted effort to capture the votes of the state's Episcopalians, a traditionally Federalist group who gradually had become frustrated with their party's entanglement with the Congregationalist Church. An 1815 controversy caused by the unwillingness of the General Assembly to grant an Episcopalian petition for funds succeeded in "making a separate party of the Episcopalians."[57] Within months, the majority of Episcopalians joined with the Republicans to form the "Toleration party." Toleration party candidates quickly won unprecedented victories, capturing the lieutenant governorship in 1816, the governorship and control of the assembly in the spring of 1817, and control of the council in the fall of 1817. None would ever be recaptured by the Federalists.

While the shift of the Episcopalians from the Federalist column is certainly the proximate cause of Federalism's defeat, that event alone cannot account for the speed or the magnitude of its collapse. To this day, no historian has offered a compelling explanation of the events that transpired in Connecticut during 1816–20. The speeches and writings of contemporary observers do, however, provide some significant clues.

During and immediately after the War of 1812, the national Republican party gradually adopted a variety of issue positions that previously had been associated with the Federalists. Many Republicans joined with the Federalists to support a navy, a national bank, higher tariff rates, and the active encouragement of manufactures. Connecticut Federalists reacted to these developments with glee. A gloating Governor Smith commented, "The administration have fought themselves completely onto Federal ground." One Federalist campaign pamphlet cast the same argument in provincialist terms: "Connecticut, once abandoned by every state in the Union, now contemplates with pleasure and pride, a recurrence to the elevated course which she has maintained. Her policy is now the policy of the nation."[58]

A similar convergence of issue positions took place in Connecticut. Putting aside decades of polarized debate, the state's leading citizens joined together to promote the development of manufacturing. As the founding address of the Connecticut Society for the Encouragement of American Manufactures commented, "The encouragement of American Manufactures is not a question of party politics" but of "national utility." According to the new political economy of the age, "commerce and manufactures are not enemies—they are friends who assist each other and give back a portion of their gains to Agriculture that provides them the means of labor and subsistence." Presumably in an effort to advertise the bipartisanship of the society, the state's unofficial Republican party chairman, Alexander Wolcott, was named a vice-president. Similarly, when the citizens of New Haven appointed a committee to lobby for a branch of the newly reestablished Bank of the United States, Republican firebrand Abraham Bishop joined arch-Federalists such as Daggett and Hillhouse on the committee.[59]

The convergence of the two parties did much to temper the bitter partisanship of the previous decades. One leading Federalist observed, "The line of distinction between the parties, appears, I think to be less definitively drawn than in former sessions, and I hope will become, ultimately, obliterated. With it, those violent passions, which blind the eyes and pervert the heart, would also vanish." An anonymous Federalist pamphleteer voiced similar sentiments: "The measures of the general government are approved by all good citizens. . . . The great questions which have so long and so unhappily divided public opinion, have been put at rest by the general peace in Europe; and harmony prevails to a degree unknown, since the establishment of the national government." Even the dedicated partisan George Washington Stanley got into the spirit of "good feelings": "Let us forget past errors; let us forgive past injuries; and, no longer deluded by names, let us sacrifice our passions and prejudices on the altar of our country."[60]

The development of Connecticut politics in the period 1816–20 reflected the breakdown of the first party system. As the ideological divide between the parties narrowed, party loyalties loosened. Leaders of both parties were faced with the dual task of retaining wavering supporters and wooing marginal opponents. Each party found its name to be a liability in its efforts to broaden its appeal. For a decade each election saw candidates nominated by parties with different names. The bulk of former Republicans usually called themselves "Tolerationists," but occasionally they were the "American party" or the "Constitution and Reform" ticket.[61] The leading Federalists backed the "State party" in 1819 and the "Union Republicans" in 1820.[62] In 1817 both sides campaigned as the "Federal Republican party."[63]

The shift away from the old party names was more than symbolic. People who would never have considered voting for a Republican cast their ballots for Tolerationists. Similarly, individuals who had vociferously opposed the Federalists joined forces with the Union Republicans. Surveying the political landscape in 1819, Simeon Baldwin concluded "that the old parties are in great measure amalgamated."[64] The successful Tolerationist candidates for governor and lieutenant governor, former Federalist luminaries Oliver Wolcott, Jr., and Jonathan Ingersoll, epitomized the transformation of Connecticut politics. Wolcott was the son and grandson of Federalist governors and a veteran of John Adams's cabinet. Ingersoll, an Episcopalian, was a leading New Haven lawyer and a former member of the council who was under serious consideration for the Federalist nomination for lieutenant governor before he received the Tolerationist endorsement. Though they supported the disestablishment of the Congregationalist Church and a constitutional convention, even the most partisan Federalist had to admit that these men were the antithesis of Jacobinism.

The available evidence suggests the outline of an explanation for the precipitous decline of Connecticut Federalism between 1816 and 1820. The successful conclusion of the War of 1812 and the developing consensus on the issues that had traditionally divided the parties freed a critical mass of voters from the pessimism and partisanship that had tied them to the Federalist party. Episcopalians and supporters of mild constitutional reform who had previously sacrificed these concerns in order to maintain a steady political course no longer feared for the immediate survival of the republic. This margin of safety allowed them to take the rash step of "experimenting" with new leadership. Once the Federalists were removed from power and their opponents had proved themselves to be cautious and competent rulers, the famous steadiness of the Connecticut electorate worked against the Federalists. As one historian of this period has noted, "Connecticut voters had not become acquainted with the principle of rotation in office." Ingersoll was reelected six times before retiring in 1822; Wolcott won reelection nine times. In a political climate of shifting coalitions, confusing nomenclature, and ideological consensus on most of the divisive issues of the previous quarter century, the majority of the voters found comfort in the moderately conservative Wolcott.[65]

During their heyday in the early nineteenth century, Connecticut Federalists articulated a sophisticated public philosophy which wove together classical republicanism, two distinct brands of conservatism, and New England provincialism. They controlled their state through the entirety of the bitter partisan struggle that is today known as "the first party system." Connecticut voters refused to abandon the Federalists as long as the debates that had divided the nation in the 1790s continued. Once the issues changed, however, Federalist ideology offered little guidance. A new synthesis of political ideas, appropriate to the challenges at hand, became necessary. The public philosophy of Connecticut Federalism was not so much rejected as retired.

11

FROM FATHERS TO FRIENDS OF THE PEOPLE

Political Personae in the Early Republic

Alan Taylor

TAKING THEIR CUE from the social order in Great Britain, most colonial Americans accepted that public authority should be exercised by men who belonged to the so-called better sort. The phrase referred to an elite who combined superior wealth with genteel manners, classical learning, and a reputation for integrity. Prior to their Revolution, Americans presumed that social, political, and cultural authority should be united in an order of gentlemen. Artisans and common farmers could vote and hold offices in their locality—offices such as surveyors of roads or viewers of fences, offices that bore little honor, no pay, but some manual labor. But it was unthinkable that any man without all the attributes of gentility should seek the more honorific and lucrative public offices at the county or provincial level. "Surely," Robert Morris of Philadelphia insisted, "persons possessed of knowledge, judgment, information, integrity, and having extensive connections, are not to be classed with persons void of reputation or character." Almost universal and unquestioning expectation, rather than formal law, underlay the unitary authority of the genteel in colonial America. For lack of an aristocratic establishment, deference in America depended almost exclusively on public acceptance. A man was a gentleman only if other people publicly conceded that he had crossed—by breeding, education, and acquisition—that critical line separating the genteel few from the common many.[1]

Sheer wealth was necessary but not sufficient for gentility. The acquisition of wealth was the easiest and usually the first attainment of public stature. The man who achieved new wealth almost invariably lagged in his acquisition of other requisite attributes: polished manners, urbane tastes, literary and legal sophistication, and a reputation for rectitude. Indeed, social mobility was vaguely suspect as subversive of a recognized and respected social hierarchy. The self-made man was vulnerable to the

biting epithet of "mushroom gentleman"—one who had sprung up over-
night from the dung. A man of new wealth needed the approval of those
already accepted by themselves and others as possessing the attributes of
gentility. Nothing was considered more foolish, more fit for satire, than
the presumptuous upstart who assumed airs he could not master.[2]

The Revolution threatened the political cult of gentility by creating
unprecedented opportunities for aspiring men—opportunities to compete for an expanded number of electoral offices, to supply armies, to
engage in privateering, to speculate in public securities, or to exploit the
rapidly inflating currency in order to pay back debts at a fraction of their
original value. Established gentlemen felt threatened by presumptuous
upstarts who pushed their way into Revolutionary committees and legislative assemblies. In 1776 James Otis of Massachusetts complained, "When
the pot boils, the scum will rise." Anxious about their own positions and
status, established gentlemen sought, as best they could, to renew the
distance between themselves and the nouveau riche by reiterating the
importance of gentility as a prerequisite for authority. Most of the new
men, they sniffed, had acquired wealth but few of the other traditional
attributes of social superiority. Insisting that every society had a natural
aristocracy, leading Whigs hoped that independence from British control would allow the meritorious to rise gradually and gracefully to their
proper honors. But this hope for a republican meritocracy meant no
abolition of hierarchical ranks with a distinct and unitary elite at the pinnacle. Those who acquired new property in the republic were supposed
to take further pains to polish themselves into cultured and cosmopolitan gentlemen and to await social acceptance by the genteel before they
sought political authority.[3]

The Federalists who dominated national and northern state politics
during the 1790s tended to be new men of the 1770s and 1780s who had
accepted the traditional expectation that power should accrue only to
those who proved their gentility to the satisfaction of the established
families of old status. Conversely, their Republican challengers in the
North were still newer men of the 1790s and early 1800s who rejected
the colonial cult of gentility in favor of a continuing revolution in social
and political status. This chapter explores the two competing political
persuasions of the early republic by examining the careers of two pairs of
opposites who struggled for power in similar confrontations set in two
different regions. In Otsego County in upstate New York, Federalist
judge William Cooper confronted Jedediah Peck; while in Hancock
County in the District of Maine (then part of Massachusetts), General

Henry Knox was challenged by Dr. Ezekiel G. Dodge. All four men began in modest circumstances and accumulated property and power over time. But the different timing of their ascents placed the two latecomers, Peck and Dodge, in conflict with the two who had enjoyed a more meteoric rise, Cooper and Knox.

Coming into wealth and power during the years of war and of national consolidation, Cooper and Knox eagerly sought acceptance into the established elite. They did not believe that the Revolution would or should disrupt the unity of economic, social, cultural, and political authority in the same persons. They accepted the necessity of cultivating genteel ways to complete and, they hoped, perpetuate their new primacy. Having exploited the Revolutionary moment to clamber to the pinnacle of the social pyramid, the Federalist arrivistes wanted to preserve the social distinctions traditionally enjoyed by the colonial elite. They meant to consolidate the Revolution and stabilize America's social flux before it elevated over their heads newer, cruder men. To preserve their tenuous supremacy, Federalists strove mightily to weave tighter hierarchical networks of dependency binding lesser men, as clients, to their betters, as patrons. Federalists wanted to sustain a society where men could clearly identify their superiors, from whom patronage flowed, and their inferiors, from whom deference was due. To that end, Cooper and Knox and their fellow Federalists posed as "Fathers of the People"—well-meaning superiors ready to assist their lessers.[4]

Jedediah Peck and Dr. Ezekiel G. Dodge accumulated property and political ambitions at the moment when Cooper, Knox, and their compatriots were striving to consolidate their new power. Recognizing the threat posed to their further assent by Federalist grandees, Peck and Dodge sensed the possibilities for themselves in promoting more explicitly democratic politics. To displace Cooper and Knox, Peck and Dodge needed to mobilize an expanded electorate among the white men of their communities. They looked to Thomas Jefferson as their national leader, called themselves Republicans, and invited the common people to reject the politics of paternalism. The Republicans of the northern states promoted a liberal vision of society where an impartial, minimal government would secure equal opportunity for all by refusing to countenance superior privileges for the elite. They promised voters that equal rights and equal opportunity would free the market to reward the industrious poor rather than perpetuate the idle rich, gradually eliminating all vestiges of hierarchy from American politics, society, and culture. Northern Republicans defended the ambitions of the common folk enhanced by the recent Revolution. They dismissed the Federalists' denunciation of social mobility and anarchy as but a pretext for their efforts to subvert the republic and substitute the rule of an aristocracy. Thus Republican challengers spoke of themselves as "Friends of the People"—equals rather than superiors.[5]

THERE WERE striking similarities in the origins of Knox and Cooper. Both men began in modest circumstances. Henry Knox was born in 1750 in Boston, the son of a Scotch-Irish master mariner whose business failed in 1756 and who died six years later, when Henry was twelve. William Cooper was born in Byberry township, near Philadelphia, in 1754, the third son of a Quaker farmer. Both men were apprenticed in artisanal trades: Knox as a bookbinder and Cooper as a wheelwright. Neither man received more than the rudiments of a grammar school education. But as young men they were physically impressive: tall, strong, heavily built, but handsome. They were hearty, gregarious, generous, and clever men who made friends easily. A political foe once conceded, "Knox is the easiest man and has the most dignity of presence. . . . Knox stayed the longest, as indeed suited his aspect best, being more of a Bacchanalian figure" (fig. 4). James Fenimore Cooper recalled William Cooper as "my noble looking, warm hearted, witty father, with his deep laugh, sweet voice and fine rich eye, as he used to lighten the way, with his anecdote and fun" (fig. 5).[6]

Knox and Cooper began their ascents with fortunate marriages to daughters of relatively wealthy and influential men. Each married at age twenty-one, unusually early for men in colonial America, especially for those with so little property. In June 1771 Knox married Lucy Flucker over the strong opposition of her shocked parents who belonged to Boston's social elite. Thomas Flucker was the provincial secretary for Massachusetts, and his wife Hannah was the daughter of Brigadier General Samuel Waldo, who had been the largest landholder in New England. In November 1774 Cooper eloped with and married Elizabeth Fenimore, the daughter of a wealthy Quaker landholder in Burlington County, New Jersey. It hardly reassured Richard Fenimore to hear his new son-in-law declare "that he was poor and she must shift for herself." In each case the new in-laws swallowed their pride and extended financial assistance that rescued Knox and Cooper from manual labor by elevating them into the ranks of shopkeeper-entrepreneurs. A month after his marriage, Knox opened a stationery and book shop in Boston. In 1776 Cooper had appeared on a Byberry tax list as a wheelwright without any taxable prop-

4. General Henry Knox, c. 1805, oil painting by Gilbert Stuart. (Deposited by the City of Boston. Courtesy of the Museum of Fine Arts, Boston)

erty; by the mid-1780s he had acquired a store in Burlington City and a tavern and several farm lots in the adjoining township of Willingboro.[7]

During the war Knox enjoyed a more dramatic ascent by virtue of his enthusiastic participation in the Revolution. As the imperial crisis deepened, Knox was smitten with military ambition. He voraciously read books about military discipline and engineering and served as an officer in Boston's elite militia units drawn from the most respectable tradesmen and merchants. When the Revolutionary War began, Knox was one of the

5. William Cooper, 1798–98, oil painting by Gilbert Stuart. (Courtesy of the New York State Historical Association, Cooperstown

new army's few officers with a sound technical knowledge of artillery and military engineering. He parlayed his knowledge and his ebullient personality into a lifelong friendship with George Washington and into a rapid promotion through the Continental ranks, rising to brigadier general within eighteen months and to major general by the war's end. Among the officer corps and war contractors he developed an extensive network of useful friends who enjoyed powerful positions in the post-Revolutionary order. Appointed secretary of war of the United States in 1785, Knox held the post, at first under the Confederation government and later in Washington's administration, until 1794. He used his clout and army contracts to nurture his friends and garner extensive interests in an array of speculative land companies spread along almost the entire frontier arc from the Ohio territory through New York's St. Lawrence Valley to Maine. By contrast, until 1786 William Cooper remained an obscure store-keeper, tavern owner, and small-scale speculator because he had invoked his Quaker pacifism to stay out of the war.[8]

During the 1780s Cooper and Knox bid for membership in the ranks of America's wealthiest and most powerful men by acting with aggressive cunning to gain control of vast tracts of land on the frontier. They exploited the postwar opportunity to obtain thousands of acres at a critical moment when frontier land values were depressed but about to soar, when frontier land titles were tangled and uncertain but about to become more secure. Before the Revolution most of the then accessible tracts of wilderness on the frontier from Georgia to Maine belonged to wealthy and politically well-connected land speculators. The years of war and po-litical turmoil ruined the plans and fortunes of many of those speculators who had gone deeply into debt to obtain their tracts or who remained loyal to the British government. The long years of brutal warfare with Indians and loyalists along the frontier drove out settlers and depressed land values. Most of the speculators who remained loyal to the empire had their land claims confiscated or at least paralyzed during the war years by the new state republics and their courts. Cooper and Knox rec-ognized that frontier lands would inevitably soar in value as young fami-lies in the relatively crowded East took advantage of the return of peace to migrate north and west to seek new farms. Both men saw an opportu-nity to make their fortunes by employing their political connections to win legal control of certain contested frontier properties in advance of the inevitable tide of settlement. During the 1780s Cooper and Knox embarked on successful land grabs that came at the expense of older, more conservative interests who had been slow to protect and develop their claims. In the process they acted as new men rather than with the restraint expected of the ideal gentleman.[9]

The centerpiece of Knox's frontier empire was his controlling interest in the Waldo Patent, a tract of over a half-million acres located in Maine along the west bank of Penobscot Bay. On the eve of the Revolution, Lucy Knox's parents owned three-fifths of the Waldo Patent. Loyalists, the Fluckers fled to England during the war. The commonwealth of Massachusetts confiscated their property, but Knox exercised his political influence to reserve one-fifth to his wife Lucy and, in 1784, to secure his own appointment as the state's agent to manage the confiscated two-fifths. As the agent, Knox was bound to satisfy the many claims by Flucker's creditors that threatened to eat up the entire value of the remaining property. In 1791 Knox used misleading advertising and intermediaries to manage the public auction of his in-laws' holdings in a manner that ultimately secured him possession at the bargain price of $3,000, less than one-sixth of the price he would pay two years later to the other heirs of Brigadier Waldo for their two-fifths of the patent. One of the intermediaries reassured the anxious general that the sale had been "well conducted and . . . I believe not more than two in the room had the least idea that it was purchased for you and I assure you not one possible reflection or insinuation has been or can be made, as it respects you in this business." The creditors had to accept payment from the auction's paltry $3,000 proceeds, less Knox's considerable expenses as agent. In the end the commonwealth netted nothing from its confiscation of Flucker's estate, because Knox's expenses and a small part of the creditors' claims exhausted the entire land sale proceeds.[10]

In a parallel set of political and legal maneuvers, William Cooper, in partnership with another Quaker merchant from Burlington, Andrew Craig, obtained a tract of 27,000 acres of fertile land beside Lake Otsego in central New York. The tract was part of a 100,000-acre domain that had been patented originally in 1769 by the province of New York to Colonel George Croghan, an Indian agent and trader. Deeply in debt and harried by multiple creditors, Croghan sold or mortgaged and remortgaged his Otsego lands in the years preceding the Revolution. He hoped to redeem the mortgages by retailing farm-sized lots to settlers, but wartime raids and counterraids by Whigs and loyalists and Indian partisans destroyed the few small, new settlements at Otsego. Suspected of loyalism, Croghan had to lie low in Pennsylvania during the war while interest on his debts continued to mount. He died in 1782, leaving behind a tangled, encumbered estate. Despairing of ever collecting from Croghan's executors, one set of his creditors, a cartel of Quaker merchants from Burlington and Philadelphia, sold their title to his earliest Otsego mortgage to Cooper and Craig. They engaged the consummate lawyer in New York State, Alexander Hamilton, another new man elevated by the Revolution who cultivated favor among the families of old wealth and status. Without notifying Croghan's executors or the other creditors, Hamilton revived a legal judgment issued in 1773 by the New York Supreme Court against Croghan. Hamilton secured a writ authorizing the county sheriff to hold a public auction of the Otsego lands in January 1786 to satisfy the unpaid debt held by Cooper and Craig. Learning of the impending auction, some of the other creditors engaged the legal services of Hamilton's archrival at the New York bar, Aaron Burr. He obtained a court order enjoining the sheriff from proceeding with the auction. But, swayed by either Cooper's threats or his promises, the sheriff ignored the injunction and the protests of Dr. John Morgan, one of the creditors who had hastened to the auction held at a crude tavern in a remote frontier hamlet. Cooper and Craig bought the tract for £2,700 (New York currency); in effect they accepted the land as part payment for the debt (£3,913.17.6) that they had purchased from the Burlington Company. By taking possession of the major asset in Croghan's estate, Cooper and Craig deprived the other creditors of the means to collect their debts.[11]

IN ACQUIRING their wilderness empires, Henry Knox and William Cooper acted within the letter of the law but violated the niceties of genteel conduct. The genteel ideal imposed a paradox on the upwardly mobile. Wealth was a prerequisite for gentility, but in a competitive, commercial America, the acquisition of great property required an aggressive, secretive cunning that was at odds with the other attributes of gentility, especially a reputation for disinterested benevolence. Dr. John Morgan bitterly denounced Cooper and Craig as "men who place self-interest the first in the list of moral virtues, and [regard] justice to their neighbors, as an obsolete command." Morgan characterized his rivals as "men void of Principle & Veracity & full of low Cunning & Deceit." Joseph Wharton was another of Croghan's creditors ruined, in part, by Cooper's maneuvers. Wharton raged against "the man called Judge Cooper, as well from the remembrance of the sufferings of a virtuous family for many years by his subterfuges and contrivances—whereby we have sustained not only the loss of a great fortune, but met miseries of body and mind—in every shape unequalled and undeserved—and by which, he hath grown rich and great."[12]

Regarding themselves as established and virtuous gentlemen who deserved to preserve their primacy in the new republic, Morgan and Wharton invoked the ideals of gentility to denounce Cooper and to express bitter frustration at their deteriorating circumstances. The son and brother of wealthy Philadelphia merchants, Wharton became an accomplished scholar of classical literature, a respected merchant, and a leading citizen. Born into a wealthy Philadelphia family and educated in medicine at the finest universities in Europe, Morgan had returned home to become a leading doctor and professor of medicine in the colonies as well as a moderate Whig active in the Revolutionary struggle. But while Cooper was on his way up the social ladder, Wharton and Morgan were on the way down. Ruined as a merchant by the change in trade routes wrought by the Revolutionary War, Wharton had to surrender his property to his creditors and withdraw into the semiseclusion of genteel poverty. Cashiered during the war from his post as physician-in-chief of the Continental army and defeated by Cooper and Craig in the scramble for the Otsego lands, Morgan became a poor and embittered recluse during the later 1780s. He blamed his declining fortunes on a weakening of deference by the common people toward the genteel. On October 15, 1789, his friend Benjamin Rush reported: "This afternoon I was called to visit Dr. Morgan, but found him dead in a small hovel, surrounded with books and papers, and on a light dirty bed. . . . What a change from his former rank and prospects in Life! The man who once filled half the world with his name, had now scarcely friends enough left to bury him."[13]

Wealth achieved, Knox and Cooper needed to prove themselves worthy of gentility: they needed to cloak their sudden and aggressive assent by cultivating the marks of gentility and thus deflect the epithets of the Morgans, Whartons, Fluckers, and Waldos. Knox and Cooper reinvented themselves to prove to themselves and others that they were natural aristocrats innately deserving of the rewards they had seized. At a minimum, they had to present their wealth in a manner that betokened urbane refinement and grandeur. Both had to demonstrate that they could not only make money but consume it in a genteel fashion. To this end, Cooper and Knox erected great houses in the midst of their crude frontier settlements. Their mansions were conspicuous monuments to their elevated tastes as well as their superior wealth, statements of their builders' mastery over both their money and the landscape. It is especially significant that both men erected their mansions atop sites identified with the founders of the land claims Knox and Cooper had usurped. Knox's Montpelier arose on the hill in Thomaston where Brigadier Samuel Waldo had built his fort, his first mark of ownership in the Maine wilderness. In his new mansion Knox hung a full-length portrait of Waldo as both a trophy of conquest and a symbol of his claim to be the brigadier's proper heir. Similarly, William Cooper built Otsego Hall precisely where Colonel Croghan had established his compound in 1769. (Cooper named the new village around his home Cooperstown.) Although barely literate, Cooper stocked the mansion with an impressive library that he had purchased out of the confiscated estate of Sir William Johnson, the prewar owner of a baronial estate in the nearby Mohawk Valley. By subsuming the old relics and displaying symbols of old wealth, the mansions insisted that the new claimants were the natural but superior successors to the previous owners.[14]

Determined to emulate the aristocratic hauteur of the great landlords of the Hudson Valley, William Cooper designed his mansion as a copy of the manor house in Albany belonging to Stephen Van Rensselaer, the wealthiest and most prestigious of New York's landed magnates. Otsego Hall was the largest and most elegant dwelling in New York's new postwar settlements north and west of the Hudson Valley. In 1803 the mansion shocked a visiting Quaker who admonished Cooper's "want of good Philosophy in Laying out Money to adorn thy House which I thought Looked more Like the Lofty Spaniard, attached to popish Immegary, than the wise and prudent American." But Cooper was willing to shock the piously plain in order to impress the secularly genteel.[15]

In 1793–94 Henry and Lucy Knox built their mansion on an even grander scale. Four stories tall, subdivided into nineteen rooms, containing twenty-four fireplaces, surrounded by a double piazza, and trailing two matching crescents of nine outbuildings, Montpelier was the largest and most ornate private building north of Philadelphia. Knox's closest friend, General Henry Jackson, was astonished at the extravagance and expense lavished on a structure situated amid the new clearings and small houses of a frontier settlement. "From the first to this moment have I *protested* and that in the most serious manner against the *magnitude* & expense of the house you propose building," Jackson wrote. "It will be much larger than a country meeting house and . . . , it will cost more money than you have an idea of or ought to be expended in that country." But Knox brushed aside Jackson's warning because the mansion bought the effect he sought. In 1796 a visiting clergyman observed, "The General's house with double piazzas round the whole of it &c exceeded all I had seen." A decade later Leverett Saltonstall, the scion of one of Massachusetts's preeminent families, visited Montpelier and remarked, "It seems to fancy the seat of a prince with an extensive establishment."[16]

In addition to displaying taste and magnificence, genteel wealth was supposed to demonstrate benevolence: gracious and obliging munificence to inferiors. Henry Knox was especially masterful at staging acts of seemingly disinterested generosity to evoke deference from his settlers.

To mark Montpelier's completion, on July 4, 1794, the Knoxes roasted a whole ox, erected temporary tables around the piazzas that sat one hundred at a time, and threw open their doors to a gaping throng of curious men, women, and children who, summoned by a public announcement, had gathered outside the grounds at dawn. "The house was so much larger than anything they had before seen, that everything was a subject of wonder," one of the Knoxes' daughters later recalled. Determined to ease settler resentments of his claims on them for land payments, Knox toured the Waldo Patent dispensing presents. In October 1794 Henry Jackson reported, "The people are now perfectly contented & happy in consequence of your late visit, and the operation of *Bibles, Rums, Spelling Books, Brandy, Primmers, Sugars and Tea.* The effect of these has worked your salvation with a little gallantry on the part of you . . . with some of their wifes & daughters." Knox also employed dozens of local men in an array of businesses he established in Thomaston and the adjoining town of Warren: barrel works, saw- and gristmills, stores, wharves, shipping, limestone quarries and kilns, brickworks, fisheries, farms, and a canal. These expensive and unsuccessful ventures drove Knox deeply into debt, but he persisted, not only because he daily expected them to yield rich returns but also because they created extensive webs of patronage that made most of the people in the two towns, directly or indirectly, his clients.[17]

Although possessed of a keener awareness of the bottom line, William Cooper recognized the importance of cultivating a paternal image with his settlers. He took unusual pains to settle his lands quickly and compactly by offering especially good terms and by investing generously in community improvements. During the late 1780s, when Otsego's new settlers endured hardship and poverty, Cooper procured emergency food supplies from the state. He also organized maple sugar production so that they could produce an immediate cash crop to purchase desperately needed supplies. Once the settlers mastered the wilderness, began to reap surpluses from their lands, and started to meet their payments to Cooper, he subsidized refined institutions in Cooperstown village: a social library, an academy, and churches.[18]

By acts of benevolent superintendence, Cooper and Knox claimed to be "Fathers of the People" meriting deference from those they assisted. In 1801 Henry Knox insisted, "My relation to the settlers as a father and guardian and my reputation ought to be the security in the mind of every settler that my intention is to be their close friend and protector and they are to be assured that all my conduct shall conform to this idea and it will be a duty they owe to themselves to suspect the man to be their enemy who shall make a contrary suggestion." For a time, Knox and Cooper enjoyed the political affirmation they longed for from their neighbors. Thomaston's citizens routinely elected Knox to represent them in the Massachusetts General Court. Running for Congress in 1794, Cooper won 84 percent of the votes cast in Otsego County. When he ran for re-election in 1796, he increased his hold on Otsego's voters to 91 percent. In 1796 Cooper's future rival Jedediah Peck lauded his landlord as "the poor man's benefactor and the widow's support—the Father of his County." Another political supporter effused that "under the guardianship of a MAN of happy genius, sent by Heaven to civilize this country," Otsego County had passed from "a dismal wilderness: a habitation for the wolf, the bear and the panther" to "a state of high cultivation—producing all the necessaries and many of the luxuries of life."[19]

A father of a rural county had to perform a delicate balancing act in mediating between his common neighbors and the political elite gathered at the state and national capitals. His standing depended upon a mix of local popularity, expressed at polling places, and social acceptance by the statewide brotherhood of gentlemen, manifested in the private circles of the elite. On the one hand, recognized standing among fellow gentlemen could endow a political intermediary with sufficient gravitas to overawe local challengers. It helped Henry Knox that he was known in the Waldo Patent as a Revolutionary War general and an intimate associate of President Washington and his cabinet. On the other hand, the intermediary who could command local popularity could win acceptance in genteel circles so long as he proved his virtue by proffering to them his political interest.

Henry Knox and William Cooper had to strike different balances in playing their roles as intermediaries. Knox had taken greater pains to educate himself, by reading the literature in his Boston bookstore and by emulating the mores and manners of gentility. He also had achieved a national reputation for public service and extensive political connections during the years of Revolution and war. Compared to Cooper, Knox could bank more on his external standing as a gentleman and concede less to the expectations of his common neighbors. Regarding public office as his due as Thomaston's preeminent gentleman, Knox refused to solicit openly votes from the common folk; he felt that hints properly placed by his managers ought to suffice with the Thomaston town meeting. Knox wanted the townspeople's honorific recognition that he was their political father to come reflexively, without overt solicitation.[20]

Compared to Knox, William Cooper was an unpolished and uneducated rustic unable to spell consistently, write grammatically, cite classical authors, or assume the dignified reserve of a complete gentleman. In 1789 he apologized to a correspondent, "P. S. Thee will at all times be Pleasd to excuse bad Spelling as I was Never Larnt to write nor Cypher but have taking [them] up my Selfe." Unable and unwilling to display the social distance from commoners expected of the ideal gentleman, Cooper frequented the taverns of Cooperstown and occasionally doffed his coat to wrestle challengers in the main street. Despite his lackluster education and rough manners, William Cooper was welcomed into the homes, correspondence, and confidence of Albany's preeminent political gentlemen—Leonard Gansevoort, Philip Schuyler, Abraham Ten Broeck, and Stephen Van Rensselaer—partly because of his boisterous charm, intelligence, and good humor, but largely because they appreciated the Otsego votes he offered them. They were willing to overlook Cooper's lack of style—of "tone"—in gratitude that he forsook the alternative political path of Anti-Federal populism. In May 1792 Schuyler lauded Cooper's success in mobilizing Otsego's voters in support of John Jay, the Federalist candidate for governor of New York. "Report says that you was very civil to the young and handsome of the [other] Sex, that you flattered the Old & Ugly, and even Embraced the toothless & decrepit in order to obtain votes. When will you write a treatise in Electioneering? Whenever you do afford only a few copies to your friends." Schuyler could celebrate Cooper's possession of popular arts that he would have found frightening either in the opposition or in himself.[21]

Cooper knew that his standing with the gentility of New York depended on his ability to deliver the votes of his neighbors. Consequently, his popular persona of bonhomie could give way to angry, uncomprehending resentment of those who declined to return deference and gratitude. In the election of 1792, William Cooper pressed a ballot bearing Jay's name into the hands of a young settler named James Moore. The young man later testified:

> I opened it, and looked at the name that was in it and made answer in a laughing manner, "Judge Cooper, I can not vote so, for if I do vote for Governor, I would wish to vote clearly from my own inclination, as I did not mean to be dictated to by any person at that time." Judge Cooper appeared in a joking manner, and in good humour until that time. He then took the ballot out of my hand; which he had given to mc, and appeared to be in a passion. Judge Cooper then said to me, "What, then young man, you will not vote as I would have you. You are a fool, young man, for you cannot

know how to vote as well as I can direct you, for I am a man in public office." He then walked away, and seemed to be in a passion.

A more aloof gentleman would have been insulated from such a frustrating encounter with an unusually independent voter. Philip Schuyler and Henry Knox could count on their friends to press ballots into the hands of common folk.[22]

Variations on a common theme, Knox and Cooper typified the early republic's several great landlords who recognized their affinities by uniting in Federalist politics. Others of this stripe were Benjamin Lincoln and Robert Hallowell Gardiner in Maine; George Cabot, Christopher Gore, and Israel Thorndike of Massachusetts; Matthew Clarkson, Thomas Morris, David Ogden, David Parish, Oliver Phelps, Robert Troup, and James Wadsworth in New York; and George Clymer, Samuel Meredith, William Bingham, Robert Morris, and John Nicholson in Pennsylvania. They were beneficiaries of the Revolution, prosperous men who had vastly increased their political and economic fortunes by aggressive speculations in public securities, government contracts, and frontier lands. But they dreaded displacement by still newer men who were ready to take a shortcut to political authority by eschewing the efforts necessary to win approving nods from those already comfortable in the ways of gentility.[23]

Identifying themselves with social order, the Federalist elite characterized their challengers as unscrupulous and ambitious demagogues whose triumph would substitute anarchy for society. In 1799 Cooper intercepted handbills that charged the Federalists with plotting to destroy the republic and establish a monarchy. He worried that "the offenders will escape unpunished—and dissatisfaction grow among the people until it is too late for the civil system." In 1800 Knox luridly warned that unless the state government sent troops to disperse his militant backcountry settlers, "a collection will soon be made of the most audacious and bloodthirsty villains that ever disgraced the surface of New England." Federalists eloquently preached the importance of a hierarchical and stable society, guided by precedent: the sort of society that America had begun to approximate before the Revolution, the sort of society that would have obstructed the rise of William Cooper and Henry Knox.[24]

COOPER AND KNOX each found his Republican nemesis in a formerly trusted lieutenant: Jedediah Peck and Dr. Ezekiel Dodge. Peck and Dodge were aggressive, ambitious men who initially enjoyed the patronage of the dominant Federalist in their respective counties. But Peck and

Dodge began to feel confined by the limits of the patronage that Cooper
and Knox believed was appropriate. To maintain the full value of their
new status, the Federalist gentlemen were obliged to be sparing of the
patronage they extended to men they could not accept as peers. By constraining the ambitions of Peck and Dodge, Cooper and Knox gave one
more proof to themselves and onlookers that they were discriminating
gentlemen. Peck and Dodge, however, came to recognize that further
advance to community preeminence required undercutting their mentors.

Peck and Dodge emigrated to the frontier in search of better opportunities to obtain property and higher status than their crowded home-
towns in southern New England could provide. Jedediah Peck began life
inauspiciously in 1748 in Lyme, Connecticut; he was one of thirteen children born to an obscure farmer. After at least one voyage as a sailor and
three years' service in the Continental army as an enlisted man, Peck
emigrated westward to settle in Burlington, one of William Cooper's
settlements in Otsego County. A frontier jack-of-all trades, Peck was at
once a farmer, surveyor, millwright, and sometime Baptist preacher. A
political associate remembered:

> Judge Peck, although a clear-headed, sensible man, was an uneducated
> emigrant from Connecticut. His appearance was diminutive and almost
> disgusting. In religion he was fanatical, but in his political views, he was sin-
> cere, persevering and bold; and although meek and humble in his de-
> meanor, he was by no means destitute of personal ambition. . . . He would
> survey your farm in the day time, exhort and pray in your family at night,
> and talk on politics the rest part of the time. Perhaps on Sunday, or some
> evening in the week, he would preach a sermon in your school house.

Although poorly educated beyond a memorization of much of the Bible,
Peck possessed a persistent, shrewd intelligence that made him very
popular among his fellow farmers.[25]

Ezekiel Dodge shared Peck's ambition but not his piety. Born in 1765
in Abington, Massachusetts, Dodge was the prodigal son of a Congregational minister. According to tradition, Dodge was an exceptionally un-
ruly boy who delighted in tormenting his elders. Once Dodge removed a
minister's pocket handkerchief from his black Sunday coat, wrapped the
handkerchief around a deck of playing cards, and restored it to the coat
pocket. That Sunday, when the minister reached for his handkerchief in
midsermon to wipe his beaded brow, he scattered the cards about his
pulpit, to his congregation's horror. At age fifteen Dodge went off to an
academy in Charlton, Massachusetts, conducted by Stephen Burroughs,
who within a few years would become the most notorious confidence

man and counterfeiter in New England. One day Burroughs found his school in an uproar because Dodge "had gone into the upper loft of the house, and had most scandalously insulted some young women, who were at the back side of the schoolhouse." Apparently impressed, Burroughs declined to punish the young man. Dodge proceeded to attend college at Harvard. To no one's surprise, the college soon expelled him. After serving an apprenticeship with a doctor, Dodge migrated in 1789 to the frontier town of Thomaston in search of his fortune. By developing the valley's leading medical practice and by investing in mercantile voyages, local land speculations, and loans to cash-strapped farmers, Dodge became one of the town's most prosperous and influential men. Unusually cunning and confrontational, Dodge frequently appeared in court to face charges of usury, assault and battery, and failure to pay his debts. Once Dodge offered to decide a disputed debt by a game of cards, but when he lost he refused to pay on the grounds that a gambling debt is not recoverable by law (a jury decided against him).[26]

Initially, Peck and Dodge got ahead with the assistance of the great men in their counties. When the New York state legislature established Otsego County in February 1791, William Cooper had Jedediah Peck named one of his associate judges in the county court of common pleas. At first Peck was a loyal subordinate who testified for Cooper in 1793 when a hostile state assembly investigated his electioneering practices and who promoted Cooper's candidacy for Congress in 1794.[27]

Dodge's services and rewards were more covert than those exchanged between Peck and Cooper. Knox liked to boast that he never brought lawsuits against his settlers: men accepted his terms for land simply because they recognized how just and reasonable they were. In August 1800 he assured the governor of Massachusetts, "I have in no instance attempted to turn off a settler nor have I yet brought a suit against an individual, deeming it most preferable to give the usurpers full time to inform themselves of the conduct that would best secure their true and permanent interests." In reality, Knox confronted many settlers who declined to play their appointed roles as grateful clients. To harry selected squatters from the land without sullying his paternal identity, Knox enlisted the services of Dr. Dodge to serve as an unscrupulous alter ego. Knox preserved his genteel image by subcontracting to Dodge the overt, aggressive acts inappropriate to a true gentleman. At bargain prices, Knox sold Dodge title to lots possessed by particularly recalcitrant settlers who refused to purchase Knox's title. Dodge then applied his considerable talents at intimidation to oust the occupants; he hired men to topple fences, seize cabins, and forcibly mow the targeted settlers' hayfields; he engaged lawyers to conduct protracted litigation that exhausted the targets' finances. It was a nasty and violent business. In July 1792 one exasperated settler shot Dodge in "the fleshy portion of his posteriors." The doctor recovered, and eventually the lands fell into his possession. This arrangement allowed Knox to highlight the disasters befalling those who failed to buy his title, and it enabled Dodge to acquire valuable land at reduced rates. Sharp-witted and ambitious, Dodge did not let any paternalistic notions complicate his relentless pursuit of individual advantage. He behaved as Knox could have behaved at an earlier stage in his ascent.[28]

Peck and Dodge became restive with their status as clients, as inferiors. They meant to become political insiders by encouraging popular resentment of the existing elite. Cyrus Eaton of Thomaston, who knew both Dodge and Knox, later explained that because the doctor was "naturally predisposed toward the Jeffersonian or Democratic party, as embodying greater latitude in thinking and action, [he] could not but chafe under the overshadowing prestige and influence of Knox. He accordingly did not scruple to foster the suspicions and charges of unfairness which he found existing in certain quarters, in regard to the manner in which the Waldo property had come into the gentleman's hands." Displacing settler resentments onto Knox, Dodge used the Jeffersonian party "as a stepping stone" to become "the acknowledged leader in the town."[29]

In 1796 Peck began to pursue his ambitions beyond William Cooper's wishes. That spring Peck boldly sought one of Otsego's two seats in the state senate without first consulting his benefactor. Although Peck ran as a Federalist, he curried Republican support and launched populist attacks on his opponents as haughty elitists who acted "as though they had all the people at their command." He preached, "In Representative Governments the people are masters [and] all their officers, from the highest to the lowest, are servants to the people." His principal opponent, Jacob Morris, was a wealthy frontier landlord and the son of one of New York's leading colonial families. He contemptuously dismissed Peck as an "ambitious, mean, and groveling demagogue." Although Peck lost the election, and the two candidates preferred by Cooper prevailed (including Morris), the bitterly contentious campaign offended Cooper who cherished harmony in his county. In 1798 Peck lowered his sights and won a seat in the lower house of the New York state legislature. He proceeded to infuriate the Federalists by breaking party ranks to vote with the Republicans on key issues. Federalist leaders concluded that

Peck was further proof that common men should not be entrusted with high office. In January 1799 a Federalist writer in the Cooperstown newspaper, the Otsego *Herald*, attacked Peck and insisted, "No minds are more susceptible of envy than those whose birth, education & merit are beneath the dignity of their station."[30]

In 1799 Cooper moved to reassert his control over his county's politics. At this critical moment he reiterated his allegiance to gentility by defining the populism promoted by Peck as sedition. Cooper desperately needed to restore his authority over his people or lose the basis for his claim to be a natural aristocrat worthy of admission to the Federalist inner circle. He knew that the Federalists in Albany expected him to act. For example, Daniel Hale wrote to Cooper about Peck, "This man appears to me and to many who know him, to be a strange, inconsistent, turbulent and I believe unprincipled Character. . . . I agree with you that it would be best for himself and for Society in general that he was reinstated in his original obscurity. This I believe will be *compleately* the case before long and I am happy to find that you are disposed to further the business." In March, with Cooper's vigorous assent, Governor Jay and the Council of Appointment removed Peck from his position as a county judge. A month later, in the midst of Peck's campaign for reelection to the assembly, Cooper published a newspaper notice warning, "Every man who circulates two seditious printed Papers, disseminated by Jedediah Peck, through this County, is liable to two years imprisonment, and a fine of two thousand dollars, at the discretion of the Court." Yet Peck won reelection, and his supporters continued to circulate provocative handbills charging that the Federalists meant to destroy the republic and establish an aristocracy in the land. Cooper announced his determination "to silence those wretches. Mercy is a cardinal Virtue, but the Public tranquility is a Consideration not to be neglected." In September 1799 Cooper had Peck arrested for sedition and hauled in irons to New York City for trial.[31]

Cooper's desperate act proved disastrous for New York's Federalists because the public regarded Peck as a political martyr. The federal district attorney released Peck on bail and never dared to bring him to trial. In Otsego, Cooper's popularity collapsed as a result of his arbitrary arrest of Peck. At the end of October, beleaguered and perplexed, Cooper announced that he would not stand for reelection to Congress and would resign his post as first judge of Otsego County. He regarded his retirement as his ultimate act of paternalism, as he sadly explained to Governor Jay: "The Great Violence of Party amongst us, makes it necessary to strive for a Cure and my withdrawing from all offices will not only make way for Others but also in some degree show that to give way and to forgive is the Onely Balsom that can heal animosities of the kind Existing among us and it will Come from no Person in the first instance better than from William Cooper, who had rather the child should be Nursed by a stranger, than that it should be hewn in pieces." Cooper hoped that the Otsego voters would rally around other, less controversial Federalists. But his retirement did not stem the steady erosion of Federalism in his county. In the spring election of 1800, a Republican slate led by Jedediah Peck won control of Otsego's delegation to the assembly. Otsego's transformation was critical to a statewide Republican triumph that had national consequences: by winning control of the assembly that would choose the state's presidential electors in the fall, the New York Republicans provided the critical margin of victory for Thomas Jefferson over the Federalist incumbent, John Adams. Thereafter, Peck dominated the Republican party in Otsego County until his death in 1821, and the county consistently voted for Republican candidates for state and national offices, except for brief interludes during the Embargo and the War of 1812.[32]

In one county after another, Republican upstarts emerged to topple the local gentry from political power. One of those upstarts was Ezekiel G. Dodge. By 1804 he saw an opportunity for himself in the emerging public longing to defy Federalist elitism. Dodge declared himself a Republican and invited his neighbors to assert their equal access to respect by symbolically smiting their preeminent gentleman. The recently shrunken employment at Knox's financially battered business enterprises helped the doctor's efforts to promote the candidacy of Isaac Bernard to replace Knox as the town's representative to the General Court. At the same time Dodge covertly persuaded another Federalist, Joshua Adams, that he ought to run, thereby splitting the potential Federalist vote. Regarding his probable defeat as an unendurable humiliation, Knox withdrew his name, and Adams prevailed. A year later the town elected the Republican Bernard as their representative. On March 28, 1805, Henry Jackson Knox broke the news to his father, "The Jacobins of this town turn out so strong & the Federalists are so lukewarm that at March meeting all the Federal officers were turned out, and such men put in (as dismal to relate) who cannot neither read nor write intelligibly." Thomaston became a Republican stronghold, and Dodge eventually supplanted Bernard as the town's representative to the General Court.[33]

Persistent but a proper Federalist gentleman to the end, Knox sent a rather plaintive note from Boston to his business manager in Thomaston on the eve of the April 1806 town meeting. "I suppose the representative will be a democrat. . . . But if it should be otherwise and the town should think proper to choose me, I should not decline, but good previous arrangements ought to be made. Of this hint you will make a discreet use." Not thinking Knox's candidacy proper, the townspeople reelected Bernard. In the summer of 1806, Charles Willing Hare, a fellow Federalist, visited Knox and reported "that his political and private influence was gone and therefore that there was no use in being longer connected with him." Where Cooper fell because he defended elite rule too aggressively, Knox fell because he remained too aloof, banking on a deference that no longer existed among the people of Thomaston.[34]

By making themselves over into elitists during the 1780s and 1790s, Knox and Cooper underestimated the legacy of the American Revolution. Indeed, they set themselves up for their falls by attempting, during the 1790s, to bring the Revolution to a premature end. It is possible to imagine the ill-educated, rough-hewn William Cooper (if not the more polished Henry Knox) taking the alternative path, allying with Jedediah Peck in celebration of social mobility and public equality, the professed values of a new liberal social order. Instead, Cooper and Knox succumbed to a mirage that prevailed at the moment (the late 1780s and early 1790s) when they achieved wealth and power: the Federalist illusion that gentlemen could restore the colonial era's unity of economic, social, political, and cultural authority. They failed to recognize the enduring potential of the American Revolution's legacy to legitimate upstarts unwilling or unable to achieve or to endure genteel authority. Until the political reorientation wrought by the Civil War and Reconstruction, America's public life belonged to the Dodges and the Pecks. The fundamental change in the politics of the early republic was in the manner of public presentation. Men no longer earned authority by parading their personae of genteel superiority. Instead, leaders had to enact publicly their friendship for the people.[35]

Afterword

The Federalists—Still in Need of Reconsideration

James M. Banner, Jr.

WHEN LINDA KERBER and I, quite independently of each other, completed our respective studies of the Federalists with the encouragement of Richard Hofstadter in the late 1960s, we hoped that our works would inaugurate a broad and fresh reconsideration of Federalism in the new nation. They did not do so. The reasons reveal much about the state of American historiography over the last quarter century, and they are filled with irony.

Kerber's work and mine, both published in 1970, had been preceded recently by David Hackett Fischer's *Revolution of American Conservatism.* Fischer's work was distinctive in two ways. It was the first study to examine the Federalist party as a fully articulated national institution that had come to its highest point of maturity after, rather than before, 1801. It was also the rare work that focused upon the many lesser Federalists who composed and led the party beyond the capital, rather than upon the Hamiltonians and other members of the Federalist national elite who were customarily the subjects of related studies. Yet as we can see more clearly in retrospect, Fischer's work lay well within the traditional framework of works about Federalism. His book held its gaze steadily upon the political and institutional dimensions of Federalism, rather than upon its ideological and social foundations. It treated Federalist ideas as discrete components of partisan policies, rather than as parts of a larger structure of thought and expression. And to the degree that it examined Federalist thought at all, it limited itself largely to political ideas, omitting those other components of thought which reflected and helped form the national political culture of which the Federalists composed a major part.

By contrast, Kerber and I sought to explore Federalism as a complex and multiseamed political and social ideology and, in the case of my work, as an ideology owing much to its relationship to the social location of its adherents. In doing so, she and I commenced the integration of Federalism into the historiography of American republicanism, just then in its early maturity; in fact, we were the very first to test the implications for post-1787 American political culture of the then recent arguments of Bernard Bailyn and Gordon S. Wood. While Bailyn and Wood had begun to explore the complexities of eighteenth-century American republicanism, whose subsequent study became a kind of cottage industry, no one had yet begun to consider the career of republicanism after the Constitution's ratification in either Federalist or Jeffersonian terms.

Surely there was no particular reason why the history of republicanism in the early nation should first be traced through Federalism, as Kerber and I began to trace it, rather than through Jeffersonian Republicanism. Yet because our interests lay with those who came to oppose Jeffersonian politics and because we sought to take seriously a group of people often dismissed because they lost the historic battle for the political and ideological future of the United States, we implicitly, although wholly unintentionally, threw down a challenge to those who were then examining Jeffersonianism and the Democratic-Republican party. We did so by implicitly suggesting the advantages of undertaking for the Jeffersonian branch of the American political lineage what we had commenced for the Federalist bloodline. That challenge was subsequently taken up by Joyce O. Appleby, Lance G. Banning, John Patrick Diggins, Isaac Kramnick, Drew R. McCoy, Thomas L. Pangle, and Steven Watts among many others. Out of it, roughly twenty-five years later, has emerged a greatly deepened understanding of the origins of early national politics and of American republicanism and liberalism, an understanding of which the chapters in this volume are evidence and to which they make a significant contribution. Out of it has also come a robust debate about the respective claims of classical republicanism and liberalism upon American politics and thought since the Revolution.

It turns out, however, that Federalism scarcely appears in this richly nuanced new historiography and that few others have undertaken to locate Federalism in its social setting, as I attempted earlier to do. Jeffersonianism, whether characterized as republican or liberal, has come to represent all that historians seem to think worth examining in the politics of the half century after 1776. When we debate the relative strengths of civic humanism, Lockean liberalism, Scottish moral philosophy, and Protestantism in early American politics, we debate their relative strengths within the Jeffersonian camp and in Jeffersonian categories. Federalism and the Federalists are missing from the story, especially in the period after 1801, save as exceptions to its main line; they are not factors in the purportedly triumphant radicalism of the American Revolution. That political Federalism might have been a conduit of particular ideological strains and traditions in the United States and that its history might thus be critical to a comprehensive understanding of everything that came afterward in American politics seems rarely, if ever, to be considered. Nor, for that matter, is the implicit deep whiggism of our unquestioning Jeffersonian triumphalism much taken into account; since we know how the story turned out, we measure its elements against its conclusion rather than against its procession. The consequences for American historiography have consequently been severe.

Some years ago it would have seemed unimaginable that the Federalists might become such comparatively forgotten subjects of history; it would have been foolhardy to predict that one would someday have to make the case that they deserve respectful attention from historians of American politics and society just as other groups, previously lost to written history, merit their own place in the public record of the nation. Yet today that case needs making against strong reigning orthodoxies. Like women, African Americans, ethnic and sexual minorities, and working people, like the "inarticulate," the voiceless, the unrecognized, and the forgotten earlier, in the last twenty years the Federalists have been lost to view. Banished not because of their silence or the comparative weakness and size of their record but rather, on the contrary, because of their "conservative" politics, their race and gender, their symbolic place in our past history, their very articulateness, and their having worked to establish a strong national state as we know it now—precisely because they lacked all exoticism and did not seem to need rediscovering, they have been excluded from the great reconsideration of American politics and society of our age. One can say without irony that it is the Federalists—those exemplars of traditional, nationalistic, commercial, often antidemocratic, as well as purportedly white and male, values—who must now be rescued from the dustbin of historiography and the condescending regard of so many historians. It is they whose stories, as we like to say of others, must still be told. And they must be told not for the Federalists' own posthumous good but for the completion of the history of the American political tradition.

Yet far more than the fact that the Federalists represent what is least fashionable in American culture today lies behind their being ignored; far more than their having been elitists, and sometimes statist elitists at that, more than our own thoroughgoing and triumphant Jeffersonianism, and more than our lack of generosity when history's losers are labeled conservatives, explains their historiographical fate. The current state of Federalist historiography owes far more to recent historiographical circumstances than to any encompassing cultural biases. Here I would like to emphasize three of these circumstances and, in doing so, at least imply a research prospectus for further understanding of the Federalists. It is a prospectus, I might add, that insists on both the significance of Federalist thought and politics well into the 1820s (as implied by many of the essayists here) and the need for a coherent presentation of the entire thickly textured worldview of Federalists, lesser as well as greater, and not just discrete aspects of it, as must be the approach of a volume like this.

Perhaps most consequential for the historiography of Federalism has been the application of the concepts of "court" and "country" to the politics of the early nation. While there can be little dispute, as Herbert Sloan reminds us again in his chapter, that the Hamiltonians were a court faction very much in the classic British mold, such cannot be said of the other—and vast majority of—Federalists, surely not of John Adams, James A. Bayard, and Harrison Gray Otis, to name only three of the most conspicuous among them; and this is to say nothing of the party leaders' adherents and followers, most of whose thoughts and actions had far more in common with "country" politics than with the politics of their Hamiltonian party colleagues. The often sharp differences between Hamiltonian and other Federalists is implicit in Doron Ben-Atar's chapter on Hamiltonian industrial espionage, an approach to economic independence and controlled industrialization which was grounded in the secretary's mercantilistic nationalism rather than in the provincial regionalism of most of his copartisans.

It may be that "court" and "country" have from the beginning of their use by American historians been meant to be metaphorical constructs, however much they may have been derived from the historical past. But if so, these metaphors have now come to be taken for established reality; and it is surely the case that their applicability has been assumed rather than adequately explained—as if the categories and realities of American politics and ideology were tied indissolubly to those of Great Britain. While a genuine "court" party did in fact exist in Walpole's Britain, where a true court, representing the state, was manifest and powerful, in the United States—where, following 1789, one had to distinguish (uniquely among then existing nations) between the state, the government, and the administration—a genuine court party could not by definition be found. Here, a party was the party of an administration, a cadre of people who were given authority for no more than four years to direct the policies of government. A strong national state—the continuous sovereign authority that embodies public power and has legitimately gained the right to protect, govern, and administer through law a unified territory for an inclusive common good—had not yet come into being to stand in for a European court and would not do so for decades.

Still, even if we are to accept the designation of "court" as being applicable to the Federalists in the 1790s, we must explain the astonishing speed with which the Federalists assumed the oppositionist coloration and ideology of a "country" party after 1801, while the Democratic-Republicans became, for over twenty-five years, the semipermanent party of government and administration—what the Federalists in effect charged with being a "court" party. (It was not the Jeffersonians, after all, whose emblematic figure was the Patriot president George Washington, whose public posture would not have failed to impress that classic country statesman Viscount Bolingbroke.) Therefore, while the very relevance of court and country concepts to American politics is questionable, surely it would make more sense to understand Federalism as a country, rather than a court, ideology for the majority of the thirty-five or so years in which Federalism was formally expressed through its organized political arm. In this way, such of its stances as its regionalism, its opposition to the Louisiana Purchase, the Embargo, and the War of 1812, even its antislavery elements begin to make more sense. At the very least, acknowledging Federalist "countryism" forces us to ask whether or not the entire American political universe had become countrified by 1801, or at least by the time of the death of Hamilton—and, if so, what that has meant for American politics, whether republican or liberal, ever since.

Accepting Federalism as a species of country politics—of which all post-1787 American politics may be considered a genus—in turn raises the nice question as to the political bequests of 1780s Anti-Federalism. It will no longer do, it seems to me, to chalk up simply to partisan opportunism—although there was much of that—Federalism's rapid changeover to localistic, opposition politics after 1801. Federalists' fearful and hyperbolic assaults on such things as concentrated and distant government, partisan organizing, and, from Federalism's principal quarter in New England, one section's excessive power over the rest of the nation were not heard for the first time in American national history from the pens of Fisher Ames, Robert Goodloe Harper, and John Rutledge, Jr. Such categories of thought were ready at hand from the 1780s, to cite only their most recent expressions; and that decade was not, after all, beyond the experience of most Federalists. In 1808, for example, Senator James Hillhouse of Connecticut proposed seven constitutional amendments—including those that would have mandated annual elections of House members, three-year Senate terms, and a single four-year term for the president—that had been proposed by Anti-Federalist opponents of ratification in 1787 and 1788. It may be difficult for historians to imagine that Anti-Federalism found a home in political Federalism in part because doing so would force us to recast our understanding of Anti-Federalism. Yet it is precisely because of this possibility—the possibility that a bloodline existed between the earliest criticism of the Constitution and attacks upon the Jeffersonian majority, the possibility that the echoes of Anti-Federalism in Federalism were organic and not adventitious—that Federalism, especially Federalism after 1801, must be forcefully reestablished as a major component of the American political tradition.

Moreover, just as it is time to read Federalism as a country ideology and as owing something to Anti-Federalism, so it is also time to read it for its liberalism. A continuing barrier to our fuller understanding of early national political culture has been the assumption, shared by almost all historians, that liberalism lodged only among the Jeffersonians. Yet as Paul Finkelman, Alan Taylor, and Steven Watts suggest in their chapters in this volume, many non-Hamiltonian Federalists held distinctly liberal, or at least protoliberal, ideas and behaved from time to time in recognizably liberal ways, even if they had a complex relationship, both ideologically and in fact, to the emerging market economy of the new century. (This seems, by the way, to represent a departure from the stance that Watts took in his penetrating 1987 study, *The Republic Reborn.*) In arguing in his chapter here that the Federalists were confused, ambivalent, and divided and that they occupied no firm and clear position on the ideological spectrum, Watts is surely correct. Yet to leave the case at that is to leave unexamined many of Federalism's discrete ideological components, including liberalism.

For instance, if, as many have argued, liberalism and liberal capitalism had begun their triumph over republicanism by the early nineteenth century, then why did not the report of the Hartford Convention, the most pointed and concerted protest against the purportedly liberal party of Thomas Jefferson, raise a single protest against liberal behavior and thought? To undertake an investigation of the degree to which post-Hamiltonian Federalism showed the marks of liberalism would of course require a close look at the words and acts of the lesser Federalists, not just of those of the Hamiltonians. Were I endeavoring now the kind of study of the Federalists that I undertook in the 1960s, I would make up for the now so obvious deficiency in that work by investigating Federalism's liberal and capitalistic, as well as republican, strains and by making much more than I did of its adherents' views of enterprise, commerce, and individualistic endeavor.

All of this is to say that the failure of Federalist historiography to mature in consonance with that of Jeffersonianism, Jacksonianism, Whiggery, and Lincoln Republicanism continues to bedevil antebellum political historiography. It is as if the Populists were omitted from the history of twentieth-century politics: Could we then make sense of progressivism or the New Deal? Yet it is not that an interest in Federalism has disappeared altogether. The work represented in the chapters of this volume reveals historians' continuing interest in that other party of the early nation. And as is made clear in the essays of David Waldstreicher, Rosemarie Zagarri, Andrew Cayton, and Rogers Smith, much remains to be learned of the tortuous origins and sometimes aborted possibilities of such modern developments as women's rights, the national state, and political style through study of Jefferson's opposition, just as the chapters of Keith Arbour and Andrew Siegel sharply portray the ways in which partisanship rapidly diffused itself, like a contagion, into all corners of the nation's culture and spared none, not even the dead.

Yet it will not do to leave it at that. It will not do to compose or reappraise the history of Federalism and the Federalists merely out of illuminating aperçus like all of those here. Nor will it do to make the Federalists appear to be no more than curious figures who here and there are worthy of our interest for the issues they raised but who, for losing out on the main political chance and dying out in the 1820s, forfeit our fuller examination of what they were and meant to be. Surely it cannot be left merely that Federalism was composed of a complex of ideas, attitudes, and aspirations, that the Federalists were little more than a diverse group of people come together at a particular moment in our history to articulate some worthy ideas. For, precisely like their Democratic-Republican opponents, they were men and women seeking to make sense of a revolutionary world. They were seeking to organize, govern, and stabilize a new nation amid world-historical changes in politics, ideology, the economy, and culture. They were political figures attempting to win and hold public office in the world's first republic and in the first constitutional system to require candidates for office to calibrate their appeals to the ideas, fears, and beliefs of voters.

Therefore, Federalism merits the same deep and nuanced extended examinations that have so enlarged our understanding of Democratic-Republicanism—and which it has not recently received, save for Stanley Elkins and Eric McKtrick's distinctive, magisterial *Age of Federalism*. It needs to be seen as a many-dimensioned ideology, as a political party, and as the public expression of a vital segment of American society in the first quarter century of the nation's history under the Constitution. It must be seen once again, as it seems to me all of the authors in this volume implicitly take it to be, as a problem—as a subject of historical inquiry about which comparatively little agreement has been reached and comparatively little still is known. Above all, it must not be taken to be just the residual and minority expression of Revolutionary republicanism; rather, it must be seen as one among many complex emanations of the American eighteenth century—republicanism, liberalism, and evangelical Protestantism chief among them—that created a political tradition too weak to withstand the forces of democratic capitalism but strong enough to imprint itself upon virtually every important issue that followed its day. It is only by understanding Federalism as such a political and ideological force in all its fullness and by integrating it into the larger history of American political, economic, and social thought that we will be able to understand fully the larger history of our political tradition and of the enduring components of American political culture.

NOTES

ABBREVIATIONS

WMQ   William and Mary Quarterly

INTRODUCTION: THE PARADOXICAL LEGACY OF THE FEDERALISTS

1. John Adams to James Lloyd, Feb. 6, 1815, in Charles Francis Adams, ed., *The Works of John Adams*, 10 vols. (Boston, 1851–56), 10:115.

2. Shaw Livermore, Jr., *The Twilight of Federalism: The Disintegration of the Federalist Party, 1815–1830* (Princeton, NJ, 1962), 10.

3. Henry Adams, *History of the United States of America during the Administration of Thomas Jefferson*, Library of America ed. (New York, 1986), 1208.

4. Robert E. Shalhope, *The Roots of Democracy: American Thought and Culture, 1760–1800* (Boston, 1990), 153. Livermore argues that the "wholesale adoption of the Federalist national program by Republicans during and after" the War of 1812 has "eliminated sharp policy divisions between the parties" (*Twilight of Federalism*, 265).

5. Gordon S. Wood, *The Radicalism of the American Revolution* (New York, 1991), 271.

6. Stanley Elkins and Eric McKitrick, *The Age of Federalism: The Early American Republic, 1788–1800* (New York, 1993), 752.

7. James Roger Sharp, *American Politics in the Early Republic: The New Nation in Crisis* (New Haven, 1993), 268–75; John R. Howe, Jr., "Republican Thought and the Political Violence of the 1790s," *American Quarterly* 19 (1987): 147–65. Michael Durey demonstrates that Federalist concern about the radicalism of some of the immigrants was justified, in *Transatlantic Radicals and the Early American Republic* (Lawrence, KS, 1997).

8. David Hackett Fischer, *The Revolution of American Conservatism: The Federalist Party in the Age of Jeffersonian Democracy* (New York, 1965); Linda K. Kerber, *Federalists in Dissent: Image and Ideology in Jeffersonian America* (Ithaca, NY, 1970); James M. Banner, Jr., *To the Hartford Convention: The Federalists and the Origins of Party Politics in Massachusetts, 1789–1815* (New York, 1970). For a highly critical view of the Federalists which excludes them from the republican consensus, see Richard Buel, *Securing the Revolution: Ideology in American Politics, 1789–1815* (Ithaca, NY, 1972).

9. Steven Watts, *The Republic Reborn: War and the Making of Liberal America, 1790–1820* (Baltimore, 1987), xxii. A striking example of how irrelevant the Federalists seem to American historians is the fact that Richard Wightman Fox

and James Kloppenberg's *A Companion to American Thought* (Cambridge, 1995) does not include a single paragraph on Federalist thought.

10. Lance Banning, *The Jeffersonian Persuasion: Evolution of a Party Ideology* (Ithaca, NY, 1978), 127–40; John M. Murrin, "The Great Inversion, or Court versus Country: A Comparison of the Revolutionary Settlements in England (1688–1721) and America (1776–1816)," in *Three British Revolutions: 1641, 1688, 1776*, ed. J. G. A. Pocock (Princeton, NJ, 1980), 405–7. Two superb studies of the Whiskey and Gabriel's rebellions portray the Federalists as aristocratic reactionaries: Thomas P. Slaughter, *The Whiskey Rebellion: Frontier Epilogue to the American Revolution* (New York, 1986), chap. 8; Douglas R. Egerton, *Gabriel's Rebellion: The Virginia Slave Conspiracies of 1800 and 1802* (Chapel Hill, NC, 1993), xi, 34–40, 114.

11. James Madison, "The Federalist No. 10," in William T. Hutchinson et al., eds., *The Papers of James Madison*, first ser., 17 vols. (Chicago, 1962–77, Charlottesville, 1977–91), 10:263–64. See also Richard Hofstadter, *The Idea of a Party System: The Rise of Legitimate Opposition in the United States, 1780–1840* (Berkeley, CA, 1969), 40–73.

12. Alexander Hamilton to Edward Carrington, May 26, 1792, in Harold C. Syrett et al., eds., *The Papers of Alexander Hamilton*, 27 vols. (New York, 1961–87), 11:429.

13. John M. Murrin, "A Roof without Walls: The Dilemma of American National Identity," in *Beyond Confederation: Origins of the Constitution and American National Identity*, ed. Richard Beeman, Stephen Botein, and Edward C. Carter (Chapel Hill, NC, 1987), 334.

14. Jefferson to William Short, Jan. 3, 1793, in Julian P. Boyd, Charles T. Cullen, John Catanzariti, et al., eds., *The Papers of Thomas Jefferson*, 27 vols. to date (Princeton, NJ, 1950—), 25:14.

15. Fisher Ames, "Laocoon I," April 1799, in W. B. Allen, ed., *The Works of Fisher Ames*, 2 vols. (Indianapolis, 1983), 1:190.

16. Alexander Hamilton, "Speech on a Plan of Government," June 18, 1787, *Hamilton Papers* 4:192.

17. Rufus King to Elbridge Gerry, June 4, 1786, in Paul H. Smith et al., eds., *Letters of the Delegates to Congress*, 25 vols. to date (Washington, DC, 1976–98), 23:332.

18. Eric J. Hobsbawm, *Nations and Nationalism since 1780: Programme, Myth, Reality* (New York, 1990), 38. See also Robert H. Wiebe, *The Opening of American Society: From the Adoption of the Constitution to the Eve of Disunion* (New York, 1984).

19. James Kloppenberg, "Republicanism in American History and Historiography," *Tocqueville Review* 13 (1992): 1–19. The tension between conservatism and future Federalists is discussed by Charles Royster, *A Revolutionary People at War: The Continental Army and American Character, 1775–1783* (Chapel Hill, NC, 1979), 353–58.

20. Bruce Ackerman, *We the People*, vol. 1, *Foundations* (Boston, 1991), 181–86; J. G. A. Pocock, *The Machiavellian Moment: Florentine Political Thought and the Atlantic Republican Tradition* (Princeton, NJ, 1974), 524; Simon P. Newman, "Principles or Men? George Washington and the Political Culture of National Leadership, 1776–1801," *Journal of the Early Republic* 12 (1992): 480.

21. Washington to Hamilton, July 29, 1795, *Hamilton Papers* 18:524.

22. Thomas M. Ray, "'Not One Cent for Tribute': The Public Addresses and American Popular Reaction to the XYZ Affair, 1798–1799," *Journal of the Early Republic* 12 (1992): 389–412.

23. James H. Broussard, *The Southern Federalists, 1800–1816* (Baton Rouge, LA, 1978), 257; Fischer, *Revolution of American Conservatism*, xix.

24. Stephanie McCurry, "The Two Faces of Republicanism: Gender and Proslavery Politics in Antebellum South Carolina," *Journal of American History* 78 (1992): 1246.

25. See also Rosemarie Zagarri, "Morals, Manners, and the Republican Mother," *American Quarterly* 44 (1992): 192–215; Joanne B. Freeman, "Dueling as Politics: Reinterpreting the Burr-Hamilton Duel," *WMQ* 53 (1996): 289–318, and "Slander, Poison, Whispers and Fame: Jefferson's 'Anas' and Political Gossip in the Early Republic," *Journal of the Early Republic* 15 (1995): 25–57.

26. Some southern Federalists, like Robert Goodloe Harper of South Carolina, publicly dismissed all notions of African inferiority and fantasized about ameliorating the state of slaves through education (Eric Robert Papenfuse, *The Evils of Necessity: Robert Goodloe Harper and the Moral Dilemma of Slavery* [Philadelphia, 1997], chap. 1).

27. Robert P. Forbes, "Slavery and the Meaning of America, 1819–1833" (Ph.D diss., Yale University, 1994), 212.

28. Gillis J. Harp, "Patrician Partisans: New York in the House of Representatives, 1789–1803," *Canadian Journal of History* 29 (1994): 479–501; Fischer, *Revolution of American Conservatism*, 205. See also Howard Rock, *Artisans of the New Republic: The Tradesmen of New York City in the Age of Jefferson* (New York, 1984); Alfred F. Young, "The Mechanics and the Jeffersonians: New York, 1789–1801," *Labor History* 5 (1964): 247–76, and *The Democratic Republicans of New York* (New York, 1967); Sean Wilentz, *Chants Democratic: New York City and the Rise of the American Working Class, 1788–1850* (New York, 1984).

29. Joyce Appleby, *Capitalism and a New Social Order: The Republican Vision of the 1790s* (New York, 1984), 73, 78, 59.

30. Drew R. McCoy, *The Elusive Republic: Political Economy in Jeffersonian America* (New York, 1980), 167.

1. CONSTRUCTING AMERICAN NATIONAL IDENTITY: STRATEGIES OF THE FEDERALISTS

1. Chisholm v. Georgia, 2 Dallas 419, 462, 465 (1793).

2. Elkins and McKitrick, *Age of Federalism*, 591–92, 694.

3. These claims are not controversial in works on nation building and nationalism. See, e.g., Benedict R. O. Anderson, *Imagined Communities* (London, 1983); Ernest Gellner, *Nations and Nationalism* (Oxford, 1983); Hobsbawm, *Nations and Nationalism*; and esp. Etienne Balibar and Immanuel Wallerstein, *Race, Nation, Class* (New York, 1991). Many scholars have also illuminated American nation building but without adequately analyzing Jeffersonian-Federalist clashes in this light. See, e.g., Samuel H. Beer, *To Make a Nation* (Cambridge, 1993); Lance Banning, "The Practical Sphere of a Republic: James Madison, the Constitution, and the Emergence of Revolutionary Federalism," in Beeman, *Beyond Confederation*,

162–87; and earlier, Paul C. Nagel, *This Sacred Trust* (New York, 1971), and Clinton Rossiter, *The American Quest, 1790–1860* (New York, 1971).

4. See, e.g., Rogers M. Smith, *Civic Ideals: Conflicting Visions of Citizenship in U.S. History* (New Haven, 1997). Portions of this essay are from chap. 6 of that work.

5. James Kettner, *The Development of American Citizenship, 1608–1870* (Chapel Hill, NC, 1978), 248–49; Edmund S. Morgan, *The Genius of George Washington* (New York, 1980), 21; Robert H. Wiebe, *The Opening of American Society* (New York, 1984), 3; Elkins and McKitrick, *Age of Federalism*, 46–50, 456, 587–88.

6. Wiebe, *Opening*, 18–19; Elkins and McKitrick, *Age of Federalism*, 4, 21–24, 27, 78–79.

7. Thomas Jefferson, *Notes on the State of Virginia*, ed. William Peden (Chapel Hill, NC, 1955), 84–85.

8. John Higham, *Strangers in the Land* (New York, 1966), 8, 19, 97, 210; Elkins and McKitrick, *Age of Federalism*, 694–95.

9. Isaac Kramnick, ed., *The Federalist Papers* (New York, 1987), 91; Max Farrand, ed., *The Records of the Federal Convention of 1787*, 4 vols. (New Haven, 1966), 1:21, 2:494, 3:61.

10. Edward Millican, *One United People: The Federalist Papers and the National Idea* (Lexington, Ky., 1990), 65–66, 75.

11. John Higham, *Send These to Me* (New York, 1975), 31–32; Moses Rischin, ed., *Immigration and the American Tradition* (Indianapolis, 1976), 43–44; Morton J. Frisch, ed., *Selected Writings and Speeches of Alexander Hamilton* (Washington, DC, 1985), 291.

12. *Annals of the Congress of the United States, 1789–1842*, 42 vols. (Washington, DC, 1834–56), 3d Cong., 64, 72, 455 (1793–95), 4th Cong., 1st sess., 1171, 1349 (1796).

13. Kirk H. Porter, *A History of Suffrage in the United States* (1918; rpt., New York, 1971), 23–24, 26; Philip S. Foner, *History of Black Americans*, 3 vols. (Westport, CT, 1975), 1:413, 462, 480; Donald E. Fehrenbacher, *The Dred Scott Case* (New York, 1978), 37–38, 84–88.

14. *Annals*, 2d Cong., 861 (1793); William M. Wiecek, *The Sources of Antislavery Constitutionalism in America, 1760–1860* (Ithaca, NY, 1977), 97–103; Fehrenbacher, *Dred Scott*, 40–42.

15. John C. Wise and Vine Deloria, *The Red Man in the New World Drama* (New York, 1971), 173–80; Wilcomb E. Washburn, *Red Man's Land / White Man's Law* (New York, 1971), 54, 162–63; Francis P. Prucha, *The Great Father*, 2 vols. (Lincoln, NE, 1984), 1:60–66; James H. Merrell, "Declarations of Independence: Indian-White Relations in the New Nation," in *The American Revolution*, ed. Jack P. Greene (New York, 1987), 203–8; Elkins and McKitrick, *Age of Federalism*, 250–55, 271–72, 436–37.

16. Washburn, *Red Man's Land*, 55; Prucha, *Great Father* 1:49–50; Merrell, "Declarations," 10; Elkins and McKitrick, *Age of Federalism*, 461–71.

17. Jefferson explained in his *Notes* how Virginia's laws claimed for the state "sole and exclusive power of taking conveyances of the Indian right of soil," including the provision that "an Indian conveyance alone could give no

right . . . which the laws would acknowledge" (136). Federal policy followed similar lines.

18. Washburn, *Red Man's Land*, 55–57, 60, 163; Reginald Horsman, *Race and Manifest Destiny* (Cambridge, MA, 1981), 106–8.

19. Elkins and McKitrick, *Age of Federalism*, counts forty-eight Federalists and four Anti-Federalists in the first House, with an eighteen to two margin in the first Senate. After a decline, Federalists resurged in the 1796 elections (33, 513).

20. *Annals*, 1st Cong., 1st sess., 1:812–13, 825–27, 836–44 (1789); Judiciary Act of 1789, chap. 20, sec. 11, 1 Stat. 73, 78; James W. Moore and Donald T. Weckstein, "Diversity Jurisdiction: Past, Present, and Future," *Texas Law Review* 43 (1964): 1–6; Elkins and McKitrick, *Age of Federalism*, 62–64.

21. Clyde E. Jacobs, *The Eleventh Amendment and Sovereign Immunity* (Westport, CT, 1972), 27–40; *Federalist Papers*, 455; John V. Orth, *The Judicial Power of the United States* (New York, 1987), 24–29.

22. 2 Dallas 419 (1793) at 434–35.

23. Ibid., 453, 455, 457, 460, 462.

24. Ibid., 470–72, 476–77.

25. *Annals*, 3d Cong., 30–31, 476–78 (1794); Orth, *Judicial Power*, 18–21.

26. See *Federalist Papers*, 447; Kettner, *American Citizenship*, 257–58.

27. Elkins and McKitrick, *Age of Federalism*, 592, 694.

28. David Ramsay, *A Dissertation on the Manner of Acquiring the Character and Privileges of a Citizen of the United States* (1798).

29. *Annals*, 1st Cong., 1st sess., 413–24 (1789).

30. Ibid., 418 (1789).

31. Ibid., 3d Cong., 1027–29 (1794), 5th Cong., 1st sess., 1:348–56 (1797).

32. I-mien Tsiang, *The Question of Expatriation in America prior to 1907* (Baltimore, 1942), 25–27, 37–41, 50; Frank G. Franklin, *A Legislative History of Naturalization* (1906; rpt., Chicago, 1969), 71, 102–3; Kettner, *American Citizenship*, 269–70, 281.

33. 11 F. 1099 (1793).

34. Ibid. at 1100–1101, 1105–7, 1118, 1120, 1122–23.

35. 3 Dallas 133 (1795).

36. Jansen v. The Christina Magdalena, 13 F. 356, 360–61 (1794).

37. 3 Dallas 133 (1795) at 139, 141, 150.

38. Ibid. at 152–53.

39. Ibid. at 162–65.

40. 29 F. 1330 (1799).

41. Ibid. at 1331.

42. *Annals*, 1st Cong., 1st sess., 1:1147–64 (1790); Franklin, *Naturalization*, 38–39.

43. *Annals*, 1st Cong., 1st sess., 1:1148–49, 1155–56 (1790); Franklin, *Naturalization*, 38.

44. *Annals*, 1st Cong., 1st sess., 1:1156, 1159–60 (1790).

45. Collet v. Collet, 6 F. 106–7 (1792); see also Portier v. Le Roy, 1 Yeates 371 (Pa., 1794); Franklin, *Naturalization*, 38, 46–47; Kettner, *American Citizenship*, 238–39.

46. *Annals*, 3d Cong., 47–53, 58 (1794).

47. Ibid., 1006–8, 1021–58 (1794).

48. Ibid., 812–15 (1795); James M. Smith, *Freedom's Fetters: The Alien and Sedition Laws and American Civil Liberties* (Ithaca, NY, 1956), 22–23; Franklin, *Naturalization*, 51–57, 67–71; Kettner, *American Citizenship*, 239–43.

49. Peter S. Onuf, *Statehood and Union* (Bloomington, IN, 1987), 68–74.

50. This bill concerned admission to citizenship "of the United States." Debates still showed support for the view that the states could admit aliens to their own citizenship, if not U.S. citizenship (*Annals*, 5th Cong., 1554, 1567–82, 1776–84 [1798]; Elkins and McKitrick, *Age of Federalism*, 694–95).

51. *Annals*, 5th Cong., 1:554–55, 564–65, 589–90, 599, 609, 2:1785–96, 1973–2028, 2049, 3:2429–35, 2986–3016 (1798–99); Smith, *Freedom's Fetters*, 22–93; Franklin, *Naturalization*, 75–81, 92–93; Elkins and McKitrick, *Age of Federalism*, 590–92.

52. Madison Grant and Charles S. Davison, eds., *The Founders of the Republic on Immigration, Naturalization, and Aliens* (New York, 1928), 42, 46–51, 89–90; Higham, *Strangers*, 8, 19, 97, 210; George Washington, "Farewell Address," in Henry S. Commager, ed., *Documents of American History*, 9th ed. (New York, 1973), 170, 173.

53. Case of Fries, 9 F. 826 (1799) at 831, 834–39.

54. Elkins and McKitrick, *Age of Federalism*, 695–99.

55. Thomas Bender, *Community and Social Change in America* (New Brunswick, NJ, 1978), 83–86; Wiebe, *Opening*, 145.

2. ALEXANDER HAMILTON'S ALTERNATIVE: TECHNOLOGY PIRACY AND THE REPORT ON MANUFACTURES

The notes in this chapter have been reduced; see the notes in the original publication. Reprinted by permission from the *William and Mary Quarterly*, 3d ser., 52 (July 1995): 389–414.

1. *Federal Gazette*, March 24, 1791.

2. Tench Coxe to Jefferson, March 14, 1791, Jefferson to James Maury, May 1, 1791, *Jefferson Papers* 19:553, 20:339.

3. Ibid., 20:340.

4. Receipt from George Parkinson, July 20, 1791, *Hamilton Papers* 8:588.

5. Anthony F. C. Wallace and David J. Jeremy, "William Pollard and the Arkwright Patents," *WMQ*, 3d ser., 34 (1977): 409.

6. Julian P. Boyd, *Number 7: Alexander Hamilton's Secret Attempts to Control American Foreign Policy* (Princeton, NJ, 1964); Albert Bowman, "Jefferson, Hamilton, and American Foreign Policy," *Political Science Quarterly* 73 (1956): 21, 19; Buel, *Securing the Revolution*, 32; Bradford Perkins, *The Cambridge History of American Foreign Relations*, vol. 1, *The Creation of a Republican Empire, 1776–1865* (New York, 1993), 108; William Appleman Williams, *Contours of American History* (Cleveland, 1961), 155; Jerald A. Combs, *The Jay Treaty: Political Battleground of the Founding Fathers* (Berkeley, CA, 1970), 33–49; Alexander DeConde, *Ethnicity, Race, and American Foreign Policy: A History* (Boston, 1992), 18.

7. Elkins and McKitrick, *Age of Federalism*, 128.

8. Doron Ben–Atar, *The Origins of Jeffersonian Commercial Policy and Diplomacy* (New York, 1993), 93–94.

9. Alexander Hamilton, "The Public Conduct and Character of John Adams, Esq.," Oct. 1800, *Hamilton Papers* 25:230.

10. John E. Crowley, *The Privileges of Independence: Neomercantilism and the American Revolution* (Baltimore, 1993), 77, 153.

11. Hamilton, "Report on the Subject of Manufactures" (ROM hereafter), Dec. 5, 1791, *Hamilton Papers* 10:266. All citations of the ROM in this chapter refer to the final draft unless noted otherwise.

12. Editorial note, ibid., 1.

13. A memo submitted to Daniel Stevens by Charleston manufacturers, Sept. 1, 1791, in Arthur H. Cole, ed., *Industrial and Commercial Correspondence of Alexander Hamilton Anticipating His Report on Manufactures* (Chicago, 1928), 90.

14. O. Burr & Co. to John Chester, Sept. 12, 1791, ibid., 22.

15. Samuel Beck to Hamilton, Sept. 3, 1791, ibid., 61.

16. George Cabot to Hamilton, Sept. 6, 1791, ibid., 62.

17. John Mix to John Chester, Oct. 5, 1791, ibid., 51–52.

18. Elisha Colt to John Chester, Aug. 20, 1791, ibid., 7–9.

19. Moses Brown to John Dexter, July 22, 1791, ibid., 72.

20. Jacob E. Cooke, *Tench Coxe and the Early Republic* (Chapel Hill, NC, 1978), 183.

21. Tench Coxe, *An Enquiry into the Principles on Which a Commercial System for the United States Should Be Founded* (Philadelphia, 1787), 19.

22. Tench Coxe, *An Address to an Assembly of the Friends of American Manufactures. Convened for the Purpose of Establishing a Society for the Encouragement of Manufactures and the Useful Arts* (Philadelphia, 1787), 13, 11.

23. Ibid., 21–22.

24. *Pennsylvania Gazette,* May 27, 1785.

25. "Extracts from the Minutes of the Board of Managers of the Pennsylvania Society of Arts and Manufactures," *American Museum* 5 (Jan. 1789): 51, 52.

26. Coxe, "Address to the Friends of American Manufactures," Oct. 20, 1788, ibid., 4 (Oct. 1788): 342.

27. Ibid., 346.

28. [John Baker Holroyd, Lord Sheffield], *Observations on Commerce of the American States with Europe and the West Indies . . .* (Philadelphia, 1783), 38, 39.

29. Coxe, "Address to the Friends of American Manufactures," 343.

30. Coxe to Hamilton, Nov. 30, 1789, *Hamilton Papers* 5:569–70.

31. Coxe's 2d draft of the ROM, ibid., 26:636.

32. Ibid., 638–39.

33. Paper "A," ibid., 10:18–19 n. 52.

34. Coxe's 2d draft of the ROM, ibid., 26:639, 646–47.

35. Hamilton, ROM, ibid., 10:271.

36. Ibid., 252.

37. Ibid., 249.

38. Ibid., 251.

39. Ibid., 272.

40. Christine MacLeod, *Inventing the Industrial Revolution* (Cambridge, 1988), 108.

41. Hamilton, "Prospectus of the Society for Establishing Useful Manufactures," Aug. 1791, *Hamilton Papers* 9:146.

42. Hamilton, ROM, ibid., 10:339.

43. John Morgan, "Whether It Be Most Beneficial to the United States to Promote Agriculture, or to Encourage the Mechanic Arts and Manufactures," *American Museum* 6 (July 1789): 73–74.

44. Hamilton, ROM, *Hamilton Papers* 10:271, 254.

45. Ibid., 270–71.

46. Hamilton, 3d draft of ROM, ibid., 82.

47. Hamilton, ROM, ibid., 254.

48. Ibid., 270.

49. Washington to Congress, Jan. 8, 1790, in Walter Lowerie and Matthew St. Clair Clark, eds., *American State Papers, Documents, Legislative and Executive*, 38 vols. (Washington, DC, 1832–61), *Foreign Affairs*, 1:12.

50. "House of Representatives Journal," in Linda G. De Pauw, Charlene Bickford, et al., eds., *Documentary History of the First Federal Congress of the United States of America*, 14 vols. (Baltimore, 1979—), 3:94; "Senate Legislative Journal," ibid., 1:269.

51. Hamilton, ROM, *Hamilton Papers* 10:296.

52. Hamilton, 1st draft of the ROM, ibid., 37.

53. Hamilton to the Directors of the SEUM, Dec. 7, 1791, ibid., 345.

54. Hamilton, 1st draft of the ROM, ibid., 36–37.

55. John R. Nelson, Jr., *Liberty and Property: Political Economy and Policymaking in the New Nation, 1789–1812* (Baltimore, 1987), 46–47.

56. Hamilton, 3d draft of the ROM, *Hamilton Papers* 10:91. For the final version, see ibid., 250–51.

57. Hamilton, 4th draft of the ROM, ibid., 228–29.

58. Hamilton, ROM, ibid., 339–40.

59. Ibid., 340.

60. Bernard Bailyn, *Voyagers to the West: A Passage in the Peopling of America on the Eve of the Revolution* (New York, 1986), 29–66.

61. Thomas Digges to Hamilton, April 6, 1792, Samuel Paterson to Hamilton, Feb. 16, 1793, *Hamilton Papers* 11:242, 14:87.

62. David J. Jeremy, ed., *Henry Wansey and His American Journal, 1794* (Philadelphia, 1970), 30.

63. Phineas Bond to Lord Grenville, Sept. 10, 1791, in J. Franklin Jameson, ed., "Letters of Phineas Bond, British Consul at Philadelphia . . . , 1790–1794," *American Historical Association Annual Report for 1897* (Washington, DC, 1898), 487.

64. George Hammond to Grenville, Oct. 3, 1792, as cited by Herbert Heaton, "The Industrial Immigrant in the United States, 1783–1812," *Proceedings of the American Philosophical Society* 95 (1951): 523.

65. Hammond to Grenville, Dec. 6, 1791, in Bernard Mayo, ed., "Instructions to the British Ministers to the United States, 1791–1812," *Annual Report of the American Historical Association for the Year 1936*, 3 vols. (Washington, DC, 1936), 3:81 n.12.

66. Quoted in *Jefferson Papers* 17:387.

67. Roger Newberry to Hamilton, undated, *Hamilton Papers* 26:828.

68. Hamilton to the Directors of the SEUM, Dec. 7, 1791, ibid., 10:346, 347.

69. Samuel Paterson to Hamilton, Feb. 10, 1791, in Cole, *Industrial and Commercial Correspondence*, 110.

70. "Loan to John F. Amelung," June 2, 1790, *American State Papers, Finances*, 9:62; *Annals* 1:1686–88.

71. Hamilton, "Prospectus of the Society for Establishing Useful Manufactures," Aug. 1791, *Hamilton Papers* 9:147.

72. Paterson to Hamilton, Feb. 10, 1791, in Cole, *Industrial and Commercial Correspondence*, 111.

73. Thomas Marshall to Hamilton, July 19, 1791, ibid., 185.

74. Hamilton, ROM, *Hamilton Papers* 10:308.

75. I. Bernard Cohen, *Benjamin Franklin's Science* (Cambridge, MA, 1990), 185, 199.

76. James L. Huston, "The American Revolutionaries, the Political Economy of Aristocracy, and the American Concept of the Distribution of Wealth, 1765–1900," *American Historical Review* 98 (1993): 1080–81.

77. William Barton, *The True Interest of the United States, and Particularly of Pennsylvania Considered* (Philadelphia, 1786), 28.

78. Hamilton, ROM, *Hamilton Papers* 10:339, 297.

79. Peter Onuf and Nicholas Onuf, *Federal Union, Modern World: The Law of Nations in an Age of Revolutions, 1776–1814* (Madison, WI, 1993), 147.

80. Jacques Necker, *A Treatise on the Administration of the Finance of France*, trans. Thomas Mortimer, 3 vols. (London, 1784), 2:475–76; John R. Harris, "Industrial Espionage in the Eighteenth Century," *Industrial Archeology Review* 7 (1985): 127.

81. Edmund Randolph to Washington, Jan. 10, 1791, Washington to Beverley Randolph, Jan. 13, 1791, as cited in *Jefferson Papers* 18:124.

82. Hamilton, 2d draft of the ROM, *Hamilton Papers* 10:60.

83. Ibid., 60. Hamilton did not include this reasoning in the report submitted to Congress.

84. Hamilton, "Prospectus of the SEUM," ibid., 9:147.

85. Hamilton, ROM, ibid., 10:296–97.

86. Jacob E. Cooke, *Alexander Hamilton* (New York, 1982), 104.

87. Hamilton, ROM, *Hamilton Papers* 10:296.

88. James Currie to Hamilton, July 1793, ibid., 15:153.

89. Harry Ammon, *The Genet Mission* (New York, 1973), 47.

90. Jefferson to William Short, Jan. 3, 1793, *Jefferson Papers* 25:14; Hamilton, "Pacificus, VI," July 17, 1793, and "The French Revolution," *Hamilton Papers* 15:102, 17:587.

91. Elkins and McKitrick, *Age of Federalism*, 258.

3. Hamilton's Second Thoughts: Federalist Finance Revisited

1. Alexander Hamilton, "Report on a Plan for the Further Support of Public Credit," Jan. 16, 1795, *Hamilton Papers* 18:58.

2. Important biographies include Broadus Mitchell, *Alexander Hamilton*, 2

vols. (New York, 1957–62); Forrest McDonald, *Alexander Hamilton: A Biography* (New York, 1979); Cooke, *Alexander Hamilton.*

3. For an overview of Hamilton's design, see Elkins and McKitrick, *Age of Federalism*, 92–131. On the Treasury, see Carl E. Prince, *The Federalists and the Origins of the U.S. Civil Service* (New York, 1977); for a study of one maverick official, see Cooke, *Tench Coxe.* On the excise and the Whiskey Rebellion, see, e.g., Slaughter, *Whiskey Rebellion*; Steven R. Boyd, ed., *The Whiskey Rebellion: Past and Present Perspectives* (Westport, CT, 1985); William D. Barber, "'Among the Most *Techy Articles of the Civil Police*': Federal Taxation and the Adoption of the Whiskey Excise," *WMQ*, 3d ser., 25 (1968): 58–84.

4. Wolcott has been little studied; George Gibbs, *Memoirs of the Administrations of Washington and John Adams . . .* , 2 vols. (New York, 1846), presents his "literary remains."

5. On eighteenth-century public finance, see J. F. Bosher, *French Finances, 1770–1795: From Business to Bureaucracy* (Cambridge, 1970), and P. M. G. Dickson, *The Financial Revolution in England: A Study in the Development of Public Credit, 1688–1756* (London, 1967); for Amsterdam, see Larry Neal, *The Rise of Financial Capitalism: International Capital Markets in the Age of Reason* (New York, 1990), and James C. Riley, *International Government Finance and the Amsterdam Capital Market, 1740–1815* (Cambridge, 1980).

6. See Simon Schama, *Patriots and Liberators: Revolution in the Netherlands, 1780–1813* (New York, 1977), for the effects of French conquest and rule in Holland.

7. On the loan and Adams's reactions, see Manning J. Dauer, *The Adams Federalists* (Baltimore, 1968), 241–42.

8. But Jefferson did pick up rumors that money might be raised in London; see Thomas Jefferson to James Madison, May 31, June 14, 1798, *Madison Papers* 17:139, 152. British investors were happy to buy up American bonds (Bradford Perkins, *The First Rapprochement: England and the United States, 1795–1805* [Berkeley, CA, 1967], 12). The financial problems and military setbacks the British faced from early 1797 (when the Bank of England suspended cash payments) through 1798 suggest chances of a loan in London were slim; though relations with the United States were fairly cordial at this point, British resources were strained to the breaking point. For British problems in 1797–98, see J. Steven Watson, *The Reign of George III, 1760–1815* (Oxford, 1960), 372–74; on suspension of cash payments, see Sir John Clapham, *The Bank of England: A History*, 2 vols. (Cambridge, 1945), 1:270–72.

9. For numbers, see Davis Rich Dewey, *Financial History of the United States*, 2d ed. (New York, 1903), 112.

10. Hamilton, "First Report on the Further Provision Necessary for Establishing Public Credit," Dec. 13, 1790, *Hamilton Papers* 7:233.

11. Jefferson to George Washington, May 23, 1792, to Madison, Dec. 28, 1794, *Jefferson Writings*, ed. Merrill D. Peterson (New York, 1984), 986, 1016.

12. Hamilton to James McHenry, March 18, 1799, *Hamilton Papers* 22:552–53.

13. Jefferson, Second Inaugural Address, March 4, 1805, *Jefferson Writings*, ed. Peterson, 519.

14. For Britain, see Patrick K. O'Brien, "The Political Economy of British Taxation, 1660–1815," *Economic History Review*, 2d ser., 41 (1988): 9; for the United States, see Dewey, *Financial History*, 110.

15. Nelson argues in *Liberty and Property* that Hamilton's policy condemned America to underdevelopment and neocolonial dependency; from a less nationalistic point of view, certainly from that of the consumer, easy access to the world's great source of manufactures may have looked different.

16. For discussions of the Republican alternative, see Merrill D. Peterson, "Thomas Jefferson and Commercial Policy, 1783–1793," *WMQ*, 3d ser., 22 (1965): 584–610, favorable, and Ben-Atar, *Origins of Jeffersonian Commercial Policy*, and Robert W. Tucker and David C. Hendrickson, *Empire of Liberty: The Statecraft of Thomas Jefferson* (New York, 1990), both unfavorable.

17. Cf. Gordon S. Wood, "America in the 1790s," *Atlantic Monthly* 272 (1993): 138. John M. Murrin's essay "Great Inversion" is the starting point for investigations of this theme.

18. For a sense of how bad things were, see John M. Norris, *Shelburne and Reform* (New York, 1963).

19. Jefferson to Madison, March 6, 1796, *Madison Papers* 16:250; for popular echoes, see William Manning, *The Key of Liberty . . .* , ed. Michael Merrill and Sean Wilentz (Cambridge, MA, 1993).

20. See Prince, *Federalists and the Origins of the U.S. Civil Service*.

21. For the tellership and other Grenville perquisites, see J. V. Beckett, *The Rise and Fall of the Grenvilles: Dukes of Buckingham and Chandos, 1710 to 1921* (Manchester, 1994).

22. Jefferson, Opinion on the Constitutionality of a National Bank, Feb. 15, 1791, *Jefferson Writings*, ed. Peterson, 416–21. On the continuing importance of Anti-Federalists, see Richard E. Ellis, "The Persistence of Antifederalism after 1789," in Beeman, *Beyond Confederation*, 295–314.

23. See David Hume, "Of Public Credit" (1752), in Hume, *Political Essays*, ed. Knud Haakonssen (Cambridge, 1994), 166–78; Adam Smith, *An Inquiry into the Nature and Causes of the Wealth of Nations* (1776), 2 vols., ed. R. H. Campbell and A. S. Skinner (Oxford, 1976), 2:907–47. Istvan Hont, "The Rhapsody of Public Debt: David Hume and Voluntary State Bankruptcy," in *Political Discourse in Early Modern Britain*, ed. Nicholas Phillipson and Quentin Skinner (New York, 1993), 321–48, illuminates this strain in eighteenth-century thought. For an Amsterdam banker's warnings that the sums available for investment in American bonds would dry up, see Nicholas Van Staphorst to Hamilton, Oct. 4, 1794, *Hamilton Papers* 17:303–6.

24. Intended to "sink" (pay off) the debt, sinking funds were used to buy up and retire government debt; in more elaborate models, the debt purchased was not retired but held in an account, its interest used to purchase more debt.

25. Hamilton, Report, Jan. 16, 1795, *Hamilton Papers* 18:109.

26. Ibid., 57–59, 101–2. The Hamilton editors note that the italicized portion of the text quotes Washington's Nov. 19, 1794, message to Congress (ibid., 59 n.49).

27. Ibid., 102–3, 103, 104–7; for Jefferson's views, see Jefferson to John Wayles Eppes, June 24, 1813, *Jefferson Writings*, ed. Peterson, 1282.

28. Hamilton, Report, Jan. 16, 1795, *Hamilton Papers* 18:108–9.

29. Ibid., 109.

30. For reactions, see the Hamilton editors' Introductory Note to the Report, ibid., 46–56; Mitchell, *Hamilton* 2:360–61, 365.

31. Hamilton, Report, Jan. 16, 1795, *Hamilton Papers* 18:115–29.

32. Joyce Appleby makes the point in several of her works; see *Capitalism* and the essays collected in *Liberalism and Republicanism in the Historical Imagination* (Cambridge, MA, 1992).

33. Hamilton to Gouverneur Morris, Feb. 29, 1802, *Hamilton Papers* 25:544.

34. Oliver Wolcott to Hamilton, Sept. 26, 1795, ibid., 19:295.

35. Dauer, *Adams Federalists*, 241–42.

36. On the Fries episode, see Elkins and McKitrick, *Age of Federalism*, 696–700.

37. Jefferson to Madison, Jan. 3, 1799, *Madison Papers* 17:193.

38. For difficulties during the War of 1812, see J. C. A. Stagg, *Mr. Madison's War: Politics, Diplomacy, and Warfare in the Early American Republic, 1783–1830* (Princeton, NJ, 1983), and, of course, Adams, *History*, e.g., 2:1058–60.

4. RADICALS IN THE "WESTERN WORLD": THE FEDERALIST CONQUEST OF TRANS-APPALACHIAN NORTH AMERICA

1. Fisher Ames, *The Dangers of American Liberty* [1805], in Charles S. Hyneman and Donald S. Lutz, eds., *American Political Writing during the Founding Era, 1760–1805*, 2 vols. (Indianapolis, 1983), 1328, 1329.

2. Washington to Congress, June 17, 1783, in John C. Fitzpatrick, ed., *Writings of George Washington*, 39 vols. (Washington, DC, 1931–44), 27:17.

3. *Federalist Papers*, 253.

4. David J. Weber, *The Spanish Frontier in North America* (New Haven, 1992), 284.

5. Washington to Henry Knox, Dec. 5, 1784, in Fitzpatrick, *Writings of Washington* 28:4.

6. Parsons to his wife, Oct. 18, 1788, quoted in Charles S. Hall, *Life and Letters of Samuel Holden Parsons* (Binghamton, NY, 1905), 533.

7. Parsons to Manasseh Cutler, Dec. 11, 1788, ibid., 543.

8. Samuel Prescott Hildreth, *Biographical and Historical Memoirs* (Cincinnati, 1852), 305.

9. John L. Brooke, *The Heart of the Commonwealth: Society and Political Culture in Worcester County, Massachusetts, 1713–1861* (Cambridge, 1989), 239.

10. John Lauritz Larson, "'Wisdom Enough to Improve Them': Government, Liberty, and Inland Waterways in the Rising American Empire," in *Launching the "Extended Republic": The Federalist Era*, ed. Ronald J. Hoffman and Peter J. Albert (Charlottesville, VA, 1996), 223–48.

11. Manasseh Cutler, *An Explanation of the Map* (Salem, MA, 1787), 14, 21, 14.

12. Manasseh Cutler, "Sermon Preached at Campus Martius, Marietta, North-West Territory, August 24, 1788," in *Life, Journals, and Correspondence of Rev. Manasseh Cutler*, ed. William Parker Cutler and Julia Perkins Cutler, 2 vols. (Cincinnati, 1888), 2:445, 444, 449.

13. Henry Knox, "The Causes of the Existing Hostilities between the UNITED STATES, and Certain Tribes of INDIANS, North-West of the Ohio," Jan. 26, 1792, Clarence E. Carter II and John Porter Bloom, eds., *Territorial Papers of the United States*, 28 vols. to date, (Washington, DC, 1934—), 2:365, 366.

14. "Report of the Secretary at War to Congress," July 10, 1787, ibid., 31.

15. Richard Kohn, *Eagle and Sword: The Federalists and the Creation of the Military Establishment in America, 1783–1802* (New York, 1975), 151.

16. Tarke, Aug. 7, 1795, Wayne, July 3, 1795, "Treaty of Greenville," *American State Papers . . . Indian Affairs* 1:580, 565–66.

17. Andrew R. L. Cayton, "'Separate Interests' and the Nation-State: The Washington Administration and the Origins of Regionalism in the Trans-Appalachian West," *Journal of American History* 79 (1992): 39–67; Cayton, "'When Shall We Cease to Have Judases?': The Blount Conspiracy and the Limits of the 'Extended Republic,'" in Hoffman and Albert, *Launching the "Extended Republic,"* 156–89.

18. McCoy, *Elusive Republic*.

19. David Hackett Fischer and James C. Kelly, *Away, I'm Bound Away: Virginia and the Westward Movement* (Richmond, 1993), 67, 97.

20. Andrew R. L. Cayton, *Frontier Indiana* (Bloomington, IN, 1996), 167–95.

21. Andrew R. L. Cayton, "Land, Power, and Reputation: The Cultural Dimension of Politics in the Ohio Country," *WMQ*, 3d ser., 47 (1990): 266–86.

22. Cayton, *Frontier Indiana*, 226–60.

23. Cato West and others to the Congress of the United States, Natchez, Oct. 2, 1799, in Carter, *Territorial Papers* 5:80, 82.

24. Malcolm J. Rohrbough, *The Land Office Business: The Settlement and Administration of American Public Lands, 1789–1837* (New York, 1968), 40, 177.

25. Mary K. Bonsteel Tachau, *Federal Courts in the Early Republic: Kentucky, 1789–1816* (Princeton, NJ, 1978), 196.

26. Cutler, Diary, April 7, 1802, in Cutler, *Manasseh Cutler* 2:105.

27. Cutler to [unknown correspondent], Oct. 31, 1803, ibid., 140.

28. Alexander Hamilton, "Purchase of Louisiana," *New-York Evening Post*, July 5, 1803, in *Hamilton Papers* 26:129, 133.

5. FEDERALISM, THE STYLES OF POLITICS, AND THE POLITICS OF STYLE

1. On political style, see Michael E. McGerr, *The Decline of Popular Politics: The American North, 1865–1928* (New York, 1986); McGerr, "Political Style and Women's Power, 1830–1930," *Journal of American History* 77 (1990): 864–85; Robert Hariman, *Political Style: The Artistry of Power* (Chicago, 1995). For cultural politics, or style as politics, see, for example, Dick Hebdige, *Subculture: The Meaning of Style* (London, 1979); John Fiske, *Media Matters: Everyday Culture and Political Change* (Minneapolis, 1994).

2. Ann Fairfax Withington, *Toward a More Perfect Union: Virtue and the Formation of American Republics* (New York, 1992).

3. Hariman, *Political Style*, 29–30. For a pathbreaking analysis of Federalist and Democratic-Republican popular political culture, see Simon P. Newman, *Parades and the Politics of the Street: Festive Culture in the Early American Republic* (Philadephia, 1997).

4. As Anne Norton observes, "Liberal theories and liberal therapies commonly turn on the neutrality of language" (*Republic of Signs: Liberal Theory and American Popular Culture* [Chicago, 1993], 161).

5. John K. Alexander, *The Selling of the Constitutional Convention* (Madison, WI, 1989); Edmund S. Morgan, *Inventing the People* (New York, 1988), 263–97; Michael Warner, *The Letters of the Republic* (Cambridge, 1990), 97–117.

6. Edward Countryman, *The American Revolution* (New York, 1985), 214–19, 226–27; *Pennsylvania Packet*, Aug. 4, 6, 7, 8, 1788; *Pennsylvania Journal*, July 5, 9, 12, 1788. See also David Waldstreicher, *In the Midst of Perpetual Fetes: The Making of American Nationalism, 1776–1820* (Chapel Hill, N.C., 1997), 53–107.

7. *Connecticut Courant*, July 20, 1789. For crowd action and spectatorship in the Revolution, see Pauline Maier, *From Resistance to Revolution* (New York, 1972); Paul A. Gilje, *The Road to Mobocracy* (Chapel Hill, NC, 1987); Barbara Clark Smith, "Food Rioters in the American Revolution," *WMQ*, 3d ser., 51 (1994): 3–38.

8. *Salem Gazette*, July 9, 1793; *Gazette of the United States*, July 18, 1796.

9. On self-regulation, education, and linguistic reform in the early republic, see esp. Lawrence Friedman, *Inventors of the Promised Land* (New York, 1975); Joseph J. Ellis, *After the Revolution* (New York, 1979); Ronald T. Takaki, *Iron Cages: Race and Culture in Nineteenth Century America* (New York, 1979), 3–36; Melvin C. Yazawa, *From Colonies to Commonwealth: Familial Ideology and the Beginnings of the American Republic* (Baltimore, 1985); Peter S. Onuf, "State Politics and Republican Virtue: Religion, Education, and Morality in Early American Federalism," in *Towards a Usable Past: Liberty under the State Constitutions*, ed. Paul Finkelman and Stephen Gottlieb (Athens, GA, 1991).

10. John P. Kaminski and Jill Adair McCaughan, eds., *A Great and Good Man: George Washington in the Eyes of His Contemporaries* (Madison, WI, 1989), 116–17, 124; Rufus Wilmot Griswold, *The Republican Court; or, American Society in the Age of Washington*, 2d ed. (New York, 1867), 339.

11. David S. Shields and Fredrika J. Teute, "The Republican Court and the Historiography of a Women's Domain in the Public Sphere," paper presented at the Society for Historians of the Early American Republic, Boston, July 15, 1994.

12. Hannah Webster Foster, *The Coquette*, ed. Cathy A. Davidson (New York, 1986), 44.

13. Wood, "The Democratization of Mind in the American Revolution," in *Leadership in the American Revolution* (Washington, DC, 1974), 73; Isaac Weld, Jr., *Travels through the States of North America . . . during the Years 1795, 1796, and 1797*, 3d ed., 2 vols. (London, 1800), 1:102; John Drayton, *Letters Written during a Tour through the Northern and Eastern States of America* (Charleston, SC, 1794), 65–67; Noah Webster to James Watson, [1794], MS no. 11327, New York State Library, Albany.

14. David Brion Davis, *Revolutions: Reflections on American Equality and Foreign Liberations* (Cambridge, MA, 1990), chap. 2; Buel, *Securing the Revolution*.

15. *Aurora*, Feb. 4, 1793; *National Gazette*, July 9, 1792. See also Newman, *Parades and the Politics of the Street*, 120–51, 154–57; Waldstreicher, *In the Midst of Perpetual Fetes*, 124–40.

16. "A New Party Dictionary," *Connecticut Courant*, Dec. 31, 1792; John Lowell, *The Antigallican; or, The Lover of His Own Country* (Philadelphia, 1797), 17.

17. This was possible in part because according to contemporary notions of rhetoric and performance, a refined style was a natural one. See Jay Fliegelman, *Declaring Independence: Jefferson, Natural Language, and the Culture of Performance* (Stanford, CA, 1993).

18. Peter Van Schaack to Loring Andrews, Jan. 26, 1796, Henry Van Schaack Papers, Massachusetts Historical Society, Boston.

19. Cyrus King, *An Oration, Pronounced at Biddeford, on the Fourth of July, 1798* (Portland, ME, 1798), 15–16; *Albany Centinel*, July 28, 1797; for a typical statement, see [Joseph Hopkinson], *What Is Our Situation? AND, What Our Prospects? A Few Pages for Americans, by an American* (Philadelphia, 1798). On the Alien and Sedition Acts, see Smith, *Freedom's Fetters*.

20. On the politics of "the revolutionary center," see Ronald P. Formisano, *The Transformation of Political Culture: Massachusetts Parties, 1790s–1840s* (New York, 1983), 57–83.

21. Jesse Appleton to Ebenezer Adams, Aug. 4, 1795, Jesse Appleton Letters, American Antiquarian Society, Worcester, MA; Buel, *Securing the Revolution*, 125–27.

22. *Gazette of the United States*, July 14, 1796; *Connecticut Courant*, July 11, 1796; *Gazette of the United States*, Feb. 26, March 5, 1796; Oliver Fiske, *An Oration Pronounced at Worcester, on the Anniversary of American Independence; July 4, 1797* (Worcester, MA, 1797), 5–6; Newman, "Principles or Men?" On the Federalist repudiation of political jealousy, see James H. Hutson, "The Origins of 'The Paranoid Style in American Politics': Public Jealousy from the Age of Walpole to the Age of Jackson," in *Saints and Revolutionaries*, ed. David D. Hall, John M. Murrin, and Thad W. Tate (New York, 1984), 360.

23. For examples, see John Andrews, *A Sermon, Delivered February 19, 1795* (Newburyport, MA, 1795); Ashbel Green, *A Sermon, Delivered in the Second Presbyterian Church . . . on the 19th of February, 1795* (Philadelphia, 1795); Thomas Baldwin, *A Sermon, Delivered February 19, 1795* (Boston, 1795).

24. *Columbian Centinel*, May 5, 1798.

25. *Times and Alexandria Advertiser*, July 6, 1798; for a similar observation a year later, see *Greenleaf's New-York Journal*, July 6, 1799. See also Steven Novak, *The Rights of Youth: American Colleges and Student Revolt, 1798–1815* (Cambridge, 1977), 39–42.

26. William Bentley, *The Diary of William Bentley, D.D.*, 4 vols. (Salem, MA, 1905), 1:196; *Gazette of the United States*, July 8, 1794.

27. *Lancaster Journal*, May 19, 1798; *Phenix or Windham Herald*, Aug. 30, 1798; *A Selection of the Patriotic Addresses to the President of the United States. Together with the President's Answers* (Boston, 1798), 12.

28. *Gazette of the United States*, May 7, 1798; *Selection of the Patriotic Addresses*, 141–42; *Aurora*, May 9, 1798.

29. *Greenfield Gazette*, May 14, 1798; *The Launch, A FEDERAL SONG* (Newburyport, MA, 1798).

30. *Columbian Museum and Savannah Advertiser*, Aug. 7, 21, 1798; *New York Globe and Commercial Advertiser*, July 12, 1798; "Spirit of the Ladies," *Portland Gazette*, July 16, 1798; *United States Gazette*, July 10, 11, 14, 1798.

31. *Oracle of Dauphin and Harrisburgh Advertiser,* Aug. 1, 1798, transcription in file 14465, Fourth of July celebrations, Historical Society of York County, York, PA; *Lancaster Journal,* July 14, 18, 1798; *Charleston City Gazette and Daily Advertiser,* Jan. 5, 1799; *Times and Alexandria Advertiser,* Nov. 29, 1798 (from Philadelphia, Aug. 8); "Female Patriotism," *Columbian Museum and Savannah Advertiser,* Aug. 14, 1798; "From the Commercial Advertiser. YOUNG LADIES—TO ARMS!," *Albany Centinel,* July 6, 1798.

32. For similar moments in the nineteenth century, see Mary P. Ryan, *Women in Public: Between Banners and Ballots, 1825–1880* (Baltimore, 1990), 24–30, 42–51, 132–41; Gaines M. Foster, *Ghosts of the Confederacy: Defeat, the Lost Cause, and the Emergence of the New South, 1865–1913* (New York, 1987), 37–46.

33. David A. Wilson, "Introduction," in Wilson, ed., *Peter Porcupine in America: Pamphlets on Republicanism and Revolution* (Ithaca, NY, 1994), 28; John C. Miller, *Crisis in Freedom: The Alien and Sedition Acts* (Boston, 1952), 6; *Augusta Chronicle,* July 14, 1798. On republican marriage, see Jan Lewis, "The Republican Wife: Virtue and Seduction in the Early Republic," *WMQ,* 3d ser., 44 (1986): 689–721.

34. Thomas Paine, *An Oration, Written at the Request of the Young Men of Boston, and Delivered July 17th, 1799* (Boston, 1799), 6; Edward St. Loe Livermore, *An Oration, in Commemoration of the Dissolution of the Political Union between the United States of America . . . and France* (Portsmouth, NH, 1799); "Sung the 17th July, 1799," *The Federal Songster* (New London, CT, 1800), 14–15; "A Card," *Columbian Centinel,* July 6, 1799.

35. Josiah Crocker Shaw, *An Oration, Delivered July 4th, 1798* (Newport, RI, 1798), 18; Alexander Graydon, *Memoirs of a Life* (Edinburgh, 1822), 381, cited in Claude G. Bowers, *Jefferson and Hamilton* (Boston, 1925), 220; Gerald Newman, *The Rise of English Nationalism: A Cultural History, 1740–1830* (New York, 1987), 71–83; Randolph Trumbach, "The Birth of the Queen: Sodomy and the Emergence of Gender Equality in Modern Culture, 1660–1750," in *Hidden from History: Reclaiming the Gay and Lesbian Past,* ed. Martin B. Duberman, George Chauncey, Jr., and Martha Vicinus (New York, 1989), 130–31; Cobbett, cited in Miller, *Crisis in Freedom,* 152, and in Wilson, "Introduction," *Peter Porcupine in America,* 32.

36. Eve Kosofsky Sedgwick, *Between Men: English Literature and Male Homosocial Desire* (New York, 1985); Sedgwick, *Epistemology of the Closet* (Berkeley, CA, 1990); Paine, *An Oration,* 10; Miller, *Crisis in Freedom,* 8; "Song. To an Old Tune," *Federal Songster,* 18–20, also as "New Yankee Doodle," *Patriotic Medley. Being a Choice Collection of Songs* (New York, 1800), 8–10; *For the Gazette of the United States. NEW VERSES—To an Old Tune,* Broadsides Collection, Library Company of Philadelphia, also as "Song VI," *The Echo: or, Federal Songster* (Brookfield, MA, 1798), 15–17. See also a song about the French bear who "would ensnare us by hugs far more fatal than blows," ibid., 164–65, also as "Columbia's Bald Eagle," *The Festival of Mirth, and American Tar's Delight* (New York, 1800), 29–30.

6. Gender and the First Party System

1. Julius Forrest, *Oration Delivered before the Republican Students of the Belles-Lettres and Union Philosophical Societies of Dickinson College,* July 4, 1815 (Carlisle, PA,

1815); Francis W. Brooke, *An Oration Delivered by Mr. Francis W. Brooke, of Fauquier Court-House, Virginia, on the Fourth of July, 1815, before the Federal Republican Students of the Union Philosophical Society of Dickinson College* (Carlisle, PA, 1815); David W. Huling, *Oration Delivered before the Students of the Belles-Lettres Society of Dickinson College, and a Number of Ladies and Gentleman of Carlisle Assembled at the College to Celebrate the 4th of July* (Carlisle, PA, 1815). Quote is in Brooke, *Oration*, 10. Up until this point, scholars have paid almost no attention to the issue of women and the first political parties, although new work promises to be forthcoming.

2. Linda K. Kerber, *Women of the Republic: Intellect and Ideology in Revolutionary America* (Chapel Hill, NC, 1980), 189–231, 269–88; Mary Beth Norton, *Liberty's Daughters: The Revolutionary Experience of American Women, 1750–1800* (Boston, 1980), 256–94.

3. Susan Branson, "Politics and Gender: The Political Consciousness of Philadelphia Women in the 1790s" (Ph.D. diss., Northern Illinois University, 1992), 116–20; Laurel Thatcher Ulrich, "'From the Fair to the Brave': Spheres of Womanhood in Federal Maine," in *Agreeable Situations: Society, Commerce, and Art in Southern Maine, 1780–1830*, ed. Laura Fecych Sprague (Kennebunk, ME, 1987), 222–24.

4. John Lambert, *Travels through Canada, and the United States of North America, in the Years 1806, 1807, 1808*, 2 vols. (London, 1813), 2:91.

5. John Morin Scott, *Oration Delivered before the Philadelphia Association for Celebrating the Fourth of July, without Distinction of Party, July 4, 1833* (Philadelphia, 1833), 8.

6. Jefferson to N. Burwell (1818), *The Jeffersonian Cyclopedia*, ed. John P. Foley, 2 vols. (1900; rpt. New York, 1967), 274; Joseph J. Ellis, *Passionate Sage: The Character and Legacy of John Adams* (New York, 1993), 187.

7. Jefferson to N. Burwell (1818), *Jeffersonian Cyclopedia*, 274.

8. Jefferson to Anne Willing Bingham, May 11, 1788, *Jefferson Papers* 13:151.

9. Quoted in Edmund S. Morgan, *The Meaning of Independence: John Adams, George Washington, and Thomas Jefferson* (New York, 1976), 61.

10. Quoted in Edith B. Gelles, *Portia: The World of Abigail Adams* (Bloomington, IN 1992), 48. See also Norton, *Liberty's Daughters*, 50; Ellis, *Passionate Sage*, 68–75; Rosemarie Zagarri, *Woman's Dilemma: Mercy Otis Warren and the American Revolution* (Wheeling, IL, 1995), 91–94, 149–55.

11. Ellis, *Passionate Sage*, 186–87; Eugene Perry Link, *Democratic-Republican Societies, 1790–1800* (New York, 1973), 172.

12. Zagarri, *Woman's Dilemma*, 63–64, 88–90.

13. John Adams to James Warren, Sept. 26, 1775, Robert J. Taylor, Gregg L. Lint, et al., eds., *Papers of John Adams*, 10 vols. to date (Cambridge, MA, 1977–), 3:168.

14. Rudolph J. Pasler and Margaret C. Pasler, *The New Jersey Federalists* (Rutherford, NJ, 1975), 70 n.56; Minor Myers, Jr., *Liberty without Anarchy: A History of the Society of the Cincinnati* (Charlottesville, VA, 1983), 185–88, 192–95; Edgar Erskine Hume, "The Society of the Cincinnati and the Tammany Society," *New York Genealogical and Biographical Record* 68 (Jan. 1937): 45–50.

15. James Tilton, "An Oration, Pronounced on the 5th July 1790," *Universal Asylum and Columbian Magazine* 5 (Dec. 1790): 372. See also Robert Porter, *An Oration to Commemorate the Independence of the United States of North-America; Delivered*

at Zion Church, in Fourth-Street, Philadelphia, July 4th, 1791; and Published at the Request of the Philadelphia Society of the Cincinnati (Philadelphia, 1791), 5.

16. James Wilson, "Lecture on the Study of the Law in the United States" (1790), Robert Green McCloskey, ed., *The Works of James Wilson*, 2 vols. (Cambridge, MA, 1967), 1:85. See also Elias Boudinot, *An Oration Delivered at Elizabeth-Town, New-Jersey, Agreeably to a Resolution of the State Society of Cincinnati on the Fourth of July, MDCCXCIII* (Elizabethtown, NJ, 1793), 23; William Loughton Smith, *An Oration, Delivered in St. Philip's Church, before the Inhabitants of Charleston, South-Carolina, on the Fourth of July, 1796* (Charleston, SC, 1796), 10. See notes 17–21 for other examples of Federalist orators addressing women directly.

17. Keating Lewis Simon, *An Oration Delivered in the Independent Circular Church, before the Inhabitants of Charleston, South-Carolina, on Friday, the Fourth of July, 1806* (Charleston, SC, 1806), 6. See also John Fauchereaud Grimké, *An Oration Delivered in St. Philip's Church, before the Inhabitants of Charleston, South-Carolina, on Saturday, the Fourth of July, 1807* (Charleston, SC, 1807), 17; Capt. James Kennedy, *An Oration, Delivered in St. Philip's Church, before the Inhabitants of Charleston, South-Carolina, on the Fourth of July, 1801; in Commemoration of American Independence* (Charleston, SC, 1801), 36.

18. William Hull, *An Oration Delivered to the Society of the Cincinnati in the Commonwealth of Massachusetts, July 4, 1788* (Boston, 1788), 5–6. See also Theodore Dwight, *An Oration, Spoken before the Society of the Cincinnati, of the State of Connecticut, Met in Hartford, on the 4th of July, 1792* (Hartford, 1792), 14; Elijah Waterman, *An Oration Delivered before the Society of the Cincinnati, Hartford, July 4, 1794* (Hartford, 1794), 19; Frederick Frelinghuysen, *An Oration, Delivered July 4th 1812, Before the New-Jersey Washington Benevolent Society, in the City of New-Brunswick* (New Brunswick, NJ, 1812), 10.

19. Tilton, *Oration*, 372.

20. David Daggett, *An Oration, Pronounced in the Brick Meeting-House, in the City of New-Haven, on the Fourth of July, A.D. 1787* (New Haven, 1787), 19. See also "An Oration, Pronounced at Roxbury, July 4, 1800, by the Request of the Inhabitants, on Commemoration of American Independence," *Columbian Phenix or, Boston Review,* July 1800, 425.

21. Philip Mathews, *An Oration, Delivered on the 5th July, 1813, in the Episcopal Church of Saint Helen* (Charleston, SC, 1813), 27–28.

22. Grimké, *Oration*, 18.

23. Linda K. Kerber, "The Republican Ideology of the Revolutionary Generation," *American Quarterly* 37 (1985): 484–85.

24. Kerber, *Women of the Republic*, 287.

25. Chandos Michael Brown, "Mary Wollstonecraft, or, The Female Illuminati: The Campaign against Women and 'Modern Philosophy' in the Early Republic," *Journal of the Early Republic* 15 (1995): 389–424.

26. Hume, "The Cinncinnati and the Tammany," 45–46; Sean Wilentz, *Chants Democratic: New York City and the Rise of the American Working Class, 1788–1850* (New York, 1984), 70, 88; Jerome Mushkat, *Tammany: The Evolution of a Political Machine, 1789–1865* (Syracuse, NY, 1971), 8–31.

27. This conclusion is derived from my reading of at least one hundred Democratic-Republican orations (especially Independence Day and Tammany

orations) for the period 1789–1815, either housed in the Rare Book Room, Library of Congress, or on microfiche in the Evans/Shaw-Shoemaker Collection of Early American Imprints, or published in Philip S. Foner, ed., *The Democratic-Republican Societies, 1790–1800: A Documentary Sourcebook of Constitutions, Declarations, Addresses, Resolutions, and Toasts* (Westport, CT, 1976).

28. *An Oration Delivered on the Fourth Day of July 1800, by a Citizen of the United States* (Springfield, MA, 1808), 12.

29. Elias Glover, *An Oration, Delivered at the Court-House in Cincinnati, on the Fourth of July, 1806* (Cincinnati, 1806), 23.

30. Ibid.

31. Richard Dinsmore, *A Long Talk, Delivered before the Tammany Society, of Alexandria, District of Columbia, at Their First Anniversary Meeting, May 12, 1804* (Alexandria, VA, 1804), 12.

32. Solomon Aiken, *An Oration, Delivered before the Republican Citizens of Newburyport, and Its Vicinity, July 4, 1810* (Newburyport, MA, 1810), 13–14.

33. Joseph Pilmore, *The Blessings of Peace: A Sermon, Preached in Christ's Church, New-York, on the Fourth of July, 1794. At the Joint Request of the Tammany Society or, Columbian Order, and the Society of Mechanics* (New York, 1794), 29. For a similar remark, see Thomas Slemons, *An Oration Pronounced at Mr. Thaddeus Broad's, on the Fourth of July, 1810, before the Republicans of Falmouth* (Portland, ME, 1810), 12.

34. Foner, *Democratic-Republican Societies*, 205, 225, 227, 229, 230, 253, 354, 392.

35. Ibid., 220.

36. *Proceedings of the Democratic Association of Gloucester County, New Jersey*, March 4, 1801 (1801).

37. Linda K. Kerber, "The Paradox of Women's Citizenship in the Early Republic: The Case of *Martin vs. Massachusetts*, 1805," *American Historical Review* 97 (1992): 349–78; Linda K. Kerber, "Making Republicanism Useful," *Yale Law Journal* 97 (1988): 1669; Newman, *Parades and the Politics of the Street*.

38. Judith Apter Klinghoffer and Lois Elkis, "'The Petticoat Electors': Women's Suffrage in New Jersey, 1776–1807," *Journal of the Early Republic* 12 (1992): 159–93.

39. Quoted in ibid., 184; Carl E. Prince, *New Jersey's Jeffersonian Republicans: The Genesis of an Early Party Machine, 1789–1817* (Chapel Hill, NC, 1964), 134 n.7.

40. Klinghoffer and Elkis, "Petticoat Electors," 191.

41. Mercy Otis Warren, *The Plays and Poems of Mercy Otis Warren*, ed. Benjamin Franklin V (Delmar, NY, 1980); "Observations on the New Constitution, and on the Federal and State Conventions," in Herbert J. Storing, ed., *The Complete Anti-Federalist*, 6 vols. (Chicago, 1981); Mercy Otis Warren, *History of the Rise, Progress, and Termination of the American Revolution Interspersed with Biographical, Political, and Moral Observations* (1805), ed. Lester H. Cohen, 2 vols. (Indianapolis, 1988).

42. Judith Sargent Murray, *The Gleaner* (1798), ed. Nina Baym (Schenectady, NY, 1992); Vera Bernadette Field, *Constantia: A Study of the Life and Works of Judith Sargent Murray, 1751–1820*, University of Maine Studies, 2d ser., no. 17 (Orono, ME, 1931).

43. Mercy Otis Warren to a very young lady, n.d., Letterbook, 114–15, Mercy Warren Papers, microfilm reel 1, Massachusetts Historical Society. See also Murray, *Gleaner*, 505–6, 636, 731.

44. Murray, *Gleaner*, 704.

45. "On Primitive Simplicity," *Plays and Poems of Mercy Otis Warren*, 228.

46. Warren, *History of the American Revolution* 1:xli–xlii.

47. L. H. Butterfield, R. A. Ryerson, et al., eds., *Adams Family Correspondence*, 6 vols. to date (Cambridge, MA, 1963—), 1:370, 382.

48. Abigail Adams to Mercy Otis Warren, April 27, 1776, ibid., 397.

49. Ibid., 418, 421. For further details on this episode, see Zagarri, *A Woman's Dilemma*, 91–94.

50. Murray, *Gleaner*, 703.

51. Ibid., 710.

52. Ibid., 452–53.

53. Ibid., 709.

54. Warren, *History of the American Revolution* 2:676.

55. Ibid., 629.

56. Ibid., 624. See also ibid., 1:14, 2:602, 664.

57. Foner, *Democratic Republican Societies*, 219.

58. Warren, *The Ladies of Castile*, in *Plays and Poems of Mercy Otis Warren*, 115.

59. Judith Sargent Murray to her brother, Feb. 13, 1796, Letterbook 9:536, Judith Sargent Murray Papers, reel 3, Mississippi Archives, Jackson.

60. Murray, *Gleaner*, 214.

61. Ibid., 636.

62. Ibid., 216.

63. Quoted in Fischer, *Revolution of American Conservatism*, 17.

64. Appleby, *Capitalism*, 74; Wood, *Radicalism*, 271–86.

65. Pauline Maier, "The Transforming Impact of Independence, Reaffirmed: 1776 and the Definition of American Social Structure," in *The Transformation of Early American History: Society, Authority, and Ideology*, ed. James A. Henretta, Michael Kammen, and Stanley N. Katz (New York, 1991), 215.

66. J. H. Hexter, "Republic, Virtue, Liberty, and the Political Universe of J. G. A. Pocock," *On Historians: Reappraisals of Some of the Masters of Modern History* (Cambridge, MA, 1979), 301.

67. Ibid. The best description of the Federalists' vision of society is in Kerber, *Federalists in Dissent*.

68. Ryan, *Women in Public*, 137; Elizabeth R. Varon, "Tippecanoe and the Ladies, Too: White Women and Party Politics in Antebellum Virginia," *Journal of American History* 82 (1995): 494–521; Norma Basch, "Marriage, Morals, and Politics in the Election of 1828," ibid., 80 (1993): 890–918; Paula Baker, "The Domestication of Politics: Women and American Political Society, 1780–1920," *American Historical Review* 89 (1984): 628–32.

7. THE PROBLEM OF SLAVERY IN THE AGE OF FEDERALISM

1. William M. Wiecek, "The Witch at the Christening: Slavery and the Constitution's Origins," in *The Framing and Ratification of the Constitution*, ed. Leonard W. Levy and Dennis Mahoney (New York, 1987), 167–84; Elkins and McKitrick, *Age of Federalism*, 163. For a recent book on this period that seems to

better understand the importance of slavery to the politics of this period, see Sharp, *American Politics*.

2. For a discussion of scholarship on Jefferson and slavery, see Paul Finkelman, *Slavery and the Founders: Race and Liberty in the Age of Jefferson* (Armonk, NY, 1996), 138–67.

3. Curiously there are a few other passing references to slavery and a significant discussion of the Haitian Revolution, but they are not indexed under "slavery." There is no serious discussion of slavery in this period despite the massive amount of secondary material on the subject written by scholars of "slavery" rather than scholars of the early national period. Elkins and McKitrick seem to have been uninfluenced by such important works as Donald Robinson, *Slavery in the Structure of American Politics, 1765–1820* (New York, 1971); David Brion Davis, *The Problem of Slavery in the Age of Revolution, 1770–1823* (Ithaca, NY, 1975); Wiecek, *Sources of Antislavery Constitutionalism*. By abruptly ending their book in 1801, Elkins and McKitrick failed to come to terms with the extensive chapter on Federalists and slavery in Kerber, *Federalists in Dissent*, 23–66.

4. See generally, Arthur Zilversmit, *The First Emancipation: The Abolition of Slavery in the North* (Chicago, 1967). The northern states passed gradual emancipation statutes as follows: Pennsylvania (1780); Connecticut (1784); Rhode Island (1784); New York (1799); New Jersey (1804). Massachusetts (1780), New Hampshire (1784), and Vermont (1791) ended slavery by their state constitutions. On the implementation of these laws, see Gary B. Nash and Jean Soderlund, *Freedom by Degrees: Emancipation in Pennsylvania and Its Aftermath* (New York, 1991); Paul Finkelman, *An Imperfect Union: Slavery, Federalism, and Comity* (Chapel Hill, NC, 1981).

5. Elkins and McKitrick, *Age of Federalism*, 4.

6. See generally Finkelman, *Slavery and the Founders*, 1–33; Wiecek, "Witch at the Christening"; Wiecek, *Sources of Antislavery Constitutionalism*.

7. In 1812 the Federalists came very close to defeating James Madison. They did so by running DeWitt Clinton, a disgruntled Republican. Had Clinton won, the Federalists would surely have gained a new lease on life. As late as 1820 the Federalists remained a political force in much of the North, even if they were already dead as a national party. Moreover, even while out of power at the national level, Federalists retained influence and power in a number of states up through at least 1821.

8. Alvin Kass, *Politics in New York State, 1800–1830* (Syracuse, NY, 1965), 4. In New York fifty leading Federalists declared an end to their party in January 1820; however, as late as 1821 Federalists still operated as a recognizable faction in the state (ibid., 80–81). It is hard to know when the "Age of Federalism" began. I would start it with the Constitutional Convention, although the Federalist party did not emerge until the 1790s.

9. Sharp, *American Politics*, 34.

10. Hornblower characterized himself as an "Old Federalist." See Paul Finkelman, "State Constitutional Protections of Liberty and the Antebellum New Jersey Supreme Court: Chief Justice Hornblower and the Fugitive Slave Law," *Rutgers Law Journal* 23 (1992): 753–87. Fessenden had been a Federalist member

of the Massachusetts and Maine legislatures, as well as being the most prominent lawyer in Maine. William Jay "was a self-described Federalist 'of the old Washington school'" (Wiecek, *Sources of Antislavery Constitutionalism*, 154). Garrison began his career as a Federalist.

11. Banner, *Hartford Convention*, 101–9; [Wendell Phillips], *The Constitution a Pro-Slavery Compact; or, Selections from the Madison Papers*, 2d ed. (New York, 1845), v–vi. Banner argues that the abolitionists represented "New England sectionalism" as well as opposition to slavery.

12. Kerber, *Federalists in Dissent*, 23–66.

13. On the ambiguous success of the ordinance, see Finkelman, *Slavery and the Founders*, 34–79.

14. Fischer, *Revolution of American Conservatism*, 245–47.

15. Farrand, *Records* 1:486, 603–4. Hamilton argued that "the only considerable distinction of interests, lay between the carrying and non-carrying States, which divide instead of uniting the largest States" (ibid., 466). For a detailed discussion of this, see Finkelman, *Slavery and the Founders*, 1–33; Wiecek, "The Witch at the Christening."

16. Farrand, *Records* 2:220–23.

17. "Letters from a Countryman from Dutchess County" (letter of Jan. 22, 1788), in Storing, *Complete Anti-Federalist* 6:62; "Fragment of Debate at New Hampshire Convention," in Jonathan Elliot, ed., *The Debates in the Several State Conventions on the Adoption of the Federal Constitution*, 5 vols. (Philadelphia, 1881), 2:203-4; "A Friend to the Rights of the People," in Storing, *Complete Anti-Federalist* 4:238-39. A few southern Anti-Federalists also complained about the clause allowing for the continuation of the African slave trade until at least 1808. For example, in Kentucky, "Republicus" thought that the slave trade provision was "an excellent clause . . . in an Algerian Constitution" (Essays by Republicus [essay of Mar. 1, 1788], ibid., 5:169).

18. Elliot, *Debates in the State Conventions* 2:484.

19. Robinson, *Slavery in the Structure of American Politics*, 299, 300. It is almost impossible to tie the slave trade to any party notions. Republicans and Federalists both supported and opposed taxes on importing slaves. Illustrative of this may be the man who proposed the first tax on imported slaves, Josiah Parker of Virginia, who was associated with the Republicans in the early 1790s but was a "half-Federalist" by the Fifth Congress and voted against Jefferson's election in 1800 (Fischer, *Revolution of American Conservatism*, 376). On one vote in 1806 on taxing imported slaves, the vote does not seem to split along coherent party lines (Gales and Seaton, eds., *The Debates and Proceedings in the Congress of the United States*, 9th Cong., p. 519).

20. Robinson, *Slavery in the Structure of American Politics*, 299–305.

21. Finkelman, *Slavery and the Founders*, 80–104.

22. This of course would culminate with the debate over the territories in the 1850s. Then Stephen Douglas, a true Jeffersonian, would declare that he did not care if slavery was voted up or down. Similarly, Chief Justice Roger B. Taney's decision in *Dred Scott* constitutionalized Jeffersonian notions of expansion. Taney's appointment to the Court, as the replacement for John Marshall, symbolized the final nail in the coffin of Federalism.

23. Although he supported Madison while in Congress, before going on the Court, Story often worked closely with Federalists. Jefferson always distrusted Story's commitment to Republican policies and believed Madison had erred in appointing him. Story spoke out against admitting Missouri as a slave state. See Paul Finkelman, "Story Telling on the Supreme Court: *Prigg v. Pennsylvania* and Justice Joseph Story's Judicial Nationalism," *Supreme Court Review*, 1994, 247–94.

24. Jefferson to John Holmes, April 22, 1820, in Paul Leicester Ford, ed., *The Works of Thomas Jefferson*, 12 vols. (New York, 1904–5), 10:157–58.

25. Garry Wills, *Cincinnatus: George Washington and the Enlightenment* (Garden City, NY, 1984), 234.

26. Samuel Flagg Bemis, *Jay's Treaty: A Study in Commerce and Diplomacy* (New Haven, 1962), 290, 284, 131; Combs, *Jay Treaty*, 127.

27. Combs, *Jay Treaty*, 161; "Resolutions Adopted on Jay's Treaty, September 28, 1795," Foner, *Democratic-Republican Societies*, 404.

28. Charles R. Ritcheson, *Aftermath of Revolution: British Policy toward the United States, 1783–1795* (Dallas, 1969), 337.

29. Donald H. Stewart, *The Opposition Press of the Federalist Period* (Albany, 1969), 180, 206–7, 320. Stewart, a fan of the Jeffersonians, adopts their pro-slavery language here, talking about the "kidnapping" of slaves. The slaves themselves might have used such terms as "liberating" or "emancipating" to describe what the British had done for them, rather than to them.

30. See generally Davis, *Slavery in the Age of Revolution*.

31. Robinson, *Slavery in the Structure of American Politics*.

32. Banner, *Hartford Convention*, 104.

33. Ibid. While I accept Banner's argument on where antislavery went, I believe that antislavery was far stronger in the North than he suggests. Part of his argument is based on what I believe is a misreading of some of the legislation passed in Massachusetts and other northern states and also fails to take into account the strong support for black voting rights among Federalists. See Paul Finkelman, "Prelude to the Fourteenth Amendment: Black Legal Rights in the Antebellum North," *Rutgers Law Journal* 17 (1986): 415–82.

34. John Quincy Adams was not elected president as a Federalist, but his pre-presidential career was as a Federalist and an opponent of Jeffersonianism. He was, arguably, the last Federalist president.

35. Van Buren was a doughface for most of his career, although late in life he abandoned the South and embraced free soil.

36. To some extent so was Madison. Both men, for example, voted to give Congress the power to regulate trade with a simple majority, something generally opposed by slaveholders.

37. Wills, *Cincinnatus*, 234; Finkelman, *Slavery and the Founders*, 105–37.

38. Zilversmit, *First Emancipation*, 205. Bloomfield was a Washington-Adams elector in 1792 (Glover Moore, *The Missouri Controversy* [Lexington, KY, 1953], 67–69).

39. Fischer, *Revolution of American Conservatism*, 165; Merrill Peterson, *Thomas Jefferson and the New Nation* (New York, 1970), 707. For a fascinating history of the defense of Jefferson, see Scot A. French and Edward L. Ayers, "The Strange Career of Thomas Jefferson: Race and Slavery in the American Memory,

1943–1993," in *Jeffersonian Legacies*, ed. Peter S. Onuf (Charlottesville, VA, 1993), 418–56. As I have suggested elsewhere, it is time to attempt to settle this debate with a DNA test on the remains of Jefferson and of the children of Sally Hemings (Finkelman, *Slavery and the Founders*, 142).

40. Both quotes from Kerber, *Federalists in Dissent*, 27, 52.

41. While beyond the scope of this chapter, it is likely that New England Federalists, many of whom still accepted Puritan concepts of morality and community, found Jefferson's marital circumstances somewhat suspect.

42. Kerber, *Federalists in Dissent*, 23, 25–26.

43. Banner, *Hartford Convention*, 276n.

44. As I argue below, the Embargo hurt free blacks disproportionately more than whites.

45. Nash and Soderlund, *Freedom by Degrees*, 136. Philip Foner claims four men were members of both the Democratic Society of Pennsylvania and the PAS: George Logan, Peter S. Du Ponceau, Dr. James Hutchinson, and Absalom Baird (*Democratic-Republican Societies*, 12). While twice as many as Nash and Soderlund found, the small number Foner found simply underscores the point that Federalists, not Republicans, supported abolition in Pennsylvania. Logan appears to be one of the few Republican leaders from the North who challenged southerners on issues of slavery.

46. Nash and Soderlund, *Freedom by Degrees*, 136; Gary B. Nash, *Forging Freedom: The Formation of Philadelphia's Black Community* (Cambridge, 1988), 181–82.

47. Edmund S. Morgan, *American Slavery, American Freedom* (New York, 1975), 327.

48. Nash and Soderlund, *Freedom by Degrees*, 136. There is some evidence of Federalists alleging that the Jeffersonians were courting the black vote. According to David Hackett Fischer, "Before 1800, even in northern states, Federalist polemicists were openly contemptuous of Negroes" (*Revolution of American Conservatism*, 165).

49. Zilversmit, *First Emancipation*, 183. See also Edgar McManus, *A History of Negro Slavery in New York* (Syracuse, NY, 1966), 175n; Dixon Ryan Fox, "The Negro Vote in Old New York," *Political Science Quarterly* 32 (1917): 252, 254. Fox argued that the vote was entirely partisan, but Zilversmit found Fox incorrectly identified as Federalists some Republican supporters of the bill (Leon Litwack, *North of Slavery* [Chicago, 1961], 81–82).

50. A few New York Republicans, including James Nicholson, Tunis Wortman, Samuel L. Mitchill, Melancton Smith, and Philip Freneau, joined that state's manumission society (Foner, *Democratic-Republican Societies*, 12). Aaron Burr voted for gradual emancipation in the New York legislature but does not otherwise appear to have taken a stand on the issue.

51. Zilversmit, *First Emancipation*, 184; Kass, *Politics in New York State*, 82, 88–89; King quoted ibid., 88; Sharp, *American Politics*.

52. Dixon Ryan Fox, *The Decline of the Aristocracy in the Politics of New York, 1801–1840* (New York, 1919; rpt. 1965), 269n.

53. McManus, *Negro Slavery in New York*, 187.

54. Foner, *Democratic-Republican Societies*, 12–13.

55. McManus, *Negro Slavery in New York*, 187; Fischer, *Revolution of American*

Conservatism, 166. I am indebted to Rob Forbes for pointing out the important connection between free blacks and maritime industry in the North.

56. Litwack, *North of Slavery*, 81–82.

57. Ibid., 82–83; Kent quoted, ibid., 83. See also Fox, "The Negro Vote," 257–63.

58. Foner, *Democratic-Republican Societies*, 13.

59. Michael Zuckerman, *Almost Chosen People: Oblique Biographies in the American Grain* (Berkeley, CA, 1993), 188.

60. Elkins and McKitrick, *Age of Federalism*, 654, 658.

61. Jefferson to St. George Tucker, Aug. 28, 1797, in Ford, *Works of Jefferson* 7:168.

62. Elkins and McKitrick, *Age of Federalism*, 659.

63. Ibid., 662. Rayford Logan, *Diplomatic Relations of the United States with Haiti, 1776–1891* (Chapel Hill, NC, 1941), 177–78, shows that the vote in both houses of Congress was almost entirely along party lines. Timothy Pickering attacks the Jefferson administration for this in a letter. Pickering was a U.S. senator from Massachusetts.

64. Charles C. Tansill, *The United States and Santo Domingo, 1798–1873: A Chapter in Caribbean Diplomacy* (Baltimore, 1938), 82–83.

65. Zuckerman, *Almost Chosen People*, 180, 185.

66. Tansill, *United States and Santo Domingo*, 104–5.

67. Zuckerman, *Almost Chosen People*.

68. Gales and Seton, *History of Congress*, 9th Cong., 117, 125, 513, 515, 516; Tansill, *United States and Santo Domingo*, 105. One New York Democrat voted no, as did the mercurial Matthew Lyon, who at the time represented Kentucky.

69. Zuckerman, *Almost Chosen People*, 186.

70. There is evidence of this in Virginia, as well, where Federalists like Josiah Parker, John Marshall, George Washington, and Bushrod Washington showed ambivalence or hostility to slavery. The Federalist congressman Charles Fenton Mercer was "an honest opponent of slavery" (Fischer, *Revolution of American Conservatism*, 384).

71. John Hope Franklin, *The Free Negro in North Carolina, 1790–1860* (Chapel Hill, NC, 1943), 106, 181, 46. Blacks also could vote in Tennessee, but little is known about how they voted.

72. Davis, *Slavery in the Age of Revolution*, 178; Finkelman, *Slavery and the Founders*, 105–37; Jordan, *White over Black*, 481.

73. David R. Roediger, *The Wages of Whiteness: Race and the Making of the American Working Class* (London, 1991).

74. James Brewer Stewart, in "The Emergence of Racial Modernity and the Rise of the White North, 1790–1840," *Journal of the Early Republic* 18 (1998): 181–236, brilliantly explores how elite whites, almost of all of whom were Federalists, cooperated with black leaders in part to create a black upper class.

75. Morgan, *American Slavery, American Freedom*.

76. Thomas Jefferson to John W. Eppes, June 30, 1820, in Edwin Morris Betts, ed., *Thomas Jefferson's Farm Book . . .* , Memoirs of the American Philosophical Society, 35 (Princeton, NJ, 1953), 45; John Chester Miller, *The Wolf by the Ears: Thomas Jefferson and Slavery* (New York, 1977), 107.

77. Sharp, *American Politics*, 22.

8. MINISTERS, MISANTHROPES, AND MANDARINS: THE FEDERALISTS AND THE CULTURE OF CAPITALISM, 1790–1820

1. See Edmund Burke, "Reflections on the Revolution in France" (1789) and "Appeal to the Old Whigs from the New" (1791), extracts from which are included in Russell Kirk, ed., *The Portable Conservative Reader* (New York, 1982), 7–47.

2. Alexis de Tocqueville, *Democracy in America* (Garden City, NY, 1969), 507, 536.

3. See Kerber, *Federalists in Dissent*; Banner, *Hartford Convention*; Fischer, *Revolution of American Conservatism*; and Elkins and McKitrick, *Age of Federalism*, for various interpretations of Federalist conservatism in the early republic.

4. The following works are among many exploring various dimensions of this socioeconomic shift: James A. Henretta, *The Origins of American Capitalism: Collected Essays* (Boston, 1991); Christopher Clark, *The Roots of Rural Capitalism: Western Massachusetts, 1780–1860* (Ithaca, NY, 1990); Thomas R. Doerflinger, *A Vigorous Spirit of Enterprise: Merchants and Economic Development in Revolutionary Philadelphia* (New York, 1986); Allan Kulikoff, "The Transition to Capitalism in Rural America," *WMQ*, 3d ser., 46 (1989): 120–44; Daniel Vickers, "Competency and Competition: Economic Culture in Early America," ibid., 47 (Jan. 1990): 3–29; Jeane Boydston, *Home and Work: Housework, Wages, and the Ideology of Labor in the Early Republic* (New York, 1990); Michael Merrill, "Cash Is Good to Eat: Self-Sufficiency and Exchange in the Rural Economy of the United States," *Radical History Review* 4 (1977): 42–71; Watts, *Republic Reborn*.

5. See Doerflinger, *Spirit of Enterprise*, 283–364; Watts, *Republic Reborn*, 2–9.

6. See Joyce Appleby, "Commercial Farming and the 'Agrarian Myth' in the Early Republic," *Journal of American History* 68 (1982): 833–49; Diane Lindstrom, "American Economic Growth before 1840: New Evidence and New Directions," *Journal of Economic History* (1979): 289–301; Thomas C. Cochran, "The Business Revolution," *American Historical Review* 79 (1974): 1449–66.

7. A vast literature exists on the transformation of republicanism. For an introduction to it, see two articles by Robert Shalhope, "Toward a Republican Synthesis: The Emergence of an Understanding of Republicanism in American Historiography," *WMQ*, 3d ser., 29 (1972): 49–80, and "Republicanism and Early American Historiography," ibid., 39 (1982): 334–56. See also a special issue of the *American Quarterly* entitled "Republicanism in the History and Historiography of the United States," 37 (1985).

8. See Jay Fliegelman, *Prodigals and Pilgrims: The American Revolution against Patriarchal Authority, 1750–1800* (Cambridge, 1982), for an excellent analysis of the demise of patriarchal authority in eighteenth-century America.

9. See Wood, *Radicalism*; Nathan O. Hatch, *The Democratization of American Christianity* (New Haven, 1989); Henry F. May, *The Enlightenment in America* (New York, 1976); Cathy N. Davidson, *Revolution and the Word: The Rise of the Novel in America* (New York, 1986).

10. Timothy Dwight, *A Discourse, in Two Parts, Delivered July 23, 1812 ...* (New York, 1812), 6–8, 40–42.

11. See William J. Taggart and William K. Bottorff, eds., *The Major Poems of*

Timothy Dwight (Gainesville, FL, 1969); Timothy Dwight, *Travels; in New England and New York*, 4 vols. (New Haven, 1821–22).

12. Timothy Dwight, *The True Means of Establishing Public Happiness* . . . . (New Haven, 1795), 7–8; Timothy Dwight, *A Discourse in Two Parts, Delivered August 20, 1812* . . . (New York, 1812), 38–39, 40–41; Timothy Dwight, *The Nature and Danger of Infidel Philosophy* . . . (New Haven, 1798), 87, 64, 70; Timothy Dwight, *A Discourse on Some Events of the Last Century* . . . (New Haven, 1801), 44–45.

13. Dwight, quoted in Kenneth Silverman, *Timothy Dwight* (New York, 1969); Dwight, *Discourse August 1812*, 49; Dwight, *True Means of Public Happiness*, 7–9; Dwight, *Greenfield Hill*, in McTaggart and Bottorff, *Major Poems*, 402 (lines 171–76).

14. Dwight, *Travels* 4:516–17, 3:473; Dwight, *Life a Race*, in *Sermons by Timothy Dwight . . . Late President of Yale College*, 2 vols. (New Haven, 1828), 1:381–402; Dwight, writing as "The Friend" in the 1789 *American Museum*, quoted in McTaggart and Bottorff, *Major Poems*, xi.

15. Dwight, *Sermons* 1:498–512, 516–33.

16. Dwight, *Last Century*, 43, 17–18; Dwight, *Discourse August 1812*, 57–58; Dwight, *The Charitable Blessed. A Sermon* . . . (New Haven, 1810), 8–9; Dwight, *On Doing Good*, in *Sermons* 1:543–44.

17. Adams to William B. Giles, Dec. 22, 1812, *Adams Papers* (microfilm edition, Massachusetts Historical Society), reel 121.

18. John Adams, *Discourse on Davila: A Series of Papers on Political History*, in Charles Francis Adams, ed., *The Works of John Adams*, 10 vols. (Boston, 1850–56), 6:232, 233.

19. Ibid., 239, 241, 237, 38.

20. Ibid., 241, 234, 245. Adams derived much of his analysis from Adam Smith's *Theory of Moral Sentiments*, as Zoltan Haraszti has demonstrated in his *John Adams and the Prophets of Progress* (Cambridge, MA, 1952).

21. C. B. MacPherson, *The Political Theory of Possessive Individualism: Hobbes to Locke* (New York, 1964), 1–4, 263–64, 270–71.

22. Adams, *Davila*, in *Works* 6:79–80, 267–70; Adams to Thomas Boylston Adams, March 18, 1794, to William B. Giles, Dec. 22, 1812, *Adams Papers*, reels 377, 121; John Adams to John Quincy Adams, Feb. 18, 1811, in Adams, *Works* 9:633–34.

23. Adams, *Davila*, in *Works* 6:242–43, 250–52, 274–76, 280; Adams to Jefferson, Nov. 15, 1813, in Lester J. Cappon, ed., *The Adams-Jefferson Letters* (Chapel Hill, NC, 1959), 398–401; Adams to Thomas Boylston Adams, March 18, 1794, *Adams Papers*, reel 377.

24. Adams, *Davila*, in *Works* 6:270–71; Adams to Jefferson, Dec. 21, 1819, in Cappon, *Letters*, 551; Adams to Benjamin Rush, Sept. 27, 1808, in Adams, *Works* 9:602; Adams to Benjamin Rush, June 20, 1808, in John A. Schutz and Douglass Adair, eds., *The Spur to Fame: Dialogues of John Adams and Benjamin Rush, 1805–1813* (San Marino, CA, 1966), 110–11.

25. Adams to Jefferson, Nov. 15, 1813, in Cappon, *Letters*, 398.

26. Josiah Quincy, review of *The Works of Fisher Ames, Monthly Anthology and Boston Review* 8 (Feb. 1810), 113; Josiah Quincy's speech of Jan. 14, 1811, in *Annals*, 22:537–38; Josiah Quincy, *An Oration, Pronounced July 4, 1798 at the Request of the*

Town of Boston . . . (Boston, 1798), 20, 24; Josiah Quincy, "A Review, Political and Literary," *Portfolio* 4 (March 1804), 82.

27. Josiah Quincy, speech of Jan. 19, 1809, *Annals* 19:1107; Quincy, "Review of Ames," *Monthly Anthology*, 114; Josiah Quincy, "Review," *Portfolio* 4:82; Josiah Quincy to John Adams, Jan. 29, 1811, *Adams Papers*, reel 41.

28. Josiah Quincy, speech of Jan. 20, 1809, *Annals* 19:1139; Josiah Quincy, *Oration of 1809*, 23; Josiah Quincy, *An Answer to the Question, Why Are You a Federalist* . . . (Boston, 1815), 3–4, 6, 16, 17–18, 20–21; Josiah Quincy, *An Oration Delivered before the Washington Benevolent Society* . . . (Boston, 1813), 4–5, 6, 20; Quincy to John Adams, Jan. 29, 1811, *Adams Papers*, reel 41.

29. Josiah Quincy to John Quincy Adams, Dec. 15, 1804, *Adams Papers*, reel 403; Josiah Quincy to Oliver Wolcott, Sept. 5, 1803, quoted in Robert A. McCaughey, *Josiah Quincy, 1772–1864: The Last Federalist* (Cambridge, MA, 1974), 35. See McCaughey's book, p. 74, for a brief discussion of the 1812 maneuver with the British.

30. Josiah Quincy, speech of April 15, 1806, and Nov. 28, 1808, in *Annals* 15:1039–41, 19:538. See McCaughey, *Last Federalist*, 17, for a description of Quincy's financial investment in the 1790s.

31. Josiah Quincy, speech of April 19, 1808, *Annals* 18:2204–5.

32. See Marvin Meyers, *The Jacksonian Persuasion: Politics and Belief* (Stanford, CA, 1957) for a shrewd assessment of American "venturous conservatives" in the middle decades of the nineteenth century.

33. See Richard Hofstadter, *The American Political Tradition and the Men Who Made It* (New York, 1974), xxxvii, and, for one example of the vast literature on Victorianism, Daniel Walker Howe, ed., *Victorian America* (Philadelphia, 1976).

9. BENJAMIN FRANKLIN AS WEIRD SISTER: WILLIAM COBBETT AND FEDERALIST PHILADELPHIA'S FEARS OF DEMOCRACY

1. Frances Wright Darusemont, *Views of Society and Manners in America* . . . *during the Years 1818, 1819, and 1820* (New York, 1821), 279.

2. This chapter draws on Keith Arbour, "Using History: Americans and Benjamin Franklin, 1790–1845" (Ph.D. diss., Univ. of Michigan, 1994), particularly chap. 4, to which the reader is referred for further documentation.

3. Deborah Norris Logan, *Memoir of Dr. George Logan of Stenton* (Philadelphia, 1899), 38–39.

4. Franklin, "Observations Relative to the Intentions of the Original Founders of the Academy in Philadelphia," in Albert Smyth, ed., *The Writings of Benjamin Franklin*, 10 vols. (New York, 1905–7), 10:9–31.

5. Arbour, "Using History," chap. 2.

6. The statue continued to elicit this response from some Philadelphians beyond the Civil War (ibid., 194–95, 213–14, 356–57, 375–76).

7. Charles Biddle, *Autobiography* (Philadelphia, 1883), 244; Arbour, "Using History," 109–10, 111–40; William Smith, *Eulogium on Benjamin Franklin* (Philadelphia, 1792).

8. Cf. James Puglia, *The Blue Shop* (Philadelphia, Aug. 1796), 11.

9. *B. Franklin: Vir Vixit Integer, Liber Obiit . . . M.DCC.XC* ([New York, 1790]), Evans no. 45624.

10. As quoted in W. J. Bruce, "The Death and Funeral of Franklin," *American Historical Record* 3 (1874): 15–16.

11. *American Museum* 7 (Feb. 1790): 100–101; Stewart, *Opposition Press*, 131; Arbour, "Using History," 166, 171–72.

12. This is not to say that the democrats themselves did not also fear the extension of political equality to these two groups.

13. "Modern Spelling *Humorously Exposed*," *Universal Asylum and Columbian Magazine* 4 (March 1790): 140.

14. *General Advertiser* (Philadelphia), Jan. 20, 1791, p. 2, cols. 1–2; *Gazette of the United States* (Philadelphia), Jan. 22, 1791, p. 1, cols. 1–2.

15. *General Advertiser*, Jan. 24, 1791, p. 2, cols. 1–2; *Gazette of the United States*, Jan. 26, 1791, p. 1, cols. 1–2.

16. Adams, *Works* 10:270.

17. Translation from the Scottish edition seditiously published by William Stewart and John Elder in 1792 (ESTC record number t 169456).

18. Francois Furet and Denis Richet, *French Revolution*, trans. Stephen Harman (London, 1970), 258 (I have modified Harman's translation of the verb phrase); William Doyle, *The Oxford History of the French Revolution* (Oxford, 1989), 118–19, 318–19.

19. Adams, *Works* 9:564.

20. Ibid., 9:570, 10:53, 4:391–92 (cf. 6:285–86), 6:490–91. Cf. Olivia Smith, *The Politics of Language, 1791–1819* (Oxford, 1984), 16.

21. Esther E. Brown, *The French Revolution and the American Man of Letters* (Columbia, MO, 1951), 34; Adams, *Works* 6:459.

22. S. W. Jackman, "A Young Englishman Reports on the New Nation: Edward Thornton to James Bland Burges, 1791–1793," *WMQ*, 3d ser., 18 (1961): 93.

23. Kenneth R. Bowling and Helen E. Veit, eds., *The Diary of William Maclay and Other Notes on Senate Debates* (Baltimore, 1988), 18; see also pp. 86, 143, 168, et passim.

24. See, for example, William Cobbett, *History of American Jacobins* (Philadelphia, 1796), 33 et seq.

25. *Gazette and Daily Advertiser* (Philadelphia), Dec. 3, 1794, p. 2, col. 1; Cobbett, *The Scare-Crow* (Philadelphia, 1796), 9; Cobbett, *History of American Jacobins*, 26. See also Cobbett, *The Bloody Buoy*, 3d ed. (Philadelphia, 1796; rpt., London, 1797), 225–26.

26. L. H. Butterfield, ed., *Letters of Benjamin Rush*, 2 vols. (Princeton, NJ, 1951), 1:278–82.

27. Brown, *French Revolution and the American Man of Letters*, 72.

28. As quoted in Cobbett, *Observations on the Emigration of Dr. Joseph Priestly*, 3d ed. (Philadelphia, 1795), 59.

29. George Spater, *William Cobbett, the Poor Man's Friend*, 2 vols. (Cambridge, 1982), 1:48, 1, 36, 33, 39, 42.

30. Cobbett, *Observations on the Debates of the American Congress* (Philadelphia; rpt. London, 1797), 27.

31. James Thomson Callender, *The Political Progress of Britain*, pt. 1, 2d ed.

(Philadelphia, 1794), 60–61, drawing on Benjamin Franklin, *Works*, 2 vols. (New York, 1794), 2:81–82, 91.

32. Cobbett, *A Bone to Gnaw for the Democrats* (Philadelphia, 1795), iv; cf. Cobbett's *Porcupine's Gazette* (Philadelphia), March 31, 1798, p. 2, col. 3.

33. Cobbett, *Bone to Gnaw*, 8–9.

34. Ibid., 19.

35. Benjamin Davies, *Tit for Tat; or, A Purge for a Pill* (Philadelphia, 1796), 30–31.

36. *Porcupine's Gazette*, July 31, 1797, p. 3 (original in italics), rpt. in *Porcupine's Works* 6:343; Cobbett, *Life and Adventures of Peter Porcupine* (Philadelphia, 1796), 11.

37. See, for instance, Cobbett, *Bone to Gnaw*, 19; *Scare-Crow*, 9, 13; *History of American Jacobins*, 24 et seq., 40.

38. Thornton, *Cadmus* (Philadelphia, 1793), v–vii, 10, 28. Cobbett called Webster and Franklin "partner[s] in the language trade," in his *Political Censor for March 1797*, 103.

39. *Porcupine's Political Censor for March 1797*, 110; Whitfield J. Bell, Jr., "As Others Saw Us: Notes on the Reputation of the American Philosophical Society," *American Philosophical Society Proceedings* 116:3 (1972): 273; Cobbett, *History of American Jacobins*, 38; Cobbett, *Bone to Gnaw*, 5.

40. Cobbett, *Bone to Gnaw*, 53; Thornton, *Cadmus*, 35, 37.

41. [Cobbett's note:] See the 28th letter of his *[New] Travels in America [Performed in 1788* (New York, 1792), 191–92].

42. Cobbett, *Bone to Gnaw*, 53; Thornton, *Cadmus*, 35, 37.

43. Cobbett, *Observations on the Emigration*, 3d ed., 70, 71; cf. Shakespeare, *Macbeth* 4.1.

44. Cobbett, *A Little Plain English* (Philadelphia, 1795), 2, 69.

45. Joseph Dennie, "An Author's Evenings," *Port Folio* 1:7 (Feb. 14, 1801): 54; reiterated in ibid., 3:11 (March 12, 1803): 87.

46. For a similar conglomeration of criticisms, minus Franklin, see William Cliffton, *The Group: or An Elegant Representation Illustrated* (Philadelphia, 1796).

47. Cobbett, *Part II, A Bone to Gnaw* (Philadelphia, 1795), 11.

48. Susanna Rowson, *Slaves in Algiers; or, A Struggle for Freedom* (Philadelphia, 1794), 73.

49. Cobbett, *A Kick for a Bite* (Philadelphia, 1795), 23–24.

50. Lynn Hunt, *The Family Romance of the French Revolution* (Berkeley, CA, 1992), chap. 5, esp. p. 138.

51. Cobbett, *Life and Adventures*, iii, cf. 14; Lemuel Hopkins, *The Democratiad*, 3d ed. (Philadelphia, 1796), 6; Cobbett, *History of American Jacobins*, 32. Sarah Franklin (B. F. Bache's mother) was born thirteen years after Benjamin Franklin "took to wife" Deborah Read; B. F. Bache was born some twenty-two months after Sarah married Richard Bache (Leonard W. Labaree, Barbara B. Oberg, et al., eds., *The Papers of Benjamin Franklin*, 33 vols. to date [New Haven, 1959—], 1:lxii–lxiii).

52. James Carey, *A Pill for Porcupine*, 61; Cobbett, *The Life of William Cobbett* (London, 1835), 111–12.

53. John Swanwick, *A Roaster; or, A Check to the Progress of Political Blasphemy* (Philadelphia, 1796), 15–16.

54. Samuel Bradford, *The Imposter Detected, or A Review of Some of the Writings of "Peter Porcupine,"* 2d ed. (Philadelphia, 1796), xiv, 26–27, 22

55. For the contents of American editions of Franklin's *Life* and *Works*, 1794–1814, see Arbour, "Using History," 166–68, 171–74, 281–84.

56. The perception that every Philadelphian "owes, or owes chiefly . . . the lights which guide him in the night" to Franklin persisted into the next century. See, for example, [J. Sanderson], *The Girard College. Roberjot's Remark's on Mr. Biddle's Discourse* (Philadelphia, 1833), 6.

57. Arbour, "Using History," 129, 309, 358n, et passim.

58. Isaac Weld, Jr., *Travels through the States of North America . . . during the Years 1795, 1796, and 1797* (London, 1799), 13.

59. Quoted in Spater, *William Cobbett* 1:91; Adams, *Works* 9:83.

10. "STEADY HABITS" UNDER SIEGE: THE DEFENSE OF FEDERALISM IN JEFFERSONIAN CONNECTICUT

1. Roger H. Brown, *The Republic in Peril: 1812* (New York, 1964), 8; William Charles White, *Avowals of a Republican* (Worcester, MA, 1813).

2. Banner, *Hartford Convention*, vii; Livermore, *Twilight of Federalism*, 12.

3. Watts, *Republic Reborn*; Banning, *Jeffersonian Persuasion*; McCoy, *Elusive Republic*.

4. For other case studies of Connecticut Federalism, see William Cullen Dennis II, "A Federalist Persuasion: The American Ideal of the Connecticut Federalists" (Ph.D. diss., Yale University, 1971); John Hastings Chatfield, "'Already We Are a Fallen Country': The Politics and Ideology of Connecticut Federalism, 1797–1812" (Ph.D. diss., Columbia University, 1986).

5. Richard J. Purcell, *Connecticut in Transition, 1775–1818* (1918; rpt. Middletown, CT, 1963).

6. On that governor, see Richard Bushman, *From Puritan to Yankee: Character and the Social Order in Connecticut, 1690–1765* (Cambridge, MA, 1967).

7. See Thomas L. Purvis, "The European Ancestry of the United States Population, 1790," *WMQ*, 3d ser., 41 (1984): 85–101.

8. [Samuel Whittlesey Dana], *Essay on Political Society* (Philadelphia, 1800), 9–10, 72.

9. *Litchfield Monitor*, June 29, 1803; [David Daggett], *Facts Are Stubborn Things or Nine Plain Questions to the People of Connecticut, with a Brief Reply to Each* (Hartford, 1803), 4; [Daggett], *Steady Habits Vindicated or a Serious Remonstrance to the People of Connecticut, against Changing Their Government* (Hartford, 1805), 20; David Humphreys, *A Valedictory Discourse, Delivered before the Cincinnati of Connecticut, in Hartford, July 4, 1804, at the Dissolution of the Society* (Boston, 1804), 17.

10. Timothy Dwight, *A Discourse in Two Parts Delivered August 20, 1812 on the National Fast in the Chapel of Yale College* (New York, 1812), 40; Noah Webster, *A Rod for the Fool's Back* (New Haven, 1800), 7; Uriah Tracy, *To the Freemen of Connecticut* (Hartford, 1803), 16.

11. Dana, *A Specimen of Republican Institutions* (Philadelphia, 1802), 78; Benjamin Trumbull, *The Dignity of Man. Especially as Displayed in Civil Government* (Hartford, 1801), 7, 14.

12. [William Coleman], *An Examination of the President's Response to the New Haven Remonstrance* (New York, 1801), 13, 17. See also Daggett, *Facts Are Stubborn Things*, 12–19, and Tapping Reeve's "Asdrubal" series appearing in the *Litchfield Monitor*, 1801–5.

13. Tracy, *To the Freemen of Connecticut*, 13.

14. [Daggett], *Count the Cost: An Address to the People of Connecticut on Sundry Political Subjects and Particularly on the Proposition for a New Constitution* (Hartford, 1804), 16.

15. Governor Jonathan Trumbull, untitled broadside proclamation, Feb. 4, 1809, Beinecke Library, Yale University, New Haven. Quotation from Secretary of War Henry Dearborn's request, dated January and also available as a broadside at Beinecke.

16. Connecticut Assembly, *Address of the General Assembly to the People of Connecticut* (Hartford 1809), 1–2; Governor Roger Griswold, *Concerning Connecticut's Refusal of Federal Requisition for Militia* (1812), broadside proclamation, Beinecke.

17. Banner, *Hartford Convention*, 51; George Washington Stanley, *An Oration Delivered at Wallingford April 4, 1814; in Celebration of the Late Glorious Events in Europe* (New Haven, 1814), 14–17; Roger Minot Sherman to Daggett, Feb. 4, 1815, Daggett Papers, Sterling Memorial Library, Yale University.

18. John Hall, *An Oration Delivered at Tolland, before the Washington Benevolent Society, February, 22, 1814, in Commemoration of Washington's Birth-Day* (Hartford, 1814), 5–7; Seth Washburne to Daggett, Oct. 26, 1814, Daggett Papers; *The Proceedings of a Convention of Delegates . . . Convened at Hartford . . . December 15, 1814* (Hartford, 1815), 4–5.

19. Hall, *Oration Delivered at Tolland*, 25.

20. Goddard to Daggett, Nov. 11, 1815, Daggett Papers.

21. David M. Roth, *Connecticut: A Bicentennial History* (New York, 1970), 105.

22. Tapping Reeve, *The Sixth of August or the Litchfield Festival, an Address to the People of Connecticut* (Hartford, 1806), 14; Dana, *Specimen of Republican Institutions; To the People of Connecticut* (Hartford, 1817), 2–3 (unattributed Federalist campaign pamphlet).

23. Daggett, *Steady Habits Vindicated*, 4, 14, 18, 16.

24. *Litchfield Monitor*, Aug. 3, 1803; Daggett, *Steady Habits Vindicated*, 7.

25. Daggett, *An Eulogim Commemorative of the Exalted Virtues of His Excellency Roger Griswold, Late Governor of the State* (New Haven, 1812), 24; Theodore Dwight, *Oration Delivered at New Haven* (New Haven, 1801), 7.

26. *To the People of Connecticut*, 2; Theodore Dwight, *Oration Delivered at New Haven*, 7; Dana, *Essay on Political Society*, 72–73; Daggett, *Steady Habits Vindicated*, 5.

27. Daggett, *Facts Are Stubborn Things*, 4–5; Reeve, *Sixth of August*, 14; Daggett, *Steady Habits Vindicated*, 6–7.

28. Benjamin Trumbull, *The Dignity of Man. Especially as Displayed in Civil Government* (Hartford, 1801), 23; Dana, *Essay on Political Society*, 72–73; Timothy Dwight, *A Discourse on Some Events of the Last Century*, 46; Reeve, *Sixth of August*, 8. Federalist praise of "the church" and "the clergy" rarely mentioned any denomination by name. However, until the constitution of 1818, the Congregational Church was the state's established church, receiving regular and generous funding from general tax revenues. The system was gradually liberalized beginning in

the mid-eighteenth century, with dissenters allowed to pay some of their taxes to alternative funds for the support of their churches and with some state money distributed to other denominations.

29. Dana, *Specimen of Republican Institutions*, 6; Dana, *Essay on Political Society*, 73; Daggett, *Steady Habits Vindicated*, 5; Trumbull, *Dignity of Man*, 21–22.

30. Daggett, *Facts Are Stubborn Things*, 19–20.

31. *To the People of Connecticut*, 2–3.

32. Timothy Pickering, *A Letter from the Honorable Timothy Pickering, a Senator of the State of Massachusetts, Exhibiting to His Constituents, a View of the Imminent Danger of an Unnecessary and Ruinous War* (Hartford, 1808), 10; Connecticut General Assembly, *Report of the Committee to Whom Was Referred His Excellency's Speech* (Hartford, 1814), 3.

33. Connecticut General Assembly, *Address of the General Assembly*, 2, 5–6.

34. Calvin Goddard to Daggett, Nov. 30, 1814, Daggett Papers; Simeon Baldwin to Ebenezer Baldwin, Oct. 27, 1814, Baldwin Family Papers, Sterling Memorial Library, Yale University.

35. Watts, *Republic Reborn*, 316.

36. Stanley, *An Oration Delivered February 22, 1815 at the Annual Celebration of the Birthday of George Washington* (New Haven, 1815), 27, 28. Early versions of these societies were known as Washington Benevolent Societies. Less well known are their later incarnation as Trumbull Benevolent Societies.

37. Lyman Beecher, *A Reformation of Morals Practicable and Indispensable: A Sermon Delivered in New Haven 10/27/12* (Utica, NY, 1813 [1812]), 4, 5, 7, 15–16.

38. Harrison Gray Otis, *Letters Developing the Character and View of the Hartford Convention* (Washington, DC, 1820), 38; Dana, *Specimen of Republican Institutions*, 5; Tracy, *To the Freemen of Connecticut*, 14; Beecher, *Reformation of Morals*, 15; Trumbull, *Dignity of Man*, 28.

39. Humphreys, *Valedictory Discourse*, 15–16; Dana, *Specimen of Republican Institutions*, 5; Timothy Dwight, *Discourse on Some Events of the Last Century*, 46. The context makes clear that the "country" to which Dwight refers is defined by his experiences in New England.

40. John Cotton Smith to Daggett, Jan. 14, 1814, Daggett Papers; Daggett, *Facts Are Stubborn Things*, 23; Daggett, *Steady Habits Vindicated*, 4.

41. Chauncy Goodrich to Daggett, Jan. 8, 1814, Daggett Papers; Daggett, *Facts Are Stubborn Things*, 7–12; Tracy, *To the Freemen of Connecticut*, 13–14; *Litchfield Monitor*, June 22, 1803; White, *Avowals of a Republican*, 19; Daggett, *Facts Are Stubborn Things*, 11; Dwight, *Discourse in Two Parts*, 34–38; *Proceedings of a Convention*, 18–24.

42. Daggett, *Facts Are Stubborn Things*, 4–5, 20–21; Webster, *Rod for the Fool's Back*, 6; Goddard to Daggett, Nov. 1, 1814, Daggett Papers. More generally, see Bernard Bailyn, *The Ideological Origins of the American Revolution* (Cambridge, MA, 1967), esp. 232–34.

43. A 1784 statute declared all slaves free at age twenty-five. The sale and importation of slaves were prohibited by laws passed in 1787 and 1790. See Roth, *Connecticut*, 126–27.

44. Benjamin Trumbull, *A Century Sermon or Sketches of the History of the Eighteenth Century* (New Haven, 1801), 20; Beecher, *Reformation of Morals*, 9; Stanley, *Oration Delivered at Wallingford*, 4; Humphreys, *Valedictory Discourse*, 35.

45. Bailyn, *Ideological Origins,* chap. 6; circular letter dated Dec. 1804, Baldwin Family Papers; Stanley, *Oration Delivered 2/22/15,* 16; *Litchfield Monitor,* June 22, 1803.

46. Humphreys, *Valedictory Discourse,* 26; Hillhouse cited in Kerber, *Federalists in Dissent,* 43; *Litchfield Monitor,* Aug. 31, 1803 (rpt. from the *Connecticut Courant*).

47. [Sereno Dwight], *Slave Representation* (New Haven, 1812), 3, 4, 5, 13, 19, 21, 22.

48. See *Proceedings of a Convention,* 19–24; Purcell, *Connecticut in Transition,* 141.

49. Kerber, *Women of the Republic,* 8; Trumbull, *Dignity of Man,* 35; Stanley, *Oration Delivered 2/22/15,* 16; Hall, *Oration Delivered at Tolland,* 23; Dwight, *Oration Delivered at New Haven,* 7; McCurry, "Two Faces of Republicanism," 1262.

50. Among the most interesting of these letters are Roger Sherman Baldwin to Emily Perkins, June 24, 1818, Perkins to Baldwin, March 28, 1820, and Baldwin to Perkins, April 17, 1820, Baldwin Family Papers.

51. Roger Sherman Baldwin to Emily Perkins, April 17, 1820, ibid.

52. On the later life of Roger and Emily, see Frederick H. Jackson, *Simeon Eben Baldwin: Lawyer, Social Scientist, Statesman* (New York, 1955), 3–35. Roger was a graduate of Yale and the Litchfield Law School, while Emily attended one of the handful of first-rate female academies springing up across the state.

53. Calvin Goddard to "Mrs. Simeon Baldwin," March 6, 1816, Baldwin Family Papers.

54. See Emily Noyes Vanderpoel, *Chronicles of a Pioneer School* (Cambridge, MA, 1903); Marian C. McKenna, *Tapping Reeve and the Litchfield Law School* (New York, 1986); and Reeve's revisionist treatise *The Law of Baron and Femme . . .* (Burlington, VT, 1846 [1816]).

55. Christine Stansell, *City of Women: Sex and Class in New York, 1789–1860* (New York, 1982), 19.

56. Purcell, *Connecticut in Transition,* 177, 188.

57. Quotation from Roger Sherman Baldwin to Ebenezer Baldwin, Jan. 9, 1816, Baldwin Family Papers.

58. John Cotton Smith to Daggett, Dec. 16, 1815, Daggett Papers; *Federal Republican Nomination for Council* (Hartford, 1817), 6.

59. Connecticut Society for the Encouragement of American Manufactures, *Address* (Middletown, CT, 1817), 3, 9, 24; [*Resolutions Passed by a Meeting of the Citizens of New Haven, 11/8/16*] (New Haven, 1817), 1.

60. Roger Minot Sherman to Daggett, Feb. 9, 1816, Daggett Papers; Trumbull [pseud.], *The Mischiefs of Legislative Caucuses* (Hartford, 1819), 3; Stanley, *Oration Delivered 2/22/15,* 21.

61. On the American party, see *Connecticut Courant,* March 26, 1816; Purcell, *Connecticut in Transition,* 211. On the Constitution and Reform ticket, see David Roth and Freemen Meyer, *Connecticut: From Revolution to Constitution* (Chester, CT, 1975), 66.

62. On the State party, see Simeon Baldwin to Ebenezer Baldwin, April 5, 1819, Baldwin Family Papers. On the Union Republicans, see Livermore, *Twilight of Federalism,* 80.

63. George Richards signed his piece in support of Wolcott "a Federal Republican"; see [George H. Richards], *The Politics of Connecticut: Or a Statement of Facts Addressed to Honest Men of All Portions* . . . (Hartford, 1817). On the other hand, the *Federal Republican Nomination for Council* listed the incumbent Federalists and attacked the "Tolerationists."

64. Simeon Baldwin to Ebenezer Baldwin, July 24, 1819, Baldwin Family Papers.

65. See Roth, *Connecticut*; Jarvis Means Morse, *A Neglected Period of Connecticut's History, 1818–1850* (New York, 1978), 71.

11. FROM FATHERS TO FRIENDS OF THE PEOPLE: POLITICAL PERSONAE IN THE EARLY REPUBLIC

The notes in this essay have been reduced; see the notes in the original publication. Reprinted by permission from the *Journal of the Early Republic* 11 (winter 1991): 465–91.

1. Gordon S. Wood, "Interests and Disinterestedness in the Making of the Constitution," in Beeman, *Beyond Confederation*, 100.

2. Ibid., 85–89.

3. Gordon S. Wood, *The Creation of the American Republic, 1776–1787* (Chapel Hill, NC, 1969), 476, 479–80.

4. Appleby, *Capitalism*, 51–53; Fischer, *Revolution of American Conservatism*, 1–17, 250–51.

5. Wood, "Interests and Disinterestedness"; Appleby, *Capitalism*, 70–78, 90–94.

6. North Callahan, *Henry Knox, General Washington's General* (New York, 1958), 16–17, 23, 281; Cooper to Susan Delancy Cooper, June 12, 1834, in James Franklin Beard, ed., *The Letters and Journals of James Fenimore Cooper*, 6 vols. (Cambridge, MA, 1960–68), 3:41; Cyrus Eaton, *History of Thomaston, Rockland, and South Thomaston, Maine*, 2 vols. (Hallowell, ME, 1865), 1:214–15; Lyman H. Butterfield, "Judge William Cooper (1754–1809): A Sketch of His Character and Accomplishment," *New York History* 30 (1949): 388, 396; James Fenimore Cooper, *The Legends and Traditions of a Northern County* (1921; rpt., Cooperstown, NY, 1936), 14.

7. Callahan, *Henry Knox*, 24–29; Cooper quoted in Joseph C. Martindale, *A History of the Townships of Byberry and Moreland, in Philadelphia, Pennsylvania* . . . (1867; rev. ed., Philadelphia, [1901]), 243; George DeCou, *Burlington: A Provincial Capital* (Philadelphia, 1945), 115–16; James Fenimore Cooper, *Reminiscences of Mid-Victorian Cooperstown and a Sketch of William Cooper* (Cooperstown, NY, 1936), 17; Cooper, *Legends and Traditions*, 221; Butterfield, "Judge William Cooper," 386–88; marriage license of William Cooper and Elizabeth Fenimore, Nov. 13, 1774, William Cooper Papers, Hartwick College Archives, Oneonta, NY; Pennsylvania state assessment ledger, Byberry Township, Philadelphia County, 1776, City Archives of Philadelphia. In 1774 Richard Fenimore Cooper owned 500 acres, 20 horses and cattle, and a small trading vessel and ranked second in taxable wealth among the sixty-eight taxpayers in Willingboro Township; see the tax ratable list for Willingboro Township, Burlington County, New Jersey State

Archives, Trenton. For Cooper's new property, see Burlington County Deeds, conveyance books E:413, H:594, R:198, A-O:30, A-Q:428, and mortgage book A:343, 392, ibid.

8. Callahan, *Henry Knox*. William S. Stryker, *Official Register of the Officers and Men of New Jersey in the Revolutionary War* (Baltimore, 1967), does not identify any service by William Cooper of Burlington, not even any militia service. This was not unusual in Burlington where Quakers dominated the economy, society, and politics.

9. For the Maine frontier during the Revolution, see Alan Taylor, *Liberty Men and Great Proprietors: The Revolutionary Settlement on the Maine Frontier, 1760–1820* (Chapel Hill, NC, 1990), 14–18. For the Otsego country during the war, see James Arthur Frost, *Life on the Upper Susquehanna, 1783–1860* (New York, 1951), 4–5.

10. Joseph Pierce to Henry Knox, July 3, 1791, Henry Knox Papers, Massachusetts Historical Society, Boston; Taylor, *Liberty Men*, 39–40.

11. Julius Goebel, Jr., et al., eds., *The Law Practice of Alexander Hamilton*, 4 vols. (New York, 1964–81), 4:91–113; Mary-Jo Kline and Joanne W. Ryan, eds., *Political Correspondence and Public Papers of Aaron Burr*, 2 vols. (Princeton, NJ, 1983), 1:21.

12. Dr. John Morgan, "To the Public," *Pennsylvania Gazette* (Philadelphia), May 17, 1786; Morgan to Jacob Morton, May 15, 1786, Aaron Burr Papers, New-York Historical Society, New York; Joseph Wharton to Miers Fisher, Dec. 15, 1796, Fisher Family Papers, Manuscript Department, Historical Society of Pennsylvania, Philadelphia.

13. Anne H. Wharton, "The Wharton Family," *Pennsylvania Magazine of History and Biography* 1 (1877): 326–29, 455–58; Whitfield J. Bell, Jr., *John Morgan: Continental Doctor* (Philadelphia, 1965), 259–64; Benjamin Rush, *The Autobiography of Benjamin Rush . . .*, ed. George W. Corner (Princeton, NJ, 1948), 180.

14. Eaton, *History of Thomaston* 1:209, Ralph Birdsall, *The Story of Cooperstown* (Cooperstown, NY, 1917), 1–2; James Fenimore Cooper, *Chronicles of Cooperstown* (1838), rpt. in *A History of Cooperstown* (Cooperstown, NY, 1929), 12, 22. For Cooper's library, see James Fenimore Cooper, "Correspondence of Judge William Cooper," James Franklin Beard, Jr., Papers, American Antiquarian Society, Worcester, MA.

15. Birdsall, *Story of Cooperstown*, 96; Cooper, *Chronicles of Cooperstown*, 22–23; quoted in Cooper, *Reminiscences*, 51.

16. Eaton, *History of Thomaston* 1:209; Callahan, *Henry Knox*, 345–48; Jackson to Knox, March 27 (quotation), 31, May 8, 1794, Knox Papers; Paul Coffin, "Memoir and Journals of Rev. Paul Coffin, D.D.," Maine Historical Society, *Collections* 4 (1856): 327; Leverett Saltonstall, Travel Journal, Aug. 26, 1806, in Robert E. Moody, ed., *The Saltonstall Papers, 1607–1815*, 2 vols. (Boston, 1972–74), 2:333.

17. Lucy Flucker Knox quoted in Thomas Morgan Griffiths, *Maine Sources in* The House of Seven Gables (Waterville, ME 1945), 8–9; Jackson to Knox, Oct. 26, 1794, Knox Papers; Eaton, *History of Thomaston* 1:209–10, 212–13, 224; Cyrus Eaton, *Annals of the Town of Warren . . .* (1851; 2d ed., Hallowell, ME, 1877), 265–67.

18. William Cooper, *A Guide in the Wilderness* . . . (1810; rpt., Cooperstown, NY, 1949), 10–11, Cooper, *Chronicles of Cooperstown*, 19–20; Otsego *Herald* (Cooperstown), May 8, 1795, June 5, 1797.

19. Knox to Robert Houston, Dec. 10, 1801, Knox Papers; Peck quoted in Alfred F. Young, *The Democratic Republicans of New York: The Origins, 1763–1797* (Chapel Hill, NC, 1967), 264; Joseph White, "Address," Otsego *Herald*, Oct. 23, 1795. For election returns, see Albany *Gazette*, Feb. 20, 1795; Young, *Democratic Republicans*, 592.

20. Eaton, *History of Thomaston* 1:260.

21. Cooper to Henry Drinker, Feb. 22, 1789, Henry Drinker Papers, Historical Society of Pennsylvania; Schuyler to Cooper, May 7, 1792, Cooper Papers; Levi Beardsley, *Reminiscences; Personal and Other Incidents; Early Settlement of Otsego County* . . . (New York, 1852), 53; Young, *Democratic Republicans*, 267.

22. James Moore's testimony, Feb. 21, 1793, in *Journal of the Assembly of the State of New-York* . . . *Sixteenth Session* (New York, 1793), 193; William Cooper to Stephen Van Rensselaer, May 2, 1792, Cooper Papers.

23. John T. Horton, "The Western Eyres of Judge Kent," *New York History* 18 (1937): 165–66; David Maldwyn Ellis, "Rise of the Empire State, 1790–1820," ibid., 56 (1975): 16; Margaret L. Brown, "William Bingham, Eighteenth Century Magnate," *Pennsylvania Magazine of History and Biography* 61 (1937): 387–434; Norman B. Wilkinson, "The 'Philadelphia Fever' in Northern Pennsylvania," *Pennsylvania History* 20 (1953): 41–56; Ronald P. Formisano, *The Transformation of Political Culture; Massachusetts Parties, 1790s–1840s* (New York, 1983), 65–68.

24. Cooper to Oliver Wolcott, Aug. 20, 1799, Oliver Wolcott Papers, Connecticut Historical Society, Hartford; Knox to Governor Caleb Strong, Aug. 15, 1800, Related Papers filed under Resolve of Nov. 15, 1800, Massachusetts State Archives, Boston.

25. Jabez D. Hammond, *The History of Political Parties in the State of New York* . . ., 2 vols. (Albany, 1842), 1:123–24. See also Beardsley, *Reminiscences*, 71–72; Throop Wilder, "Jedediah Peck, Statesman, Soldier, Preacher," *New York History* 22 (1941): 290–94.

26. Stephen Burroughs, *Memoirs of the Notorious Stephen Burroughs of New Hampshire* (1811; rpt., New York, 1924), 7–8; Eaton, *History of Thomaston* 1:181; Joseph Thompson Dodge, *Genealogy of the Dodge Family of Essex County, Mass., 1629–1894*, 2 vols. (Madison, WI, 1894–98), 1:77–78; Clifford K. Shipton, *Biographical Sketches of Those Who Attended Harvard College in the Classes 1690–1771*, 17 vols. (Boston, 1933–75), 12:367–69; Jasper Jacob Stahl, *History of Old Broad Bay and Waldoboro*, 2 vols. (Portland, ME, 1956), 1:423–24; Commonwealth v. Dodge, June 1804, Lincoln County Supreme Judicial Court Records, Lincoln County Courthouse, Wiscasset, ME, 2:142.

27. John Lee Frisbee, "The Political Career of Jedediah Peck" (M.A. thesis, State University of New York, Oneonta, 1966), 2–5; Young, *Democratic Republicans*, 510.

28. Knox to Governor Caleb Strong, Aug. 1, 1800, Knox Papers; settler quoted in Eaton, *History of Thornaston* 1:240; Henry Knox and Ezekiel G. Dodge, "Memorandum of Agreement," Oct. 31, 1795, Henry Knox Papers, Maine Historical Society, Portland.

29. Eaton, *History of Thomaston* 1:260.

30. Peck and Morris quoted in [Jedediah Peck], *The Political Wars of Otsego: or Downfall of Jacobinism and Despotism* . . . (Cooperstown, NY, 1796), 41, 17; "Otsegonius," Otsego *Herald,* Jan. 3, 1799; James Morton Smith, "The Sedition Law of 1798 and the Right of Petition: The Attempted Prosecution of Jedediah Peck," *New York History* 35 (1954): 63–65.

31. Hale to Cooper, Jan. 9, 1799, Cooper Papers; William Cooper, "Caution!" Albany *Centinel,* April 23, 1799; Cooper to Oliver Wolcott, Sept. 16, 1799, Wolcott Papers; United States v. Jedediah Peck, Sept. 1799, Southern District of New York, United States Circuit Court, RG 21, National Archives and Records Service, Washington, DC; Smith, "Jedediah Peck," 65–66.

32. Cooper to Jay, Oct. 25, 1799, Document 1550, New York State Library, Albany; William Cooper, "To the Electors of the Western District," Albany *Gazette,* Nov. 14, 1799; Hammond, *History of Political Parties* 1:131–32.

33. Henry Jackson Knox to Henry Knox, Mar. 28, 1805, Knox Papers, Massachusetts Historical Society; Eaton, *Thomaston* 1:260; William A. Robinson, *Jeffersonian Democracy in New England* (New Haven, 1916), 46.

34. Henry Knox to John Gleason, April 24, 1806, Knox Papers, Massachusetts Historical Society; Charles Willing Hare to the Trustees of the Bingham Estate, Feb. 11, 1807, in Frederick S. Allis, Jr., ed., *William Bingham's Maine Lands, 1790–1820,* 2 vols. (Boston, 1954), 2:1215. For the identity of Thomaston's representatives, see *The Massachusetts Register and United States Calendar* . . . (Boston 1804), 35; ibid. (1805), 24; ibid. (1806), 26.

35. Fischer, *Revolution of American Conservatism;* Alexis de Tocqueville, *Democracy in America,* ed. Phillips Bradley, 2 vols. (1866–68; rev. ed., New York, 1960), 1:182-87.

Contributors

Keith Arbour, a Ph.D. in history from the University of Michigan, is an independent scholar.

James M. Banner is an independent historian in Washington, D.C.

Doron Ben-Atar is associate professor of history at Fordham University.

Andrew Cayton is professor of history at Miami University in Oxford, Ohio.

Paul Finkelman holds the John Seiberling Bicentennial Chair in Constitutional Law at the University of Akron School of Law.

Barbara B. Oberg is editor of the Benjamin Franklin Papers and a senior research scholar in history, Yale University.

Andrew Siegel, M.A. in history from Princeton, is completing his J.D. at New York University Law School.

Herbert Sloan is associate professor of history at Barnard College.

Rogers M. Smith is professor of political science at Yale University.

Alan Taylor is professor of history at the University of California, Davis.

David Waldstreicher is an assistant professor of American studies at Yale University.

Steven Watts is professor of history at the University of Missouri, Columbia.

Rosemarie Zagarri is professor of history at George Mason University.

INDEX

Republicans *(cont.)*
commercial banking in New York
and Pennsylvania, 12; win control of
Connecticut, 221–24; criticism of for
corruption and degeneracy, 171–72;
oppose deference, 131, 226; described
as new men who reject deference, 226;
description of, 21, 153–54; domestic
political culture of, 7–8; replace
Federalist officials in territories, 93,
94; retain some Federalist policies, 95,
222, 255; Germans in Pennsylvania
support, 39; oppose Hamilton's
financial plan, 62–63; oppose
Hamilton's sinking fund, 72; oppose
hierarchical society, 12, 131–32, 183,
227; historiography of, 2–3, 247; hostile to Indians, 22; oppose Jay Treaty,
5; leadership of, 11–12; espouse liberalism, 73; reject paternalism, 227;
dispense with taxes, 66; oppose internal taxes, 6; perception of government by, 68; assert that Americans are
too heterogeneous for a consolidated
republic, 23; support for, 4; support
free markets, 227; less likely than
Federalists to oppose slavery, 9–11,
40, 140, 144, 147; support slavery, 22;
style of criticized, 107–8; attitude of
toward women, 118–34
Resident requirements: for citizenship, 36,
37, 38
Rhetoric, 99–117
Rhode Island: passes gradual emancipation act, 135, 275; Federalist strength
in, 13; manufactures in, 45–46.
See also New England
Rigaud, André, 150
Robinson, Donald, 144
Rousseau, Jacques, 8
Rowson, Susanna, 193
Rush, Benjamin, 186, 234
Rutledge, John, Jr., 250

Sade, marquis de, 193
St. Clair, Arthur: and citizenship in Northwest Territory, 38; defeated by Indians, 25, 87; interprets prohibition of
slavery in Northwest Territory, 24; local opposition to, 92
St. Domingue. *See* Haitian slave rebellion

Salem, MA, 103, 146
Saltonstall, Leverett, 235
Sargent, Winthrop, 92–93
Schuyler, Philip, 147, 238, 239
Scottish Enlightenment, 161–62, 247
Secession: Federalists threaten, 2, 13; pos-
sible in West, 7. *See also* Union
Sedgwick, Theodore, 31, 36, 37
Sedition Act (1798). *See* Alien and Sedi-
tion Acts
Senate, U.S.: openness of sessions wanted,
107
Sevier, John, 91
Shakespeare's *Macbeth*, 179, 191, 194
Sharp, James Roger, 137
Shawnee Indians, 81, 87, 88
Shays's Rebellion, 75
Sheffield, John Baker Holroyd, Lord, 47
Shields, David S., 104
Siegel, Andrew, 11, 13, 13–14, 252
Silliman, Benjamin, 124
Simon, Keating L., 123
Sinking fund, 70–73, 265
Slater, Samuel, 45–46
Slavery, 21, 135–56; and Constitutional
Convention, 135, 136, 139; defense
of, 25; divisiveness of, 143–44; emancipation acts, 135–36, 141, 147, 275,
287; Federalists hope for end of, 22,
152, 155; Federalists oppose, 9–11,
24, 30, 40, 140; Federalists do little to
abolish, 25; and First Federal Congress, 140, 276; and miscegenation,
145–46; New England opposition to,
216–18; northern opposition to, 277;
in Northwest Territory, 91; opposition
to in Northwest Territory, 24; prohibited in Northwest Territory, 10, 83;
Republicans support, 22; and expansion into territories, 10, 11, 153, 276;
and three-fifths clause, 138, 139. *See
also* Abolitionists; Antislavery societies;
Slaves; Slave trade
Slaves: ameliorating condition of, 257;
British refuse to pay for those evacu-
ated, 24, 142; Congress bans export
of, 24; education of, 257; Federalists
more sympathetic to, 10–11; and Fugitive Slave Act (1793), 25, 141; newspaper ads for sales of, 146; patriarchal
society needs dependency from, 91;